THE PICKERING MASTERS

SELECTED WORKS OF
ROBERT OWEN

Volume 3. *The Book of the New Moral World*

SELECTED WORKS OF
ROBERT OWEN

EDITED BY
GREGORY CLAEYS

VOLUME
3

THE BOOK OF THE
NEW MORAL WORLD

Routledge
Taylor & Francis Group
LONDON AND NEW YORK

First published 1993 by Pickering & Chatto (Publishers) Limited

Published 2016 by Routledge
2 Park Square, Milton Park, Abingdon, Oxon OX14 4RN
605 Third Avenue, New York, NY 10017

Routledge is an imprint of the Taylor & Francis Group, an informa business

British Library Cataloguing in Publication Data

Owen, Robert

Works of Robert Owen. – (Pickering Masters Series)

I. Title II. Claeys, Gregory III. Series

335.0092

ISBN 13: 978-1-851-96088-0 (set)
ISBN 13: 978-1-138-64643-8 (hbk)

Typeset by Waveney Typesetters
Norwich

CONTENTS

INTRODUCTORY NOTE

The bibliographical details of the various Parts of *The Book of the New Moral World* are as follows: Part One editions, Glasgow 1836; Glasgow, 1837; Glasgow, 1840; abridged editions 1838 and 1840. A French edition of Part One was published at Paris, c. 1838. Parts Two and Three appeared in 1842, Parts Four to Seven in 1844. The first American edition was published in 1845, and another edition of the complete work appeared in 1849. An abridged French edition, *Le Livre du Nouveau Monde Moral* appeared in 1848 and it was reprinted in 1849 and 1852. There was a German translation, *Das Buch der neuen moralischen Welt* in 1840.

The 1842 edition of Parts One to Three is reprinted here; it has been reprinted in 1970.

THE BOOK

OF THE

NEW MORAL WORLD,

CONTAINING THE

RATIONAL SYSTEM OF SOCIETY,

FOUNDED ON DEMONSTRABLE FACTS, DEVELOPING THE CONSTITUTION AND LAWS OF

HUMAN NATURE AND OF SOCIETY.

BY

ROBERT OWEN.

Truth, without Mystery, Mixture of Error or Fear of Man, can, alone, emancipate the Human Race from Sin and Misery.

IN SEVEN PARTS.

PART I.

London:
PUBLISHED BY THE HOME COLONIZATION SOCIETY,
AT THEIR OFFICE, 57, PALL MALL,
AND SOLD BY ALL BOOKSELLERS.

MDCCCXLII.

TO

HIS MAJESTY, WILLIAM IV.,

KING OF GREAT BRITAIN, etc.

Sire,

Circumstances, not under your controul, have placed you at the head of the most powerful association of men for good or for evil, that has hitherto existed in any part of the globe; and other circumstances are about to arise, also beyond your controul, which will render it necessary for you, Sire, and those whom you may call to your councils, to decide whether this power shall be now directed to produce the good or the evil.

The book, the first part of which, with this letter prefixed, I submit to your Majesty, contains truths, of the highest import to you, Sire, to every member of your family; to every subject of the wide-spread empire over which you preside; to every human being, high or low, now living and to all those who shall live hereafter. It unfolds the fundamental principles of a new moral world, and it thus lays a new foundation on which to re-construct society and re-create the character of the human race. It opens to the family of man, without a single exception, the means of endless progressive improvement, physical, intellectual, and moral, and of happiness, without the possibility of retrogression or of assignable limit.

Society has emanated from fundamental errors of the imagination, and all the institutions and social arrangements of man over the world have been based on these errors. Society is, therefore, through all its ramifications, artificial and corrupt, and, in consequence, ignorance, falsehood, and grave folly, alone govern all the affairs of mankind.

Under your reign, Sire, the change from this system, with all its evil consequences, to another founded on self-evident truths, insuring happiness to all, will, in all probability, be achieved; and your name, and the names of those who now govern the nations of the world will be recorded, as prominent actors, in a period the most important that has ever occurred in the history of mankind.

The world, in its present mental darkness, will rashly pronounce this change to be impracticable; or, if practicable, that it will be the work of ages. Herein all men err. The great circumstances of nature, and the existing state of human affairs, are full ripe for the change; no one material is deficient, and man cannot longer govern man without forming a union of governments and nations to effect this change.

As the change will be permanently beneficial for high and low, rich and poor, it may be effected by wise general arrangements, in peace, in order, and with high gratification to all nations and people.

At the termination of the late war of, what are called, the civilized nations, an alliance was formed by the leading governments to protect each other from individual national revolutions;[a] and it was a wise measure to prevent premature changes in each state – changes desired by the people before they had acquired wisdom to give such changes a right direction.

The world has undergone a revolution of principle since that alliance was formed; the folly and wickedness of all wars, civil or national, have become too glaring not to be opposed by the cultivated mind of Europe and America. The empire, Sire, over which you preside, can no longer be governed by party proceedings, and, in consequence, your present administration, as well as any other that can now be formed, must be one of mere necessity; because, in the present state of society, individuals cannot be found to constitute one that shall be efficient. Difficulties of a similar character are arising in all countries; the old prejudices, or errors of the world, have been shaken to their foundation, and are tottering previous to their fall and final destruction.

A union of governments and nations is now required, to reconstitute society upon a new and solid basis, and to secure to the human race peace and happiness, through the right application of the discoveries, both scientific and moral, made within the last century.

Your ancestors, Sire, a hundred years ago, directed a mixed manual and scientific national power for the production of wealth and happiness, equal together to the exertions of about fifteen millions of men, to supply a population of about fifteen millions: the population and power being equal, or as one to one. You, Sire, have the direction of a mixed national power of production more than equal to the exertions of six hundred millions of men, with no assignable limit to its rapid increase, to supply a population of twenty-five millions, or as twenty-four to one. This enormous new power of the British Empire may be most advantageously given to all other populations in proportion to their number, and it is the immediate interest of Great Britain that this

[a] The Napoleonic Wars ended in 1815. Austria, Prussia, Russia and Britain were allied against France.

new power should be spread, as rapidly as possible, over all the nations of the earth. It is a boon that will be more beneficial to the givers than to the receivers.

The British nation is in the most advantageous position to propose and negotiate this alliance, now called for by an irresistible necessity, arising from the progress of knowledge. This alliance is imperative, to protect, alike, both the governments and people from the effects of ignorant violence, and to insure their progressive improvement and happiness.

Two conditions only are required to found this alliance upon a basis that will insure its permanence and success; conditions, too, that will be highly advantageous to all governments and people.

The first, That the contradictory parties shall abandon, by the most public declaration, the fundamental error on which society has been hitherto based: and second, that they shall adopt the opposite truth for base of all their future measures.

The *error* is unsupported by a single fact, and opposed by all facts bearing upon it; the *truth* is supported by every fact, and opposed by no one fact having reference to it. The necessary consequence of acting upon the error is misery; the necessary consequence of acting upon the truth will be happiness. The change may now be effected from the one to the other without injury to the mind, body, or estate of a single individual of any age, class, or rank, in any country; and every material to effect the change now, is at the controul of society, almost without effort, but certainly, with only agreeable and beneficial exercise. Neither will it be necessary to disturb private property, as now existing, or to require any labour from those who have not been trained to employment.

I offer to make all these matters plain in principle, and easy of practice, to your Government and to all civilized Governments. The whole subject has been long familiar to

Your Majesty's faithful Friend,

ROBERT OWEN

1, Crescent Place, Burton Crescent,
1st August, 1836

AN ADDRESS

FROM THE

ASSOCIATION OF ALL CLASSES OF ALL NATIONS,[a]

TO THE

GOVERNMENTS AND PEOPLE OF ALL NATIONS;

BUT ESPECIALLY TO

THE FIVE LEADING POWERS OF EUROPE, AND TO THE UNITED STATES OF NORTH AMERICA

You are now in the midst of a conflict which involves the deepest and dearest interest of every individual of the human race; and upon its result depends the misery or happiness of the present and future generations.

It is a contest between those who believe that it is for their individual interest and happiness that man should continue to be kept in ignorance, and be governed, as heretofore, by force and fraud; and those who are convinced, that for his happiness, he should be hence forward governed by truth and justice only. The increase of knowledge renders the ultimate result of the contest no longer doubtful; but it is greatly to be desired that it should speedily terminate to the satisfaction of all parties: and it may now be made so to terminate, by the union of the six leading nations of the more civilized part of the world. For were they united to adopt simultaneously national measures, to give a wise direction to modern discoveries in the sciences of physics and of mind, they could accomplish the most magnificent results for themselves and for the entire family of man.

The inexperienced will hastily conclude that these results are impracticable, or if practicable, that men are too ignorant, vicious, and selfish to promote a change which would ensure equal privileges to all, although the benefits,

[a] Owen's main organisation in the last phase of his active career. Founded in 1835, the AACAN co-ordinated branch activities and was chiefly concerned to raise funds for a new community.

thereby arising to each, should far exceed the advantages which any one can enjoy, under the existing constitution of society. We believe, that through the self-interest of man, these objections may be overcome. For the experienced know that all nations might, now, easily adopt arrangements to produce more of all kinds of wealth, essential to human happiness, than would satisfy all to the full extent of their desire, and also establish new institutions, in which the natural faculties and powers of each might be cultivated from birth, to be greatly superior to any character ever formed, or that can be formed, under any of the old institutions of the world. This vital change in the condition and character of the human race, may now be effected with only light, healthy, beneficial, and agreeable manual labour, combined with the most desirable and pleasant mental exercise; and this change may be effected in peace, with universal consent, without injury to the mind, body, or estate, of a single individual, in any rank or country.

This is the revolution which the progress of knowledge now requires from those who have hitherto ruled the destinies of nations; a revolution in the fundamental principles, and in the arrangement of society, which will essentially promote the interest, and secure the progressive happiness of all, from the highest to the lowest.

We undertake to explain the principles of nature, and to unfold the practical measures consequent upon them, by which this great revolution in human affairs may be now effected, without disorder, or evil of any kind, not even disturbing existing private properties.

We proceed one step further; and confidently state that the progress of knowledge now renders this revolution, in the general condition and character of mankind, so irresistible, that no earthly power can prevent or much retard its course; and it will be effected either by reason, or by violence forced upon society by the mental degradation of all, and the extreme misery of the many. We, therefore, as the disinterested friends of all Classes of all Nations, recommend to all Governments and People, that the old prejudices of the world, for or against class, sect, party, country, sex, and colour, derived solely from ignorance, should be now allowed, by the common consent of all, to die their natural death; that standing armies of all nations should be disbanded, in order that the men may be employed in producing instead of destroying wealth; that the rising generation should be educated from birth to become superior in character and conduct to all past generations; that all should be trained to have as much enjoyment in producing as in using or consuming wealth, which, through the progress of science, can be easily effected; that all should freely partake of it; and that, thus, the reign of peace, intelligence, and universal sympathy, or affection, may, for ever, supersede the reign of ignorance and oppression.

DEDICATED

TO THOSE WHO PREFER A SYSTEM

OF SOCIETY WHICH WILL ENSURE THE HAPPINESS OF THE

HUMAN RACE THROUGHOUT ALL FUTURE AGES,

TO A SYSTEM WHICH,

SO LONG AS IT SHALL BE MAINTAINED,

MUST PRODUCE MISERY TO ALL.

PREFACE

The time approaches, when, in the course of nature, the evil spirit of the world, engendered by ignorance and selfishness, will cease to exist, and when another spirit will arise, emanating from facts and experience, which will give a new direction to all the thoughts, feelings, and actions of men, and which will create a new character of wisdom and benevolence for the human race.

The present work, the first part of which is now given to the public, has been written to hasten the period of this all-important change, by explaining the cause of human evil, the means of removing it, and by unfolding a new moral world, in which evil, except as it will be recorded in the past sufferings of mankind, will be unknown; a new moral world, in which truth alone will govern all the affairs of men, and in which knowledge, unchecked by superstition or prejudice, will make an everlasting progress; – a world in which justice, for the first time, will be done to human nature, by every feeling, faculty, and power, inherent in each child, being cultivated to its full extent; and cultivated, too, by the concentrated intelligence and goodness of the age. By these measures all the external circumstances, under the controul of man, will be re-arranged, and so wisely combined, that they will give full efficiency and excellence to every thought, feeling, and action of the human race.

Thus, by the superior arrangements which, through experience, man will be enabled to make, all will attain the best dispositions, habits, and manners, and the most valuable knowledge that each can be trained from infancy to receive.

In this simple, straightforward, and rational manner; in peace, and by universal consent, through conviction of its incalculable advantages to each individual, will the great change be effected, from evil to good, from misery to happiness.

To explain the principles and practices which will work out, and which must be consequent upon this change, and to make their vast superiority over the existing imaginary notions, and consequent practices of all the nations of the earth, apparent and familiar to man, is the object to be now accomplished.

The perusal, however, of this work, will be unavailing to those who are incapable of viewing the subject as comprehending an entirely new system to re-form man, and to re-constitute society. For a more limited conception of this all-important subject will only perplex the intellect, between old prejudices and new truths, and, therefore, make it less competent to understand arrangements designed to constitute a new state of human existence, one founded on the laws of nature, in direct opposition to the erroneous notions on which the arrangements of the world have been hitherto conceived, based, and constructed.

New and strange as this statement will appear, even to the most learned and experienced of the present day, let no one rashly pronounce it to be visionary; for it is a system the result of much reading, observation, and reflection, combined with extensive practical experience, and confidential communication with official public characters in various countries, and with leading minds among all classes; a system founded on the eternal laws of nature, and derived from facts and experience only; and it will be found, on full examination by competent minds, to be the least visionary, and the most easy of practice, of all the systems which have been proposed, in ancient or modern times, to improve the character and to insure the happiness of the human race.

INTRODUCTION

The religious, moral, political, and commercial arrangements of society, throughout the world, have been based, from the commencement of history, upon an error respecting the nature of man; an error so grievous in its consequences, that it has deranged all the proceedings of society, made man irrational in his thoughts, feelings, and actions, and, consequently, more inconsistent, and perhaps more miserable, than any other animal.

This work is written to explain, first – the cause of this universal error, which has produced the derangement, degradation, and misery of the human race; and secondly – to open to the present generation a new moral world founded on principles opposed to this error; and in which, the causes producing it will cease. In this new world, the inhabitants will attain a state of existence, in which a spirit of charity and affection will pervade the whole human race; man will become spiritualized, and happy amidst a race of superior beings.

The knowledge which he will thus acquire of himself and of nature, will induce and enable him, through his self-interest, or desire for happiness, to form such superior external arrangements as will place him within a terrestrial paradise.

As in this new world, all will know, that far more happiness can be obtained by union than by disunion, all opposition and contention between man and man, and nation and nation, for individual or national advantages, of any kind, will cease.

The overwhelming power, which, through the progress of knowledge, may be now obtained by the external circumstances under the controul of society, to form the general character of the human race, will become evident to all, and in consequence, no child will be permitted to grow up in ignorance, in superstition, or with inferior dispositions or habits; or without a knowledge of his own organization, of its laws, of the laws of nature generally, of the useful sciences, and of the practical arts of life.

The degradation, therefore, of mind and body, hitherto produced by a general training in error, regarding the organization or natural powers of man, and the innumerable errors thence arising, will be altogether unknown.

The evils, also, which are now produced by the desire ignorantly created to obtain individual superiority in wealth, privileges, and honours, will not exist; but advantages much superior to these will be secured to all, and feelings of a higher character than individual distinctions can create, will be universally experienced.

Scientific arrangements will be formed to make wealth everywhere, and at all times, superabound beyond the wants or wishes of the human race, and all desire for individual accumulation, or any inequality of condition, will consequently cease.

The necessity for a never-ceasing supply of wealth for the use and enjoyment of all, and the right of each to produce and enjoy his fair share of it, will be obvious and admitted. It will be equally evident that the unwrought materials to produce manufactured wealth exist in superfluity, and that scientific aids may now be constructed to procure and work up these materials without any disagreeable, unhealthy, or premature manual labour, into every variety of the most useful and valuable productions.

With means thus ample to procure wealth with ease and pleasure to all, none will be so unwise as to desire to have the trouble and care of individual property. To divide riches among individuals in unequal proportions, or to hoard it for individual purposes, will be perceived to be as useless and as injurious as it would be to divide water or air into unequal quantities for different individuals, or that they should hoard them for their future use.

As more wealth will be produced through scientific aid, by healthy exercise, and as a gratifying amusement, than the population of the earth can require or advantageously use, no anxious thoughts, or care for a continued supply, will perplex the minds, or injuriously occupy the time of any one. And as sufficient wealth will be so easily produced by scientific arrangements to effect whatever riches and knowledge can accomplish by the union of mankind, a far better education than any which has ever yet been proposed or conceived in the old world, will be given from birth to every one. In consequence of the ease with which wealth and scientific knowledge will be obtained, and made abundant for the most ample use and gratification of all, the inferior existing circumstances will be abandoned, and man will no longer live in crowded cities, or in seclusion from enlightened and superior society; but other arrangements will be formed to enable all, as soon as they shall be made rational, to live in superior habitations surrounded by gardens, pleasure-grounds, and scenery, far better designed and executed than have yet been possessed by the monarchs of the most powerful, wealthy, and extended empires. The human race will also be surrounded by other very superior circumstances, which, now, by the progress of knowledge, can be placed for the first time under the controul of man; circumstances of a far higher character than any which have yet existed in any part of the globe.

Ignorance, therefore, and poverty, or the fear of it, now the fruitful causes of crime and misery, will no longer disunite man, and be the bane of his happiness. These evils will be known only in the history of the past, or of the irrational period of human existence.

Money, which has hitherto been the root, if not of *all evil*,[a] of great injustice, oppression, and misery to the human race, making some slavish producers of wealth, and others its wasteful consumers or destroyers, will be no longer required to carry on the business of life: for as wealth of all kinds will be so delightfully created in greater abundance than will ever be required, no money price will be known, for happiness will not be purchaseable, except by a reciprocy of good actions and kind feelings.

Consequently, the present classification of society will be not only useless, but it will be discovered to be unjust and productive of every kind of evil; necessarily destructive of sincerity, honesty, and of all the finest feelings and most valuable sympathies of our nature. This artificial and most injurious classification will be superseded by one derived immediately from nature – one that shall insure sincerity and honesty; that shall cultivate, foster, and encourage the finest feelings, the best sympathies, and continually call into action the higher qualities of our nature, and that shall insure to every one the full amount of happiness that his original constitution, under the most favourable circumstances, shall be capable of receiving. These effects can be obtained, only, by a natural classification into employments according to age and capacity. All, at the same period of life, will pursue the same general occupations, for the public benefit, for which all, by their superior training and education, will be made more than competent; and all will have a large portion of each day to employ, according to their peculiar capacities and individual inclinations, without interfering with the happiness of others.

By these arrangements, and this classification, all will become superior, physically, intellectually, and morally; each will know all the duties of life, and will have the greatest desire to execute them in the best manner. In this classification, however, none will be trained to teach incongruities or mysteries, which must derange the mental faculties, and disorder all the transactions of mankind – none will be engaged in devising or administering laws in opposition to the laws of nature; or, in adjudging artificial rewards and punishments to counteract those of nature, which are all-wise and efficient. It will be obvious, even to children, thus rationally educated, that all human laws must be either unnecessary, or in opposition to nature's laws, that they must create disunion, produce crime incessantly, and involve all transactions in inextricable confusion. None will be trained in idleness and uselessness to waste extravagantly the productions of others, to which no just law can give them a shadow of right or title; and no unjust law will be admitted into the code of the new moral world. None will be trained and set apart to attack, plunder, and

[a] See 1 Timothy 6:10.

murder their fellow-men; this conduct will be known to be irrational, and the very essence of wickedness; nor yet, will any be trained to bargain with, or even to attempt to take advantage of another, or to desire individual privileges or distinctions of any kind. The individual who is trained to buy cheap, sell dear, and seek for individual benefits above his fellows, is thereby degraded – is unfitted to acquire superior qualities – is deprived of the finest feelings of our nature, and rendered totally incompetent to experience the highest enjoyments of human existence. Nor will any be permitted, by society, to be trained in an *inferior manner*, or for *inferior purposes*; because one such example will be injurious to every one; – but all will have the original powers and faculties of their nature directed and cultivated, in such a manner, as shall make it unavoidable, that each shall become, at maturity, superior in mind, manner, and conduct.

In this new world, the sympathies of human nature will be rightly directed from infancy, and will engender a spirit of benevolence, confidence, and affection, which will pervade mankind.

The impurities of the present system, arising from human laws opposed to nature's laws, will be unknown. The immense mass of degradation of character, and of heart-rending suffering, experienced by both sexes, but especially by women, will be altogether prevented, and the characters of all women will, by a superior, yet natural training, be elevated to become lovely, good, and intellectual. Of this state of purity and felicity few of the present generation have been trained to form any correct or rational conception.

In this new world, founded on universal and everlasting truths, no attempts will be made to falsify any of our physical or mental feelings; they will be known to be instincts given, as necessary parts of our nature, to be beneficially exercised and enjoyed.

Thus will be attained perfect truth, the great desideratum of human life, to prepare it for the enjoyment of happiness; – truth, which, in this new world, will be, upon every subject, the sole language of man to the full extent of his knowledge.

There will, therefore, be an undeviating unity between all the thoughts, feelings, language, and actions of the human race. It will be distinctly perceived, that falsehood necessarily produces misery, and that truth necessarily produces happiness; consequently, no motives will arise among beings rationally educated, and possessing a knowledge of their own nature, to induce any one even to imagine a falsehood.

In this regenerated state of human existence, all will be trained from birth to attain physically, mentally, and morally, very superior qualities, and to have them regularly exercised up to the point of temperance, according to the constitution of each.

Thus will the well-being, the well-doing, and the happiness of each be insured, and permanently maintained.

It must now be evident, that the new moral world will have little in common with the old, excepting humanity as it comes into existence at birth, and the simple materials of nature; and even these will be made to receive forms and qualities so superior to those which have hitherto been given to them, that the inexperienced would scarcely believe their natures to be the same.

In this book the difference between the two states of existence, and also the mode by which the change from the one to the other will be effected, without injury to person or property, will be made so plain as easily to be understood.

The First Part contains an explanation of the Constitution of Human Nature, and the Moral Science of Man, in order that a solid foundation may be laid at the commencement. In the succeeding parts of this book the conditions requisite to insure the happiness of man will be stated, with the reason for each condition. Having considered what individual man is by nature, and what is necessary to the happiness of a being so constituted, an explanation will be given of the arrangements which are necessary for the social condition, which will lead to the consideration of the best mode to *Produce and Distribute Wealth – to Form the Character, and to Govern Men in the aggregate, so as to insure their happiness*. The religion and morals of the new world will then be explained, and their superiority shown over the mysteries and inconsistencies of the religions and morals of the old world. The principles on which to found a rational government for mankind will next follow, with its laws, the reasons for each law, and the consequences of such a government to the population of the world. To these will succeed an explanation of the practical arrangements by which *all* the conditions requisite to happiness may be obtained for, and *permanently* insured to, the human race; together with the mode of effecting the change from the old to the new world.

CONTENTS

THE BOOK

OF THE

NEW MORAL WORLD

CHAPTER I

The Five Fundamental Facts on which the Rational System is founded

1st. THAT man is a *compound being*, whose character is formed of his constitution or organization at birth, and of the effects of external circumstances upon it from birth to death; such original organization and external influences continually acting and re-acting each upon the other.

2nd. That man is compelled by his original constitution to receive his *feelings* and his *convictions* independently of his *will*.

3rd. That his *feelings* or his *convictions*, or both of them united, create the motive to action called the *will*, which stimulates him to act, and decides his actions.

4th. That the organization of no two human beings is ever precisely similar at birth; nor can art subsequently form any two individuals, from infancy to maturity, to be precisely similar.

5th. That, nevertheless, the constitution of every infant, except in case of organic disease, is capable of being formed into a *very inferior*, or a *very superior*, being, according to the qualities of the external circumstances allowed to influence that constitution from birth.

The Fundamental Laws of Human Nature, or First Principles of the Science of Man

1st. Human nature is a compound of animal propensities, intellectual faculties, and moral qualities.

2nd. These propensities, faculties, and qualities, are united in different proportions in each individual.

3rd. This diversity constitutes the original difference between one individual and another.

4th. These elements of his nature, and their proportions, are made by a power unknown to the individual, and consequently without his consent.

5th. Each individual comes into existence within certain external circumstances, which act upon his peculiar original organization, more especially during the early period of his life, and, by impressing their general character upon him, form his local and national character.

6th. The influence of these general external circumstances is modified, in a particular manner, by the pecular organization of each individual; and thus the distinctive character of each is formed and maintained through life.

7th. No infant has the power of deciding at what period of time, or in what part of the world, he shall come into existence, – of what parents he shall be born, – in what religion he shall be trained, – what manners, customs, or habits, shall be given to him, – or by what other external circumstances he shall be surrounded, from birth to death.

8th. Each individual is so organized, that, when young, he may be made to receive either true ideas derived from a knowledge of facts, or false notions derived from the imagination, and in opposition to facts.

9th. Each individual is so organized, that he must necessarily become irrational when he is made from infancy to receive, as truths, false fundamental notions; and can only become truly rational when he shall be made to receive true fundamental principles, without any admixture of error.

10th. Each individual is so organized that, when young, he may be trained to acquire injurious habits only, or beneficial habits only, or a mixture of both.

11th. Each individual is so organized, that he *must believe* according to the strongest conviction that is made upon his mind; which conviction cannot be given to him by his will, nor be withheld by it.

12th. Each individual is so organized, that he *must like* that which is pleasant to him, or which, in other words, produces agreeable sensations in him; and *dislike* that which is unpleasant to him, or which, in other words, produces in him disagreeable sensations; and he cannot know previous to experience, what particular sensations new objects will produce on any one of his senses.

13th. Each individual is so organized, that his *feelings and his convictions* are formed *for him*, by the impressions which circumstances produce upon his individual organization.

14th. Each individual is so organized, that his *will* is formed *for* him by his feelings, or his convictions, or both; *and thus his whole character – physical, mental, and moral – is formed independently of himself.*

15th. Each individual is so organized, that impressions, which at their commencement, and for a limited time, produce agreeable sensations, will, if continued without intermission beyond a certain period, become indifferent, disagreeable, and ultimately painful.

16th. Each individual is so organized, that when, beyond a certain degree of rapidity, impressions succeed each other, they dissipate, weaken, and otherwise injure, his physical, mental, or moral, powers, and diminish his enjoyment.

17th. Each individual is so organized, that his highest health, his greatest progessive improvement, and his permanent happiness, depend upon the due cultivation of all his physical, intellectual, and moral, faculties, or elements of his nature, – upon their being called into action at a proper period of life, – and being afterwards temperately exercised, according to his strength and capacity.

18th. Each individual is so organized, that he is made to receive what is commonly called a *bad character*, when he has been placed, from birth, amidst the most unfavourable circumstances.

19th. Each individual is so organized, that he is made to receive a *medium character*, when he has been created with a favourable proportion of the elements of his nature, and has been placed, from birth, amidst unfavourable circumstances: –

Or, when he has been created with an unfavourable proportion of these elements, and when the external circumstances in which he is placed are of a character to impress him with favourable sensations only:

Or, when he has been created with a favourable proportion of some of these elements, and an unfavourable proportion of others; and has been placed, through life, in varied external circumstances, producing some good and some evil sensations. This compound has hitherto been the general lot of mankind.

20th. Each individual is so organized, that he is made to receive a *superior character*, when his original constitution contains the best proportion of the elements of human nature, and when the circumstances which surround him from birth, and through life, are of a character to produce superior sensations only; or, in other words, when the laws, institutions, and customs, under which he lives, are all in unison with the laws of his nature.

These are fundamental laws of nature, not of man's invention; they exist without his knowledge or consent; they change not by any effort he can make; and, as they proceed solely from a cause unknown and mysterious to him, they are *divine* laws in the only correct sense in which that term can be applied. These laws, considered separately and unitedly, and viewed in all their bearings and consequences, form a perfect foundation for a true Moral Science – for that science, the knowledge of which is necessary to secure the happiness of mankind.

CHAPTER II

'That man is a *compound being*, whose character is formed of his constitution or organization at birth, and of the effects of external circumstances upon it from birth to death; such original organization and external influences continually acting and re-acting each upon the other.'

No one will dispute the truth of this fact; because there can be only the original organization of the individual at birth, and the influence of external circumstances upon it, afterwards, to form its character at every moment of its existence. But it may be useful here to remark, that the influence of external circumstances upon the organization, partakes more of the character of a chemical action than of a mere mechanical impression. Impressions made upon the organization form a new compound with it, and, more or less, alter its powers of reacting upon external circumstances; producing thereby, a change in the character of the individual. This change is frequently effected by the sudden appearance of a new, disagreeable, or lovely, object, producing very powerful effects on the feelings, thoughts, and actions.

The effects of the action of external circumstances upon the original constitution, may be thus described. Suppose the organization at birth to be represented by A; and the first circumstance acting upon it to be represented by B. A and B unite, and make a compound, represented, we will suppose, by C. The second circumstance which influences the organization shall be called D; which then unites with the last compound C, making a new compound of character, which we will call E. The next external influence, which we will call F, must now make another compound – not however by uniting with A or C, (which peculiar compounds have been lost for ever,) – but with the last new compound E; making, together the fourth compound, which we will denominate G. And in this manner the character of each individual undergoes a continued change, or makes a constant advance towards maturity, and afterwards to old age. Now it should be always held in remembrance, that the individual, after each new combination has been effected, has had some change made in his character; and his power and inclination to react upon external circumstances will be in accordance with this change.

From the knowledge elicited by this first fact, man discovers that he himself knows nothing of the formation of his own original nature; that he is, previous to birth, passive and unconscious – his mechanical and chemical organization gradually forming; and whether, at birth, his nature is good or bad, perfect or imperfect, the being, thus, unconsciously to himself, formed, cannot rationally be the subject of either merit or demerit; or be justly made responsible for the general or particular qualities of the organization or constitution, which it has been thus made to possess.

The peculiar organization of each individual is the sole foundation of his matured character, and always modifies the effects of external circumstances; but the external circumstances may be made to possess either a weak or a strong influence over the original organization, in forming the character. Thus, arrangements may be devised to make the character of every one, more or less under the power of his *original constitution*, or more or less influenced by external circumstances. *Savages* are extreme examples of the former; and the *Society of Friends*[a] the best specimens we have yet had of the latter. This difference in the influence of external circumstances upon different individuals, has perplexed most men who have thought and written upon the subject. They have not understood the science of the influence of circumstances upon human nature; and, in consequence, they have not known how to educate or to govern man, as a rational being, or how to create circumstances sufficiently powerful to form a superior matured character for *all* individuals.

It is necessary to the right understanding of the moral science of man, that this first fact, relative to the formation of his character, should be accurately known; and that all the consequences to which it leads, should be fully comprehended. For this first fact is the foundation upon which the science is erected; and no one passing it over superficially, can proceed with advantage in the investigation of the subject. The results which necessarily follow from this first fact, are most momentous to individuals and to society. These consequences will be gradually developed in the progress of the work, and they will be found to decide the *happiness* or *misery* of the human race.

CHAPTER III

'That man is compelled by his original constitution to receive his *feelings* and his *convictions* independently of his *will*.'

This is a fact or law of nature which has puzzled the learned of all ages to the present time, and perplexed their reasoning faculties more than any other law of nature which they have attempted to investigate; it is yet unknown, unexplained, or misunderstood by the public; and more evil has arisen and

[a] On the importance of the Quakers to Owen's social theory, see the general introduction to this edition (vol. 1, pp. xlix, lviii).

exists in consequence of erroneous notions in the human mind relative to this fact, than from any other cause.

This most lamentable source of error has perpetuated ignorance, poverty, disunion, wars, and massacres, and engendered most, if not all, of the inferior passions, vices, and crimes, with which the human race has been afflicted: while a right understanding of this fact, will dispel ignorance, withdraw the cause of division, establish confidence, secure peace and good-will, charity and affection and render these virtues permanent throughout society.

The feelings and convictions experienced by man are not produced or regulated by his will, but are the necessary effects of the action of circumstances upon his physical and mental nature. Hitherto the world has been governed under the supposition that the feelings and convictions have been produced by the *choice* of the individual, and that they are under the immediate countroul of what is called *free-will*. The languages of all nations are filled with the terms, that you must love or hate, believe or disbelieve, certain qualities and creeds, or, if you disobey, you will be punished here and hereafter; and for so loving, hating, believing, or disbelieving, men are now praised and rewarded, as though there were great merit in so doing.

Yet, from an investigation of the facts connected with this subject, it appears that the feelings and convictions are *instincts of human nature*, – instincts which every one is compelled to possess or receive, and for which no man can have merit or demerit, or deserve reward or punishment.

That the feelings *are* instincts of human nature, every one may ascertain for himself, by trying what power he possesses to change, by his will, his present feelings towards those persons and things which he most likes or dislikes, loves or hates.

A few such experiments will convince those who make them, that it is in vain to attempt, by our will, to like what we dislike, or to dislike what we like, – to love what we hate, or to hate what we love. These feelings are created in us without the consent or controul of the will, which is, itself, formed essentially by these feelings, and only exists in consequence of them and of our convictions. It is for acts of the will that men are punished or rewarded by men; because they have hitherto imagined that the will was formed by the voluntary impulse of the individual; and they never suspected that it was as much created *for*, and independent *of*, him, as any part of his physical frame or mental faculties.

Similar experiments relative to the convictions made upon the mind, will demonstrate the powerless nature of the will over our opinions or belief; will demonstrate that these depend not upon the *will* of the individual, but are, alone, formed by the strongest impressions made upon the mind; and that the *will* has no power to force the mind to believe what it has been made to disbelieve, or to disbelieve what it has been made to believe. Every effort, thus made, will prove the fallacy of the general opinion. There can, consequently, be no merit or demerit in conviction, when, in every case, we are *compelled* to have the conviction which we possess.

But it is said that man has the power, or the free-will, to *seek for evidence* to enable him to love or to hate contrary to the feelings, and to believe or disbelieve contrary to the convictions, which he has been compelled to receive, and that he is therefore culpable for not searching for this evidence. Now, the will to seek for this kind of evidence must first be created by the feelings or the convictions, or both, generating the desire to investigate additional or new evidence, which may tend to provide new feelings and convictions: and unless the will shall be so excited through the convictions or feelings, or both, none can exist upon the subject, and even the chance of effecting an alteration cannot be obtained.

But suppose the feelings or convictions, or both, have been excited, by some new impressions, to desire and will to investigate other evidence or facts, with a view to change love into hate, or hate into love – belief into disbelief, or disbelief to belief; it is not the *will* of the individual which decides whether he can do either. Counter feelings must *first* be created by some *other* means than the *will* to effect the change, and impressions stronger than those already existing, must be made upon the mind, by new evidence, before a different opinion can be formed; and it is not the *will* which determines whether or not that evidence can be obtained.

It is also evident, that in this case, as in that of the former fact, there is nothing but the original organization and the external circumstances acting upon this organization, to produce whatever sensations the individual is conscious of experiencing. The feelings, therefore, whether strong or weak, good or bad, as they are termed, must influence the being as instincts totally independent of the will. In like manner, we see any object before us in connexion with all the circumstances by which it is surrounded; that object makes an impression on our minds of its existence in combination with the circumstances by which it is surrounded. It is an instinct of our nature thence to be convinced that the object does so exist, surrounded by such external circumstances: it is a *fact* to us, which we are compelled to believe, without any reference whatever to what is called the *will*: and thus is man under the necessity of receiving his convictions, respecting all external objects of nature, without the action of the *will* having any power to direct; it has, in fact, no decision whatever in forming any one of these convictions.

So, also, with regard to convictions arising from reflections upon the previous impressions made on the mind. By the organization of man, the senses first convey the impression of objects, – their qualities or relations to other things, – to that quality or power denominated our *consciousness*. Many of these impressions are thus received at various periods, and remain to be recalled by another faculty of our organization, called *memory*. These different impressions are then compared by another faculty or power of the organization.

These comparisons are more or less numerous or complex, according to the number of ideas to be compared with each other; they are of longer or shorter duration, depending upon the similarity or dissimilarity of the ideas, and the consequent difficulty or facility of detecting all the differences between them. When this comparison has been made, a faculty of the organization, commonly termed the *judgment*, decides upon the result. If the comparisons be hastily executed, and decided upon, it is said to be a hasty conclusion or imperfect judgment; if the ideas be carefully examined, under all the variety of comparisons that can be made with them, and a decided conviction follow, then it is said to be a sound judgment after due examination. But it sometimes happens, that by the most calm and deliberate examination and comparison of all the impressions made upon the mind, or ideas received into it, no decision can be made by the judging faculty: the balance, as to the result of comparison, is equal, relative to two or more conclusions; and without additional impressions from new facts, the subject of comparison remains in the mind without any decision. Now in each of these cases the convictions are made independently of the *will* of the individual, and these decisions, thus made, produce the sensations which create the will. In all this there is nothing which acts but the organization, changed as it has been, in its increasing formation, by the action of external circumstances upon it. The convictions, therefore, made on the mind by external objects, acting immediately through the senses, or by the power of reflection, comparison, and judgment, whether they are one faculty of the organization, or more, *are so made independently of the will*: and as the will has not the power to form the convictions in the first instance, neither has it the capacity to change them. The convictions remain fixed in the mind unless removed by new evidence sufficiently strong to overcome the previous opposing conviction.

In the next chapter it will be discovered, not only that the feelings are received, and the convictions formed, independently of the will; but that the *will itself* necessarily emanates *from* the feelings and convictions.

CHAPTER IV

'That his *feelings*, or his *convictions*, or both of them united, create the motive to action called the *will*, which stimulates him to act, and decides his actions.'

THIS, also, is a fact most important to be fully comprehended in all its parts, and which requires an exact development. Man's feelings include his convictions or mental inclinations – indeed, man may be said to be a compound of feeling of varied descriptions, engendered by different parts of his organization, physical, intellectual, and moral, and all of which are instincts of his nature. When man shall have his character so formed that he shall become a rational being, these instincts will be, probably, always, or very nearly always, in unison with each other; but if opposition should ever arise between them, the physical instinct will be completely under the guidance and controul of the mental and moral.

Calm reflection upon human motives to action will develope the causes which give strength to all these instincts; and by a due investigation of the circumstances upon which these causes depend, a much more accurate knowledge of the motives to human actions will be obtained.

In the present irrational state of society, the physical, mental, and moral instincts, are almost continually opposed to each other, and thus is nature thwarted throughout the whole life of every individual. There is a strong desire on the part of every child to express all its sensations – to say, 'I like this, and dislike that,' with regard to all inanimate circumstances; and to say to those who surround it, 'I love you,' or, 'I am indifferent,' or, 'I dislike you.' It is contrary to the natural feelings of children to have any mental reservations whatever. The love of truth is an instinct of human nature which would be always exercised in simplicity, were not individuals praised and blamed for particular feelings, and were not rewards and punishments ignorantly and arbitrarily awarded for them.

The direct and only road to a knowledge of man and of human nature, and to the attainment of happiness, is through the development of truth, by every individual, upon all occasions, expressing his thoughts and feelings as they are experienced by him. When this is done, and then only, can human nature be known; then, and then only, can arrangements be formed to give to man the superiority over all terrestrial animals, for which, by his organization, he is adapted; then, and then only, can man be so placed amidst his fellows, that he may enjoy in security all the happiness of which his nature is so susceptible. It is truth alone, developed by each individual expressing his sensations as they arise, that can elevate man to that rank in the creation to which his faculties entitle him; and it is the impossibility of adopting this practice, under the existing mistaken notions respecting human nature, that now keeps man the irrational being that he is, and which he ever has been: but when he shall acquire such an insight into the formation of his own character as to enable him to know *how* it is formed, he will discover that his *will* is as much created *for* him as any other quality or faculty which has been given to him; that it is the result of his physical feelings overpowering his mental feelings, or the reverse, or of an union of both. When the physical feelings are too strong for the mental, and a will is thus formed to act in opposition to the latter, it is sometimes said by the individual thus influenced, that he did so contrary to his will, that is, contrary to the sensations produced by his mental feelings; which, having reference to ulterior consequences, produced in his mind one will or motive, while the physical feelings, being at the moment of action stronger than the mental, produced another will or motive stronger than the former, and the action followed. At other times it is said by an individual, 'I did so and so contrary to my feelings or desire; I was strongly impelled to act according to my feelings (the physical motive or will to action), but my convictions (or mental feelings), by placing before me the ultimate consequences of yielding to those feelings, enabled me to resist them, and my better will prevailed.' That is, the individual is, according to circumstances, impelled to action by his physical or his mental feelings, whichever present or create the strongest motive, when they are in opposition to each other; and when they are so, the mental feelings of the individual are perplexed and injured, or the physical feelings are unnaturally restrained, and, consequently, an anxiety is experienced, always injurious to health and happiness. The present system of the world places man almost perpetually in the condition to have opposing feelings, to live in a daily contest between two feelings; sometimes one is victor, sometimes the other, and in consequence, man appears to be 'born to evil as the sparks fly upwards.'[a] Now, the physical as well as the mental feelings are capable of being made beneficial to man, both in his individual and his social character; they are both, under proper arrangements, calculated to produce health, satisfaction, and enjoyment, and to be made, at all times, to harmonize together; and it is not, perhaps, going too far to say that they need never be placed in opposition to each other.

Nature's laws require that the physical, mental, and moral, feelings, should be satisfied or exercised, up to the point of temperance, and if arrangements were made for this practice to be universal among mankind (and the experienced know that these arrangements could be easily effected), then there would not be two opposing feelings; and harmony would obtain throughout the human race. It is the erroneous supposition that the will is free, and not the necessary result of physical or mental feelings, or both united, that creates these two opposing feelings in every individual, or makes him the sport of two sets of motives; and this irrational state of human existence is produced by the want of knowledge relative to the mode of guiding and directing the physical and mental feelings, as they increase from birth to maturity, and change from that period to dissolution; for the physical feelings are excellent in themselves, and, although so much decried by those trained in religious mysteries and errors, are as essential to health and happiness as the mental feelings. The germs, only, of the physical feelings, or the *powers* of feeling, exist at birth; but these are capable of being made either to produce only evil and misery continually, or to become the source of daily and hourly benefit and pleasure

[a] See Job 5:7.

to the possessor and to society. The individual, however, is at the mercy of society for the guidance of these physical feelings; and upon the ignorance or intelligence of governments or of public opinion, relative to the formation of character and the science of society, will depend the right or wrong direction which shall be given to these feelings.

The due exercise of the physical feelings, at the times when nature requires them to be put into action, is essentially requisite to the health of both body and mind; and without such exercise, at the proper periods indicated by nature, the body will become diseased, and the mind confused and weakened. Society, as it is now constituted, is full of error on this subject, both in principle and practice; and man can never become either rational or happy, until the errors in both shall be removed.

As the physical feelings are capable of being trained so as to have a right or wrong, a beneficial or injurious, tendency, so are the mental and moral feelings. These mental feelings or convictions of the mind, may be founded on imaginary notions – on conjectures made at random without regard to facts; they may, indeed, be formed to be the most incongruous in their nature, the most contrary to all existing facts, and, consequently, the most opposed to reason: and such, generally speaking, are the mental feelings which have been given to the human race, through all known periods of its past existence. The time, however, seems approaching, when the human mind will be impressed with a very different character; when its feelings will be in accordance with facts; when none of them shall be incongruous, none mere conjectures, or wild fancies of the imagination; but when all of them shall be in perfect unison each with the others, and harmonize with the whole of external nature.

It, then, depends on the governing power, in directing the circumstances by which the physical and mental feelings are trained from birth, what shall be the kind of *will* each person under that government shall possess; and, of course, whether the prevailing will of the individual shall be essentially good or bad, superior or inferior: also, whether the stimuli to act shall be strong or weak – for this likewise depends upon the manner of forming the will – and, also, what shall be the nature of the actions which shall be performed. The strength of the action, and the action itself, are both decided by the will; and as the will is formed by the physical or the mental feelings, or both, the whole process of deciding human actions is, thus, resolvable into a knowledge of the mode by which superior physical and mental feelings may be given to the individuals from their birth.

Man is not, therefore, to be made a being of a superior order, by teaching him that he is responsible for his will and his actions. This is putting the most formidable obstacle in the way of his attaining the most valuable knowledge that man can acquire: it is the direct mode to prevent him from knowing himself; and it teaches him to believe himself another kind of being from that which he really is, and, in consequence, to err in all his thoughts and actions, respecting his own nature and human nature generally. No! the stimuli to action will henceforth not be the uncertain and inefficient influences of *deception* upon the human race, forcing them to imagine, contrary to every fact recorded in history, that each individual *himself* forms his feelings, thoughts, will, and consequent actions. It will be known that man is, altogether, a being whose organization, feelings, thoughts, will, and actions, are predetermined for him by the influence of external circumstances upon his original constitution; and that he is, therefore, irresponsible for the character formed for him, whatever it may be. Those who imagine, that the notion of individual responsibility is calculated to produce a better or more virtuous state of society, than the knowledge that every part of the character of man is formed for him, by circumstances pre-existing to the will which decides his actions, have yet to learn the laws of nature respecting man individually, and the science of society or the laws relative to man in a social state.

The first notion has formed man and society as they have been described by history, as they are found to be to-day over all the earth. We know, then, from *experience*, that this notion does not prevent the great majority of mankind from being ignorant or irrational, unjust to their fellow-men, and miserable themselves. What the knowledge of the true formation of human character may produce, we have only partial experience of; but from reasoning *a priori*, from facts as they exist, there can be no doubt that this knowledge will speedily lead to a practice which will enable the adult population, fully instructed in the principles of the formation of character, to train their descendents to become, physically, mentally, and morally, a superior race of beings, living in the most delightful harmony together, without any individual pride or vanity arising from their conscious superiority to their predecessors, or their imagined superiority to each other.

CHAPTER V

'That the organization of no two human beings is ever precisely similar at birth, nor can art subsequently form any two individuals, from infancy to maturity, to be precisely similar.'

It is well known to those accustomed to children, in infancy, that there is a decided and palpable difference between them at birth; occasionally there have been approximations so near, that, when seen apart from each other, superficial observers have imagined that there was no difference between them; but whenever any of those most nearly alike have been compared accurately together, a decided variation, in many particulars, has always been discovered. In fact, an accurate investigation, by persons competent to such examinations, will always detect a decided difference in the physical and mental organs of all human beings, such a difference as naturalists discover to exist in all the works of nature, whether organized or unorganized.

This variety in the organization not only exists at birth, but it is after birth daily and hourly increased by the influence either of circumstances different in their kinds or qualities, or varied in their order of succession; or even the same circumstances, acting, of course, in a different manner upon two different organizations, will produce different results, and thus each man is made to differ essentially from all other men.

It is indeed fortunate that there is this double guard to prevent exact similarity in the formation of any two individuals. The inconvenience of such similarity would be great; the monotony would be most disagreeable and prejudicial; and, altogether, the consequences of a greater resemblance among men, would be pernicious in every point of view in which the subject can be considered. It is, however, of great practical utility to know, 'that nature does not produce two human organizations alike at birth, and that art cannot subsequently form any two characters to be the same.' The difference between men exists by nature, and in opposition to all art, and is, therefore, inevitable. This difference, however, whether it be more or less, is not made by the individuals; it is made *for* them, by pre-existing circumstances, and no one can justly or rationally take merit or demerit to himself for any difference which may exist between him and any of his fellows.

The knowledge of this fact, when followed through all its consequences, will effectually destroy all motives to individual pride or vanity. No one versed in this knowledge of his nature, will think more highly of himself than of any of his fellow-men; selfishness, therefore, from personal considerations, will cease to exist, and a new mind, in this respect, will be formed. Man will discover, through a knowledge of the laws of his nature, the true cause of all differences among his fellow-men: he will not think it necessary that all should be alike at birth, or that attempts should be made to force them, contrary to their original and acquired nature, to feel, to think, or to act, precisely alike, seeing that these differences are created for them, and when created are inevitable.

The knowledge of the fact that this difference among all individuals exists by nature and from external circumstances, and that it is not caused by the individuals themselves, combined with a knowledge of the three preceding fundamental facts, will, of necessity, lay the foundation, in every mind trained to trace all the consequences to which these facts lead, of true morality and real virtue; that is, to have universal charity for the personal appearance, for the feelings, thoughts, actions, and general character, of all individuals, whatever may be their colour, language, religion, habits, or conduct. This knowledge will also prepare the mind of every one to entertain kind feelings towards all men; and when the children of one generation shall be educated to possess all these lovely qualities in body and mind, – which they *must* acquire as soon as they shall be trained, from birth, on the principles of the Rational System of Society, – they will, also, of necessity, possess that universal sympathy of feeling, which will compel each one to love his neighbour, not merely as well as, but much better than, himself. For if some are now made to love a few of their fellow creatures better than themselves, although both parties have been formed with all the inferior qualities of irrational beings, how certainly will this pure and superior affection be generated among mankind, when *all* shall be trained, from infancy, to be rational in their looks, thoughts, words, and actions; to be, in fact, compared with the past and present generations, a race of superior beings, physically, intellectually, and morally.

The mind accustomed to examine facts accurately, and to generalize its own ideas, will perceive the practical importance of this difference, made by nature, between all human beings; that its endless variety must of itself be a perpetual source of enjoyment to all, when in a rational state of existence; and that the difference between individuals, whether chiefly made by nature at birth, or afterwards by the influence of external circumstances, can never become among rational beings, a cause of pride, envy, or jealousy, and much less of any exclusive privileges.

The knowledge of the fact under consideration, united with the three preceding facts, will also destroy the germs of all mere personal ambition, or desire, in any one, to obtain rule over his fellows, or to possess any power or authority superior to that to which all, at the same age, will be acknowledged to be equally entitled.

As all receive the various physical, intellectual, and moral, qualities, whether produced by nature at their birth, or from the influence of external circumstances afterwards, independently of any power which they can create, the knowledge of this perpetual dependence upon causes which do not originate with themselves, will destroy the germs of all self-righteousness, self-importance, or arrogance of any kind. Egotism, also, of every description, and ignorant selfishness, the great banes of society, must disappear, under the practice of a system founded on a knowledge of these fundamental facts. Such feelings can have no place in minds fully comprehending these facts; there can be no germs of them; they cannot exist, for there will be nothing to create them. Thus, by an accurate knowledge of these few and plain, but eternal, laws of human nature, the causes which have hitherto given origin to the inferior feelings, erroneous judgments, and injurious passions, will be for ever removed from the human race.

CHAPTER VI

'That, nevertheless, the constitution of every infant, except in case of organic disease, is capable of being formed into a *very inferior*, or a *very superior*, being, according to the qualities of the external circumstances allowed to influence that constitution from birth.'

THE four previous facts relate to the general theory of the formation of the human character; they develope, step by step, the modes by which the infinite diversity of this extraordinary compound is created; they make it evident that the whole character or man is formed *for* and not *by* the individual: and these four fundamental facts, or principles, must be thoroughly understood before men can either think or act rationally, with respect to themselves or to their fellow-men.

The fifth and last of these fundamental facts, which now remains to be explained, is one of principle combined with practice; and with practice more important and comprehensive in its nature than any that has ever been presented to the world.

Its *principle* is, that every human being that comes into existence, with an organization not diseased, may be made to be either very inferior or very superior throughout life, unless accident or disease should affect the original constitution: and that the one or the other is to be accomplished through the instrumentality of inferior or superior circumstances, acting upon the organization possessed by the individual at birth.

The *practice* which the acknowledgement of this principle will necessarily induce, will be the removal of the existing inferior circumstances, which keep men in ignorance and poverty, which generate bad feelings and passions, which regularly train men to become vicious and to live in opposition to each other, and which compel them to become irrational and to suffer all manner of miseries. It will, also, occasion the removal of all those injurious influences by which mankind are now surrounded, by creating an entirely new combination of such external circumstances as are under human direction, and preventing every unfavourable influence, subject to the controul of man, from acting upon any individual from birth to death.

This will be the universal practice of man, as soon as he shall be taught to know what manner of being he is, and how he is to act in order to train his offspring to become rational.

What this new combination of external circumstances under human controul and direction *ought* to be, and *how* it is to be formed, will be explained in subsequent parts of this work.

CHAPTER VII

THE FUNDAMENTAL LAWS OF HUMAN NATURE, OR FIRST PRINCIPLES OF THE SCIENCE OF MAN

SECTION I

'Human Nature is a compound of animal propensities, intellectual faculties, and moral qualities,or the germs of them.'

WHEN men attend to the evidence of their senses, and observe what passes around them among the other productions of nature, they cannot fail to discover that they possess much in common with the vegetable and animal creation; – the desire for food to support their existence, for sleep to recruit their exhausted power, for union with the opposite sex to continue their species. These, therefore, may be considered *the animal propensities* of man, which he possesses in common with other animals, and from those of which they do not differ in their general character.

Similar observations will discover other faculties in man, analogous, in some degree, to the instincts of animals, with this remarkable difference, that the instincts of animals remain nearly the same through the life of every succeeding generation, while the mental faculties of the human race are continually enlarging, through experience, or the acquisition of new knowledge, leading to new discoveries in every department of life. This power of adding to the number of ideas in the mind, of comparing the previous ideas with those more lately received, to ascertain their agreement or disagreement, and thereby attaining a knowledge of permanent general principles, and deducing sciences from them, constitutes what are termed *the intellectual faculties* of man; and it is this power in human nature that distinguishes man from all other animals and earthly productions. These faculties have hitherto been far less beneficial in promoting his happiness than the instincts of other animal appear to have been to them; and it is probable that, in consequence of the errors of the inexperienced intellects of man, he has hitherto possessed less enjoyment than any other tribe of beings.

The third division of the elements of human nature comprises *the moral feelings*, or those sensations which are produced when the individual feels conscious that he has added to, or deducted from, the sum of happiness in the creation; producing pleasure in the former, and pain in the latter case.

Man is thus constituted a being altogether of physical, intellectual, and moral, feelings; and his happiness can arise only from the harmony existing between these component parts of his nature. When these elements of human nature are in their best proportion to each other, man is prepared to enjoy the greatest degree of happiness through life, provided the external circumstances around him are in unison with his nature. But these circumstances are now, and ever have been, so much in opposition to human nature, that, it is probable, the individuals who have hitherto possessed the finest compound of the elements of human nature, for the acquisition of all excellence and enjoyment, have been made, through the counteraction of external circumstances formed by man through mistaken notions of his own nature, to experience more pain and misery than those individuals who have been less favoured in their proportions of the original elements of their nature.

The practical application of this first law of human nature will be to use the most rational means to secure, to future generations, the best proportion of these elements, in the original constitution of every child at birth; which will be effected, on the same general principles as those which men now pursue in obtaining superior vegetable and animal productions, by a scientific knowledge of the methods most proper to be applied to attain the object proposed.

SECTION II

'These propensities, faculties, and qualities, are united in different proportions in each individual.'

This law of human nature has been, in part, considered in Chapter V.

The evidence of our senses, the strongest evidence possessed by man, proves the universality of the law. No two infants have ever yet been known to possess, at birth, the same proportions of physical, intellectual, or moral elements. It appears, indeed, from all the facts of which we have any knowledge, that no two senses of any two individuals, have ever been precisely alike; and as no two things in nature have yet been found the same, it may be concluded that no two senses of any two infants have been yet formed without some difference. Every consideration relating to the question, clearly proves that it would be absurd, as well as useless, to imagine that there could be any intention on the part of the Power that gives existence to man to form any two of them alike. It is highly improbable that human beings ever have been made to appear externally, to feel internally, or to think and act, in any particulars, alike; they are, evidently, so formed as to make it impossible that they ever should do so; and in so forming man, his happiness has been the most effectually secured. When men shall be trained, from infancy, to become rational beings, their highest social enjoyment will arise from the endless variety of useful and agreeable qualities which will be possessed by the human race, and which will be delightfully natural in each individual. There will be no affectation, no attempt to copy the appearance or actions of conspicuous individuals, no forced, unnatural, character, arising from these awkward attempts; but each one will be independent, unaffected, and naturally graceful in the free and unconstrained expression of his own thoughts and feelings; and it is thus that intelligence, grace, dignity, and benevolence, in all their varied natural combinations, will become the common characteristics of mankind.

It is this endless variety in the compound of the original elements of human nature in each separate person, that forms but one being in the whole of mankind, and, with an ever-ending diversity of qualities in the *individual*, produces a perfect equality of rights, privileges, and happiness, among all of the human race. All thus come from the same *general* elements, in infinitely mixed proportions; all live upon the same general atmosphere; and, at dissolution, each particular organization returns to the same general elements, to give new life to new compounds, and to reanimate continually improving organizations; thus forming the future life eternal, to which, probably, there will be no termination. It is thus that the good or evil done in one generation benefits or affects future generations; and hence the utility of making the greatest possible progress in every kind of amelioration, and in every species of government during each successive generation; that the offspring which proceeds from us, – which is, in fact, part of ourselves, or ourselves continued through succeeding ages, – should have the greatest amount of advantages and enjoyments.

Thus, when reason shall prevail over superstition, the different proportions of the elements of our nature which are united in different individuals, will be calculated to produce harmony among mankind, and infinitely to increase the happiness of the human race.

SECTION III

'This diversity constitutes the original difference between one individual and another.'

The diversity of the human race is necessary to the happiness of man. In the very few instances in which there has been a strong resemblance between two individuals, living at the same period, in the same district, the inconveniencies which have been experienced have been sufficient to prove the endless confusion that would arise if the individuals of the human race were formed to be more nearly alike than they have been. This diversity is, then, not only a necessary result of the organization of man, but should be found, and in a rational state of society *will* be found, a potential cause of his greatest happiness. Without this diversity, society itself would be a mass of confusion, and universal disorder would pervade all the transactions of mankind; the business of life could not be continued without this variety among the human species.

It is irrational to suppose, then, that all men, or that any portion of mankind, can be justly governed under any complicated system of human laws which presupposes men to be influenced alike by the same external circumstances. Nothing can demonstrate more forcibly the irrational state in which men have hitherto existed, and the little knowledge of human nature which their rulers have possessed, than the modes by which they have been governed in, what is called, the civilized world.

It is now quite evident, that the legislators and lawgivers of former times were themselves *totally ignorant of human nature*, and, consequently, of all the practical measures necessary to be adopted, in order to insure its well-doing, well-being, and happiness.

In consequence of the human mind not having been directed to the study of itself and of human nature generally, every imaginable error has been committed in forming society in those countries which have been called civilized. Some individuals, ages ago, supposed that human nature ought not to be what it ever has been, and is, but something quite different, and they set about inventing various devices of religions, laws, and governments, to force it to become what they conceived it should be, and could be made to be. But through every device hitherto adopted to change and improve human nature, it has remained unchanged in its original character, and has been made to act infinitely worse by all the attempts to compel it to become unnatural.

Until men shall be induced by reason, to desist from these absurdities, human nature will continue vicious or unnatural, and men will still exhibit all manner of irrationality in their public and private transactions, and render each other as miserable as their nature will admit. When the error of this proceeding shall be made manifest, all attempts to govern men on the notion that they ought to feel, think, and act, alike, or that each individual ought to feel, think, and act, alike at all times, will cease; and the natural diversity of man will be acknowledged and provided for, as well as the natural change of feelings, thoughts, and actions, of the same individual, as he grows in experience, or is altered by the presence of successive and differing objects.

The knowledge of the fact that men are made to differ one from the other in the proportions of all the elements of their nature, and that this difference is the source whence infinite excellence and happiness may be derived, will induce those who shall, hereafter, direct the public and private proceedings of mankind, to adopt such general laws, regulations, and arrangements, as will allow this natural diversity among men to have its full scope of action, and to produce all the endless benefits and enjoyments which must, necessarily, flow from its existence and encouragement.

SECTION IV

'These elements of his nature, and their proportions, are made by a power unknown to the individual, and consequently without his consent.'

The evidence of our senses demonstrates this to be a fact. The ignorance of a child when born, of himself, how he was formed, how he came into existence, what are his qualities, physical, intellectual, and moral, is obvious to the most common observer. No one can, for a moment, imagine that the infant possessed any power to direct or controul his formation, or gave his consent, in any manner, to become what he is. A being, therefore, thus brought into existence, cannot be made, with any degree of justice or of common sense, accountable for the qualities of his nature, or for the particular proportions of the different elements which have been united in his individual formation.

To make him accountable for them, to form arrangements in society upon the supposition that he ought to be accountable for them, to make laws in conformity with this supposition, and to educate and govern men under such a notion, is to adopt a system erroneous in its whole combination; a system, which must engender all the bad passions, keep men ignorant, continually produce poverty, crime, disease, and misery, and make man an inconsistent and irrational being. Under a system founded upon this supposition, men must become irrational in their feelings, thoughts, and actions; they must become enemies to one another, and they must, in all their transactions, counteract each other's happiness. But all the systems of the world have emanated from this error, and, consequently, they have all produced anger, hatred, and uncharitableness. The notion that human nature in the aggregate is bad, and that each individual is accountable for that portion of it which has fallen to his lot, is the source of the present ignorant and wretched condition of the human race, in all parts of the world.

Before man can begin to perceive what is rational – before he can in any degree understand what manner of being he is, he must distinctly know that he cannot become accountable for what human nature is, or for what he has himself been made to be; that, in like manner, none of his fellow-men can be justly or beneficially made, in any degree, accountable for what they have been formed to be at their birth. He must know that their organization is their nature, and as this is, so must they be. It will be vain to attempt to form man to become a rational creature, until he can be taught, by reason, to give up the absurd notion that his nature is bad, and that, to become virtuous and happy, he ought to act in opposition to it. The beginning of wisdom is to know ourselves; and the commencement of this knowledge is clearly to understand that human nature, in the abstract, is neither better nor worse than any other organized nature, and that it is better or worse only as it possesses superior or inferior qualities for the acquirement of knowledge, and the enjoyment of happiness, compared with other terrestrial organizations.

A superior state of human society, therefore, can be formed, only, upon a knowledge that man is not the former of his own nature; that it is organized in a manner unknown to him, and without his consent; and that, when it is comparatively ill-formed in any particular instance, the individual is an object of compassion, calling for our kindest exertions to remedy the evil, and never once for blame or punishment. It is this knowledge of our nature, alone, which can lay the foundation of charity and affection for our race. No other view of human nature can create the feelings of pure charity and sincere affection for the whole family of mankind. This is that knowledge which alone can produce the love which casts out fear, and the confidence which knows no limits. It is that knowledge by which alone error, ignorance, vice, or misery, for they are but one, can be removed, and be replaced by an accurate comprehension of man and nature, and by a consequent state of human society which shall be virtuous and happy. Let us, then, openly acknowledge the innocence of man, with respect to his original nature and the superstructure of character which society has raised upon it, and also, the ignorance and injustice of making the individual accountable for that which nature and society have compelled him to become.

The contrary notion is an error, which, so long as it shall be retained, will be destructive of virtue and happiness among the human race, and will compel them to remain irrational, and ignorant, and wretched.

SECTION V

'Each individual comes into existence within certain external circumstances, which act upon his peculiar original organization, more especially during the early period of his life, and, by impressing their general character upon him, form his local and national character.'

This, also, is a fact evident to our senses, and confirmed by all our reasoning faculties. We see every infant come into existence within certain external circumstances. The kinds or qualities of these circumstances depend upon the country in which he is born, and especially upon the particular district – upon the character and class in life of the parents – upon the comparatively good or ill success of the parents in their class – upon the other inmates of the family – upon those in connection with it – and, generally, upon the peculiar laws, customs, and prevalent public opinion, of the immediate neighbourhood in which the being lives during infancy, childhood, and youth. These external circumstances continually act upon the organization of the child, and by their unceasing impressions, during every moment of its existence, train it, in a manner unknown to itself, to acquire the local language, habits, and manners, of the class, district, and country, in which it lives. So effectually will these impressions be made upon the organization of any individual, that should he, at matured age, remove to a distant part of the same country, the experienced will easily discover in what local district he has formerly lived; and if he should go into a foreign country, men of the world would know of what localities he was a native, or that he had been a localized being belonging to a certain district; and they would be competent, by noticing the effects which external circumstances had produced upon him, to ascertain the general character of those external circumstances. So true is it that 'man is the creature of the circumstances in which he is placed.' It is thus that the Frenchman is so easily distinguished from the Englishman; the Spaniard from the German; the

Portuguese from the Russian; the European from the African; the Asiatic from the American, etc; that the inhabitants of northern latitudes are so easily known from those of the southern; and it is owing to this cause that there is so much less difference between the higher classes of different countries than between the lower classes of the same countries, the former being usually under a greater number of similar general external circumstances than the latter.

It is owing to the same cause that a native of Yorkshire is so readily known from a native of Wiltshire, a Welshman from an Englishman, or a Scotsman from an Irishman, a countryman from a citizen, or one who has lived all his life in Glasgow from one who has lived all his life in Edinburgh, although there is only a distance of forty-two miles between them.

These facts, which may be multiplied to an unlimited extent, prove, beyond all doubt, that the external circumstances existing around individuals form their local, national, and general, characters.

SECTION VI

'The influence of these general external circumstances is modified, in a particular manner, by the peculiar organization of each individual; and thus the distinctive character of each is formed and maintained through life.'

Observation and reflection prove, not only, as stated in the previous section, that the external circumstances in which the individual is placed from birth through childhood and youth, form his local, national, and general, character, but, also, that this local, national, and general, character, is diversified in every one, by reason of the difference between one organization at birth and another.

As organizations are made to differ from one another, as explained in the second section of this chapter, so is there necessarily a consequent difference in the effects produced upon them by the same general and local external circumstances.

It is owing to this law of human nature, combined with the impracticability of placing any two human beings under precisely the same external circumstances, for a single day, or even an hour, that no two children are alike in the same family, that brothers and sisters differ in what are called their *natural* dispositions, and in their capacities to acquire a knowledge of certain things, or to perform certain operations.

It is owing to this, and the preceding laws of human nature, that the natives of particular countries, though so much alike in their general character, differ so much from each other individually; that Quakers, Jews, Mahommedans, Hindoos, etc, resemble each other so much generally, and yet, when seen together, are in many particulars so different.

SECTION VII

'No infant has the power of deciding at what period of time, or in what part of the world, he shall come into existence, – of what parents he shall be born, – in what religion he shall be trained, – what manners, customs, or habits, shall be given to him, – or by what other external circumstances he shall be surrounded, from birth to death.'

None will dispute the truth of these facts or laws or our nature; for each fact is a self-evident proposition, and admits of no difference of opinion. They are facts of the highest importance for the human race to comprehend and act upon; and yet they appear to be unknown and unappreciated by all tribes and people; for none have hitherto regulated their laws, institutions, or practices, in conformity with them.

This law of our nature developes the chief causes which influence the destiny of all individuals, and which form them to be what they are.

An essential part of the character of all men proceeds from the age of the world in which they are born. If, for instance, all the philosophers and men of letters whom we have any knowledge, had lived at a period previous to the invention of the alphabet, their characters would have been altogether different from those in which they now appear by their writings. They would have been savages, perhaps of weak physical powers, and, therefore, despised by their stronger associates, and kept in abject subjection by them.

Socrates, Plato, Aristotle, etc, in former times, as well as Shakespeare, Milton, Bacon, Locke, Newton,[a] etc among the moderns, would, in all probability, if they had lived before the invention of letters, have been ordinary men, occupied in performing the common drudgeries of savage life, to supply their physical wants.

Or, if the heroes of former and modern times had lived in other ages, and been trained under the circumstances existing in those other ages, they might have been no heroes, from the want of the exciting and favouring causes which drew forth their powers in the countries in which they became celebrated.

Again, an essential part of the character of all men depends upon the country of their birth. Had the celebrated men of Greece and Rome, of Great Britain, France, Europe generally, and the United States, been born in

[a] Socrates (c. 470–399 BC): Greek philosopher.
Plato (428–348 BC): Greek philosopher.
Aristotle (384–322 BC): Greek philosopher.
William Shakespeare (1564–1616): playwright.
John Milton (1608–74): poet.
Francis Bacon (1561–1626): philosopher and statesman.
John Locke (1632–1704): philosopher and statesman.
Isaac Newton (1642–1727): mathematician and scientist.

Siberia, Turkey, or under the Spaniards in South America, or in the Islands of the Pacific Ocean, previous to their discovery by Europeans, how different would have been their employments – how different their associations of ideas, and how different, beyond a doubt, would have been their acquirements and their fate!

Another, and a very important, part of the character of all men, is produced by the individual character of their parents. An infant born of, and trained by, parents who have themselves been ill-trained, whose powers of mind are weak, or, if strong, mis-directed, whose habits are bad, and who generally associate with the inferior or worst members of their class in life, will become, at maturity, a very different being from one whose parents were well-trained, their powers of mind strong and well-directed, their habits comparatively good, and their general associates among the superior and better members of their class.

Again, infants nearly similar in their natural faculties, born of either royal or pauper parents, would become, at maturity, so different in general appearance, language, manners, and general mode of feeling and thinking, that they might easily be mistaken for beings of a separate species, and almost of another nature. A difference, although not quite to the same extent, will arise from infants of nearly similar natural faculties, being born of parents engaged in agriculture, in trade, or commerce, or in any of the professions, if the children are trained in the same pursuits. How different become the habits, manners, feelings, thoughts, actions, and appearance, of a human being living within circumstances to make him a working chimney-sweeper, a dustman, or a scavenger, and one living in other circumstances, to become an archbishop, a lord chancellor, or a commander-in-chief of armies or navies. The associations of ideas in the minds of these opposite parties, form them, in fact, to be totally ignorant of the thoughts and feelings of each other, and to have scarcely anything in common, except the general physical constitution of human nature; and yet, if the circumstances in which the parties have been placed from birth, had been reversed, the thoughts, feelings, manners, habits, appearance, and conduct, of both parties, would have been also reversed.

It is thus, by the quality and quantity of external circumstances, properly applied for the purpose, that the character of every human being, after he comes into existence, may be principally formed, whatever may be his organization, short of organic disease, to become, at maturity, very inferior or very superior. It is thus that future generations may be placed and trained, from their birth, upon principles as certain and permanent in their nature as those of the fixed sciences, to become, without exception, beings of an order altogether different from the past generations of men, and greatly superior to them, physically, intellectually, and morally.

The proper business of man, hereafter, will therefore be to make himself thoroughly acquainted with 'the science of the influence of circumstances over human nature;' and by a knowledge of this science, he will hold the destinies of future ages, as to their inferiority or superiority, their misery or happiness, under his controul; and the love that parents have for their children will secure superiority and happiness for all future generations.

Thus is the path to truth opened; and it may soon be made so clear and plain to all understandings, that men, by steadily pursuing it, must remove sin and misery, or ignorance and vice, for ever from the world, and establish in place thereof, knowledge and happiness, which will continually increase, without a chance of retrogression, except by some unforeseen and unavoidable convulsion of nature, beyond the power of the human faculties to controul.

It is thus, and thus only, that pure charity and sincere affection can become universal among men; that peace, knowledge, and an ever-active kindness, can be made to pervade the earth; and that man shall be able to live without fear of man or other animals, and in perfect confidence with all the superior agencies and powers of nature.

Death itself will be considered simply as a change of one organization for others; and perceiving thus a common interest in all animated nature, all will endeavour to prevent pain and to give pleasure to whatever has life and feeling.

Thus will that long-anticipated period of happiness, so often foretold by our ancestors, be enjoyed by all of the human race.

SECTION VIII

'Each individual is so organized, that, when young, he may be made to receive either true ideas derived from a knowledge of facts, or false notions derived from the imagination, and in opposition to facts.'

The human mind, in its infancy, is passive in receiving its first impressions. These may be the most opposed to facts, or the most in unison with them; they may be derived from the wildest fancies, falsifying all that is true, and so impressed on the confiding unresisting faculties of the child, that, by degrees, it shall possess no power of reasoning accurately, or consequently, from any fixed or certain data; or they may be so true to nature, so consonant with all facts, so completely in accordance with each other, so uniformly consistent in all parts, that before the child shall attain his eighth year, he shall have so many true impressions, in unison and strict accordance with all the facts by which he is surrounded – they shall form within his mind so many ideas, each proving the truth of the others – that they will become to him a '*Standard of Truth*,' by which he can afterwards examine all new ideas which shall be presented to his mind; and by which he will be enabled, in most cases, to say, at once, whether they are ideas derived from facts, and certainly true – whether they are *probabilities*, the confirmation of whose truth or fallacy requires a more extended knowledge of facts – or whether they are mere visions of the fancy, proceeding from illusory impressions.

By a knowledge of this law of our nature, and of the science of the influence of circumstances over human nature, measures may be adopted to surround all children with those circumstances which shall make true impressions only on their minds; and not only make those impressions which are true, but make them in the order in which they ought to be received; so that, conformably with the nature of the human faculties and the wants of man, the whole mind may be based upon a right foundation, and built up in such a manner that the fabric shall possess, at maturity, its just proportions of firmness, unity, use, and ornament.

It is only when human beings shall be thus trained, and placed within external circumstances all in accordance with such training, and shall be permitted to act in unison with their nature, that it will be discovered what men may be made to become, generally and individually. No man now living can form an adequate conception of the difference that will exist between human nature trained and placed as it has ever yet been, and as it will be when each individual shall be trained, from infancy, in that only which is in accordance with facts, well educated in all that is known, and placed within circumstances all in unison with his nature.

This change is necessary to insure to man all the improvement and all the happiness of which his nature is susceptible; the most ample means now exist by which this state of human society may be attained in a very few years.

SECTION IX

'Each individual is so organized, that he must necessarily become irrational when he is made from infancy to receive, as truths, false fundamental notions; and can only become truly rational when he shall be made to receive true fundamental principles, without any admixture of error.'

If it be true that consistency in thought and action constitutes that which is rational, and that inconsistency of ideas and actions is the character of irrationality, then this fact is a self-evident law of human nature, and becomes a truth most important for practice.

All men, hitherto, have been made from infancy to receive false notions as truths, and often as truths of the highest import; as truths on which the whole fabric of their mind must rest, as on a sure and solid foundation; as truths in opposition to which no other impressions ought to be made or received.

The consequence of this mode of proceeding has been to make all men inconsistent in their thoughts and actions; to create prejudices the most opposed to facts; to fill the mind with the most vague impressions of its own nature, and to give the most erroneous notions respecting the thoughts and feelings of others; and thus, to compel all the human race to become at mature age irrational.

By this system of error, continued from one generation to another, during the whole period of history, human nature has been maltreated and grievously abused; the infants and children of every generation have been the mental slaves of the preceding generations. None have been permitted to have their reasoning faculties cultivated free from parental and national prejudices; but, on the contrary, all have been compelled to become – what their fathers had been previously compelled to be – slaves to the most gross and inconsistent errors, which rendered them, to all intents and purposes, much more irrational in their thoughts, feelings, and actions, than any other species of animals, yet claimants to a superiority of intellect over the unerring instincts of the latter.

It is thus, and thus only, that ignorance of human nature has so long prevailed; that vice has been created; that the propensities of men, healthy and beneficial when regularly and duly exercised, have, by encountering an unnatural opposition, been forced into violent and injurious passions, engendering innumerable diseases, and leading to premature old age and death. It is thus that uncharitableness, unkindness, and hatred, have been made to spring up, where, under a rational cultivation of the reasoning faculties, charity, kindness, confidence, and affection, would have been alone known. It is thus that man has been cheated of his birthright, made to suppress all the finer feelings of his nature, and to sacrifice high intelligence and permanently increasing happiness, to the wildest fancies of a disordered imagination. It is thus that he has been made a physical and mental tyrant, a moral coward, and a being full of every kind of deception. It is thus that man, in despite of his wonderful discoveries in some of the fixed sciences, or general laws of nature, has continued, as he is found at this day, an ignorant and miserable being, devoting all his faculties to the acquisition of what he deems wealth – wealth which, in a rational state of society, might be obtained to satiety for all, by the most easy and simple of all arrangements.

It is by thus training man from infancy, to compel him to become an irrational being, that he is made an enemy to himself and to his species; that irritation and anger are engendered between man and man; and that tribes and nations are made to delight in war, and in wreaking their vengeance on defenceless women and children. It is thus that man is made a deceitful slave and a ferocious savage, covering the enormity of errors producing these results, by the term civilization, which term, in fact, means nothing more than an extended association of human beings, acting systematically in opposition to their own nature, and to their own happiness, individually and collectively.

Instead of longer pursuing this insane course, it now behoves all men, who have discovered the enormous magnitude of the errors which have hitherto formed the mind and governed the conduct of the whole population of the world, to consider, in good earnest, what practical measures are necessary to put an immediate stop to these melancholy and miserable proceedings, and to put men, hereafter, in a condition to become rational creatures; that they may acquire charity and affection for, and have full confidence in, each other, in order that they may live in union, peace, and harmony, through all succeeding generations.

This improvement in the condition of mankind will be easily introduced into practice as soon as the proper arrangements shall be formed to teach *only truth, in accordance with facts*, to the young mind, and to permit all of human kind to act in conformity with the unchangeable laws of their nature.

SECTION X

'Each individual is so organized that, when young, he may be trained to acquire injurious habits only, or beneficial habits only, or a mixture of both.'

Observation and experience will convince those who notice and reflect upon what they see and hear, that the fact now stated is an unchanging law of human nature, – one the most important to be understood, in order that it may be practically and effectually applied to prevent future generations from experiencing the evils necessarily arising from injurious and inferior habits, and to secure to them the unknown and inestimable advantages to be derived from a whole people being trained in superior habits only.

It is seen, that the general habits of any country are invariably given to those who are born and brought up in that country; – that the particular habits of local districts are also, as regularly, given to those who constantly remain secluded within them; that the habits of a court are given to courtiers, and the habits of the aristocracy to those who are daily under their influence; so, also, the habits of St Giles's are given to those unfortunate beings who are compelled by ignorance and poverty to remain subjected to the influence of peculiar circumstances which, in such a district, are sure to be produced.

It is equally observable, that those beings who live in the middle stations of life, have neither the habits of courtiers nor of paupers, but mixed habits, altogether the result of the peculiar class in which their daily and hourly associations take place, modified by the thousand nameless differences which are found to exist in every district and family. The slight degree of difference between the habits of one individual and another, in the same family, is owing, in part, to the variety in the compound of elements which formed the constitution at birth; and also, in part, to the variety in the order in which the impressions from external circumstances are made upon them, and to the degrees of strength, or to the frequency, with which they happened to be impressed upon the different parties. If, then, it be a law of human nature to receive habits from external circumstances around it, that vicious and inferior habits shall proceed from vicious and inferior circumstances, mixed habits from circumstances of a mixed character, and good and superior habits from good and superior circumstances, how necessary is it that all the nations of the world should now begin to consider in what manner they may most beneficially remove the injurious and inferior circumstances, and substitute those only which are beneficial and superior!

Whenever men shall take a correct view of their condition – shall well understand their own nature, and ascertain the real causes which engender vice and misery, and those which produce virtue and happiness, they will also clearly perceive the overwhelming advantages of training all, without exception, in the best habits only, in order that no example of vicious or inferior habits should be seen, to corrupt, in any degree, the purity of character which will be formed by the example of virtuous and superior habits only.

The easiest mode of training men to be intelligent, superior in their habits, manners, and conduct, and to enjoy progressive happiness from birth to death, is to adopt decisive measures to prevent the formation of vicious or inferior habits in a single individual. And when all the laws of human nature, the conditions requisite for happiness, and the science of society, or the social state of man, shall be fully understood, it will be discovered to be for the interest of every one, that not a single individual shall be neglected in the formation of his habits from infancy to maturity, and that it will be much more easy to form arrangements to make *all* really superior, than to train a *few* to be what are now ignorantly considered superior, while the many around them are neglected and allowed to grow up inferior.

Good habits must be given to *all*, or the *best* cannot be given to *any*.

SECTION XI

'Each individual is so organized, that he *must believe* according to the strongest conviction that is made upon his mind; which conviction cannot be given to him by his will, nor be withheld by it.'

This law of human nature has been already explained in considerable detail under the head of the second fundamental fact; but it may be useful here to enlarge somewhat more upon it, because the mistake which our ancestors made respecting this and the succeeding law, has given rise to all religions among nations calling themselves civilized – religions which, for so many generations, have caused endless divisions among mankind, and produced, in consequence, so much misery.

It is necessary, therefore, that all doubt respecting the fact stated in this law of our nature should be for ever removed from the human mind; and, until this shall be effectually done, it will be impracticable to train men to become rational in their thoughts, feelings, and actions, and equally impossible to form arrangements to train them to become intelligent, sincere, and permanently happy.

Men have been taught by the priests who have been at the head of every worshipping sect, that they ought to believe the particular dogmas of the religion which they teach; that men are good, and deserve, and will receive, reward, in proportion as they believe in those dogmas; and that they are bad, and deserve, and will receive, punishment, according to their disbelief.

Theology, when stripped of useless words, and of the mysteries with which all religions are veiled from the common eye, is founded upon this single dogma; and, as the law of human nature, stated at the head of this section, is a true law, confirmed by all known facts, then, of necessity, all the religions established on a false notion of human nature, directly opposed to this law, must be errors of the imagination, and must lead, as they have done, to every evil experienced through the past ages of the world. This error is, at this moment, the real cause of all anger, hatred, and division among mankind. It induces men to suppose that others *can* believe the same unfounded and fanciful notions that *they* have been taught; and that their fellow-men *ought* to believe these same fanciful notions. It induces men to suppose, that, if others do not express their belief in the same words which they use, with respect, often, to the most incomprehensible incongruities, they are justified in applying to such unbelievers all manner of opprobrious terms. It also induces them to excite the worst feelings of society in opposition to those whom they term heretics; to inflict every kind of cruelty upon them; and not unfrequently to sacrifice their lives under the most excruciating torments. And this solely because those who have been compelled to differ from them, have possessed too much honesty and firmness to become hypocrites, and to say that which is contrary to the convictions which have been made upon their minds, and which, according to this law of their nature, it is utterly impossible that they of themselves could change. Anger, hatred, and cruelty have been and are thus engendered by the religious against those among their fellow-men who cannot make themselves believe sectarian doctrines, solely because these latter are too sincere and strictly conscientious to express in words – though it be to promote their interest or save their lives – that which is opposed to their calm and deliberate convictions; convictions forced upon them by the strongest evidence that has been presented to their minds, and which, by an unchanging law of their nature, they must receive.

This error, with another to be explained in the succeeding section, is the evil genius of the world, the Devil of the Christians, and the real and the sole cause of all lies and hypocrisy. Remove these two errors, and the Devil will no longer have the power to torment human kind; he will take his flight from earth, and, with all the imaginary evil existences conceived by the ancients, be no more heard or thought of. The world will then speedily become, in reality, that paradise about which so much has been said and written. And, until this demon of ignorance shall be unmasked and removed from human society, mankind must remain – as they have been, as they are to this day – beings who have been made to prefer darkness to light, falsehood to truth, vice to virtue, misery to happiness; beings taught to contend against their nature, and made to believe that they are thereby obeying the author of their own and of all nature! beings, in fact, who, by ignorance and error, acting upon the most noble and capable qualities of mind and body, have been forced for innumerable ages to live the life of vicious, localized, irrational animals.

Who, then, can calculate the extent of the interests which are now involved in seeing this cause of all human errors and evils brought to light, exposed to all, and for ever removed from every district of the world? All, all, from the highest to the lowest, from the oldest to the youngest, have the deepest interest – an interest combining their happiness as individuals, the happiness of their offspring, and of all future generations, – in striking a deathblow now and at once against this hydra of human ills; in rooting up, without farther delay, this tree of evil, which bears poisonous fruits only, and which produces not a single blossom of good to counteract its ever-increasing evil and destructive effects.

SECTION XII

'Each individual is so organized, that he *must like* that which is pleasant to him, or which, in other words, produces agreeable sensations in him; and *dislike* that which is unpleasant to him, or which, in other words, produces in him disagreeable sensations; and he cannot know, previous to experience, what particular sensations new objects will produce on any one of his senses.'

Next to the law of human nature which has been described in the preceding section, the one now to be considered is the most important to be understood in principle, and to be pursued, through all its ramifications, fully, honestly, and fairly in practice. No one law of human nature, except the one preceding, has been so little understood; and of no one law, with the same exception, has the infringement produced such direful consequences to mankind. The misery inflicted on the human race, by the errors respecting this law of human nature, has been of a peculiar character; producing bodily diseases, mental aberrations, concealed torments afflicting even unto death; and engendering falsehood, hyprocrisy, and crime, to an extent which cannot be appreciated by the most powerful imagination, even to a tithe of its real amount.

This is a law of nature which the great mass of the world have never yet been put into a condition to examine. They have, from infancy, been taught the most absurd notions respecting it; their minds, individually, and in association, have been, most unnaturally, trained to acknowledge an error completely opposed to this law; and hence all manner of unjust laws, unwise regulations, and cruel arrangements have been adopted and acted upon, in direct opposition to all the most plain, obvious, and powerful feelings of human nature; feelings always exerting themselves as instincts of man's organization, to direct him in the right course to health, virtue, and happiness; but which, until now, in all countries termed civilized, have been met and turned out of nature's course by the prejudices implanted in all, from infancy, through ignorance of the everlasting laws of the universe. And thus, that law which, when known, and acted upon in conformity with nature, will produce the finest, highest, and most exquisite feelings of pleasure and satisfaction to the human race, has been made, through the grossest ignorance, the means of corrupting those feelings to the basest purposes, and of poisoning all their enjoyments, making earth a pandemonium instead of a paradise, as it so easily might be made by acting in obedience to the simple and unerring instincts of our organization; an organization formed purposely to direct man, in the same manner as the general instincts of nature, to those movements, exertions, and feelings which are necessary to his sustenance, health, and enjoyment.

This law of nature is evidently intended to induce, impel, or compel one portion of organized matter to seek some other portion of matter necessary to its best state of existence, and this law seems to pervade all nature, except when man by his absurd aritificial laws, opposed to nature's laws, interferes, and says to the Power which animates and organizes the universe, 'I am more wise and holy than thou, and I will therefore oppose thy laws with all my might, and endeavour to frustrate thy weak and foolish decrees. I will force into union, according to my notions, bodies and minds, contrary to thy laws, and compel the continuance of the union, however thy laws may repel or loathe the connection.'

Thus has the ignorance of man, with regard to his own nature and universal nature, interfered in opposition to his own happiness, and to the happiness of all surrounding nature, as far as his limited powers extend.

He has decreed that man shall love that power which animates the universe, before he has any knowledge of what that power is. He has endeavoured to compel man to love his neighbour as himself, before he has ascertained the nature of man, or of his neighbour, or how love is produced. He has decreed that men and women, whose natural sympathies and affections unite them at one time, and repel each other at another, shall speak and act in opposition to these unavoidable feelings; and thus has he produced hypocrisy, crime and misery, beyond the powers of language to express.

It is thus that disunion, crime, and misery, are always engendered by man in attempting to oppose the laws of human nature, and to interpose his own imaginary notions.

If man had attentively examined facts, he would long ago have ascertained, that liking or disliking, loving or hating, or indifference, with regard to any of the human senses individually, or to the whole collectively, is never in a single instance an act of the will, but always an instinct of human nature, and made an instinct for the most important of all purposes – to lead the organized being to unite with those objects which its own nature may require, to fill a void, or satisfy a want, which, by its nature, for some wise end or necessary purpose, it is compelled to experience.

It is in reality, therefore, the greatest crime against nature, to prevent organized beings from uniting with those objects, or other organized beings, with which nature has created in them a desire to unite.

Nature, when allowed to take its course through the whole life of organized beings, produces the desire to combine or unite with those objects with which it is the best for them to unite, and to remain united with them as long as it is the most beneficial for their well-being and happiness that they should continue together; and Nature is the only correct judge in determining her own laws. It is man, alone, who has disobeyed this law; it is man, alone, who has thereby brought sin and misery into the world, and engendered the disunion and hatred which now render the lives of so many human beings wretched.

It is to secure the performance of this law, that nature rewards, with so much satisfaction and pleasure, the union of those organized beings, who often, in despite of man's absurd artificial arrangements to the contrary, contain between them, the pure elements of union, by being the most perfectly formed to unite together physically, intellectually, and morally.

Man, then, to be permanently virtuous and happy, from birth to death, must implicitly obey this law of his nature, and of universal nature.

SECTION XIII

'Each individual is so organized, that his *feelings and his convictions* are formed *for him*, by the impressions which circumstances produce upon his individual organization.'

This law of human nature has also been considered, in part, under the head of the second of the fundamental facts, upon which the whole of the Rational System of Society is founded.

It is, however, a law of human nature so little thought of by most men, and so much misunderstood by the comparatively few who have turned their attention to the subject, that the further development of it in this place will be useful.

The evidence of our senses informs us, that man is an organized being, possessing in his organization the germs of all the faculties, qualities and powers, which are afterwards brought out and matured, by the effects of external circumstances acting upon the organization.

The germ of feeling exists at birth, but the direction which that germ shall be made to take, will greatly depend upon the kinds and qualities of the external objects which shall be around the individual from his birth to maturity, and especially in the early part of his life.

When the organization shall be surrounded by the kind of circumstances proper for the purpose, it may be made to like, to be indifferent to, or to dislike, any certain class of objects or persons, and any one class of objects or persons as well as any other. An English Christian, for instance, may be made to dislike, or even violently hate, a French Christian, an English Jew, or an

Irish Christian, as well as the distant Mahommedan or Hindoo, whom the English Christian has never seen; or he may, unconsciously to himself, be made to like some other class of beings, possessing qualities which many other classes of men have been taught to consider greatly inferior to those of the French Christian, the English Jew, or the Mahommedan or Hindoo. But these partialities or dislikes are made artificially, by the active exertions of the parties around the individual. It is from this kind of influence from infancy, of the adult population over the rising generation, that so much error and evil are produced in the world, and that the succeeding generation is held in mental bondage by the generation immediately preceding it, and that prejudices of various kinds have been, for so long a period, transmitted from one age to another. The feelings of human nature are, therefore, instincts of a peculiar class; instincts capable of receiving a direction contrary to that intended by nature, by the direct influence of external circumstances created by society before man himself knew what manner of being he had been formed to be. Human feelings are, consequently, instincts formed by nature, but capable of being well or ill directed by the influence of the old over the young; thus putting it into the power of experienced man to perform the most important benefits for the inexperienced infant, child, and youth.

In fact, as nature has implanted in man so powerful a love of his offspring, as often, very often, to make it stronger than the love of life itself, the unlimited power thus prepared for the adult in directing the feelings and convictions of the child, and in forming, or, rather, almost recreating the character of the man, will become, at a future period, one of the most important privileges of human nature.

This power in the adult, to create so large a portion of the character of his offspring, will enable one generation to see and enjoy the great improvements secured to the coming generation. It will enable those now living, to adopt a decisive system of progressive and unlimited advance towards human physical, intellectual, and moral perfection. It will secure to them the means of witnessing, in the rising generation, a constant and daily change for the better; a regular movement forward towards excellence of every description; a satisfying progress in the annual acquirement of superior habits and dispositions, and in new and valuable knowledge – knowledge which, as soon as it shall be ascertained to be practically beneficial, will be rapidly spread through every part of human society, enabling every one to rejoice, without any alloy, at every step of improvement in the whole circle of the sciences made by any one in any country.

But our convictions are instincts of human nature, as well as the physical feelings of which we have been speaking; and in this respect, also, are as capable of receiving a wrong or right direction from the adult, as are the physical feelings.

When the moral science of man, and the science of society, or social science, shall be generally known, the means will become obvious by which the adult part of society will be enabled to teach the young truth only; that is, to make all the impressions which produce conviction on the mind to be in accordance with facts. By this mode of procedure, the human mind will be gradually supplied with ideas, all of which will be in unison with each other, and in strict accordance with nature, and thus will confusion and perplexity of mind be avoided. As the knowledge of facts extends, the mind will be put into the best condition to search for new knowledge, and also to acquire patience not to draw conclusions until it has accumulated a sufficient number of facts to have sufficient evidence that the deduction is sound, or free from all incongruities.

It is to this part of the formation of the human character, or education of each child from birth, that the utmost care should be applied. The future superiority or inferiority of the whole character and conduct of the child will depend upon the right or wrong direction which shall be given from birth to his capacity for feeling, and his power for receiving convictions. The first may be made so humane, and be so directed, that the matured man shall be compelled to feel considerable horror at accidentally injuring the limb of the smallest insect, or be made to experience the greatest pleasure and delight in first killing, afterwards roasting, and then eating, one of his fellow-men; and be made equally, in either case, to think that he is acting right. Such are the varied directions that may be given to the germ of feeling, and to the capacity for receiving convictions, which exist in the organization of every child at birth; and by attending to these laws of human nature, we shall arrive at the knowledge of the means by which the best direction may be given to the feelings and convictions of every individual of the human race.

When these laws shall be known and acted upon, there will be no occasion to find fault with the direction given to the feelings or convictions that shall exist in society. The cause why they exist will be distinctly known. If they are injurious, or inferior, or false, the parties experiencing the inconvenience from them will feel the necessity of removing the causes which produced them; they will not waste their time in unavailing attempts or regret, but they will actively bestir themselves to withdraw the cause or causes creating the evil, and they will replace them by others that will be fully competent to effect the changes for good which they desire. Thus will the science by which man shall be made intelligent and happy become well known to the human race.

SECTION XIV

'Each individual is so organized, that his *will* is formed *for* him by his feelings, or his convictions, or both; and *thus his whole character – physical, mental, and moral – is formed independently of himself.*'

This law of human nature has been in part considered under the head of the third fundamental fact; but as it is the law of human nature the least understood, and the most overwhelmed with early prejudices, and as errors regarding it have been of the most direful consequences to the human race, it will be useful more fully to examine the facts on which this law is predicated, and the consequences to which it leads, and also to consider it under new aspects.

It has been stated that the will is sometimes formed by the physical, and sometimes by the mental feelings, and sometimes by both united. The conflict between the physical and the mental feelings has been, by the religious, called, 'the war between the flesh and the Spirit.' They felt the opposition between the two, and not knowing that this was a necessary consequence of supposing the feelings and convictions to be formed by the will, nor comprehending in what manner the will was formed by the feelings and convictions, their imaginations have taken the wildest range, and they have conjured up every possible inconsistency to account for this difference between our physical and mental feelings; and when once the imagination is allowed to take flight, unguided by facts, it is impossible to know to what extent of error it may lead, both in principle and in practice.

The error respecting this law of human nature has led man to imagine a personal Deity, author of all good; and a personal Devil, author of all evil; to invent all the various forms of worship of the former, and, in many instances, of the latter also; and the modes of propitiating the favour of the one, and avoiding the supposed evil doings of the other. And yet, when the mind can be relieved from the early prejudices which have been forced into it on these subjects, it will be discovered that there is not one single fact known to man, after all the experience of the past generations, to prove that any such personalities exist, or ever did exist, and, in consequence, all the Mythology of the Ancients, and all the Religions of the Moderns, are mere fanciful notions of men, whose imaginations have been cultivated to accord with existing prejudices, and whose judgments have been systematically destroyed from their birth. There is no practical advantage to be derived from the supposition that the Power of the Universe is an organized Being, or that it should be personified in any manner whatever; but, on the contrary, all attempts which have been made to describe the Cause of Motion, Life, and Mind, have been injurious to the true interests of the human race, and every attempt to force a belief upon mankind, on this subject, can lead only to error, confusion, and crime. But the notions of a personal Deity will be considered more in detail when we come to explain the principles and practices of the Rational Religion. It is evident, from the past history of mankind, that the natural course of events has forced man to receive his first impressions of externals, and of himself, through his imagination; and that the whole experience of his existence has not yet been sufficient to disabuse him of all the false impressions which this erroneous medium of knowledge has left in his mind. It is only of modern date that the importance of facts in developing knowledge has been known; it is only now that the necessity of comparing fact with fact, to a great extent, to gain accurate and valuable knowledge, has been ascertained. It is only now, for the first time in the known history of mankind, that the mind has been permitted to examine facts, in order to discover truth upon the subjects which have the greatest influence on the happiness of the human race; and upon many of these subjects, even now, there are but a few very small districts, over the whole earth, in which one portion of society will permit another to declare the truths which the examination of facts has made certain to them; and it is only now that the Government and Church of Great Britain have attained sufficient rationality to permit the most important truths, respecting the real formation of the human character, to be publicly disseminated among the population of these islands and the colonies depending upon them.

It is only now, that the government feels the necessity for allowing the free circulation of the writings which tend to prove that the whole character of man, physical, mental, and moral, is formed *for* him; and formed independently of any power which he can exert, that is not first given him by his organization, or by the influence of external circumstances acting upon the organization.

And it is only now, in consequence of the circulation of these writings, that the public are beginning to investigate the facts, from a knowledge of which, alone, man can discover his own nature, and how it can best be conducted, from birth to death, to make each individual a being of superior feelings, intelligence, and conduct; also to ascertain what every one has been made to be by the power or powers which formed his organization, and which created and continued the external circumstances which acted upon it, from its birth, to create the reaction from the organization to the surrounding circumstances; and by thus tracing, step by step, the actual formation of man as now demonstrable from facts, we are compelled to come to the conclusion, that he is a wonderful and curiously contrived being, a being whose physical, mental, and moral feelings are formed *for* him, through his organization acted upon by external circumstances. The sensations produced by the impressions of the first external circumstances give a new character to the organization; other external circumstances then act upon this altered organization, and further change it, until it acquires power to react upon the external circumstances. The power, however, thus acquired, is the combined result of the original organization, formed without the knowledge of the individual, and of the influence upon it of the peculiar external circumstances which happened to exist around the individual, in consequence of the age of the world in which he was born, of the country in which he lived, of the district in which he was trained and educated, and of the class, sect, and party, of his parents and early associates and instructors. And these circumstances united, direct the feelings, thoughts, and conduct of every one; and therefore we reiterate that the whole man, physical, mental, and moral, is formed independently of any original will and choice of the individual; and that he is consequently irresponsible for what he is formed to be, and made to do; and that this accurate knowledge of human nature will necessarily engender in every one the purest charity for the feelings, thoughts, and conduct of all, and will also speedily disclose the means by which a sincere affection will be experienced by every one for all; and thus, in a short period after these important truths shall be openly and generally promulgated, will peace and good-will pervade the whole human race, and the earth be changed, in consequnce, into a terrestrial paradise.

SECTION XV

'Each individual is so organized, that impressions, which at their commencement, and for a limited time, produce agreeable sensations, will, if continued without intermission beyond a certain period, become indifferent, disagreeable, and ultimately painful.'

The object of human existence, as of all that has life, is to be happy; and the highest attainment of human wisdom is to know how to obtain and to secure that degree of happiness which can be most permanently enjoyed.

This knowledge is only to be discovered by experience; and experience has now demonstrated that any impressions made upon human nature, and repeated without intermission, will become, however delightful at first, less and less agreeable, until they produce not only indifference, but pain, which may be increased till it produces insanity or death. Innumerable instances might be adduced to prove the truth of this statement; any one of our five senses may be thus delighted, diminished in its pleasure, made to feel indifferent, be fatigued, over-fatigued, and be ultimately destroyed. Either seeing, tasting, hearing, smelling, or feeling, may be thus continued through all these gradations from exquisite pleasure to insufferable pain. Or these senses may be so exercised up to the point of temperance, that, from each, pleasure only shall be derived; and instead of these powers being weakened and destroyed, they may be, to an advanced period of the life of every individual, strengthened and improved.

It is not, however, the physical powers only that may be thus enjoyed, over-exercised, and destroyed; the intellectual faculties and the moral feelings are also subject to the same law of nature; any particular course of mental investigation, the most pleasant at its commencement, may be persevered in until it absorbs the whole mind, becomes a mental disease, and finally destroys both mind and body. So the moral feelings – that portion of our nature which, when duly exercised, is capable of producing pleasure of the highest character, and durable throughout the whole existence of the organization – may be carried to such excess as to derange the animal functions, and put a sudden termination to life itself.

In all compounds in nature there is a certain point at which they attain perfection; anything short of that point is deficient; anything beyond it becomes detrimental. This point, in all that have life, may be called the point of temperance, or the point of the highest possible perfection. It will be the business of those who direct the affairs of mankind, to discover the means by which every individual may ascertain this point in his own organization, and to form the whole social arrangements in such a manner as to induce, or morally compel, all men to act in conformity with this knowledge.

SECTION XVI

'Each individual is so organized, that when, beyond a certain degree of rapidity, impressions succeed each other, they dissipate, weaken, and otherwise injure, his physical, mental, or moral powers, and diminish his enjoyment.'

When, through the attainment of much wealth, men acquire the power of indulgence, without at the same time increasing their knowledge of human nature, they often attempt to increase their happiness by procuring a quick succession of those sensations from which, at first, they derive much pleasure; expecting that their enjoyment will go on increasing with the number of their sensations. Experience has always proved these expectations to be fallacious, and demonstrated that wealth, or the means of procuring these quick successsive sensations, either of sight, hearing, smell, taste, or touch, without the acquisition of real knowledge to direct the manner, order, and time of these sensations, to produce the most permanent health and happiness, is highly pernicious to the possessor, destructive of his own well-being, and in too many cases highly injurious to those around him. This, in fact, is real vice, and leads to all kinds of human miseries, to endless disease of body and mind, to dissatisfaction with the best things that wealth can command, to desires, the gratification of which would still farther increase all the evils which unrestrained luxury produces.

This is the very reverse of that state of society which an accurate knowledge of human nature will create among mankind. It is a habit which, with that knowledge, never can be acquired by a single individual; all the arrangements of a rational state of society will, of necessity, be formed to guard against it. All should, therefore, have their attention early directed to acquire a knowledge of the number of sensations, of every kind, that prove the most beneficial for their own constitution; for in all probability, the number will vary, not only in every organization, but also, at different periods of life, in the same organization.

SECTION XVII

'Each individual is so organized, that his highest health, his greatest progressive improvement, and his permanent happiness, depend upon the due cultivation of all his physical, intellectual, and moral faculties, or elements of his nature, – upon their being called into action at a proper period of life, – and being afterwards temperately exercised, according to his strength and capacity.'

The elements of human nature, combined as they are in man, form him to be what he is at his birth. These elements, as society at present exists, are sometimes more and sometimes less favourably united to produce excellence of character; but whether the individual shall, at maturity, become a very inferior or a very superior being will depend upon the manner in which the various compounds of his nature shall be cultivated and exercised; in other words, whether he shall be made to be unhappy himself, and make those around him unhappy, or whether he shall be trained to acquire real knowledge, to enjoy happiness, and to dispense it to those within the sphere of his influence.

The highest virtue is that which produces the greatest happiness that human nature can experience; and the highest and most permanent happiness that human nature can experience, arises from all parts of each man's nature being satisfied, without being over-excited or over-exerted; or when each faculty exists at the point at which it contributes the most essentially to the health of the individual, and to the sound action of all the other faculties.

This state of human society has never yet been known to exist in anything like perfection; it appears to have been the best known and practised by the Greeks, who exercised their physical and mental powers more equally than any other nation of antiquity whose records we possess. The Romans, during the best days of their republic, endeavoured to follow their example; but modern nations have greatly degenerated in this respect. And now, generally speaking, the moderns cultivate but very imperfectly the physical powers of human nature in one portion of the population, and the intellectual faculties very imperfectly in another portion of the population; thus, through ignorance, making modern man a diseased, distorted, and miserable being.

The religious and political governments of the world have, for many centuries past, caused this degeneracy in the education of the human race; and they have now proceeded to such an extreme of error, that a radical change in the mode of forming the character and of governing man, has become absolutely necessary to prevent society from being totally demoralized, and falling into utter confusion.

The proper business of human life is to form man to attain the highest degree of physical, intellectual, and moral perfection; to remove from around him every impediment to the acquisition of happiness; and to create new circumstances which shall contribute most essentially to promote his permanent enjoyment. He must, therefore, be well-educated, physically, mentally, and morally; he must be beneficially employed and occupied; and so trained as to act cordially with his associates, who must be equally well trained and occupied. He will thus be formed to know the truth, to feel it, and to look and act uniformly in accordance with it. He will then know and feel the importance of exercising all the faculties of his nature, in their due order, to the point of temperance, and of never exceeding that point. He will thus discover that all parts of his nature are equally necessary to his happiness; that his physical propensities require to be as regularly exercised as his intellectual faculties, and these, again, as his moral feelings; and that, as the health of each part is essential to maintain the health of all the other parts, no one portion of human nature can be inferior to another, because, although composed of many parts, it is one individual whole, and perfect only in proportion as all its parts approach perfection.

Those systems, therefore, which have thrown discredit upon the physical propensities or intellectual faculties and enjoyments of human nature, have been formed in gross ignorance of what manner of being man is, and of the mode of creating and securing his happiness.

In a rational state of society, arrangements will be permanently formed to cultivate and regularly exercise the physical propensities, the intellectual faculties, and the moral feelings, each in subserviency to the other, and thus keep the health of body and mind, through life, in the best state for action and enjoyment.

As nature gives the organization to man, so will nature best direct when any of the functions of that organization should be exercised. In fact, no other law can be acted upon without injury to the individual and to society. And in proportion as human laws and customs have interfered with the dictates of nature, in the same proportion has man been forced to become a vicious and miserable animal, and to have the finest and highest qualities of his nature deteriorated.

In consequence of the various religious and political institutions of society being formed to interfere unnaturally with the physical propensities and the intellectual faculties of human nature, the moral feelings have been always demoralized; and where pure health, simple truth, and unsuspecting confidence, could alone have prevented disease, hypocrisy, falsehood, and distrust, these have become, of necessity, so general, that men now think these vices are natural to man; whereas they are solely the effects of religious and political errors.

Let arrangements, then, be formed to admit of the due and regular exercise of all the propensities and faculties of our nature, according to the strength and capacity of the individual, and disease, vice, deception, and misery, will soon disappear from the earth.

SECTION XVIII

'Each individual is so organized, that he is made to receive what is commonly called a *bad character*, when he has been placed, from birth, amidst the most unfavourable circumstances.'

In different ages of the world, different qualities of human nature have been called good and bad; and now a like variety of opinions exists in the various nations of the world, according to the political and religious dogmas which prevail in each, and the unnatural customs which these dogmas have generated. A man who is called bad or good in one country, will not therefore be considered so in another; and there is a considerable shade of difference in the meaning of these terms, not only in distant nations, but in different classes and sects in the same country. In fact, there is no fixed standard, in any part of the world, of a good or a bad man; both terms have ever been the creation of the prejudices and imaginations of the human mind, according to the education it has received; and men have been punished and rewarded, and promised future eternal rewards and threatened with future eternal punishments, in one age and country, for qualities and conduct, which, in another age or country, would have subjected them to opposite treatment.

It is probable, from present appearances, that this error is destined to be speedily removed, and that these terms will no longer be applied as heretofore; that arrangements for punishing mankind for being what they are formed to be by nature and education, will soon appear to be too glaringly absurd and unjust to be permitted to remain, and that the language of abuse will no longer be applied to our fellow-men who have been compelled to possess or to acquire qualities which are inferior.

Men are made to be what they are, by their organization and the external circumstances which act upon and influence it. None are or can be bad by nature; their education is always the business of work of society, and not of the individual. The individual is thus, evidently, a material of nature, finished and fashioned by the society in which it lives, according to the ignorance, or intelligence, or the knowledge of human nature, which that society has been made to possess, and by the influence of other external circumstances with which the individual may be surrounded. Man cannot, therefore, be bad by nature; and it must be a gross error to make him responsible for what nature and his predecessors have compelled him to be. If his original organization has been the most unfavourable in its combinations, and if the circumstances by which it has been surrounded, from birth, have been of the most inferior description, the individual is more an object for the pity and commiseration of those who have received a superior organization, and who have been placed in more favourable circumstances. It is, therefore, cruel and unjust, in the extreme, still further to punish and afflict a poor individual, after he has been already ill-treated by nature and the society in which his character has been formed from birth.

The characters which are now called bad, would, in most cases, under a rational system of society, become the most useful, and often the most delightful members of their circle. They often possess strong powers of body and mind, too strong to be restrained in a course opposite to their nature by existing human contrivances, and they therefore break through them, and are made amenable to artificial laws. Thus, to the injury of every individual of the human race, is man made to oppose man, and to adopt measures which defeat the continual desire of human nature to attain happiness.

The time cannot be far distant when the terms bad and good, relative to man, will have a very different signification from that which they now possess.

The term bad will convey the idea only, that the individuals to whom it is applied have been most unjustly and ignorantly treated by the society in which they have been trained and educated; that, in consequence, they call upon us, individually, for our pity and deep commiseration, and upon society, to remedy the evil with the least pain or inconvenience to the injured parties. Terms of reproach or abuse will no longer be applied to them; feelings of separation and avoidance will no longer be created against them; much less will any arrangement exist to punish them for possessing qualities which nature, or the ignorance of man, forces them to have, or to acquire. Inferior qualities in individuals will thus cease to arouse anger, and all the worst feelings that can be given to man; they will, on the contrary, call forth all the energy and best feelings of our nature to remove those inferior qualities, or, if from long habit that be impracticable, to improve the individual to the extent to which he is capable of being improved.

Such conduct being uniformly pursued by those who govern society and who influence public opinion, inferior characters will soon cease to exist; nor will there be occasion for prisons, penitentiaries, or courts of law. The immense waste of human labour and means thus saved will be applied to more rational purposes; the feelings of the comparatively well-informed and reflecting, will not then be daily lacerated by seeing the time and wealth of the people squandered upon trials, relative to the lives and properties of their fellow-men, for no other real object than that the few may rule over and plunder the many – that error and injustice may be perpetuated under the plausible terms of law and religion. No! instead of bad men being punished, no bad or inferior characters will be formed; or, if formed through any practical ignorance of human nature which may yet exist for a short period, measures will be adopted to improve, and not to punish them, for defects emanating from others over whom the sufferers had possessed no controul.

Thus, by degrees, will an *universal system* for the *prevention* of *evil* supersede that which has existed for numberless ages to *punish* it, by the instrumentality of the very parties who were themselves the immediate cause of the evil, and of the miseries which evil must always produce.

Thus will the system of injustice and cruelty terminate for ever; and man will attain to that scale in the creation, to which the original faculties of his nature prove him to be entitled.

By these measures alone, can the world attain to that state in which peace and goodwill shall universally prevail, and knowledge everywhere supersede ignorance and superstition.

SECTION XIX

'Each individual is so organized, that he is made to receive a *medium character*, when he has been created with a favourable* proportion of the elements of his nature, and has been placed, from birth, amidst unfavourable* circumstances: –

'Or, when he has been created with an unfavourable* proportion of these elements, and when the external circumstances in which he is placed are of a character to impress him with favourable* sensations only: –

'Or, when he has been created with a favourable* proportion of some of these elements, and an unfavourable* proportion of others; and has been placed, through life, in varied external circumstances, producing some good and some evil sensations. This compound has hitherto been the general lot of mankind.'

The causes which produce a medium character in the human race are so various and numerous, that thus a *very* bad character has seldom been formed, and a good one never.

Under the universal error in which the character of man has been formed, it often happens that those born with proportions of the elements of their nature approximating to perfection, are placed within very unfavourable circumstances. As when, for example, individuals with superior natural formations are born in districts in which ignorance, poverty, and the grosser vices abound – in which the greater part of the external circumstances are calculated to produce inferior impressions, which counteract continually the superior organization of the individuals. With external circumstances thus opposed to the superior organization of the individual, a character full of mental perplexity, and of opposing physical feelings, will be formed. The superior natural intellectual faculties of the individual, and his natural good feelings, will be perpetually injured by the never-ceasing unfavourable influences which the inferior or vicious external circumstances make upon his organization, and there will be a constant warfare between these opposing forces. In the mystical language of the Christian Scriptures, 'the spirit appears to war against the flesh;' when the simple fact is, that the institutions of society have been formed, through ignorance, to oppose one part of human nature to another, when no such opposition ought to have been thought of. Every part of human nature is the work of the same power, and every part is equally necessary to the well-being and happiness of the individual; it is, therefore, only a popular and vulgar error, to believe that any of our propensities, faculties, or feelings, are bad by nature; the idea intended to be expressed by the term is an absurdity, proceeding, at

* The terms 'favourable and unfavourable proportions of the elements of human nature,' are here used with reference to what are now called good or bad characters, for it is probable that those organizations, which, under the universal system of error in which all nations are now involved, make the worst, would, under a rational system of society, be made to acquire the most valuable qualities in high perfection.

first, from the overheated imagination of some fanatic, who was totally ignorant of the facts or laws of his own nature.

It also now often occurs that inferior organizations, for the present views of society, are born in families in which comparatively favourable circumstances prevail, and these acting, from birth, upon the child possessing the inferior organization, the individual, at mature age, appears to much greater advantage than the less fortunate superior-organized being, who, from his birth, had been under the continual influence of inferior and vicious circumstances. Thus, often, the organizations now esteemed inferior by nature rise to elevated situations, to wealth and honours, while others, esteemed superior by nature, are depressed to the lower conditions in society, and their lives sacrificed to the laws made by the mistaken and prejudiced rulers of states; – rulers who have been altogether ignorant of the valuable prize they possessed – rulers who had not the knowledge to cultivate and rightly apply the good and superior qualities which were inherent in those superior organizations. Thus, often, are the naturally inferior for governing, made to rule over and direct those who are naturally superior, and confusion of every description is the necessary result.

But the most common medium character, as it now exists, is produced by mixed qualities in the organization, and mixed qualities in the external circumstances by which it is influenced from birth, and subsequently matured.

The character, however, which is now considered a medium character, will, in a state of society in which measures shall be adopted to form all men to be rational, not appear to be medium, but a most inferior and irrational character, full of error and vice.

Inferior and superior are relative terms, referring only to an acknowledged standard. But as all past and existing human characters have been chiefly formed by the irrational circumstances which have surrounded them from birth, the false notions which they have thus been made to receive, upon the most important subjects connected with human happiness, have compelled them, one and all, to be irrational in their feelings, thoughts, and actions. The time is approaching when the existing errors will be made evident to the public, and when, in consequence, all past and present characters will be considered a variety of inferior characters only, and that which is now called medium, will be known to be a character very inferior to all that will be made in future from the same average organization. It will be afterwards seen how this organization itself may be materially improved.

SECTION XX

'Each individual is so organized, that he is made to receive a *superior character*, when his original constitution contains the best proportion of the elements of human nature, and when the circumstances which surround him from birth, and through life, are of a character to produce superior sensations only; or, in other words, when the laws, institutions, and customs, under which he lives, are all in unison with the laws of his nature.'

A superior human being, or any one approaching a character deserving the name of rational, has not yet been known among mankind. A man intelligent and yet consistent in his feelings, thoughts, and actions, does not now exist even in the most civilized part of the world. Therefore, we know only from history or personal acquaintance, human beings who have been considered superior under the irrational system in which the human race has existed up to the present period; beings possessing comparatively superior organizations, and who have been placed through life amidst the least irrational circumstances. The most excellent of these characters, however, the most choice specimens that ever lived in the artificial and unnatural state which these circumstances have produced, have been but irrational beings – men who have been a little rational in a few points, while their fellow-men were made to be irrational in all their feelings, thoughts, and actions.

Before a truly superior character can be formed among men, a new arrangement of external circumstances must be combined, all of which must be in unison with human nature, and calculated to produce rational impressions only upon the human organization. Every external circumstance, too, must be superior of its kind; and there must be also the absence of slavery and servitude, that no inferior impressions may be made upon any of our faculties.

Before this character can be given to the human race, a great change must occur in the whole proceedings of mankind; their feelings, thoughts, and actions, must arise from principles altogether different from the vague and fanciful notions by which the mental part of the character of man has been hitherto formed; the whole external circumstances relative to the production and distribution of wealth, the formation of character, and the government of men, must be changed; the whole of these parts must be remodelled and united into one system, in which each part shall contribute to the perfection of the whole; nothing must be left to the ignorance or inexperience of individuals or of individual families, whose apparent interests are made to oppose those of their fellows and neighbours; a false interest which diffuses a spirit of jealousy and competition among the members of every class, sect, and party, in every nation, city, town, and village, and too often in families.

No! a rational and superior character can be formed only by changing the whole of the existing irrational circumstances, now everywhere prevalent in the domestic, commercial, political, literary, and religious arrangements of mankind, for an entirely new and scientific combination of all these separate parts into one entire whole; and this so simplified and arranged, that all may be trained, even at an early period of life, to comprehend it, and also the reason for the formation of each part of this new and scientific machine of society. But this change can never be effected during the continuance of the laws, institutions, and customs of the world, which have arisen from the belief that the character of the individual is formed *by* himself – that he possesses within himself the power to form his own will, and the inclination or motives which induce him to act. These errors of the imagination have produced the most lamentable consequences in leading men to form institutions, codes of laws, and customs, in accordance with them, and fatally for the happiness and improvement of mankind, in direct opposition to the laws of human nature, and to all the natural feelings of the human race. Ignorance, poverty, cruelty, injustice, crime, and misery were sure to follow from this opposition to the laws of that Power which pervades the universe, and gives man his nature, his feelings, and all his attributes. This opposition, however it may have arisen, is, in fact, a direct denial of wisdom, or design, in the Cause which creates. That Cause gives man an organization or constitution, with propensities, instincts, and faculties, necessary for the well-doing, well-being, and happiness of the individual and of society; but inexperienced man says, 'No; these instincts, propensities, and faculties are bad; Nature has made them, it is true, but Nature is ignorant of the means to accomplish her own ends; we will instruct her better, and will therefore counteract her blind, or foolish, or injurious laws, by all the artificial and unnatural measures our wisdom can devise.'

By these vain and futile attempts to oppose Nature, and improve himself, man is made the greatest obstacle in the way of his own happiness, and of the happiness of his race.

CHAPTER VIII

Deductions from the preceding Facts and Laws.

These facts and laws make it evident that human nature is a compound of qualities, different from that which it has hitherto appeared to be; that these qualities have been misconceived, and that the true nature of man has been, to the present time, hidden from the human race; that this want of all knowledge of himself, from which man has hitherto suffered, is now the great, and almost the sole cause of all crime and misery. He has mistaken the most important instincts of his nature for the creations of his will, whereas facts now prove that his will is created by these instincts. This fundamental error respecting the qualities of the material of human nature, has, of necessity, deranged all the proceedings of mankind, and prevented the whole race from becoming rational. Man has imagined that he has been formed to believe and to feel as he likes, by the power of his will, and to be, to a great extent, independent of external nature. All past society has been founded on these erroneous assumptions, and, in consequence, the human mind has been a chaos of perplexing inconsistencies, and all human affairs a compound of the most irrational transactions, individually, nationally, and universally.

The stronger members of every association have tyrannized over the weaker, and by open force or by fraud made them their slaves; – such is the state of society over the world at this moment. But tyrants and slaves are never rational; nor can such a condition of society ever produce intelligence, wealth, union, virtue, and happiness, among mankind; or place man in a condition of permanent progressive improvement.

This division into tyrants and slaves, has produced a classification of society, which, however necessary in its early stages, is now creating every kind of evil over the earth, and prevents the possibility of any one attaining that high degree of excellence and happiness which, otherwise, might be so easily secured to the whole of the human race; a classification which must be destroyed before injustice and oppression, vice and misery, can be removed. For while men shall be divided into castes of employers and employed, masters and servants, sovereign and subject, tyrant and slave, ignorance, poverty, and disunion must pervade the world, and there must be alternate advance and retrogression in all nations. The division of the inhabitants of the earth into tyrants and slaves has produced, not only the general classification which has been mentioned, but others, subdividing these into emperors, kings, and princes; into legislators and professors of divinity, law, medicine, and arms; into producers and non-producers of wealth and knowledge; into buyers and sellers of each other's powers, faculties, and products, and into the respective servants of all these divisions. Thus making a heterogeneous mass of contending interests among the whole human race, which, while these opposing feelings shall be created, must sever man from man, and nation from nation, to the incalculable injury of every individual of all nations.

It is now, therefore, evident that man has committed the same mistake from the beginning, respecting the power and faculties of his own nature, as he did for so long a period in relation to the laws of motion which govern the solar system; and from the same cause – the want of a sufficient number of facts accurately observed and systematically arranged, to enable him to draw sound deductions, and discover the truth. It is equally evident, that while these fundamental errors respecting the powers and faculties of human nature shall be entertained by, and shall controul the conduct of, those who govern the nations of the world, the same confusion of ideas, in the conception and direction of human affairs, must prevail, as existed in all minds respecting the solar system, when it was generally believed that the earth was the centre of the universe, and that the sun, stars, and planets moved round it.

Those who discovered the principles which now so beautifully explain the motions of the heavenly bodies, were deemed by the Priesthood of those days, infidels, because this knowledge of nature's laws was opposed to their superstitions and ignorance; and Galileo, to save his life, was compelled publicly to deny, in words, what he was forced, through the knowledge which he had acquired, to believe, by an irresistible instinct of his nature.[a] Thus the Priesthood forced him, in order to escape a death of excruciating torment, to give a public denial to those truths which he was compelled to believe.

In like manner, now, the promulgators of those divine principles of truth which must produce charity, kindness, and affection, unlimited, and harmonize all minds as well as all human affairs, are called infidels by the Priesthood of the present day; and the Priests now desire to make them also deny the truth, by inflicting on them fines and imprisonment, or by using all the influence which they possess to destroy the only means of living within the power of these lovers of truth. Knowledge, however, progresses; the opinions of mankind on these subjects are rapidly changing; the errors and evils of the Priesthood are seen and felt by the intelligent over the world; and all the signs of the times make it evident that the æra approaches when mental truth shall be as free as physical truth, and when the far greater benefits to be derived from the former will be experienced and universally acknowledged.

Men will then recur to the present state of mental imbecility, relative to human nature, as we now do to the notions formerly entertained of the form of the earth, the solar movements, and the principles of mechanics and chemistry.

It seems extraordinary, at first, that the physical sciences, requiring so much accurate observation of external nature, so much profound thought and reflection, and, often, such an extended, unbroken chain of close reasoning, should have made the advance the world now witnesses; and that so little progress should have been made in mental knowledge, which can alone insure happiness to the human race. This is, however, explained by the fact, that the Priesthood in all countries, in all times, have opposed the barrier of their hitherto all-powerful influence, to stifle inquiries and prevent investigations, which they perceived would undermine their power over the human mind, and, consequently, over the fortunes of men.

Thus the most intricate and important discoveries have been made in some of the physical sciences, while the mental and moral sciences have remained in

[a] In 1632, Galileo was forced by the Inquisition to renounce his belief that the earth revolved around the sun.

total darkness. Even now, upon these latter subjects, the most erroneous assumption, in opposition to all facts, are taught to the mass of mankind, who are, in consequence, made imbecile and mentally blind.

This injurious state of human affairs will remain as long as the authorised teachers of the people are made to believe that they (the teachers) have an interest in keeping the people in mental darkness. And the teachers will continue thus to instruct, until they shall be themselves better instructed with respect to their own interest and happiness.

Thus the errors of the world relative to these facts and laws of human nature, have kept past generations in the ignorance, poverty, disunion, crime, and misery which have hitherto pervaded all parts of the earth; and while these errors are retained, the evils must continue to increase. But it is, and always, without a single exception, has been the highest interest of all men, in all countries, that these errors should be removed; and happily men now begin to perceive this truth.

We have, in this chapter, stated a few only of the most obvious deductions from the facts and laws, or constitution of human nature. Were we now to enter fully upon this wide field of new knowledge, a volume would be insufficient to contain that which might be advantageously written; but the subsequent parts of this book will afford a better opportunity to place the subject gradually before the mind, when it will be more habituated to follow this train of reasoning.

CHAPTER IX

'The influence of these facts and laws in forming the general character of the human race, and their effects upon society.'

THESE facts and laws of nature, whenever they shall be fully understood and generally adopted in practice, will become the means of forming a new character for the human race. Instead of being made irrational, as they have hitherto been, they will be made rational, they will be formed to become, of necessity, CHARITABLE to their fellow-men of every clime, colour, language, sentiment, and feeling, and KIND to all that has life. When a knowledge of these facts and laws shall be taught to all from infancy, they will know that the clime, colour, language, opinions, and feelings, are the necessary effects of causes over which the individuals, subject to their influence, have no controul; they will not, therefore, be angry with their fellow-men for experiencing influences which are unavoidable. These different effects will be considered varieties of nature, useful for observation and reflection, for instruction and amusement. Such varieties in the character of man, as now produce opposing feelings and interests, and thence anger, violence, wars, and disunion, and all manner of oppression and injustice, crimes and misery, will, on the contrary, elicit knowledge, friendship, and pleasure. Hence characters the most opposite by nature will seek each other, unite and form intimate associations, in order that the most extended knowledge of human nature, and of nature generally, may be acquired, one interest formed, and affection made everywhere to abound.

The necessary result of unions of opposite varieties of character, will be, speedily to remove prejudices of every description, to dispel ignorance, root out all evil passions, destroy the very germs of disunion, and make men wise to their own happiness. Thus there will be no opposing interests or feelings among men in any part of the globe; the spirit of the world will be changed, and the selfishness of ignorance will be superseded by the self-interests, or, which is the same, the benevolence of intelligence.

The individuality of man, unavoidable by his nature, which is now, through ignorance, a cause of so much of the disunion of the human race, will become the cause of the more intimate union, and of the increase of pleasure and enjoyment. Contrasts of feelings and opinions which have been hitherto causes of anger, hatred, and repulsion, will become sources of attraction, as being the most easy and direct mode to acquire an extended knowledge of our nature, and of the laws which govern it. The causes which produce these differences will be examined with affection by the parties, and solely with a view to discover the truth; for all will be lovers of truth, and no one will feel, or think of being, ashamed of truth. They will know assuredly, and without a shadow of doubt, that truth is nature, and nature God; that 'God is truth, and truth is God,' as so generally expressed by the Mahommedans. And when men shall be made wise, by acquiring an accurate knowledge of the facts and laws of their nature, and can pursue a lengthened rational train of reasoning founded upon them, no one will shrink from, or be ashamed of the discoveries which nature will thus unfold. It will be known to all, that our individual physical feelings, and mental convictions or feelings, are instincts of our nature; all will, therefore, express them as such; nature will be justified, man's false shame of declaring the truth will be removed, and all motive to falsehood will cease. As each human being will have the knowledge which will enable him accurately to express and explain the real power, state, and condition of his own mind, and will always speak the truth; his character will be fully known to every one. It is solely the want of an accurate acquaintance with the science of human nature, or the individual and social character of man, that has given rise to the motives which have engendered falsehood, uncharitableness, and unkindness.

The effects which will be produced on society, by those facts and laws being known and publicly taught, are far too great to be comprehended by the faculties of men as they have been hitherto cultivated. When truth, in every department of human knowledge, shall supersede error and falsehood – when, by common consent, from conviction of the injury produced, men shall abandon falsehood, and speak the language of truth only, throughout all nations – then, indeed, will some conception be acquired of what human nature is, and what are its powers and capacities for improvement and enjoyment.

Under this change, man will appear to be a new-created being. The powers, capacities, and dispositions, cultivated under a system of falsehood, arising from ignorance of the laws of his nature, will assume another character when cultivated from infancy under a system of truth – a character so different in manner and spirit, that, could they now be seen in juxtaposition, they would appear to belong to opposite natures; the one, irrational, actively engaged in measures to defeat its own happiness, and in making the earth a pandemonium; the other, rational, daily occupied in measures to promote and secure the happiness of all around, and in making the earth a paradise.

Thus will the present irrational arrangements of society give place to those which are rational. The existing classification of the population of the world will cease. One portion of mankind will not, as now, be trained and placed to oppress, by force or fraud, another portion, to the great disadvantage of both; neither will one portion be trained in idleness, to live in luxury on the industry of those whom they oppress, while the latter are made to labour daily and to live in poverty. Nor yet will some be trained to force falsehood into the human mind, and be paid extravagantly for so doing, while other parties are prevented from teaching the truth, or severely punished if they make the attempt. There will be no arrangements to give knowledge to a few, and to withhold it from the many; but, on the contrary, all will be taught to acquire knowledge of themselves, of nature generally, and of the principles and practice of society, in all its departments; which knowledge will be easily made familiar to every one. The whole business of life will be so simplified, that each will understand it, and will delight in its varied practice.

Thus will the effects upon society of a knowledge of these facts and laws, remove the causes of all evil, and establish the reign of good over the world.

CHAPTER X

The harmony, unity, and efficiency of this Moral Science.

The proof of the truth of any science is the harmony of each part with the whole, and its unity with all nature; for, of necessity, each truth upon any subject must be in strict accordance with every other truth; it being contrary to the laws of nature for any one truth to be opposed to any other truth.

Thus, if these facts and laws be nature's facts and laws, then, of necessity, there will be perfect harmony and unity between them, and they will be also in accordance with every part of nature.

Accordingly, it will be found that the five fundamental facts, and the twenty facts and laws of human nature, on which the Moral Science of Man is founded, are in perfect unison with each other, and with nature; for each fact and law, commencing with the first, leads on to its successor, and gradually advances until the science is complete, and thus is the truth of the science demonstrated.

How opposed are the harmony and unity of this science, to all the religions and codes of laws invented by the past generations of men, while ignorant of their own organization, and of the laws of nature! All human laws are opposed to nature's laws, and, therefore, discordant, disunited, and perplexed, and always producing more evil than good.

The religions founded under the name of Jewish, Budh, Jehovah, God, or Christ, Mahomet, or any other, are all composed of human laws in opposition to nature's eternal laws; and when these laws are analyzed, they amount only to three absurdities – three gross impositions upon the ignorance or inexperience of mankind – three errors, now easily to be detected by the most simple experiment of each individual upon himself. The fundamental doctrines or laws of all these religions are, first, – 'Believe in my doctrines, as expounded by my priests, from my sacred books; second, Feel as these doctrines, thus expounded, direct you to feel; and third, Support my ministers for thus instructing you.' 'If you faithfully perform these three things in my name,' – say the priests of all these religions – 'you will have the greatest merit in this world, and an everlasting reward in the next.'

All religions and all codes of laws are built on the preceding dogmas, and all presuppose the original power in man to believe and to feel as he likes.

Now the facts and laws of nature, which constitute the Moral Science of Man, demonstrate that all belief or mental convictions, and all physical feelings, are instincts of human nature, and form the will; it follows, that the three fundamental dogmas of all religions have emanated from ignorance of the organization of man, and of the general laws of nature. Hence the confusion in all human affairs, the inutility of all human laws, and the irrational and miserable condition of all human society.

It follows, that – as all religions and codes of laws are founded on the error that there is merit or demerit in belief and in feeling – religions and laws must have originated in some error of the imagination, similar to the universal error, maintained through unnumbered ages, that the earth was flat, immoveable, and the centre of the universe.

But unity and harmony could never be found in any religion of codes of laws founded on the mistaken notion that instincts were free-will, while all facts prove that the will of man is the necessary result of the action of those instincts.

Those who have acquired a knowledge of the Moral Science of Man, are enabled, thereby, to perceive the cause of past evils; to detect the source of disunion, of crime, and their consequent misery; to perceive every step of the process by which these evils may be in future prevented, and by which all men may be educated to become rational and superior beings. This knowledge is the necessary result of the instincts of nature, acting upon the reasoning faculties of the individuals, who, through its effects, are compelled to exert the full extent of their powers, in order that the present generation may be made to understand it, and be induced to commence the practice of it, for the partial benefit of themselves, and for the permanent good of their offspring. And they are compelled thus to act, without the slightest merit on their part, although it appears, that, by so doing, they pursue a line of conduct directly opposed to their immediate individual interest.

They are made to perceive, that if the *Great Truth*, that all physical and mental feelings are instincts of human nature, and that these instincts create the will, could be impressed upon the present generation, so as to induce them to make it the foundation of another system, a high degree of excellence and happiness would be, thereby, permanently secured to the human race. It is the unavoidable deep impression of the inestimable blessings which this change would confer upon the human race, now and for ever, that compels these individuals to lose sight, altogether, of their own individual condition, that the great purposes of Nature may be accomplished upon earth, by man being made rational and happy.

It is the general knowledge of this invaluable truth, that is alone wanting to complete the great change in humanity, from irrationality, pain, and misery, to the most delightful state of existence. For men of experience know, that all the materials to over-supply the inhabitants of the world, now and for ever, with all that is necessary for their happiness, superabound; and that there is also far more power in the labour and skill of man, were they wisely directed, than is necessary to work up these materials into the most valuable products, and that all contests for their use and enjoyment will be unnecessary.

In the formation of man and woman there is the most evident harmony and unison of design, as well as the most efficient means to produce, in form and figure, beings physically, intellectually, and morally fitted to attain the highest excellence in all these divisions of their nature. But whence the Power which designs, or what its attributes, no man has yet ascertained; and upon this hitherto mysterious subject, the human mind must, of necessity, wait until new facts, explanatory of the mystery, shall be discovered. It is sufficient, at present, to deduce from the facts which *are* known, that there *is* this harmony and unity of design in the formation of human nature. There is not only the unity of many parts, possessing extraordinary faculties and qualities, physical, mental, and moral, to produce a race of beings far superior to all other terrestrial organizations; but sufficient power has also been given to this wonderful Compound, to multiply its own powers, by making discoveries in various sciences, without assignable limit to their progress, and to attain a very high degree of excellence in every division of its nature, whether of body or mind. For these facts and laws which demonstrate what human nature is, develope, also, a sufficiency of power to accomplish results far more extraordinary than any miracles which the wild fancy of superstition has yet imagined.

Here is a being, with a finely proportioned physical form, which in the early stages of society was evidently inferior in prowess, or physical strength, to many animals, and living in the daily fear of them, formed to acquire, although by slow experience, powers many thousand times greater than those of any other living creature. This being has already acquired the knowledge by which he has increased his own powers, to an extent which has given him the full controul over the animal creation, sufficient to subdue them, and to make millions of them obedient to his designs, and to contribute largely to his gratification.

Yet, extended as these powers have been, by slow degrees, from the period of man's most inexperienced state to the present time, it seems as though he were still in the infancy of his progress in the acquisition of power; for even now he appears to be on the eve of some great moral and intellectual advance, which will give him, not only additional controul over all other animals, but also over the elements of nature, and enable him to subdue them to his purpose upon the most magnificent scale of operations; and, what is yet far more important, to re-create a new and greatly superior matured character for all the future generations of men.

This second creation or regeneration of man will bring forth in him new combinations of his natural faculties, qualities, and powers, which will imbue him with a new spirit, and create in him new feelings, thoughts, and conduct, the reverse of those which have been hitherto produced.

This re-created or new-formed man will be enabled easily to subdue the earth, and make it an ever-varying paradise, the fit abode of highly intellectual moral beings, each of whom, for all practical purposes, will be the free possessor and delighted enjoyer of its whole extent; and that joy will be increased a thousand-fold, because all his fellow-beings will equally enjoy it with him.

Man could not attain this excellence and happiness in his first or irrational state of existence, which has been a state of repulsion and weakness; while the change of his condition which he approaches, will produce a state of attraction and strength, or unity and efficiency, that will insure the universal peace, intelligence, and happiness of mankind.

As soon as man shall be thus regenerated, he will discover that the present classification of society into the various grades of the Aristocracy, Professions, Trades, and Occupations, is fit only for man in his irrational or first state of existence; that it is the greatest of all errors to form permanent arrangements to train all men to become at maturity, irrational – to be either of the class of fools or knaves, or fools and knaves, to be oppressors of their fellows, or to be oppressed by them, to thus insure the inferiority and misery of both; for the existing classification can form only fools and knaves, the oppressor and the oppressed; men contending against each other to destroy, or to prevent the creation of, that which is essential to their happiness; one portion being purposely trained to keep the other in gross ignorance, that the latter may be easily deceived and made the slaves of the former, while these are trained in refined ignorance, and are made slaves to their own feelings, passions and injustice.

This chaotic state of existence will be changed for the rational state, in which a classification of society will arise, based on a correct knowledge of the newly acquired powers of human nature; a classification that will train all, at maturity, to be neither fools nor knaves, oppressors nor oppressed, but, on the contrary, men and women abounding in the most valuable knowledge of themselves and nature, living under arrangements to insure their own happiness, and the increasing happiness of their offspring; directing the powers or agencies of nature to perform all the affairs of life which are unhealthy, or in any manner disagreeable, or which have hitherto been the work of servants or slaves. When the present ascertained powers of science shall be wisely directed, there will be no necessity for any human being to become the servant or slave of another, or to perform that which to him would be disagreeable; and thus, harmony and unity of feeling, and efficiency of power, would be permanently retained.

It thus appears, that however human nature has been degraded in the first or irrational stage of its existence, it possesses the germs of faculties and qualities, which, when rightly directed, are sufficient to overcome ignorance, and sin, and misery, and to work out its own salvation from all the evil which it has hitherto suffered; and thus the harmony, unity, and efficiency of the constitution of human nature, to produce high intelligence and permanent happiness to the human race, will soon become obvious to all.

The beauty or harmony of this constitution of man arises from its unity and efficiency, and from such extraordinary powers being combined in a frame so small and finely proportioned.

When it is considered that human nature, in the aggregate, consists of certain faculties, propensities, and powers, of all of which each individual receives certain proportions; that the proportions vary in each individual, thus producing an endless variety of natural character, while the variety continually increases the happiness of each, the beauty and harmony of the device and arrangement must be admitted, and more especially when it is discovered that by this contrivance the greatest possible extent of human acquirements is insured for the benefit of all.

This provision of nature secures the most extraordinary advantages of the human race; for man acquires, by means of this endless diversity, of new proportions of the same original elements of his nature, a continual, never-ending increase of power. Each child having thus, at birth, a new combination of these faculties and qualities, would, were they rationally cultivated, bring into action new powers to enable it to invent or discover something new, to improve, or to add to, the previous experience and happiness of the population of the world.

No arrangement can be conceived more beautiful and harmonious than this simple device of Nature to secure an everlasting advancement in knowledge and happiness, without any counteracting evil. For human nature being understood, through a knowledge of the Moral Science of Man, each new variety of character will become a source of additional pleasure, and a sure means of increasing progression towards the perfection of happiness.

But man has not formed the elements of his nature, or combined their proportions in each individual; these wonderful operations are the work of a power hitherto unknown and mysterious to him. He, therefore, cannot be responsible for the original quality of the elements of his nature, or for the proportions combined in each individual. Were these elements and their varied proportions in each human being the worst of all created compounds, man would be blameless, being what he has been formed to be by a power superior to himself, and over whose operations he can exert no controul.

These elements, however, instead of being inferior, contain the germs of high physical, intellectual, and moral excellence, to the gradual increase of which no limits can be assigned; but, seeing that they are combined in each individual by a power unknown to man, no one can justly claim merit to himself for any fanciful superiority which he may possess over others. Whatever merit exists, belongs solely to the Power which creates the elements and forms the compound of them in each individual. All pride and vanity, therefore, in a being so formed, is irrational, and will cease as soon as he shall be trained to know himself, or to become a rational being, to which character, hitherto, he has not had the slightest pretension.

The ignorance of man relative to the origin of his formation, is also a strong stimulus to induce him to exert himself, without ceasing, to investigate Nature through her most secret recesses. He is thus urged on to the acquisition of the most varied and valuable knowledge, making him daily better acquainted with his own powers, by which he will, ultimately, learn to know himself. Who that has examined the physiology of man, and ascertained, as far as known, the manner in which his various powers of body and mind are united to perform their different functions, could suppose human nature to be bad or inferior?

These powers and qualities are so harmoniously arranged, united, and held together, that each part appears perfect in itself, and yet, the whole combined forms one of the most wondrous contrivances for the concentration of physical, intellectual, and moral power, into a finely proportioned being.

The combination of so many varied parts, concentrating such extraordinary powers, physical and mental, within a frame so small and finely proportioned as man and woman, constitutes a perfection of design and execution unequalled by any other known result of nature. The extent and value of this design, however, will not be understood until these extraordinary powers shall have their course of action in every individual, nor until the effects of a rational education shall manifest the wisdom of nature in committing to the experience of age the formation of the entire acquired character of the young.

By the wondrous, and hitherto mysterious, organic construction of man and woman, the adults of the first generation that shall acquire a practical knowledge of their own powers to re-form the matured character of each individual, will be enabled almost to re-create the character of succeeding generations; to re-create it by training each individual from birth, by a new and very superior arrangement of external circumstances, to have a sound physical constitution, to have superior dispositions, habits, and manners, to have much valuable knowledge, and to make a daily progress towards physical, intellectual, and moral perfection.

It is obvious, through a knowledge of the constitution of human nature, or of the moral science of man, that to form the highest character in man and woman, no inferior example must be seen in any one of the adult population; therefore, the formation of an inferior character will be prevented; the superior external circumstances which alone will be permitted to act upon and to influence each individual, will, of necessity, form all to be superior, according to the organization which they receive from nature.

By this simple, easy, straightforward mode of proceeding, measures, the most effectual, will be adopted to *prevent one* human being from acquiring a single inferior quality, either of body or mind; and it is believed that the concentrated wisdom of society, in this rational state of existence, will be competent to effect this all-important object.

As in this state all must perceive it to be for their interest and happiness, that the most superior character which circumstances under the controul of man will permit, shall be formed for every one, without a single exception, it would be most unwise to suffer one human being, in any part of the world, to be so placed as to acquire any inferior qualities; because, it will be obvious that if any inferior qualities should be permitted to be formed in any one, all will be injured by the contaminating effects that such an example will have, not only upon adults, but more especially upon the children of the rising generation.

When, therefore, all the institutions and arrangements of society shall be formed in accordance with the constitution of human nature, and with the principles which constitute the Moral Science of Man, the harmony, unity, and efficiency of this science will be demonstrated, and its value understood, and then only will it be duly appreciated.

END OF THE FIRST PART

THE BOOK

OF THE

NEW MORAL WORLD,

EXPLANATORY OF THE

ELEMENTS OF THE SCIENCE OF SOCIETY

OR

THE SOCIAL STATE OF MAN,

BY

ROBERT OWEN.

Truth, without Mystery, Mixture of Error or Fear of Man, can, alone, Emancipate the Human Race from Sin and Misery.

PART SECOND.

London:
PUBLISHED BY THE HOME COLONIZATION SOCIETY,
AT THEIR OFFICE, 57, PALL MALL,
AND SOLD BY ALL BOOKSELLERS.

MDCCCXLII.

PREFACE

THE first part of this Book explains what human nature has been made to be by the power which has created it; and unless man shall cease to imagine that the wild conjectures of his inexperienced ancestors are divine truths, which may not now be examined and compared with unchanging facts, so as to arrive at certain and fixed conclusions, he can make no useful progress in real knowledge.

This first part of 'The Book' should, therefore be read and studied by the disciple of truth until it is understood and he is prepared to think and act in accordance with the principles of his nature.

Until this part of the subject is understood so as to form the base or foundation of all the ideas and associations of ideas which constitute the human mind, to proceed another step in the investigation, or to open this second part, will be useless.

While the first part, explanatory of human nature, is hidden from the capacity of the student, he need not open this Second Part. Unless the mind is capable of understanding the First Part, this Second must remain a dark page, and it will be a waste of time to attempt to comprehend it.

The First explains the science of human nature; the Second the science of society. The First is the inlet to the means by which, without failure, a good and valuable character may be ensured for every human being. The Second developes the means by which all may be amply supplied with all that is requisite, when men shall be trained to be rational beings, to ensure health, prosperity, and happiness to all of the human race.

The two sciences united, will lift up the veil which has so long kept man ignorant of his own nature, of his powers, and of the means of enjoying his existence. They will explain to him the cause why he has been so long kept in bondage to error, and therefore made the child of sin and misery.

When men shall learn how to form a superior character for their race, and to surround them, as now they easily may, with superior external circumstances, to the exclusion of all inferior, then will the days of rejoicing come, and man will be the intelligent inhabitant of a terrestrial paradise.

When the disciples of the system shall have made themselves – or more correctly, when by studying these part of 'The Book,' they shall become –

masters of these two sciences, they will be prepared to enter upon the study of the succeeding or third division of the subject.

Regent's Park, March, 1842

THE BOOK

OF THE

NEW MORAL WORLD

SECOND PART

THE PRINCIPLES OF SOCIETY

THE elements of the science of society, or the social state of man, contain –

1st. A knowledge of the principles, and their application to practice, of the laws of human nature; laws derived from demonstrable facts, and which prove man to be a social being.

2nd. A knowledge of the principles and practice of the best mode of *producing* in abundance the most beneficial necessaries and comforts for the support and enjoyment of human life.

3rd. A knowledge of the principles and practice of the best mode of *distributing* these productions beneficially for all.

4th. A knowledge of the principles and practices by which to form the new combination of circumstances for *training* the infant to become, at maturity, the most rational being.

5th. A knowledge of the principles and practice by which to *govern* man under these new arrangements in the best manner, as a member of the great family of man.

6th. A knowledge of the principles and practice for uniting in one general system, in due proportions, these several parts of the science of society; to effect and secure, in the best manner for all, the greatest amount of permanent benefits and enjoyments, with the fewest disadvantages.

Without a knowledge of the principles of these elements, in their whole extent, as a foundation for the future fabric of society, it will be unavailing and useless to commence practical measures. These elements form the architectural materials with which to build up a new state of human existence; and without a distinct knowledge of this outline, the builder will be wholly at a loss how to proceed with the superstructure.

It must, therefore, be clearly understood, that until the disciples of the rational system of society shall have acquired a correct knowledge of this outline, they cannot be competent to form a right conception of the subject, much less to become teachers of it, either in public or private. Hitherto, the premature teaching of those who have called themselves disciples of these new views of society, and who have imagined that a very small part of the rational system was the whole of it, has more retarded its progress, and effected far more injury to the cause they intended to support, than all its open opponents united. In fact, these partially informed persons can alone injure, by their injudicious advocacy, a system which, when fairly and fully explained in its own spirit, and with the calmness and patience which a knowledge of it always must produce, cannot fail to convince every one, except those who are so far prejudiced by some of the old mysteries, that they are incompetent to attend to facts, or to reason respecting them.

Too much, therefore, cannot be said as to the necessity for those who desire to understand this system, with a view to instruct others, to compare it fairly, in all its parts, to its full extent, with the old system, in which they have been educated and prejudiced, before they attempt to express an opinion whether it is erroneous and visionary, or true and practicable; and especially before they attempt to instruct others.

CHAPTER I

'I. A knowledge of the laws of human nature, derived from demonstrable facts, which prove man to be a social being.'

It is, alone, by attention to these laws, that man can acquire an accurate and extensive knowledge of himself. And without this knowledge, he is a mere animal, governed by an imagination, arising from inexperienced instincts, which have hitherto led him through a maze of error; a maze in which almost all men are still involved; for few, if any, have yet acquired a knowledge of the laws of human nature, and are, therefore, capable of knowing 'what manner of beings they are.'

Truly, then, was it said, by the ancients, that the highest and most important attainment of man was that he should 'know himself.'[a]

This knowledge is yet to be acquired by the human race; for they have, hitherto, devised their religions, laws, and institutions, not only not in accordance with this knowledge, but in direct opposition to it.

And yet, if the human mind had once been directed in a right course, the attainment of this invaluable knowledge would have been far more easy than many of the acquirements which it has long since made. But, to speak in the language of men with the limited knowledge yet acquired by the human race, it appears most unfortunate, that from the beginning of time known to us, man has been impelled to take a wrong course, and, in consequence, to wander for unknown ages in a maze or circle of error; being led, by the most wild and crude imaginations, from one gross absurdity to another; until now, when every reflective person cannot but feel astonishment as he contemplates the antics and folly of those who have been blindly compelled to feel, think, and act, in opposition to the truth and their own interest.

And it is now evident that a state of insanity exists, in which all are made to believe themselves and their immediate party right, however small that party may be, and all the world besides to be poor deluded fools; and so to believe, without any of the parties being yet made conscious how themselves and their own party have been compelled to feel, think, and act with equal or perhaps more folly. The laws of human nature, which so beautifully open this knowledge to man, and which, when fully understood, will so easily enable him to 'know himself,' have been generally explained in the various chapters of the first part of this book, which was first published by Effingham Wilson, and since has passed through several editions.

For the advantage of those who have not seen the first part of this book, it may be useful here to re-state the outline of the facts from which those laws are deduced. They are,

1st. that man is born now, as through all past time, helpless and ignorant, but with the germs of physical, mental, and moral faculties.

2nd. That he makes not any of these faculties, nor knows by what power they are formed or combined in his organization.

3rd. That the germs of these faculties are combined in varied proportions in every individual, previous to birth, and without his knowledge or control.

4th. That these faculties, thus formed and combined, gradually grow and expand, and, as they increase, become the recipients of impressions, by which knowledge or experience is given to each individual.

5th. That it does not depend on the knowledge, power, or control of the

[a] Attributed to Seneca, among others. Pope's version was perhaps the best known at this time: 'Know then thyself, presume not God to scan / The proper study of mankind is man' (*Essay on Man*, Ep. 2, l.1).

individual, what shall be the qualities or combination of his physical, mental, and moral faculties, at birth, which then constitute the individual, and which are the original material of, or foundation on, which his subsequent character is formed. Nor yet what shall be the kind or qualities of the objects which, subsequently, make their impressions on these faculties as they grow and expand. Nor yet what shall be the effects which these objects produce upon the peculiar qualities and combination of the faculties which have been given to each individual.

Thus the number and kind of faculties, their qualities and combinations, the objects which produce impressions on those faculties, and the capacity for receiving those impressions in the manner peculiar to the individual, are all formed *for* each human being; and thus is his whole character *forced* upon him, and formed *for* him, without his consent or knowledge.

It is also a law of God that man *must believe* according to the strongest convictions made upon his mind, and *must feel* as he is compelled by his organization to feel, or to like or dislike instinctively. These, then, are the unchanging laws of nature respecting humanity, or the everlasting laws of God, regarding man, as they have been known to have existed from the beginning, even until now.

But man, previous to experience, has also been formed with instincts to force him to make various efforts to acquire knowledge, by the exercise of the powers of imagination which have been given to him. He, therefore, when new impressions are made upon him, imagines, guesses, or conjectures vaguely, respecting their causes and results; often, at first, wide from the truth; and it is only by repeated impressions and extensive comparisons, that he gradually acquires an accurate knowledge of any subject.

Thus has it been with man respecting his own nature. He has imagined, guessed, and conjectured, various notions; acted upon them, and made laws under the supposition of their truth. Yet not only is it now discovered that these laws have been based upon errors, most fatal to the well-being and permanent happiness of the human race, but facts and experience, the test of truth, prove, that they have been in direct opposition to nature's laws, and in defiance, as it were, of the laws of God, written, as they have been from the beginning, in unchanging characters, in the language of nature alike intelligible to all nations.

The laws of man, made from misconception of his own nature, have, of necessity, produced over the world a general state of society, in which he continually endeavours to falsify his nature, and, in consequence, lives in a constant system of deception; each one endeavouring to hide from others his natural feelings and real impressions; and, thus, an universal conviction is made, 'that man is bad by nature;' humanity, although the direct work of God or Nature, is traduced; and thus the human race have been until now divided, opposed, and rendered vicious and irrational. The laws of man, too, are all calculated to train men to become unsocial in their character, to create separate and opposing interests, and to excite competition and contest among the human race.

With these laws of man, founded, as they are, in direct opposition to the never-changing nature of humanity, it is utterly impossible that he should ever become wise, or charitable, or competent to love his neighbour as himself. These laws, so long as they shall govern society, will be an effectual bar to the acquirement of the most important knowledge that man can attain; they must imbue his whole mind with uncharitable feelings for all who differ from him in opinion, and make him to hate and despise them. They will, for ever, prevent mind speaking to mind, in the delightful fulness of confidence, devoid of all fear and reserve. They will, as long as they shall be maintained, be a bar to the universal simplicity of truth. They will disfigure the human form and features, and prevent the formation of minds that will express in each countenance intelligence, simplicity, charity, confidence, and kindness, with the total absence of all fear or suspicion; and expression never yet seen in man; but which, when his character shall be formed under the laws of nature, in accordance with his nature, will be the universal expression of the human race; but varied as these qualities shall be differently compounded in each individual.

The laws of God or of Nature are, therefore, all calculated to make man a social being; to unite him most cordially with all his fellows; to *destroy* all anti-social feelings; and to prevent the existence of opposing feelings or interests.

In fact, no two states of existence can be imagined to form a stronger contrast than will exist between the state of society which has been formed under the laws of man, and that which will arise under the laws of nature or of God. Nor will it be possible for the present wretched state of human existence to be changed, and man to be made to know himself and become a rational being, until he shall be sufficiently enlightened to be induced entirely to abandon his own insane laws opposed to his nature, and to adopt the consistent and wise laws of the power that gives him existence, and which every moment supports his life; laws which are in perfect accordance with his nature; and, which, if faithfully acted upon, would insure his permanent happiness, and enable him speedily to make this earth a continually improving paradise.

CHAPTER II

'II. A practical knowledge of the best mode of producing, in abundance, the most beneficial necessaries and comforts, for the support and enjoyment of human life.'

To know how to produce abundance of wealth of the most useful and best qualities, in the manner most beneficial to the producers and consumers, or, in other words, to insure, from this process, the greatest amount of happiness to both, is an important fundamental element of the science of society.

But this knowledge is not to be attained without an extensive and varied experience of society as it has been constituted, and an intimate acquaintance with the natural and scientific powers which are, or may be made to be, under the control of those who influence and direct the operations of society.

The first consideration, previous to entering upon the more practical part of this division of the subject, is to ascertain –

1st. What constitutes the most useful, and consequently, that which is intrinsically the most valuable, wealth to man and to society?

This question almost answers itself.

That which is the most necessary for man's existence and the well ordering of society, is the most useful; and the most useful is, intrinsically, the most valuable.

The most necessary wealth is air, water, food, clothes, shelter, instruction, amusement, the affections of our associates, and good society.

These are required, and, excepting air and water, are obtained in the early stages of society, generally of a coarse and rude description, or of inferior qualities; and as the population of the world progresses in knowledge derived from facts and experience, the quantities and qualities of these varied kinds of wealth increase and improve, or may be made to do so, because the powers of production continually increase beyond the advance of population. Now, were the inhabitants of all countries, at all times, amply provided with good air and water, and superior food, clothes, shelter, instruction, amusement, with the means to enjoy good society and to acquire the affections of their associates and the esteem of their fellows, they would have all the materials that could be desired to insure their health and happiness.

It is of deep concern to all, that it should be well ascertained whether the means exist, by which the population of all countries may be thus supplied with all the superior kinds of wealth requisite for their health and happiness.

The means consist in land, water, labour, skill, capital, and knowledge.

These exist, in superfluity, to supply the present population of the world, and for its unrestrained increase for unnumbered ages. Man has now obtained possession of all the materials requisite for his health and happiness, except the knowledge *how to apply* the materials to procure these results and maintain them through succeeding ages.

But it is the interest of every human being that he should be healthy and happy, and that all other human beings should be equally healthy and happy.

If, then, it be the interest of each that all should be healthy and happy, and the materials superabound to enable society unitedly to produce these most desirable results, how is it that these results have not been attained, and the well-being and happiness of the human race have not been secured?

There is but one true reply, which is, that for reasons yet unknown to man, he has been hitherto kept too ignorant to understand his own interest, or to unite with his fellows to apply the abundant means around him to secure his own happiness and the happiness of his race.

He has also erred in his estimate of what is the most valuable wealth, and he has not known the short, easy, and simple mode of obtaining it. He is to-day, over the earth, greatly deficient in knowledge on both these subjects.

The misapplication of the medium by which, conveniently, to exchange wealth, has greatly tended to assist to derange the human intellects upon the subject of wealth. Money has truly been made the cause of innumerable errors in society, even to induce some to deem it 'the root of all evil.'[a]

The latter expression is erroneous – the root of all evil in human society, has been the adoption of the laws of man, made by him while ignorant of his own nature, and the continual rejection of the laws of God, although these laws have been declared in language spoken to the human race, age after age, without ceasing; but which laws, man, in his ignorance, would willingly obliterate, but has hitherto been foiled in the mad attempt, and now finds himself, for this purpose, more powerless than ever.

To produce the greatest amount of the most valuable wealth, in the shortest time, with the least amount of labour, and with the greatest benefit to the producers and consumers of it, money will be required but for a short period; after which it will become unnecessary and useless. For intrinsic wealth, that is, good air and water, superior food, clothes, shelter, instruction, and amusement, may be easily obtained, under other arrangements, without money, and also without the endless injustice, oppression, and other evils, now produced solely by money.

But previous to this change in the feelings and conduct of society, it must be enabled to understand how easily and certainly intrinsic wealth may be made, everywhere, without competition and contest, to abound beyond the possible wants or desires of any population. And, also, that that which has not intrinsic worth, will gradually cease to be esteemed or sought for, until it will become valueless.

---

[a] See 1 Timothy 6:10.

But to produce the greatest amount of the most valuable wealth, in the shortest time, and in the best manner, man must be cordially united with his fellows, and the spirit of contest and competition must die within him. The period for its natural extinction is near at hand.

To obtain this cordial union, the laws of man, which generate all manner of division and contest, even to death, must be, for ever, abandoned, and the everlasting laws of God adopted for the government of society.

This change being effected, the cordial union of all, not only for the creation of wealth, but for the attainment of every object connected with the well-being and happiness of society, will necessarily follow.

The laws of God make it evident to all who are enabled to think rationally, that man is formed *directly*, by the power whence he derives his physical, mental, and moral faculties, and *indirectly*, by society, or external circumstances of man's immediate production. And that, thus, the character of every one is formed *for* him, and may be well or ill formed, to a very great extent, by society.

It being, then, a law of God, that the physical, mental, and moral faculties, and practical character, of each individual, shall be formed *for* him, and this law being made the base of society, and the superstructure being, in all its parts, in undeviating unison with this base, there will be no difficulty in cordially uniting the human race, in destroying all the causes which have hitherto produced sin and misery throughout the world, and in creating the most valuable wealth for all, far beyond the possible wants or rational desires of any.

It has been stated that the most valuable wealth consists in good air and water, superior food, clothes, shelter, instruction, and amusement; and that the materials for the production of wealth are land, water, labour, skill, capital, and knowledge; and that all these materials, except the last, exist, or may be easily obtained by union, in all countries. The last is that which we now seek to obtain; for – as this superior wealth in its *whole* extent is not now enjoyed by any, and *partially* only by a few compared with the mass of population who are deprived of all superior wealth – it is most certain that the requisite knowledge to ensure a regular supply of superior wealth for all, has not yet been made known to the public, if it has ever existed in any mind.

And, yet, when we once commence to proceed on the true base of society, that which, hitherto, has appeared impracticable or utterly impossible, will speedily become obvious, simple, and easy of execution.

To produce at all times, without fluctuations, except depending to a limited extent upon the seasons, the greatest amount of the most valuable wealth, in the shortest time, with the least labour and capital, and with the greatest pleasure and benefit to the producers and consumers, it is necessary that upon a certain proportion of land, there should be united labour, skill, capital, and population; and that these materials should be combined and directed by those who understand the laws of God, that they may be enabled cordially to unite the people, and who are familiar with the principles of society, that they may be enabled to unite, in their due proportions, the materials for the creation of wealth, and thus effectually to obtain the desired results. The parties, thus informed, cannot avoid being alive to the enormous waste and extravagant useless application, under all the existing arrangements, of the materials and all the powers possessed by society to create wealth, in all countries, from those arrangements having emanated, as they have done, from the erroneous, unwise, and most injurious, laws of man.

The greatest loss and waste arise from the disunited minds and feelings which these laws create and perpetually maintain among all people and nations.

By this universal division of the convictions and feelings of the human race, the enormous expense to create and maintain the armies of the world has been rendered necessary. But for these laws, there would be no use for these armies; and these armies, alone, by what they consume and waste, expend more of the materials and capital for the creation of wealth, than, if wisely applied, to direct the labour and skill of the individuals composing these armies, would, under the government of the laws of God, be much more than sufficient to well supply all the wants of the population of the world.

By this universal division of the convictions and feelings of the human race, made solely by the laws of man, the opposing, conflicting, and grossly absurd theocratic mystical notions whence all the religions of the world have originated, have been introduced and maintained, at an expense which, if now wisely applied to give a right direction to the physical and mental power of the individuals engaged, directly or indirectly, in the innumerable swarms and armies of the priesthood of the world, would, also, be much more than equal to the full supply of the most valuable wealth for all the population of the earth, were they under the government of the laws of God.

But the direct waste of wealth, and the indirect loss of the creation of wealth, by the secular and religious armies of the world, enormous as these evils now are, are, yet, not to be compared with the sufferings which they daily and hourly inflict upon the human race, by the hypocrisy, vice, crime, and universal immorality, which they create, foster, and encourage.

By these universal divisions, made by the insane and horrible general laws of man, creating endless opposition between the convictions and feelings of the same individual, and the convictions and feelings of individuals trained in different sects, parties, and classes, in different countries and having different colours of skins, universal disorder is made to reign and ride triumphant over all people and nations, until national and more local laws in detail, but founded on the same insane general laws of man, become necessary to keep society together in some way or other, even as it now is. But these national and local laws of man, again create an expense, direct and indirect, of labour, time, and capital, and immorality and misery, frightful and hideous to contemplate.

Now those who are directly or indirectly employed in making, executing, and aiding to support these most wicked and oppressive laws of man, as they now exist in the various codes over the world – and exist in direct defiance, as it were, of the just, wise, consistent, and most benevolent laws of God, as hourly declared, throughout nature, to all who attend to the unchanging laws by which the operations of nature proceed through all time – even these persons, for they are very numerous, would form an army, if under the government of the laws of God, of superior and happy producers of valuable wealth, that in amount, aided by the improved machinery of modern times, would go far towards the relief from poverty of all who now suffer, in all countries, from the want of the necessaries and comforts of life.

By the perplexities arising in men's minds from the inconsistent and opposing laws of man, especially respecting the necessity, thus imposed upon him, to endeavour to believe and feel contrary to his power to oppose the laws of God or of nature upon these subjects, and from the universal physical and mental disorder and confusion throughout society which human laws are perpetually producing, man has become a diseased animal, instead of being formed, as he would be if he were under the government of the laws of God, into a superior physical and mental, healthy, rational, and happy being.

The result of this portion of error is to create a necessity for a numerous medical profession, and for loads of artificial medicine, for neither of which would there be any necessity, if the human race were trained and placed as they might be from their birth, and governed, in all their proceedings, by the laws of God in conformity with their nature. As the change from the laws of man to the laws of God shall be gradually made, so will diseases of body and mind diminish, until both will be unknown except as a matter of history. Now the expense of this profession is also considerable; and if the parties who are now, directly and indirectly, engaged in it, were judiciously employed as superior producers of wealth, or cultivators of the human faculties, in accordance with the laws of nature, an immense saving of wealth would be made and obtained, and the health and happiness of all would be greatly improved and increased.

Again, by the derangement of the human faculties produced solely by the insane laws of man being opposed to the wise laws of God, an immense loss and waste of wealth is produced by all the existing institutions for the education, as it is called, of the higher and now of the middle classes of the population. For instance, the immense annual expenditure in Oxford and Cambridge, and similar institutions, said to be for the good education of the students sent there for instruction; while all who are let into the secret, know, that these universities are seminaries to teach ignorance and hypocrisy, and to derange the rational faculties of all within their influence, training the individuals to become in too many cases the most presumptuous, vain, conceited, immoral, and yet ignorant oppressors, of their much superior fellow men, whose minds have escaped this excess of misdirection.

All the principal seminaries are compelled in certain degrees to follow these sad examples, or they would be so discouraged by the parties thus miseducated at the universities, and those whom they influence, that the directors of these seminaries would have no chance of pecuniary success, however superior their arrangements and instruction might be.

The loss of wealth, by non-production, ill-production, and waste, arising from this mal-education in the malevolent and insane laws of man, instead of the benevolent and wise laws of God or Nature, is beyond all human calculation, to say nothing now of the extent of the hypocritical immorality which these poor deluded, presumptuous creatures spread throughout all countries. How many parents are at this moment in the British dominions bewailing their misfortune in having sent their children to these universities, or other fashionable public institutions called seminaries of instruction, to have them in reality taught to squander their wealth most viciously, instead of being trained to assist them honestly to create more for useful purposes!

So, also, by the divisions and derangement of the human faculties by these insane laws of man, is there a great loss and waste of wealth in the existing arrangements and institutions established with the view to amuse the people of every grade in society. These, although in many cases conducted at a great expense, are more calculated to produce disease, vice, and misery, than the rational relaxation and amusement which human nature always requires to preserve it in the best state of body and mind for healthy and beneficial occupation and exercise.

But it will be endless to proceed with the causes in daily action, under this old wretched and most immoral system, which prevent the production of superior wealth, create inferior and useless, or destroy the wealth that has been created.

Suffice it to say that the whole of the existing system for the creation of a full supply of the most valuable wealth with the least labour and capital, the most beneficially for producers and consumers, is a heterogeneous mass of absurdity added to absurdity, founded on no principle except that of counteracting the object which all have in view, which is, to obtain the command over the greatest number of advantages that can be used or enjoyed in human society. These have been stated to be 'good air and water, superior food, clothes, dwellings, furniture, implements, instruments, machinery, instruction, amusement, good society, the affections of our associates, and the friendship or esteem of our fellows.'

Having at all times, unmolested and without fear, a full supply and command of these advantages, we should be in reality more wealthy than any human being has ever been known to be at any time in any country.

Yet by the most simple and beautiful scientific arrangements, which may be easily formed with a capital less than is now required to accommodate and support middle-class society, these advantages may be gradually secured for the whole of the human race, and enjoyed without retrogression, except and until they shall be disturbed in them by the irresistible and overwhelming operations of the elements of nature which man can neither foresee nor prevent.

Now, to obtain a constant full supply of good air and water, superior food, clothes, shelter, furniture, instruments, implements, complicated valuable machinery, instruction, amusement, the affections of our associates, and good society, none of the professions will be required; on the contrary, the army, war navy, the church, the law, and physic, are the most formidable obstacle to the attainment of these advantages, and will continue to be so as long as the ignorance of the world shall encourage or permit them to remain.

Instead of these useless divisions of a most ignorant and irrational state of human existence, by which all the superior elements to construct an enlightened, prosperous, and happy society are always kept in abeyance, and those inferior are elevated, by continual vulgar contention, to assume the supremacy, another and totally different arrangement of the divisions of society, founded on opposite principles, will arise, in which the members of these useless and most injurious professions – professions which fill the members of them with the spirit of hypocrisy or oppression – shall, for their own benefit and happiness, be delightfully occupied, under most desirable arrangements, to produce and distribute wealth, or in forming a superior character for the rising generation; or in governing locally or generally; or in the immediate enjoyment of a superior existence, such as rational beings, with the means now under the control of society, ought, and might, by the most simple yet beautiful arrangements, always enjoy.

These arrangements will be formed by uniting land, labour, and skill, in such a manner, in separate yet united establishments, throughout all countries, that, everywhere, there shall be the due proportion for the benefit of all, of production and distribution of wealth, of instruction and amusement, and of all other advantages that the present knowledge of the world can supply.

The principle, if there be any principle, in the present random and disordered state of society, is to separate agriculture from manufactures, trades, and professions – to isolate the former, by position and habits, from immediate connexion and intercourse with the latter – to crowd the latter into streets, lanes, alleys, and courts, forming towns and cities, to which the food is conveyed from the country – to give apparent separate interests to the innumerable divisions into which agriculture, the professions, trade, commerce and manufactures are divided, and again to oppose the interest of each member of these divisions to each other; thus forming a heterogeneous mass of as much opposing absurdity in principle and practice as can be combined to work together, in any manner that will bear a moment's calm and unprejudiced reflection.

The true object of society is to obtain health and happiness for the human race, to the extent which the means furnished by nature and the knowledge or experience acquired by man will admit.

To obtain these results other principles must be adopted; the late acquirements in practical knowledge have terminated the possibility of the working classes being prosperous, as long as the old principles and practices of society shall be maintained.

To insure health and happiness to the human race, men must not be isolated from their fellows – nor crowded into streets, lanes, and alleys, – nor must their general food be carried long distances to them – nor must their faculties and habits be confined to single objects, or even a few – nor trained to oppress or despise any one – nor to be idle and useless, or wasteful and extravagant – nor to have their characters formed in any manner as they have been heretofore.

But, on the contrary, to produce the greatest amount of the most valuable wealth in the best manner, to insure the highest health of body and mind, and to give continually increasing happiness to the human race, an entirely new combination of arrangements must be formed, to avoid and prevent the existence of any of the evils which have been enumerated.

These arrangements will constitute a state of society, the essential character of which will be great simplicity and high excellence. A state of society so simple, that all shall be gradually trained, from their birth, to comprehend it fully, in principle and practice, before they attain the age of majority in this old world. At twenty-one, males and females will understand society in its full extent, both in principle and practice – it will be open before them as a map in which they are familiar with the details of its latitude and longitude.

To form this simple and superior organisation of society, we dismiss at once all the existing divisions, institutions, and arrangements, which are too complicated and absurd to deserve any consideration, when a superior state of society is to be formed, and men are to be made to think and act wisely and consistently, and to become rational beings.

The whole business of life will be comprised in four departments, and these, in every case, will be united, in their due proportions, in separate establishments; and these separate establishments, like the railways, will be made gradually to supersede the old arrangements, but without creating loss or derangement as they advance, to any portion of existing society.

These four departments will consist of production of wealth, its distribution, formation of character, and governing. And these four departments will be intimately united in every establishment, in their due proportions, and, thus combined, form separate societies.

These societies will be, to a great extent, independent of all other similar societies, although, according to distance, intimately or more remotely connected with them, in the most friendly manner, by frequent intercourse and mutual exchange of kind and useful services.

The individuals born within these societies will be educated to understand the principles and practices of the four departments which form the society, and which include the chief knowledge and business of life.

When made familiar with the principles, practices, and knowledge, obtainable in their own society, they will be well prepared easily to comprehend the principles and practices of all other similar societies, and without loss of time, or much subsequent teaching, to take an useful, active part, according to age, in any of their departments.

Under this general arrangement, no portion of society will be isolated or crowded. There will be no street, or lane, or alley, or any such inferior object or external circumstance to be seen.

All will be in the most convenient union with their fellows, to produce wealth and to distribute it in the best manner, to have their characters, from birth, well formed, to be entirely alone when nature requires quiet and retirement, and to be easily, and without expense, in the midst of the best society, when the mind is in the proper state to benefit by, and to enjoy it.

In each of these societies there will be a due proportion of agriculture, which will always be formed to be the foundation of each, and carried to the highest point of perfection; because all the manufactures and trades in the world cannot enable one individual to exist beyond the number which the land can be made to support. The land will, therefore, be highly cultivated to produce the greatest amount of valuable wealth from it; but, as the great object of wealth, after the support of animal existence, is to procure happiness to the human race, the land will be laid out, in connection with the buildings upon it, to be the most convenient for all, and at the same time to present as much beauty by its general arrangement and in detail as the locality and other circumstances will permit.

In these separate societies there will be no contest or competition between the members; nor yet will there be any between the societies, however near, or distant, or numerous they may be. There is no arrangement that can be conceived more destructive of wealth and happiness than the present system of individual and national contests and competition.

All will be trained and educated to acquire the greatest amount of useful and valuable knowledge; and then, possessing the spirit of charity, kindness, and love for all their fellows – which spirit will be given to them by their new mode of instruction from birth – all will of necessity feel the greatest desire to aid and assist each other to the full extent of their powers, and their greatest pleasures will arise from being thus occupied.

There will also be in each of these societies the due proportion of manufactures, trades, and commerce, for the number of members and their wants; but manufactures, trades, and commerce will be established and conducted on principles very different to those prevalent throughout present society.

The greatest economy will arise from having the best of whatever society requires. This principle, carried into practice throughout the whole of these new establishments, will create a saving in time, labour, and capital, of which the members of old society can scarcely form a rational conception.

And this saving of labour, time, and capital, added to the saving that will arise, directly and indirectly, from the absence of all the professions – which are of incalculable cost and injury to the whole of society, – will create a reduction in the general expenditure of labour, time, and capital, of from fifty to sixty per cent. at least; besides adding, beyond all estimate, to the knowledge, charity, morality, virtue, and good feeling, throughout all these societies.

In this manner will these societies, being always supplied with the latest and best machinery for performing whatever it can be made to well execute, produce the greatest amount of the most valuable wealth, in the shortest time and in the best manner, or so as to produce health and enjoyment to all while engaged in the department of production; and which department, instead of being as now, a low, degraded and degrading, unhealthy, and most disagreeable and severe labour, will be a moderate exercise of an elevating and pleasurable character, in which all will ardently desire to have their full share, and be at all times ready to take more, provided any of their companions will from any cause permit.

The detail of the peculiar agriculture, manufactures, trades, and commerce, within each society, will materially depend on its soil, climate, and other local peculiarities. The distribution of the wealth so produced will be considered in the next chapter.

Suffice it to say, generally, that under the new arrangements for creating wealth, proposed in this chapter, combined with the further advantages to be added, and which will be hereafter explained in this division of 'The Book,' all wealth will be created and put into the hands of the consumer at less than one-fourth of the present cost of time and labour. Besides which, the whole of it will be of superior quality, and enjoyed without the fear of adulteration.

No parties appear to be so erroneous in their ideas of real economy in the production and distribution of wealth, as the persons who, for some years, have conscientiously thought themselves the best informed upon the subject. These are the Modern Political Economists,[a] who, by their writings and practices, prove that they have yet to acquire the rudiments or first principles of economy in the production of wealth to promote the happiness of society, or to give lasting advantages to posterity.

[a] E.g., David Ricardo, James Mill, J. R. McCulloch.

CHAPTER III

'A practical knowledge of the best mode of *distributing* wealth most advantageously for all.'

Previous to ascertaining what this knowledge is, it will be useful to consider the principles and practices of the distribution of wealth, as they now exist, generally, throughout old society, and the effects resulting from them, as they are now experienced.

The principle now in practice is to induce a large portion of society to devote their lives to distribute wealth upon a large, a medium, and a small scale, and to have it conveyed from place to place in larger or smaller quantities, to meet the means and wants of various divisions of society and individuals, as they are now situated in cities, towns, villages, and country places. This principle of distribution makes a class in society whose business it is to *buy from* some parties and to *sell to* others. By this proceeding they are placed under circumstances which induce them to endeavour to buy at what appears at the time a low price in the market, and to sell again at the greatest permanent profit which they can obtain. Their real object being to get as much profit or gain between the seller to, and the buyer from them, as can be effected in their transactions.

There are innumerable errors in principle and evils in practice which necessarily proceed from this mode of distributing the wealth of society.

1st. A general class of distributors is formed, whose interest is separated from, and apparently opposed to, that of the individuals from whom they buy and to whom they sell.

2nd. Three classes of distributors are made – the small, the medium, and the large buyers and sellers; or the retailers, the wholesale dealers, and the extensive merchants.

3rd. Three classes of buyers thus created, constitute the small, the medium, and large purchasers.

By this arrangement into various classes of buyers and sellers, the parties are early trained to learn that they have separate and opposing interests, and different ranks and stations in society. An inequality of feeling and condition is thus created and maintained, with all the servility and pride which these unequal arrangements are sure to produce. The parties are regularly trained in a general system of deception, in order that they may be the more successful in buying cheap and selling dear.

The smaller sellers acquire habits of injurious idleness, waiting often for hours for customers. And this evil is experienced to a considerable extent even among the class of wholesale dealers.

There are, also, by this arrangement, many more establishments for selling than are necessary in the villages, towns, and cities; and a very large capital is thus wasted without benefit to society. And from their number opposed to each other all over the country to obtain customers, they endeavour to undersell each other, and are therefore continually endeavouring to injure the producer by the establishment of what are called cheap shops and warehouses; and, to support their character, the master or his servants must be continually on the watch to buy bargains – that is, to procure wealth for less than the cost of its production.

The distributors, small, medium, and large, have all to be supported by the producers, and the greater the number of the former compared with the latter, the greater will be the burden which the producer has to sustain; for as the number of distributors increases, the accumulation of wealth must decrease, and more must be required from the producer.

The distributors of wealth, under the present system, are a dead weight upon the producers, and are most active demoralizers of society. Their dependent condition, at the commencement of their task, teaches or induces them to be servile to their customers, and to continue to be so as long as they are accumulating wealth by their cheap buying and dear selling. But when they have secured sufficient to be what they imagine to be an independence to live without business, they are too often filled with a most ignorant pride, and become insolent to their dependants.

The arrangement is altogether a most improvident one for society, whose interest it is to produce the greatest amount of wealth of the best qualities; while the existing number of distribution is not only to withdraw great numbers from producing to become distributors, but to add to the cost of the consumer all the expense of a most wasteful and extravagant distribution; the distribution costing the consumer many times the price of the original cost of the wealth purchased.

Then, by the position in which the seller is placed by his created desire for gain on the one hand, and the competition he meets with from opponents selling similar productions on the other, he is strongly tempted to deteriorate the articles which he has for sale; and when these are provisions, either of home production or of foreign importation, the effects upon the health and consequent comfort and happiness of the consumers are often most injurious, and productive of much premature death, especially among the working classes, who, in this respect, are perhaps made to be the greatest sufferers, by purchasing the inferior or low-priced articles. A moment's reflection must now make it evident that the distribution of wealth under the present system of society, is most erroneous in principle and highly injurious in practice, to the producer, distributor, and consumer.

The expense of thus distrbuting wealth in Great Britain and Ireland, including transit from place to place, and all the agents directly and indirectly engaged in this department, is perhaps little short of one hundred millions annually, without taking into consideration the deterioration of the quality of many of the articles constituting this wealth, by carriage, and by being divided into small quantities, and kept in improper stores and places, in which the atmosphere is unfavourable to the keeping of such articles in a tolerably good and much less in the best condition for use.

In fact, the arrangements as they exist in old society for the distribution of the wealth which it produces, are, like all the other general arrangements of this system, false in principle, and most injurious in practice; they seem, indeed, as though they were purposely devised to be as imperfect and deficient for the attainment of the objects to be desired in the distribution of wealth as man's ingenuity could invent; for they are first-rate contrivances to add to the cost of production – to deteriorate the qualities – to require a large amount of most unnecessary capital and labour – to demoralize the character of the parties occupied in the department – and to train men to become servile slaves to their customers and ignorant tyrants to their dependants. In short, to assist most materially to make society a system of falsehood, deception, and of swindling of the weaker or less cunning by the stronger in position and intellect.

From what has been written it must be now evident that the sooner this division of society can be superseded by other arrangements, founded on true principles, and practices in accordance with those principles, the better will it be for producers, distributors, and consumers.

We will now examine what are the *true* principles for the distribution of wealth, and the *right* or *best* mode of applying them to practice.

In a right or rationally constituted system of society, if one shall ever be established, the most efficient arrangements will be formed to enable its members with health, pleasure, and enjoyment to themselves, to produce the greatest amount of the most valuable wealth that can be required for the use of all, and to have it distributed with economy while in the best condition for use. Distributors add nothing to the value of wealth, but add to its cost by the whole expense of their living and that of the people whom they employ. All the distributors in society do not create a particle of wealth. They are therefore a burden to the producers, to the whole extent of their consumption and waste by transit and keeping.

It becomes, then, the direct interest of all society, that there should be the least amount of labour that is practicable employed in distributing wealth; and that there should be the least transit and waste of wealth, after it has been completed in its stages of production. Under such arrangements as may be now introduced into regular and systematic practice, it is very probable that one per cent. of the capital and labour applied to distribution under the existing system, would be more than sufficient for a much better distribution.

Under a wise and scientific arrangement of society, the loss and waste of much transit and improper keeping in shops and stores would be avoided.

Then the ninety-nine per cent. of capital and labour, that would be thus saved, would be advantageously employed in production, greatly to the benefit of society, by the increased amount of wealth which these additional numbers and the increase of capital would assist to create. But by far the most important gain to society and to the individuals taken from the present system of distribution, would be the improvement in the thoughts, feelings, and entire character of all the producers, distributors, and consumers. They would know that their producing occupations were beneficial to society and to themselves, that it was a healthy and honest employment; and every reflection connected with it would be satisfactory to themselves and to all around them.

Under a properly constituted scientific arrangement of society, for producing and distributing wealth in the best manner, the producers and distributors would be also the chief consumers of it, on the premises where it was grown and made. It would be kept in quantities in granaries, stores, and warehouses, properly placed and constructed to keep each kind of wealth in the best state for preservation, and to be consumed when in the best condition for use.

In a properly constituted arrangement for producing and distributing wealth, for forming the character, and for local government, the distribution of the wealth would be, very generally, at once from the granaries, stores, and warehouses, for the immediate daily consumption and use of those who had produced it. And thus the loss arising from frequent transit, and subdivision, and deterioration, would be saved, and the whole expense of distribution would be the conveyance of the daily consumption from the places of keep to the culinary apartments, or to the rooms of the makers of garments, or to other places where the different kinds of wealth would be required for use.

Under these arrangements there would be throughout the whole of society no retail shops or wholesale warehouses with the parties within them engaged in schemes to buy cheap and sell dear. These establishments, as now conducted in old society, are neither more nor less than expensive wasteful arrangements, to produce the least amount of good, with the greatest amount of evil. They, with the appendages dependent upon them, create the necessity for streets, lanes, alleys, and courts, constituting villages, towns, and cities; each of which as now constructed is an evil, an unfavourable and vicious external circumstance, which assists to ill-form the character of man, woman, and child from birth, and to exclude them from the health and pleasure of the benefits and delights of the country; and more especially when it shall be laid out and cultivated as it ought to be everywhere now, with the acquired knowledge and capital in the possession of society.

Instead of thus congregating masses of half-formed human beings within streets, lanes, courts, and alleys, to deteriorate wealth, deprive themselves of the glorious scenery of the atmosphere and earth, and of their natural benefits to the human mind and constitution, production, distribution, and consumption will be very gradually united, under arrangements that will ensure to all the greatest amount of advantages that can be, with our present knowledge, derived from them, when they shall be combined with a direct view to promote the permanent happiness of producers, distributors, and consumers.

When these arrangements shall be well executed and in full operation, then will be seen the difference between the principle in practice of taking food and other kinds of wealth to man, and bringing man to his food and the enjoyment of wealth where the food and other wealth are chiefly produced and created.

In fact, every department of society as it is now constituted or organized – if such a compound of heterogeneous absurdity as society now is can be said to be organized – it would seem as though our ancestors had maturely considered, in making their arrangements, how they could contrive to produce the most vice, crime, and misery, to the mass of the population of the world, and the least amount of real virtue and happiness; for if they had so deliberated, while in possession of great knowledge upon the subject, they could scarcely have succeeded better than, or indeed so well as, they have, in producing the maximum of crime and misery, and the minimum of virtue and happiness.

And one of their great aids to produce the maximum of evil and the minimum of good, has been their invention to distribute wealth by means of arrangements which create a never-ending desire to buy cheap and sell dear, through the medium of an artificial representative of wealth, which has no power to expand or contract as wealth expands or contracts; but which is, on the contrary, the continual cause of disturbing all sound principles for the production and distribution of wealth, and the unceasing cause of incalculable misery to the human race, with the destruction, also, of all their faculties to enable them to distinguish right from wrong in any of their proceedings.

In a rightly constituted or rational state of society, gold or silver, or paper money of credit, will never be used as a medium by which to distribute wealth.

The medium for the easy, and advantageous, and just exchange of wealth, as long as any medium shall be required, must possess the quality of expansion and contraction to a fractional accuracy as wealth for exchange expands or contracts. It must, also, while it represents wealth, be unchanging in its value.

And this medium may be now easily made, and to be, at all times, equal to the wants of society, and to set industry free and at work over the world, now and for ever; and thus prevent, in future, the complaint of a single individual for want of useful and profitable employment, and put an end also to poverty, or the fear of poverty, among any portion of the human race, for ever.

How instructive of the error of the monetary system of the world, and how amusing would it be, were it not for the overwhelming misery which this error produces, to observe the results of the working of the system in the two most powerful commercial nations in the world, that is, in the British Empire and in the United States of North America!

These two nations possess the most unbounded means for the creation of wealth; and much more than fifty fold beyond the possible wants of their respective populations, when they can be made tolerably rational on the subject of wealth.

Neither of these people make the slightest complaint that they cannot produce all that they can possibly require, if they had but plenty of what they call money; nay, even without a surplus or supposed sufficiency of this magic something called money, which it sadly puzzles all their wise men to comprehend, they somehow or other do contrive to produce, by their arrangements, even a surplus of real wealth; and so great a surplus that they are at a loss to know what to do with it, for want of this money, and it makes them full of fears and alarms that so much surplus wealth or production will ruin them outright, for lack of this money to represent it; and having so much real wealth, and being competent to make so very much more, they are apprehensive they must all come to poverty and die of want; and of want of those things of which they can, with so much ease, produce abundance, and spend half their time, if they so thought fit, in the improvement of their minds or in rational amusement.

But no; this state of prosperity can never be, as they suppose, if they cannot procure gold and silver money, or paper money of credit. Poor souls! (if it be possible to conceive they ever had any) what would become of them if they had no gold or silver, or paper of credit money? Why, with their present notions and insane monetary impressions, if they had plenty of food they must starve; if they had abundance of clothing they must go naked; if they had a superfluity of dwellings and furniture they must remain in want of both. In short, if they had an over supply of all things which constitute real wealth, and had not as money, gold, silver, or paper credit, which are not wealth, they must starve and go out of existence; such being the principles on which the esteemed wisest men, as well as all others, in these two great commercial nations, are now acting.

Until society shall become sane and be competent to create a *real*, instead of an *imaginary* representative of wealth, with which to make exchanges, as long as a representative for an exchange shall be required, extremes of riches and poverty will exist and increase, and the crime, misery, slavery, and oppression, which they produce, with ignorance and every attendant upon an irrational state of existence, will increase in like proportion; society will be kept in continual turmoil; and immorality of every description will more and more extend over the earth, until it becomes a worse pandemonium, if possible, than Great Britain is rapidly becoming.

Wealth can never be beneficially distributed under the present monetary system of society, which, with the extraordinary new means required to produce wealth, is the most injurious to the population that can be well conceived, and a complete bar to all the advantages which would otherwise arise to all parties from an increase of wealth, that would soon be made superabundant for all the desires of the human race.

By far the most simple of the divisions of society, whenever it shall be rationally constituted, and a real representative of wealth shall be introduced, will be its beneficial distribution without contest or competition, and probably with less than one per cent. of the loss and cost of it under the existing malarrangements of an old worn-out system.

As an immediate step between an irrational and a rational state of society, banks of real wealth will be made to supersede banks of imaginary wealth and of paper credit. When these banks of real wealth shall be arranged and conducted as they easily may be, idleness, poverty, crime, and misery will gradually disappear, and all complaining in our streets will soon cease. United in due proportion with arrangements to produce wealth and to form the character of the population, the improvement of society would be so rapid and continuous, that to the men of this old worn-out immoral system, it would appear the greatest of all miracles that has been performed, since the creation of the world in its present form and with its present species of inhabitants.

And of all the divisions of society the distributive will be the most simple, easy, and economical; requiring little labour, but good systematic arrangement. Its operations will also afford healthy exercise and pleasant occupation to all engaged in them. And as, under these arrangements, it will be in reality 'more pleasant to give than to receive,' all will rejoice when they arrive at the age for distribution.

CHAPTER IV

'A knowledge of the principles and practices requisite to form the new combination of circumstances by which to train the infant from birth, to become, at maturity, the most rational being that his organization and our present knowledge of the science of the influence of external circumstances over human nature, will admit.'

THIS division of the subject, taken to its whole extent, in all its bearings on the well-being, well-ordering, and happiness of the population of the world, is, next to the attainment of means to continue existence, the most important; and second to the support of existence only because without the support of the being there could be no formation of character, good or bad. The organization of the individual and continued life, may be said to be the prepared material for the manufacture of the human character.

Upon education, as the term is generally understood throughout the civilised world, much, through past ages, and up to the present period, has been said, written, and published. Education, as commonly understood, constitutes but a very small portion of the science of the formation of character. And education hitherto, so far as it has gone, has tended much more to ill-form than to well-form the human character, for its evidently ultimate destined existence.

Under the circumstances which, until now, have existed among all the nations of the earth, ancient and modern, none appear to have understood the science of the cultivation of the human faculties, to form the possessor of them into an healthy, intelligent, a reasonable, rational, good, and happy being.

Lycurgus, of all whose history has been given and preserved to us, appears to have approached nearer to the conception of the principles to form a science for the formation of character, than any other lawgiver, statesman, or philosopher.[a] But so little, upon correct authority, has reached our period respecting the reasons for the practices which he introduced into Sparta, that it is now impossible to ascertain, with certainty, what was the extent to which his knowledge of the science of the formation of character has attained. It is evident, if the facts of his history, respecting the great change of character and condition which he caused to be made throughout the Spartan population, be true, that he had gone far towards the discovery of the principles by which any character, not inhuman, might be forced upon the human race, so as to make the individuals to be either Spartans or Quakers, intelligent or foolish, grossly irrational or highly rational.

But, excepting Lycurgus, no one appears to have had a conception of this first of all sciences; a science destined, and ere long, to ensure the permanent well-being and happiness of the human race.

Nature has now advanced so far in her progress, that, from henceforth, she places the power of well or ill-forming the general character of one generation, in the preceding, through all future time, or as long as man shall be an inhabitant of this globe.

In consequence of the fundamental errors on which society has ever been based, arrangements exist not, at this day, in any part of the world, to well-form the human character, by cultivating in their due proportions all the faculties of our nature; or which evince a knowledge of how to provide due and healthy and beneficial exercise for body and mind, or to give a right direction to the propensities and other natural qualities of our common nature.

But the period approaches for society to be placed on its true base; when man, for the first time in his history, shall know himself, and in consequence shall speedily learn how to form arrangements to secure a superior comparative character to all of his race; when he shall distinctly perceive what external

[a] Lycurgus: semi-mythical Spartan legislator who gave political stability to Sparta by establishing a Senate to avoid both arbitrary power and extreme democracy; divided the lands to lessen inequality, introduced common dining, and abolished lawsuits for money. His chief aim, according to Plutarch, was to exterminate the love of riches and luxury.

circumstances are good, and what are bad, for him and his offspring; and when he shall have the power to combine the superior for his use and enjoyment, and to reject the others, until none of the inferior shall be allowed to remain to disturb or injure any of his race.

This is the prospect which is now opening to man; it is the day of great things, of glad tidings, and not for a sect, or class, or a colour, but for all who live or may yet live; when man may say to ignorance, to poverty, to division, to fear, to jealousy, to revenge, wars, contests, and to all other crimes of ignorance – and there are none others – 'So far have you gone, but no further shall you go. Here, in the nineteenth century, is your boundary fixed.' All future centuries shall be years of increasing knowledge and enjoyment. And the cry of the beggar, the prisoner, and the oppressed of Britain, shall be the immediate cause of the emancipation of nations, and of man over the world, from the tyranny and wickedness of ignorance. Hail, friends of man, the approaching day when the knowledge of the science of the formation of character of man shall be universally known and practised. When it shall be so well known and so well practised, that not an inferior human being shall be formed at maturity to walk the earth, or disturb the universal happiness of man, or his progeny, in whatever country or clime he may be found!

Your miseries have proceeded from a false and most defective education; your happiness will arise from a true and superior education.

Hitherto, at no time, nor in any place, has there been an approach towards a true and superior education; the best education existing is based on false principles, and is necessarily most defective and inferior.

To well educate and wisely form the human character, requires a length and breadth and depth of knowledge, on the parts of those who are to direct and perform this task, such as none engaged in it have hitherto had the slightest conception of.

To know how to well form the human character is to know human nature; how it has been formed to acquire all the varieties of past national and local characters; how any of the human race may now be compelled to receive any similar characters; how they may be made to acquire a general character far beyond all comparison with the best ever yet formed for man; is to know the hitherto hidden science of the overwhelming influence of external circumstances over human nature; overwhelming to so great an extent, as to be capable of being applied with ease to form all individuals of the race into beasts or superior rational beings; to know how to create the external circumstances which shall effect either the one result or the other.

Where are the teachers with these qualifications to be now found? Have they ever existed? And is this science of forming man for happiness or misery, to be yet entrusted to those who are not only grossly ignorant of human nature, and of themselves, but without any useful knowlege of the application of the science of circumstances to the formation of character, and who have no power to create those circumstances which are absolutely necessary to well educate man and to make him a rational being?

How long is this weak and irrational course to be continued, to effect the greatest possible detriment, without exception, to all of the human race?

The creation of the circumstances to well educate man, is a national work, to be directed by national wisdom, and executed by national capital.

It is true, it may be imperfectly effected by the union of individuals seeing the importance and advantages of such arrangements even for the superior production and distribution of wealth; and an approach towards something rational may be attained by such associations, provided they are sufficiently extensive, and directed by a knowledge of the science of influence of circumstances in forming the character of man.

But, as the great change from an entire system of error and consequent misery, to one of truth and consequent happiness, must come, it would be far better that the arrangements for a superior formation of character for all should be, at once, made to emanate from the government; in order that the education for all should be the most useful and the best that national means can give, and that there should be harmony throughout the nation, and with other nations.

At present, the arrangements intended for and called education, as they are applied to form the character of the lower, middle, and upper classes, as these are now made to exist in Great Britain, are anything but arrangements to well educate either, or to form men to become rational beings.

The existence of these arrangements is a proof how very little is yet known of a rational mode of education, or of the only means by which man can ever be made a reasonable and happy being. Yet it is said that the object of the present mode of education is to make man reasonable and happy. The present state of society in Great Britain, in which, in proportion to numbers, more is expended, said to be to well form the character of the people, than in any other country, is proof that hitherto no sound or correct principles of education have ever been known.

Note the circumstances as they now exist in Oxford and Cambridge, and the preliminary schools and colleges connected with them; these form the prime seats of learning for the British Empire. The circumstances existing in these establishments for forming the character of the upper classes, are arranged chiefly to teach the languages, customs, habits, and ideas, of barbarians; to create early impressions in favour of them, and a desire in the taught to acquire the same ignorant and barbarous characters; to form men without any accurate knowledge of society as it now exists; to fill their minds with false notions and absurd mysteries; to create the most ridiculous feelings of presumption over those who have not been rendered irrational in the same manner that they have been; and to form beings at maturity to become the very pests of society. Poor creatures! – they know not the injury which has been done to them, and through them to society at large; for they are the men, from their position and possession of much wealth, who now, in the present irrational state of human affairs, influence the national proceedings and the general condition of the people in this country and in other countries.

These results are the necessary consequences of the teachers of Oxford, Cambridge, and the other most fashionable seminaries of learning, so called, being themselves totally untaught in all that is requisite to well teach others, to form in them a good and superior character. These teachers at an early period have been forced to receive impressions strongly in favour of words and of mysteries which soon cloud the mind, and, for all useful and superior purposes, render it of no value; but which, on the contrary, are sure to create a false view of man and society, and in consequence a false estimate of the relative importance of men and measures, and of all things around them. It is, therefore, no matter for surprise that men have become the miserable beings which they are, and the earth the pandemonium which it is; seeing that the directing minds under this old system of error, are thus made to become useless and irrational by all their training, teaching, and instruction.

All the seminaries for forming the character of the middle and lower classes partake more or less of these and other errors, and are calculated to make just the men and women who now constitute the various classes throughout society. And while these arrangements for disordering and deranging the human faculties from birth shall be encouraged or permitted to exist, no better results can ever arise. As these circumstancers are, so will the character of man be.

It is not, however, the teachers at Oxford, Cambridge, and the other seminaries for malforming the human character, who can rationally be blamed for the disastrous results which they produce. The real cause is in the error of the system in which our ancestors and this generation have been involved. These teachers are as much to be pitied as those whom they irrationally teach, and whose characters they malform.

Before any substantial or permanent change can be made in this respect, the directing *minds* of this and other countries must be born again; they must be made to see all things through a new medium; hitherto they have seen all things through a glass darkly[a] – through a mist which has falsified all things to their senses. This dark glass must be withdrawn – this mist of error must be removed – all old associations of ideas must be unassociated – the fundamental errors first forced into their minds, and on which all these associations of ideas have been formed, must be rooted out to their lowest foundation – and fundamental truths, respecting human nature, the formation of individual character, and the elements of society, must be made to replace them, and to

[a] See 1 Corinthians 13:12.

constitute the new base on which the new associations of ideas are to be formed. It is thus that the dark glass is to be withdrawn, that the mist of error is to be removed, that false associations of ideas are to be unassociated, and it is thus, and thus alone, that the *mind* can be born again, while the body lives; and this is now the destined change for man and for the human race.

It is for this generation now to arouse all its energies, to shake off the outward garment of the old man, with its frailties and defects, and with it to let all old things pass away, that all may become new, and man may arise a reasonable creature, with a new heart, a new mind, and a new spirit, which shall make him a rational being, fit inhabitant of the new moral world, and the terrestrial paradise which this new knowledge will speedily form the globe we inhabit to become.

The first practical step now to be taken to effect this great and glorious change for humanity, is to adopt efficient measures to open, enlarge, and expand, the minds of the present rulers of the earth, to enable them to see and comprehend the causes which are necessitating this great event, that they may be induced to accelerate and not to retard its progress.

And this course must be adopted, because it will be much more easy and much better to effect the change with the aid and hearty concurrence of these parties, than by any other means; and from their position in society, they will be made more easily to comprehend the whole subject, than those confined within a more limited sphere of action. It will also be, most strongly, their immediate interest to acquire a knowledge of it, and to take active measures to guide and direct all the requisite practical operation, to ensure speedy and general success to the entire change, without violence or disorder.

And this course with regard to the governments is the more necessary, because the government in each country is an essential ingredient in well or ill forming the character of all under its influence and control. In fact, it is the government and religion of any country, that, next to the fundamental principles on which society in all countries has been hitherto based, have been the most powerful circumstances in moulding man to be what he is in each country – for these together chiefly form his national character.

The second great step in forming a superior and rational character for man, will be to reform the religions of the world, and to bring them gradually over by kindness to that which can now be easily demonstrated to be the only true religion calculated for man, or that can ever be of substantial permanent benefit to him or to his race.

True religion, it may be demonstrated, is not a religion of any name. It is a principle, and the most glorious of all principles. This principle is TRUTH. TRUTH IS RELIGION, AND RELIGION IS TRUTH. All other religions have had a beginning among and by men, and all will speedily cease to exist, and ere long, will be known only as being recorded among the strange events which occurred during the history of the irrational period of human existence, before the mind of man was born the second time, to make him a reasonable and rational creature.

But how, it may be enquired, is this TRUTH AND TRUE RELIGION to be known for a certainty, when all the varied and opposing religions now in the world claim to be each the only true religion?

From the fact that not one of these religions can convince those who have been trained in any of the others, to abandon in a body their supposed true religion and adopt that one, it is evident that not one of these supposed true religions contains sufficient internal or external evidences to convince the educated and better informed opponents of its truth. And it would be the greatest of all imagined miracles if one such could be found among them, when they are, one and all, filled with endless contradictions and opposing statements, the internal evidence of all being superabundant to prove the error of their origin, and the continued ignorance and irrationality of all their trained followers.

And until the human mind can be born again, and trained to acquire sufficient power, strength, and elevation of intellect, to attain this knowledge, it will be useless to speak to it in the language of common sense, or to address it, except in accordance with its acquired absurd local prejudices. 'But,' it will be reiterated, 'how is the TRUE RELIGION to be known from all the pretenders to it?'

This is indeed a question of the deepest import to all; and it requires and shall have a reply which cannot be mistaken.

TRUE RELIGION IS TRUTH; and truth is that which changes not with time; that which is, at all times and seasons, in accordance with every fact known or that may become known; which is never opposed to itself, but always, in all its parts, however these may be multiplied, in perfect unity, without the shadow of incongruity.

But Truth has not yet been known or understood by man; his infant mind first imagines or conjectures; and hitherto he has been in his infancy, and has conjectured all manner of errors, and imagined all manner of frightful and grotesque and incongruous nonentities; and so far he has been the child of error, creating fears and alarms of ghosts, witches, and hobgoblins, and the train of misconceptions and miseries which such a crude state of the infant mind of man naturally and necessarily engenders.

The gradual progress of experience has now given man knowledge to attain another stage in the growth of his existence – to discover the mist of falsehood and error in which he has been hitherto enveloped, and in which he perceived all things darkly. Until now he has been inclosed as it were in a shell of ignorance, in which a perforation has just been made to admit the first rays of intellectual truth.

While he remained in this unperforated shell of ignorance, truth was hateful to him; he detested it, and, to the extent of his power, he persecuted it, and if he had known how, he would have destroyed it for ever.

So blind has man been made to be to his chief good! He has, from some cause or other, been made the greatest enemy to his best friend; for it is truth alone that can make man wise, and good, and happy.

But this dismal era in human existence is rapidly passing; the sun of Truth has, at length, arisen; and will now shine more and more gloriously as it approaches perfect day, when not a vestige of falsehood shall remain to cloud or disturb the harmony and happiness of man.

Yet again it is asked – 'What is the *Religion of Truth*?'

The Religion of Truth consists 'in consistent and undeviating *practice* in accordance with the now ascertained laws of nature respecting humanity, which are alone the laws of God.'

This practice, and this practice alone, will admit of and require the strict language of Truth, in the words and actions of all men.

When the Religion of Truth shall be established, all motive to falsehood, in the looks, words, or actions of men, will cease over the earth. It is the Religion of Truth that can, alone, set man free from disease of body and mind, or from sin and misery.

Hitherto, falsehood has reigned over the destinies of man; it is now the language, in look, word, and action, of the human race; it has involved all in its intricacies, perplexities, and miseries. It hates and fears the Religion of Truth, above and beyond all other of its hates and fears; and especially now when it is in its last struggles for existence.

It is only now, therefore, when the laws of human nature are ascertained – when the Religion of Truth has been made known – when the mind of man has acquired sufficient strength to bear the light of Truth – and when the era in his existence has arrived in which he dares no longer openly to persecute truth, that there is utility in talking about forming a good and superior character for man.

To form a useful, valuable, good, and superior character for man, the Religion of Truth, or the practice of man in accordance with the principles of his nature, must be the foundation on which his mind and conduct must be based.

The next layer of the superstructure must be a government, itself based on the Religion of Truth, and governing in accordance with the laws of man's nature.

Without these for the foundation and base of the superstructure, there can be no good, or valuable, or rational character formed for man.

With these two first steps secured, those which succeed will be easily attained.

Hitherto, it has been the false religions, and irrational governments, that have created the external arrangements formed by man around man. They have created or caused to be created all human institutions.

These have been combined from the false principles of the one and the irrational notions of the other. A more complicated compound of folly than that which has emanated from these errors, in all parts of the world, but especially in the British Empire, no one, without seeing or knowing the wretched effects which they have produced through past ages, and which they now produce, could have imagined that beings, thinking themselves to be reasonable creatures, could have established, and so long maintained.

These errors, however, highly mischievous as they are now in all respects, it will be necessary for some time to support, on the same principle and like necessity that the old roads for slow travelling upon were continued, until the corresponding and superseding railways were completed and ready for full action upon them.

With the Religion of Truth, with Governments prepared to adopt and carry into every day's consistent practice the laws of human nature or of God, the next means for forming a rational and superior character for man will be the local arrangements by which he is to be surrounded from his birth.

To form man to become a rational being, these arrangements must be combined in accordance with the Religion of Truth, and the governments founded upon it; and, of course, these local combinations will be in perfect unison with the Religion and Government and the laws of human nature.

These three circles of external circumstances will go far to bind and overrule all individuals who shall be within them, if not malformed at birth, to become wise, good, and happy. And malformations at birth must, under these circumstances, rapidly diminish, until they entirely cease.

That which will be required in addition to these three great and powerful circles of external circumstances to well-form the human character at birth, will be a selection of properly trained individuals to be around those who are to have their characters formed, from their birth.

As the forming of the characters of the human race will be, by far, the highest and most important business of human life, the individuals possessing the most accurate and extended knowledge of human nature and of society, with interminable patience and perseverance, and a love for children, will be selected as assistants to form and well manufacture, from the materials of human nature, the best character for each individual, that the natural compound of humanity of each at birth will admit. But as the most indelible benefit or injury is effected in the first years after birth, even at the commencement of the manufacture, the individuals having the finest minds, best spirit, and highest qualifications, will be selected for the formation of the character during infancy and childhood; the first six years of life being the period when the foundation for good or evil can be the most easily laid; the first year of the series being the most important, and the last the least so. How dreadfully is poor human nature mangled during this period, among all classes, under the existing insane system of forming or manufacturing a character for man by man!

To think, even under what are deemed the best modes of early instruction, of forming the character to be rational in childhood, by entrusting the care of the infant to the most inferior in mind, manner, and knowledge, and by placing the child within four walls, to sit quietly on a seat, and to ask no questions, is proof how totally ignorant the public have been and now are, on the subject of forming or manufacturing a superior character for the human race.

It was the observing of this idiotic proceeding among the children of the working class at New Lanark, that suggested the necessity of a new kind of infant school,[a] and a new mode of instruction, by something that the infants could see and be easily made to understand; and that their minds, manners, spirit, and conduct, should be formed under the principle of unceasing kindness, directed by judgment, instead of harshness, directed without knowlege of human nature, as had been previously the general practice of society in all ranks and conditions; of harshness and ignorance united, endeavouring to force infants and children to like that which is opposed to their nature, and to enable them to acquire that which they could not comprehend, and of which the teachers themselves were often equally ignorant.

But before the individuals who have been trained in the old immoral world of ignorance and mystery, can understand how the character of man is to be manufactured to form him into a good, wise, rational, and happy being, they must acquire a knowledge of the principles of human nature, and of the elements of a rational system of society; for until they shall have made these acquirements it will be useless to attempt to explain to them the mode by which a superior rational character is to be formed for man.

Until this change shall be effected within them, they will be incompetent to understand the overwhelming influence of external circumstances in forming the human mind and body, and spirit and conduct; they will not be capable of perceiving that this character is not to be formed by ill-educated persons, in a space within four walls, only furnished with seats and desks; but that it must be created in the midst of a well-organised and full society, by its realities, and its own previous well-formed rational characters; and in which society that which is inferior in mind, manner, spirit, or external appearance, will not exist, to give an inferior impression to the being who is intended to be formed, physically, mentally, morally, and practically, to be superior.

To have the superstructure of a superior character formed, great care must be taken in laying the proper foundation, and in placing the right layers of knowledge and physical powers in their due order, so that none shall be erroneously placed, either by being premature, or too long delayed.

It will require the experience of the best informed mind, or minds, to adjust

[a] See *infra*, vol. 1, pp. 120–42.

the details of this order and arrangement; and when a more general rational character can be given to the public, then may more of this system to form men and women into rational beings, and society into a rational state, be made known.

CHAPTER V

'A knowledge of the principles and practice by which to govern man, under these new arrangements, in the best manner, as a member of the great family of man.'

THE government to aid in forming man into a rational being, and the government when man shall be so formed, will be different.

The first must be an active government, to change man from an irrational to a rational state of mind and condition. The second a watchful and observing government, to prevent aught irrational being at any time introduced to disturb the order and harmony of a superior mode of existence.

The first must be a government knowing the causes of good and evil; a government of energy and decision, to overcome and remove the evil, and to introduce the good. It must unite unceasing attention to the movements of the old world and the new, with a spirit of justice, derived from an accurate knowledge of human nature, in order to prevent collision between the two, and to effect the change from the one to the other in the shortest practicable period compatible with the maintenance of good feeling between the members of each.

The first government must be wise as serpents and harmless as doves.[a] It must be wise to perceive and understand quickly the *causes* now producing evil throughout society, and to know how, with the least injury to all parties, those causes may be the most easily removed.

It must thoroughly understand human nature to the extent that past facts enable man to comprehend it; in order that the laws, rules, and regulations, which may be necessary in this transition state may be in accordance with it, and never opposed to it; because to act in opposition to the unchanging laws of human nature, must be a certain mode to create crime and inflict misery on the human race.

It must understand the science of the influence of external circumstances over human nature, generally and individually; generally, that those superior

[a] See Matthew 10:16.

circumstances may be created which are necessary to the well-forming of the character of all men; and individually, that it may know how to direct the formation of the character of those men and women to whom the educating of infants, children, and youth, is to be entrusted in the detail, and who must apply the influence of particular circumstances to well-form the character of each, according to the peculiar combination of general faculties of human nature as they have been given at birth to the individual.

This first or transition government must also be well informed on the science of producing, distributing, and consuming wealth, the most beneficially for all the people.

It must have a clear conception of what wealth is, and of the various gradations in its *intrinsic* value; that that which is the most necessary to existence, to a superior condition of society, and to the happiness of all, may be the first and most abundantly cultivated or produced, and the less intrinsically valuable may be brought forth in the regular order or gradation of real utility.

It must see and feel the necessity of forming arrangements to produce wealth, at all times, abundantly for all; and it must know what those arrangements should be, and how to direct their application to practice.

It must not only know how to produce wealth of the most intrinsic value and with its various gradations in due order, but how to produce it in the best manner; that is, in the shortest time, with the least labour or capital, and with the most health and enjoyment to all occupied in its production.

This first or transition government must know how to form efficient arrangements to preserve in the best manner all the various kinds of wealth after they have been produced, in order that they may not be injured by being placed in situations or within buildings not adapted to retain them in their best or most healthy condition for use. It is little understood by the public at large, how much unnecessary inferior wealth is produced under the existing system of disorder and confusion, and how much of the wealth even thus inefficiently or injuriously produced, is deteriorated in quality, wasted in quantity, or totally lost.

The quantity deteriorated, wasted, and lost, forms a considerable portion compared with the whole amount used in its best condition; and this proportion is a real loss to society, which by scientific arrangements may be prevented.

But arrangements must be not only made to preserve all kinds of wealth in proper places in the best manner, but also to have them *distributed* in such a manner that there shall be the least waste or loss in quantity or quality, and also in the time and expense incurred in its transit from its place of production to its consumption.

Now the waste of time and loss and deterioration of quantity and quality, arising from dividing and subdividing, and sending wealth first to one place, then to another, through many successive changes, adds to the labour of the producers one-third, if not one-half, more than would be required for well-arranged production. Nine-tenths of the cost and labour now required to *distribute* the inefficient and inferior wealth created under the present wretched system of competitive individualism, might be most beneficially saved, under a principle of governing which rendered it necessary that the governors should understand the true theory and practice of governing for the mutual benefit of the governors and governed.

Indeed, no mistake can be more fatal to the unity, harmony, and well-being of any people than for the government to be based on the principle that it has nothing to do with the production and distribution of wealth, or with forming the spirit, mind, and conduct, or character of the people. It is a principle admirably calculated to create division, disorder, and contention, and to waste the most valuable useful materials, and the powers of the population. It is to place the production and distribution of wealth, as well as its preservation, in the most inefficient hands, with the most scanty means to ensure success; it is to place the forming of the character of the people at random, with the greatest probability that it will be physically, mentally, morally, and practically ill-formed; while all the superior means which might be brought into most advantageous action are allowed to remain dormant or unused, or to be misapplied to some other very inferior purpose.

A rational government will have the most ample means of collecting for every purpose the best information, to enable it to learn what is the most advantageous mode to produce and distribute wealth, and to form general and individual character, as well as to govern the most beneficially for all, both at home and abroad; and the great duty of government is so far to superintend and direct these departments, as to see that they are established on sound principles, and carried into execution in a statesman and business-like manner, through all the districts of their government.

In short, to govern well, the government should be so constituted that it should be formed to consider the territory to be governed an estate, and the population upon it, its family; and that every proper means should be put into active practice to make the estate the most productive and beautiful, and the family the most powerful in intellect, the most superior in physical form, and the best in mind, manners, spirit, and conduct.

As the principles and practices of government will have to be more extended in another form, in one of the general divisions of 'The Book,' which will appear in due order of place and time, it is not necessary to add to this chapter the details which will be better placed in that division.

CHAPTER VI

'A knowledge of the principles and practices for uniting in one general system, in their due proportions, these separate parts of the "science of society;" to effect and secure, in the best manner for all, the greatest amount of permanent benefit and enjoyments, with the fewest disadvantages.'

Society, hitherto, over the world, has been a chaos. It is now one scene of disorder and utter confusion; there is no union of its parts, no order, or harmony, or foresight, in any of its general proceedings. There is no rational object defined for its attainment; no end in view, that any one can comprehend. Man is now everywhere an isolated being, having in all his thoughts, directing all his actions, his own limited notions of his supposed interest, or, at most, the supposed interest of his immediate family or sect, and small local district.

It is true that man, like all that have life, has an inward strong desire to be happy. This is the instinct of all life; but he is and has been so far, mentally blind on this most important never-failing object of his nature.

He has, however, now attained a new position in his existence; the progress of events, of which his own blind activity has been a powerful agent, has placed him in a situation which most sorely perplexes him; he has witnessed, latterly especially, the creation of new powers and materials around him, which his present faculties are incapable of appreciating or understanding. This misconception of his position has created in his race an insatiable desire for what he has been taught to call wealth; and previous to the possession of what he deems masses of it, he has been led to imagine that wealth and happiness are names for the same object; or that, if wealth can be obtained, happiness will necessarily follow.

That which is now called wealth can be so easily collected in masses by some individuals, favourably placed for that purpose, that this experiment has been tried with sufficient frequency to demonstrate that there is no necessary connection between wealth and happiness; and that wealth and misery are much more frequently united than wealth and happiness; indeed, it has been proved again and again that there is no approach to anything like a satisfactory state of human existence to be attained by any parties, under the chaos of confusion, counteraction, opposition, and universal deception, which pervades the population of all the districts into which the world has been divided, by language, religion, customs, and apparent varied interests.

It is now, however, discovered for the first time, that the materials from which to form order and harmony, and a very superior state of society, exist in unnecessary superfluity, amidst the chaos in which all are now, to all appearance, inextricably involved.

And as it has been proved to demonstration that individual accumulations of what is now called wealth, more frequently bring care and anxieties, and great disappointments, than content or satisfaction, the more advanced in real knowledge are beginning to consider whether the materials for ensuring the general well-being and happiness of society – materials which exist abundantly in many places, and which may be made so to exist in all places where it is necessary or desirable that man should live – cannot be collected, arranged, and harmonised scientifically, so as to form a superior and rational state of human existence; a state in which, instead of all being, as at present, opposed to all, all shall be wisely and cordially united to promote the well-being and happiness of all; by which the power of each to produce and enjoy happiness will be multiplied by the difference between all individuals opposing, and all assisting, each other – a difference so enormous as to be difficult to estimate to its real ultimate amount; but which may safely be stated to be equal to the multiplication of the powers of each individual at least by three or four thousand; that is, each one would have the means of progress and enjoyment increased, at the least, three or four thousand times beyond the means of happiness possessed by any potentate or subject now living, or who ever may live, so long as the present irrational and immoral system of competition, contest, and individualism, shall be maintained.

Before the whole subject of producing and distributing wealth, of forming a superior character, and of governing well and wisely, can be ascertained, it is necessary to discover the proportions in which these departments can be most advantageously united to ensure the greatest happiness throughout society.

No parties, hitherto, have been initiated in a knowledge of the sciences of human nature and of society – a knowledge without which it is impossible to form a correct notion of any combination of the elements of society, by which individualism can be successfully superseded by the union of permanent united feelings and interests.

Individualism is a necessary result of ignorance respecting these two at present unknown sciences; unknown except by the founder of the Rational System of Society. And to attempt to form a general permanent system of united feelings and interests, without a knowledge of these sciences, and of the mode of applying them successfully to practice, would be labour lost and time uselessly expended, except to prove the error of the attempt.

Unity of feeling and action will be the necessary result of the proper application of these two sciences to practice. Alone or singly they would be inefficient; united, they are competent to direct man to gradually attain universal unity and happiness, in which there will be no contest for money or power in individual privileges; in which the only contest will be who shall the most extensively secure the well-being and happiness of all society.

Various Utopias, from the time of Plato[a] to the present, have been imagined and strongly desired for practice; but hitherto they have been but Utopias, because the principles upon which alone society can be founded to be made permanently united, and all made excellent and happy, were unknown to any of the projectors of them. Let these Utopias be now separately examined, and the most opposing and contradictory principles and practices will be discovered to be recommended for adoption in each of them, from Plato, to Fourier[b] – principles and practices which never can be united, and which it is impossible to introduce into permanent successful practice.

Men of experience discovering and fully detecting these inconsistencies, have necessarily rejected them, and given to these imaginary schemes the character of Utopias, and from being thus disappointed in all the measures to secure the general happines of society, by any system of union or equality hitherto proposed, they have naturally come to the conclusion in their minds that it is impracticable to devise a state of human existence to produce permanent unity, virtue, and happiness, and that there must be individual collision and contest to the end of time.

It is admitted that no such system has ever yet been offered to mankind, either in ancient or modern times; that the principles in combination, on which alone such union could be formed, have until now remained unknown, and that the application of those principles to practice, until the unity of these principles was discovered, could not be effected.

Many of these principles have been known, and their truth strongly felt, by philosophers and wise men of deep reflection through past ages; but they knew them only in parts, separately, and without being competent to unite them so as to form a science applicable to practice, and to explain what that practice should be, and how it could be carried into execution.

Philosophers, men of sound, sober, and calm reflection, who could patiently collect and examine facts, and trace cause and effect to some extent, have discovered more of the principles which are requisite to form the Science of Human Nature, but have been deficient in the discovery of those elementary principles which are necessary to constitute the Science of Society.

In fact, learned men, or men of words, seldom knew anything of practical measures, or of the principles which should direct them; while men engaged in the practical operations of society and general business of life, seldom, knew or

[a] Plato, *The Republic* (c. 375 BC).

[b] Charles Fourier (1772–1837): early French socialist whose plans for small-scale communities paralleled Owen's at many points. He had few followers in Britain, but by the early 1840s, more than Owen in the United States. For his life and ideas, see Jonathan Beecher, *Charles Fourier. The Visionary and His World* (Berkeley, University of California Press, 1986). On his American followers, see Carl J. Guarneri, *The Utopian Alternative. Fourierism in Nineteenth-Century America* (Ithaca, Cornell University Press, 1991).

troubled themselves about the principles of human nature, or the causes which regulated the formation of the human character.

Thus the two sciences, which are the foundation on which alone a superior society can be formed, which require to be well known and to be intimately united, to form in practice, a system of individual excellence and of general happiness, remained unconnected in any mind; and the learned men who endeavoured to imagine such a system without practical knowledge, committed, in attempting to form such a combination, errors so palpable, that experienced practical men could easily discover them; while, when men of mere mechanical minds and habits, unacquainted with the Science of Human Nature, or the principles of forming the general and individual character of man, attempted to imagine or put together the materials for creating human happiness, they were equally unfortunate; the men of learning being competent immediately to detect the incongruities in principle of the practical men, as easily as these latter could perceive the errors and fallacies in practice of the men of mere mental theories, uncorrected by the experience of extensive practice.

From the continuation, through so many ages, of the errors of theoretical men without practice, and those of practical men without any accurate or extensive knowledge of principle, it will be now difficult, except by practical demonstration, to convince these two classes that by a union of principles derived from unchanging facts, with the practice emanating from extensive experience in accordance with those principles, an intelligent, united, wealthy, virtuous, and happy society, may be now formed and be made permanent in the gradual increase, through unknown thousands of years, in knowledge, riches, and happiness.

Happily for man, the Science of Human Nature and the Science of Society have been discovered; still more fortunate is it, that the mode by which they can be united and formed into a practical system for the benefit of the human race, has been conceived and prepared for practice.

This practical system is to be formed by uniting in their due proportions the production and distribution of wealth, with the means of well educating and governing all men, and by creating through these means a new and very superior arrangement of the general business of life, to constitute a nucleus to supersede the present most defective family nuclei, and thus form a new organization of society altogether different from any hitherto known.

By thus forming the nucleus to consist of the due proportions of these elements of society, wealth will be produced easily, abundantly, and of the most superior qualities; it will be distributed at the least expense of time and waste; the character of each individual will be the best formed; and the direction of the practical arrangements with the best government of the people, will be obvious, simple, and complete.

When these nuclei shall have been formed, and society shall have been reorganized in accordance with them, ignorance, poverty, division, and all the inferior and bad passions, now so prevalent throughout the world, will speedily disappear.

The causes which now produce these, and almost all other human evils and sufferings, will be withdrawn, and other causes will be introduced to supersede them – causes which will ensure knowledge, wealth, and superior conduct in all, and, for the first time in human history, make man just to man, and, thereby, secure to all, happiness, continuing to increase through every succeeding generation.

These subjects will be extended in the chapter on 'A General Constitution of Government, and Universal Code of Laws, derived from the Constitution of Human Nature.'

END OF THE SECOND PART

THE BOOK

OF THE

NEW MORAL WORLD,

EXPLANATORY OF THE

CONDITIONS REQUISITE FOR HUMAN HAPPINESS,

WHICH WILL ULTIMATELY BE SECURED TO ALL UNDER THE

RATIONAL SYSTEM OF SOCIETY.

BY

ROBERT OWEN.

Truth, without Mystery, Mixture of Error or Fear of Man, can, alone, emancipate the Human Race from Sin and Misery.

PART THIRD.

London:
PUBLISHED BY THE HOME COLONIZATION SOCIETY,
AT THEIR OFFICE, 57, PALL MALL,
AND SOLD BY ALL BOOKSELLERS.

MDCCCXLII.

PREFACE

Hitherto the population of the world has been advancing from total ignorance, by slowly acquired isolated facts, and gradually combining more or less of these on particular subjects, until various limited sciences have been discovered. These sciences are necessary results from fixed and unchanging facts, and are therefore real knowledge, in contradistinction to conjectures of the imagination, unsupported by such facts.

With a knowledge of facts sufficient only to form limited views of isolated subjects, the population of the world has been so far kept in a state of mystery and random conjectures; and, while passing through this state, there has been a blind universal contest for the means of a secure and permanent existence, not only for the life of the contending parties, but for their own descendents through, if possible, all future time; and the world, in consequence, has been kept in a continual state of opposing interests and warfare. It is only now, at this important period of human history, that the human mind has been competent to advance from uniting isolated facts to form a single science, to unite the sciences to form a new state of human existence.

In the first state, men contended for the means of mere animal existence, through savage violence; they now contend for it by deceptive arts of half-civilized existence; but it has been discovered that there is more to be obtained than mere animal existence; – that, by uniting the hitherto isolated sciences, not only may a superior animal existence be secured for all without contest, but a life of rapid improvement and high enjoyment may be obtained and secured for the human race, and, for the first time in the progress of humanity, happiness is placed within the reach of all men.

Until now, the anxious inquiry, as each individual advanced in years, has been, 'What measures must I adopt to become rich, or how shall I become wealthy?' This has been now answered for all – 'By the right application of the illimitable powers of science to enable society united to produce a vast superfluity of wealth for all.' The question now is, not how are we to become rich, but how are we to attain happiness, and secure it permanently throughout our lives? This is the question now to be answered; and this question leads to others requisite to be first answered – and without a knowledge of which all replies must be given in random conjectures.

The second question, then, is, – 'What are the general conditions necessary to insure happiness to humanity?' – The third, 'Are the conditions attainable?' – The fourth, 'If attainable, how are they to be obtained and secured?'

Now, as the motive principle to all action in all that have life or conscious sensation on earth, if not throughout the universe, is the desire to be happy, and as man possesses this instinct of nature in an eminent degree, it is somewhat extraordinary that he has been hitherto so far groping in the dark on this subject, that for thousands of years he has been involved in the errors of a system, which, while it shall continue, must prevent the attainment of the very object of his existence.

It now appears, from the experience of the past, that there are thirteen general conditions requisite to insure the permanent happiness of the human race; and that, under the system of society which has alone hitherto existed, not one of these conditions can be insured to one individual; and that, yet, by the errors of this system, he has been made so accustomed to it, that with all its gross ignorance, errors, and evils, many would now rather part with their lives, than permit this system to be changed for another, superior, beyond all comparison, in principle and in practice.

Such is the strong natural force of habit upon human nature – and an excellent habit it will prove as soon as mankind shall be taught true principles and consistent and superior practices – that at present the old errors are pertinaciously maintained, although not one of the conditions requisite to happiness can be secured under the system which they have created, and that system which would in a short period make all these conditions attainable for all, is rejected, and by many, who are the most ignorant, even with horror.

1st. The existing system cannot secure, but is itself an effectual bar to the attainment of 'a good organization, physical, mental, and moral, at birth;' while the proposed system would speedily prepare the way for the human organization at birth to be gradually improved through future generations, in a manner far superior to what man has yet effected in the improvement of any of our domesticated animals.

2nd. The existing system most ignorantly prevents all from obtaining that which is requisite, to preserve the organization in the best state of health; while the proposed system would insure these means to all.

3rd. The existing system will not permit a good education to be given to any; while the new will secure it to all.

4th. The existing system may not prevent all from having the inclination continually to promote the happiness of our fellow-beings, but it puts every obstacle in the way of carrying such inclination into practice by any; while the Rational System proposed, will not only create the inclination, but will continually afford the means to put the inclination into practice.

5th. The existing system creates the desire in the few to increase their stock of knowledge, but destroys it in the many, and limits to a small amount the means of all to effect a substantial increase; while the Rational System will greatly increase the inclination of all to add continually to their stock of knowledge, and will afford the most ample means to attain their object – means which the men of the old world have desired, and, while it continues, must desire, in vain.

6th. The existing system is wholly incompetent to form any association of men and women that can deserve the name of 'good society.' The best it can form is a wretched artificial society of deception and of counteraction of happiness; while the Rational System will form a superior society wherever man, so trained and placed, shall be. Again, under the existing system few can associate at pleasure with those for whom they have the most regard and the greatest affection; while under the new all will be so educated, trained, and placed, that all may, advantageously for all, enjoy this highest of all enjoyments.

7th. Under the existing system, few, if any, can travel pleasure with pleasure; while under the new, the most convenient and advantageous arrangements will exist to admit all at pleasure to travel with pleasure.

8th. Under the existing system superstition, supernatural fears, and the fear of death, more or less torment the human race; while under the Rational System they will never be created, and will therefore remain unknown.

9th. Under the existing system no men or women dare freely and fully to express their thoughts and feelings on all subjects; while under the new, all will be encouraged so to express them, and all will derive the most substantial and permanent benefit from the practice.

10th. Under the existing system, freedom of thought and of action is limited most injuriously for all; while in the Rational System both will be encouraged to the utmost extent compatible with the permanent happiness of others.

11th. Under the existing system a character of ignorance, error, injustice, uncharitableness, and unkindness, is forced upon all, even upon those now deemed the best throughout society; while, under the Rational System, most especial care will be taken, as the first object of society, to insure from birth a character which shall be pervaded with the spirit of universal charity and kindness, and with the most lovely and superior qualities.

12th. Under the existing system no society can be found upon earth in which its laws, institutions, and arrangements, well organized and well governed, are all in unison with the laws of human nature; while under the Rational System every division of society will have its laws, institutions, and arrangements, well organized and well governed, at all times, in perfect unison with the laws of human nature. And

13th. Under the existing system no arrangements exist to create the desire or means to effect the happiness of all that have life, as far as may be practicable; while under the Rational System these arrangements will exist, and all will be trained to have great pleasure in assisting to apply them to practice.

Such is the difference between the irrational system which has hitherto prevailed throughout the world, and the Rational System recommended in 'The Book' for immediate adoption.

Broughton, Hants, May 3, 1842

THE BOOK
OF THE
NEW MORAL WORLD

THIRD PART

CONDITIONS REQUISITE FOR HUMAN HAPPINESS

CHAPTER I

On the universal desire for happiness in all that have life.

From all the facts yet known to man, it appears to be an universal law of Nature or of God, that all life, in whatever form or organization it may appear, desires to be happy; or, in other words, that, by its natural instinct, it continually makes every effort in its power to avoid or be relieved from pain, and to attain the enjoyment, according to its individual nature or organization, of agreeable and pleasurable sensations. Thus man endeavours to avoid pain, physical and mental, and to enjoy physical and mental pleasure. This is the secret motive or instinct to all physical or mental movements in each individual of the human race. This motive all must have by their nature, as beings with life. There is, therefore, no real merit or demerit in anything that has life.

There appears to be, from the accumulation of facts now collected by the human race, this one universal instinct or cause of action throughout all living nature. This instinct is the immediate cause of all the living movements throughout this world, and probably throughout the universe. This instinct or power is called 'Providence' by some – 'God' by others – 'the Power of God' by a third party.

It is, however, most evident now, that by whatever name men may call this Instinct of the Universe, the knowledge that it exists is the present boundary of human attainment on the subject. Man has discovered through, to him, long experience, that there is an universal principle throughout nature, which impels all that have life to action, through the desire to avoid pain and to enjoy pleasure.

Whether that principle *is* the ETERNAL CAUSE whence proceeds all that is effected throughout the universe, or whether it *proceeds from* the Eternal Cause, no man has yet discovered. It is now uncertain whether man will ever be enabled, through his future experience and acquisition of facts, to make this discovery.

But there is, at present, a general principle, probably this universal instinct, in action, to compel society to apply its late large acquisition of the knowledge of new facts, to diminish the pain and increase the pleasure of all its members, by terminating local prejudices, and elevating man above the errors and evils arising from geographical sects, parties, and classes; – in fact to arouse him from the existence of a mere irrational localized animal, which he has ever yet been, to become a being of enlarged powers, with a new mind and a new spirit, competent speedily to become a superior rational inhabitant of the earth; – a being who shall understand what humanity is, in the aggregate and in its detail – who shall talk no more about vice and virtue, merit and demerit, of individuals – who shall discontinue the irrational language and conduct of free-will, converse in the phraseology of rational made minds, and act, daily and hourly, in accordance with the laws of human nature.

These beings, so formed, will no longer occupy themselves with finding fault with the small detail of matters necessarily emanating from a system itself fundamentally erroneous; but they will, at once, apply their powers to discover the causes that produce evil in society, and to remove those causes with the least possible delay and injury to all. They will also ascertain the causes that will produce happiness to the human race, and whether those causes can be brought so far under the direction of man, isolated or united, as to ensure to him the conditions requisite for his happiness. We will therefore proceed in the next chapter to investigate the causes of human error and misery, and to ascertain the conditions requisite for human happiness.

CHAPTER II

Without a correct knowledge of the CAUSE of human misery, it will be impossible to ascertain whether it can or cannot be removed by the power inherent in human nature, through its organization, or the circumstances which surround it or which may be made to surround it.

To all who have the powers of steady observation and extended reflection, it will soon become evident that the sole cause of the misery of man has been, and is now, not only a total ignorance of his nature, but a total misconception of it; – that his nature is *one thing*, and that he had imagined it to be something the *reverse* of what it is. Our ancestors, to account for the error and evil which have ever been the lot of man, after numberless fruitless attempts to make him, according to their notions, what they deemed to be good, came to the conclusion that he was *bad by nature*, and that he never could be made *good or happy* in this world.

Yet have they always continued to endeavour to act in opposition to this conclusion. In fact, man has been hitherto, through this misconception of his nature, a most irrational animal, calling himself a reasonable being, and, over the whole earth, daily and hourly acting against reason, with the most incongruous, inconsistent, and fantastic notions, upon all things appertaining to his happiness.

That which is most evident is, that humanity has been formed by the same power, whatever it may be, which has formed all other organized beings; – that, by its nature, it possesses certain general qualities, which constitute its nature; – and that these general qualities are varied in their quality and combination in each individual. Also that it is as useless to call human nature *good* or *bad*, as to call the organization of the tiger or the lamb good or bad. The man, tiger, and lamb, have been, by some power unknown to either, made to be what they are, generally and individually; and merit or demerit for what they are, belongs to neither; because they could not avoid being what they are.

Nature cannot rationally be spoken of as being bad or good; man knows not what he is speaking about when he says that anything is by nature good or bad.

Man, the tiger, and the lamb, have been made to be what they are; and why they were so made, man knows not. They are formed to desire their individual happiness, and all their movements are to obtain it, by avoiding pain and seeking pleasure, which may be said to be the UNIVERSAL MOTIVE OR INSTINCT OF NATURE.

Man has been formed to be a progressive animal, and to be gradually advancing, from a state of perplexity, confusion, and disorder, of ideas and conduct, towards a more sane state of mind, and more rational conduct; in fact, he is now beginning to know better than heretofore, what his own nature really is.

He has been hitherto blindly seeking happiness in various ways, by wars and fighting, by robbery and murder, by various superstitious and fantastic notions, by dress and equipages and distinctions of varied kinds, by power and rule over others, and by the accumulation of wealth, as the means of attaining power and rule. Experience, however, has now proved that, upon trial, none of these means have yet produced the kind or extent of happiness that man desires. He ever has been dissatisfied with all these attempts to attain his object. He now seems lost in bewilderment.

Latterly he thought that great riches would satisfy him; but he has experienced his usual disappointment. Great riches have been obtained, without happiness, or anything approaching to a rational state of happiness, being attained. Great riches can satisfy only certain of our wants and desires, leaving essential parts of our nature unprovided for, and consequently dissatisfied.

There are certain conditions which are necessary to the happiness of human nature, made as it is; and it is useless for man to expect happiness, unless permanent arrangements can be obtained for him to secure these conditions for all of the human race. For if one shall be known to be unhappy, the knowledge of this fact will diminish the happiness of all who know it.

The general conditions necessary to happiness are –

1st. The possession of a good organization, physical, mental, and moral.

2nd. The power of procuring at pleasure whatever is necessary to preserve the organization in the best state of health.

3rd. The best education, from birth to maturity, of the physical, intellectual, and moral powers, of all the population.

4th. The inclination and means of promoting continually the happiness of our fellow-beings.

5th. The inclination and means of continually increasing our stock of knowledge.

6th. The power of enjoying the best society; and more especially of associating at pleasure with those for whom we are compelled to feel the most regard and greatest affection.

7th. The means of travelling at pleasure.

8th. The absence of superstition, supernatural fears, and the fear of death.

9th. Full liberty of expressing our thoughts upon all subjects.

10th. The utmost individual freedom of action, compatible with the permanent good of society.

11th. To have the character formed for us to express the truth upon all occasions, and to have pure charity for the feelings, thoughts, and conduct, of all mankind, and a sincere good will for every individual of the human race.

12th. To reside in a society, whose laws, institutions, and arrangements, well organized, and well governed, are all in unison with the laws of human nature. And

Lastly, to know that all that have life are as happy as their natures will admit, but especially all of the human race.

Now the great question to solve is, how many of these conditions can be permanently secured for the whole of the human race, and these conditions shall be examined separately in the following chapters.

CHAPTER III

1st. The possession of a good organization, physical, mental, and moral.

Of course, this condition can apply to those children only, who shall come into existence after arrangements shall have been purposely formed to have an influence, such as is required, upon the organization of those who shall be born under the new state of society which will arise when it shall be devised to obtain, if possible, all the conditions that are necessary to ensure the permanent happiness of the human race.

As it is of deep interest to all, that there should be the greatest amount of good and superior organizations throughout society, it is most desirable, on this account, alone, that the change from the present system – in which no arrangements have ever been formed, with knowledge of the subject, to improve the physical and mental organization, at birth, of the human race – should be superseded, with the least possible delay, by a system which, in all its arrangements, will have this important object in view.

Under the existing system of society over the world, no efficient arrangements for this purpose could be effected. The fundamental errors on which it is based, preclude the possibility of any such arrangements being formed, and they have never been thought of. While men are taught from their birth that they have the power to believe or disbelieve, to like or dislike, and to love or hate, at their will and pleasure, they can form no rational arrangements for their happiness, or for the happiness of their children.

While they are taught that they must believe that which is opposed to facts and to all nature, and that they must disbelieve that which is in accordance with all facts and with nature – while they are taught that they must like that which their nature compels them to dislike, and that they must dislike that which their nature compels them to like, it is utterly impossible that any arrangements they may form, can ever be reasonable or rational, or that virtue can be introduced and vice prevented. These fundamental errors keep the minds of all in a state of constant injurious excitement, or of depressed and dissatisfied feelings; and, combined with all the necessary evil effects produced by the competition and contests of the individual system.

1st. They prevent the union of the sexes as it would be made in a rational state of society:

2nd. They prevent the formation, and continuance after marriage, of the state of mind and feelings which is so essential to the production of offspring, healthy and superior both in body and mind:

3rd. They create among all parties a state of hypocrisy, destructive of any approach to a virtuous, moral, or rational state of existence; and

4th. They make it necessary for the sexes to live together and procreate children, not only when, by their nature, they cannot have the affection for each other which should exist to enable the parents to have infants well-formed in body and mind, but when they have strong repulsive feelings towards each other, and when it is most injurious to society, as well as to the individual, that they should be so placed as to have children born to them under such unfavourable circumstances.

It is these unnatural unions, forced upon the individuals by the present most vicious state of society, that are the chief causes of the birth of infants who are malformed, or who have inferior organizations. There are other causes also arising from the state of society necessarily emanating from the same fundamental errors.

Superstition, bigotry, and other religious or mystical perplexities, are most unfavourable to the production of infants with a sound mind in a sound body. Such states of mind are always verging towards particular insanities, in addition to the general destruction of the human intellects which is necessarily effected in all minds made to receive the fundamental errors respecting belief and love, previously referred to.

The disappointment of the affections on the part of one or both of the parents, is also a cause of the production of malformed or ill-formed infants. Few circumstances more derange the functions of the mind, and speedily, in consequence, those of the body, than strong disappointment of the affections. All who understand these subjects, even in the imperfect manner in which the present malformation of society admits them to be understood, know that from this cause alone more dire disease of body and mind is engendered, directly and indirectly, than from any other cause, except that of religious perplexities, terminating in madness, or the insanities of superstition and bigotry. Experience has proved that, through past history of the human race, that which the various people of the world, at various times, have called religion, has been the cause of more insanity and madness between nations and individuals, and has tended more to retard society, and perpetuate gross ignorance and folly, than all other causes combined. While these religious perplexed feelings, and those arising from the disappointment of the affections, shall be permitted to proceed as heretofore and at present, from parents so afflicted it will be useless to expect healthy infants, with superior physical and mental organizations.

Another cause which materially tends to fill the world with inferior and malformed infants, is the poverty and fear of poverty with which so large a portion of society is now afflicted.

This is an evil of the third magnitude. It now severely afflicts society throughout the civilized world; and such is really the insanity of the existing system, that those nations in the actual possession of the most abundant means to preclude poverty or the most distant fear of it, now suffer the most extensively from this cause, even to the gradual starvation of multitudes of their industrious population. And this state of suffering has been gradually increasing for some years, in proportion as the means for diminishing it, if wisely applied, have increased.

The pecuniary difficulties of many of the upper and middle classes, and the actual poverty or fear of immediate poverty among the working class, are at this moment producing suffering among the population of the British Empire, such perhaps as was never experienced from poverty, except when actual famine raged and destroyed the weakest and poorest among the multitude. And this suffering is now experienced in Great Britain and Ireland, when the most abundant means that any nation ever possessed are hourly at the command of the government, the capitalists, and the experienced men of business, and indeed, if they had wisdom to know how to unite their weekly means for the purpose, at the command also of the working classes.

There can be required no stronger evidence of the irrationality of the present system of society, than the daily and hourly afflictions experienced by the multitude, and the misery arising to the middle and upper classes, from their senseless contests and competition for wealth and power, when both may be obtained for all, and by all, to a greater extent than any parties, having any rational conception of what humanity is, and what it is desirable society should be, and what it now easily might be made to be, would desire, or could beneficially use.

While these pecuniary difficulties shall be allowed to remain, while this poverty and the fear of immediate poverty shall haunt the minds of the multitude, and while the feelings of these parties are thus, and thus so unnecessarily, lacerated, it is not probable that many, if any, really superior physical and mental organizations, can be born to parents so afflicted.

But the first introduction of rational or true fundamental principles among civilized nations, will speedily terminate poverty, the fear of poverty, and all pecuniary difficulties.

The next general cause of perplexity and suffering to parents, which tends to deteriorate the organization of their offspring at birth, is the great anxiety which many experience respecting the well-being, well-doing, and health, of their children.

As society is now constituted, no children can by possibility be really well educated.

The fundamental errors on which it has been based, filling the early mind with error and hypocrisy and all manner of conflicting ideas, opposed to facts and to nature, render it impracticable for any child to be rationally trained or treated by society. And the more education of this kind is given to children, the more they will be estranged from a knowledge of themselves, or of human nature generally, and the less competent will they be to understand what society has been made to be, and yet less what it ought to be, and how it may be made what it is desirable it should be, for the well-being and happiness of all.

Mothers and fathers thus taught, are incompetent to teach and educate their children in the spirit, manner, and conduct, which should, for the benefit of all, be given to all children. Their affections also, especially the strong natural animal affections of the mother, are, in almost all cases, too strong for the very limited powers of judging accurately respecting their own children and those of other parents, which females now acquire from their present mal-education.

The individual family arrangements confining the children to the limited number of ideas among them – to their exclusive and isolated feelings – to their early deep impressions in favour of family interests and supposed rights – to the narrow and partial experience of a family and its usual small connexions, are equally destructive of a good sound practical education or well-training of children.

The individual system of society which has so long prevailed in all nations, and among almost all people, is also a strong barrier to the proper education of beings intended to be made rational. The individual system of society is injurious to man now, under every point of view in which it can be considered; but especially in the education of the children of all classes. It confines all their strongest feelings to self first, then to family, afterwards to kindred, and then to small neighbourhoods and district, regularly and systematically training each child to become at maturity a mere localized ignorantly selfish animal, filled with family and geographical prejudices.

As long as this individual system shall be continued, it will be vain to expect that any child can be well educated, or properly trained to become a rational being – a man with the full physical and mental powers of humanity, intelligent, moral, and virtuous. The isolated character formed by the individual system will, as long as children shall be educated under it, and in accordance with all its innumerable errors in principle and practice, render it impossible for any child to be so educated and placed in society as not to become, more or less, a cause of anxiety to its parents. Every child under this system comes into society, at its birth, opposed by the capital and experience of society; and as it advances in its progress, and has to take its part in the jostle, bustle, and business of life, it has to contend for itself, often, not only against these general powers of society, but, on the death of parents, or sometimes even before, with brothers and sisters, for individual property or other advantages.

Besides, children, before they have any resisting powers of mind, being forced to receive the errors of their parents and other early instructors respecting their supposed faculties of believing and disbelieving, loving and hating, are, by this process, placed through life in direct opposition to their nature; and, as vice has been made, by the gross errors of our ancestors, to consist in acting in accordance with nature, and virtue in acting in opposition to it, and as nature continually impels the individual to desire to act in accordance with its own laws, in defiance of man's unwise and unjust laws, the great probability is that children will be more liable to obey nature than man; and thus, where there are children, they must be a source of constant anxiety to parents; and that anxiety must be injurious to the best formation or the organization of the remainder of the infants who may be born to them.

Under these united deranging circumstances of the existing malformation of the character of the present generation, and of the consequent malformation of society, it is impossible that the parents of infants can be now in a condition, either of mind or body, to procreate children to have the superior physical, mental, and moral organization, which it is so desirable that all infants should possess, for their own happiness, and for the benefit of the state and of the world.

To secure a superior organization for future generations, it is necessary that the causes which produce and continually reproduce these evils, should be altogether withdrawn from society. But they cannot be withdrawn under the continuance of old society. They all may easily be withdrawn under the new; and it therefore becomes the most evident interest of every individual that the change from the one to the other should be effected in the shortest possible period.

CHAPTER IV

2nd. The power of procuring at pleasure whatever is necessary to preserve the organization in the best state of health.

It is not only necessary for the happiness of the human race, that a superior organization should be produced in each infant at his birth, but also that during his growth, and through life, he should have the means to preserve it, physically, mentally, and morally, in the best state of health, during its longest natural existence.

What, it may be asked, are those things which are necessary to keep the organization in a constant state of good health, until its natural period of old age and decomposition? They are –

1st. Kind treatment, with judgment, from birth.

2nd. Pure air.

3rd. Wholesome food in proper quantity, and at proper times.

4th. Regular exercise in the open air through life.

5th. Due cultivation of the faculties, powers, and qualities, physical and mental.

6th. The temperate exercise of all the natural propensities, at their proper periods through life.

7th. Healthy alternate occupation of body and mind; temperate in proportion to the strength and capacity of the individual.

8th. Extensive real knowledge of ourselves, society, and nature, in accordance with facts and external nature, without mysteries to confound the understanding and judgment, or any of the other faculties of the mind.

9th. Full, genuine, and pure charity, derived from an accurate knowledge of human nature, which produces kindness for all, and destroys all the inferior passions and all motives to vice and crime; generating a serenity of mind and feeling, self-possession, and satisfaction, from which alone a constant good state of physical and mental health can proceed. And

10th. The esteem and affection of all our neighbours and friends, and of the human race.

Now there can be no approach to the attainment of these united objects under the existing individualized state of society; but, on the contrary, the system itself, from which all the arrangements of society have emanated, precludes the possibility of their accomplishment. While on the other hand, the Rational System of Society, from both its principles and its practices, readily affords all the means that can be desired to secure the whole of these objects to all of the human race.

1st. The knowledge of the real formation of the human character, before and after birth – the knowledge of the principles on which depends the conviction of the truth or the untruth of anything, the liking or disliking, loving or hating – will create a new spirit in man, new form his character, make him kind and forbearing to all, and give him a sound judgment to direct his kindness beneficially for the infant, child, and man, and for the whole of society; for society, if it understood its best, its highest and most permanent interest, is deeply interested in the well forming of the body, spirit, mind, manner, and conduct, of every infant of the human race, in order that, in process of time, there should not be one inferior human being to be found on the earth, or any irrational transaction performed by man. It is this knowledge of human nature, which alone can create continued kindness directed by judgment in all adults to all children from their birth, and it is this treatment which will lay the foundation of the right spirit in the infant, to increase with the child, and, when he acquires a knowledge of his own nature, to be perfected in the man. And, unless the foundation of this spirit shall be commenced from birth, and systematically continued through the growth of the infant, child, and youth, to maturity, he will not be as perfect as it is desirable for society that he should be made. It is this spirit, to be derived alone from an accurate knowledge of human nature, that can regenerate the old corrupt world, and make man a moral and happy being, fit inhabitant of such a terrestrial paradise as may now be created for him, by the abundant means at his disposal, whenever he shall acquire sufficient knowledge to use them in accordance with the plain dictates of common sense.

Now this spirit cannot be acquired under the individual system, which has hitherto prevailed among all people calling themselves civilized. The placing of children from their birth in a condition to be opposed by the accumulated capital and experience of the world, and making it necessary that they should, through life, contend against both, render a uniform kind treatment of any parties impracticable, and the creation of the right spirit for humanity to acquire impossible. Were an attempt to be made under the existing system of society to train and educate children to be moral and virtuous, it would be soon discovered that such made beings could not exist, but for a short period, in the present corrupt, demoralized, and individual system. Were they taught to be natural, and to express the truth, in look, word, and action, upon all occasions, the old world would be made to appear, as it is in reality, so utterly absurd, incongruous, immoral, and irrational, that such truth speaking and acting persons could not be allowed to live. It would be similar to placing what is now called a sane individual in a large lunatic asylum, who should be continually employed in telling the inmates of their madness, and enabling them to discover that he spoke the truth. The consequence would be, that all would be so irritated, that their madness would be increased beyond all bounds, and only to be restrained by bonds and straight waistcoats. Kind treatment of children from birth can only be administered in another state of society; – in one in which all shall be trained to abandon individual interests, and to derive their highest and daily enjoyment from the prosperity, superior character, and happiness of everyone around them. There can be no really kind treatment where there is insincerity, and individualism and sincerity can never be united in the same system. It is, therefore, impossible, under the present degraded and degrading system of falsehood and deception, that any individual 'can procure at pleasure that which is necessary,' even in this first step, 'to preserve the organization in the best state of health.'

2nd. To obtain and preserve health in the best state to ensure happiness, pure air is necessary.

It is at once obvious that large cities and extensive manufactories are not well calculated to permit pure air to be enjoyed by those who live in the one, or who are employed in the other. Neither are they well adapted to give anything approaching to a state of full practical happiness to man, woman, or child. Both conditions are unnatural, or, in other words, are opposed to the well-being of humanity. To ensure the enjoyment of pure air to all the members of society, large cities and towns, and extensive manufactories, must be abandoned; and abandoned they will be, as soon as man can be formed into a rational being.

All the benefits now to be derived from populous cities and extensive manufactories, may be obtained in much higher perfection, and at half their present cost of capital, without their unhealthy defects in destroying the purity of the atmosphere, which all within them must continually experience through every moment of their existence. The advantage of pure, and disadvantage of impure, air, are experienced each time we breathe, and all who understand the causes of disease know that an impure atmosphere is most unfavourable to the enjoyment of health, and an efficient cause to shorten human existence within the natural life of man.

It is, therefore, most desirable that decisive measures should be devised and generally adopted to ensure to all a pure atmosphere, in which to live during their lives – at least as pure as is compatible with superior production and distribution of wealth, the superior forming of character, and good governing.

In forming each separate part for the improvement of society and the happiness of all, every part must be taken into due consideration, for no one part can exist without the others. It is not only necessary to devise measures to ensure a pure and healthy atmosphere for all, but to ensure this result in connection with all the requisite operations of society.

It is not sufficient to say that an impure atmosphere is unfavourable to health, and that crowded populations and extended manufactures must create an impure atmosphere; it is also requisite to prove not only that both are unnecessary, but that other arrangements may be formed more easily than either, that shall secure to society, permanently, all the advantages ever derived from these defective combinations, without the extensive deterioration of the vitality of the air, which large towns and large manufactories create.

It is practicable by uniting, in their due proportions, the four elements of society – which are, as previously stated, production, distribution, and the formation of character, and governing – to preserve the atmosphere almost as pure as it is produced by nature in the localities in which these operations may be established. And unless this result were practicable, the second ingredient requisite to 'procuring at pleasure whatever is necessary to preserve the organization in the best state of health' could not be obtained. And a pure atmosphere is one of the most necessary conditions to health and happiness, and in all arrangements for carrying forward the operations of society, the parties making them should have this primary object in view.

3rd. 'Wholesome food in proper quantity, and at proper times.'

Diet, although so essential to the health of body and mind, has been little studied on rational principles by the mass of people. As superstition and bigotry make their gains from the diseases of the mind, through the ignorance of the multitude, so do the medical profession make their gain from the diseases of the body, arising from the same cause. And well do these parties assist each other, as the mind and body act and react on each other in producing an extension of disease. Health, it has been well said, consists of having a sound mind in a sound body; but the mind of man has ever been under the disease of ignorance – the most fatal of all diseases; and he has not in the civilized world been rationally taught the best means of preserving health by the proper use of meats and drinks. It has not been made to appear to be the interest of any party to discover and give to society this knowledge; but, on the contrary, it has been made the apparent interest of a whole profession, that disease should generally and permanently prevail throughout society, and that their pecuniary success through life should depend upon its amount.

By this arrangement of society, which makes it the apparent interest of a numerous, influential, and comparatively well-educated class, to extend and perpetuate disease, one of the first principles of wisdom in conducting the affairs of men is directly opposed; for it is the duty of all to endeavour to diminish disease to the greatest extent, even, if possible, to its entire termination. But, by the establishment of a medical profession, under the individual system and for individual gain, it is made to be the interest of all the individuals of the profession to act in opposition to their duty, or, in other words, in opposition to the interest of the human race. One of the clearest principles for the adoption of society, as soon as it can be made to approach a rational state, will be to make the interest and duty of all to be always united. That is, that the individual and general interests shall never be separated. At present they are almost continually opposed; and they will continue to be opposed as long as the individual system shall be maintained. Fortunately, however, the time draws nigh, when the irresistible laws of necessity will compel the abandonment of this system of insincerity, division, and crime, with all the misery which these hourly produce.

This individual interest of the profession, opposed to the general interest of the population, has hitherto prevented those who by their education have been the most likely to understand in part the subject of diet, from giving even their partial knowledge to the public; and, in consequence, the comparative and limited amount of knowledge upon this subject, which the present most defective system of society has permitted them to acquire, has been withheld. This evil is not the fault of the individuals, but of society, in creating and sustaining such a profession, in direct opposition to the interest of the whole population, not excluding every member of the medical profession, with the doubtful exception of surgery.

Every individual has a constitution by nature differing more or less from every other constitution. It is the interest of the individual and of all society, that he should be made, at the earliest period, to understand his own construction, the proper use of its parts, and how to keep them at all times in a state of health; and especially that he should be taught to observe the varied effects of different kinds of food, and different quantities, upon his own constitution. He should be taught the general and individual laws of health, thus early, that he may know how to prevent the approach of disease. And the knowledge of the particular diet best suited to his constitution, is one of the most essential laws of health. In fact, in the various kinds of food, now generally to be obtained in most parts of the world in which there is a moderate amount of population, every useful quality of what is called medicine may be found for each constitution; and by the parties being trained from birth, as all might be, and as it is now the interest of society that all should be, each may be instructed, as most animals appear to be instructed, when in a state of nature, each by its nature, to know the particular kind and quantity of food which is the best for them, at their various periods of life.

But it will be said that man has attained to a state of society so highly artificial, that the food, both in kind and quantity, which is beneficial to him under some circumstances, will not produce the same beneficial effects under other circumstances, and that this essentially changes the influence of food when taken under these altered circumstances, and disease follows.

This is true; if the mind be disturbed by fears, alarms, sorrows, or great perplexities, or much distress from any cause, the stomach refuses to perform its functions in the same manner as previous to the mind being so disturbed.

To preserve permanent good health, the state of the mind must be taken into consideration; and if afflicted with great perplexity or distress, the diet should be, in most constitutions, altered in quality and quantity. But the best, bcause the most effectual remedy, will be, in this as in almost all other cases, to go to the root of the evil; and by training and educating all individuals from birth, which may now easily be accomplished, to become intelligent, reasonable, and rational creatures, and by constituting society scientifically to perform all its functions in due order and proportion, there would be little if any unhealthy perplexities or distress, to disturb the regular usual action of the stomach.

Were all thus trained and educated, they would soon discover by experience that very generally a simple diet would keep mind and body in the best state, and all their proceedings, individually and generally, would contribute so effectually to promote continued physical and mental activity and satisfaction of mind and feelings, that disease would rapidly diminish, until, in two or three generations, it would be unknown; for, were well-formed healthy infants alone born, and were these rationally treated, trained, educated, and properly placed, as they advanced in years, there would remain no cause to generate disease either of body or mind.

A full supply of the most wholesome kinds of food would be always produced and in store, under the system of combined production and distribution of wealth, as stated in the previous part of this book. When scientific arrangements shall be once formed to contain all the elements of a rational system of society, in their due proportions, with the education stated, then will it be impossible that want, or the fear of want, of any necessaries or beneficial comforts of life, should ever be experienced by any member of society.

Therefore, to insure a supply of wholesome food in proper quantities, at all times, for the whole population, and the state of mind and feelings necessary to permit such food to continue to digest beneficially to keep the organization of all in a sound healthy state, the individual system must be abandoned, and the united rational system must be adopted.

4th. 'Regular exercise in the open air through life.'

The general system of society adopted in the state of civilization to which men have now attained, is unfavourable to the due extent of exercise in the open air, which nature requires to produce a sound full state of health in mind and body, which will be the first consideration in the arrangements to form a rational state of society.

Again, large towns and extensive manufactories are most unfavourable to give health to the populations within them; in fact, neither have been formed with any consideration of giving health to the masses employed in them.

They are wrong in principle; and both must be abandoned, to make room for the arrangements by which the whole business of life may be well conducted, and yet all individuals may have the benefit of regular exercise in the open air through life: and without these arrangements being so made, society will be unjust to itself, and, of course, unjust to each of its members.

Now, by forming society on the principle of uniting its four elements in their due proportions, the 'regular exercise in the open air through life' will be easily obtained, combined with means to insure 'wholesome food in proper quantity' – 'pure air' – and 'kind treatment, with judgment, from birth.' And this regular exercise in the open air, as it is essential to secure continued good health, is an important consideration when forming the arrangements for a rational system of society.

5th. 'Due cultivation of all the faculties, powers, and qualities, physical and mental, of each individual.'

If there be one condition more essential than another to forming a sound mind in a sound body, it is attention to this part of the subject before us.

It is in consequence to this part of our subject being misunderstood, in fact unknown, that man has been deemed by a large proportion of his fellow-men to be '*bad* by nature.'

These mistaken individuals have never known what human nature is; they have taken a small part of it for the whole; and knowing but this small part, and knowing even this very imperfectly, they have consequently deemed it insufficient to be formed into a good and happy being.

And knowing the whole so very imperfectly, and mistaking the value of one part compared with another, from not knowing the true use and intent of any of these parts, they have imagined that some parts of human nature were more excellent than others, and, of necessity, that some were of less, and almost of no value, if they were not a degradation to humanity. These erroneous notions, leading man to the conclusion that his nature was bad, and that it would remain so while upon this earth, have led him into the wilds of imagination, regardless of all the facts around him, and into every kind of absurdity; no folly or fantastic notion, or combination of such notions, being too gross for him to entertain.

These are the errors which have led man step by step from one absurdity to another, adding to them through every suceeding generation, and being the more strongly attached to them the longer they have been entertained. Hence the various religions of the world, and the wars, massacres, and murders, which they have generated, and the demoniacal feelings which they have produced, and the hatred of one sect of these poor made maniacs for all other sects, through past ages, and at the present time.

Hence the insane denunciations of minds made puritanical, against some of the qualities of the physical parts of our nature, as well as of some of the mental, when these happen to be preoccupied with superstitions differing from those filled with puritanical incongruities.

Facts have now disclosed that human nature is one whole, composed of many parts; and each part absolutely necessary to the perfection of the wonderful compound of each individual. And that, unless each part is duly cultivated, according to the use for which it is evidently designed, man must remain, as heretofore, an imperfect specimen of human nature.

Until now the necessity has not been experienced, nor the means known, nor the circumstances created, to train, educate, and well cultivate, at the proper periods of life, all the powers, faculties, and qualities, of our common nature.

Human nature possesses physical, mental, moral, and practical powers. The physical may be highly cultivated, exclusively of the mental, moral, and practical; the mental, to the exclusion of physical, moral, and practical; the moral, to the neglect of the physical, mental, and practical; and the practical, to the exclusion of the mental and moral, and also, in many cases, of the general physical also.

Now man will remain extremely imperfect, while this most erroneous formation of the human character shall be continued. The physical, mental, moral, and practical divisions of human nature, are all essential to be cultivated, and well cultivated, to make each individual into the being that it is the highest interest of society that each should be formed to be.

Since the advance of the knowledge of facts over useless or rather injurious mysteries, and the progress made in the various arts and sciences, to extend the powers of production so extensively and enormously as they now exist, the necessity for the division of manual labour, as previously advocated, has ceased, and all such division is become far worse than useless, except under great modification; that is, unless it shall be based on a previous cultivation of all the faculties, qualities, and powers of our common nature; and even then, that the practical, physical, mental, or moral division of our nature, shall not be entire, but shall allow sufficient daily exercise to the other less required faculties, to keep the whole being in its proper state of health, and for having its healthy share of the enjoyments of existence.

In a rational state of society there will not be any mere physical, or mental, or moral, or practical beings, or mere imperfect parts of humanity; but all will be trained, from birth, to become at maturity full formed men and women, having every portion of their nature, and every one of their natural qualities, well cultivated and duly exercised at the proper periods of life.

Machinery and chemistry will supersede the necessity for the longer continuance of the manual division of labour, by which, now, the invaluable human being is sacrificed to the needle or pin,[a] or some other less useful and more insignificant object.

Human nature consists of numerous propensities, faculties, powers, and qualities; and the whole, when united in certain proportions in the living being, is called man. Now these varied powers are, every one of them, necessary and useful to man's existence and enjoyment. They are, indeed, apparently formed for this double purpose for upon the investigation of all that is now known connected with humanity, man and woman appear to be purposely formed to exist, and to enjoy existence; but that they should pass through various preparatory stages of infant and childish existence, before they should acquire sufficient knowledge, through slow experience, to enable them to enjoy their existence.

And it is only now that sufficient experience has been acquired to enable them to know that without health there is little chance for happiness, and that without the due cultivation and proper exercise of all the faculties, health of body and mind cannot be obtained, nor the full happiness of life be enjoyed. Nature has given all the propensities, faculties, and powers of humanity, to be used and exercised according to the peculiar quality of each kind of power, and the individual suffers when any one of these powers is not duly cultivated, or when it is under or over exercised.

It is, therefore, of the first importance for the health of the human race, that society should now make efficient arrangements to have the physical, mental, moral, and practical portions of our nature, in every individual, well cultivated

[a] Pin-making was Adam Smith's chief example of the advantages of the division of labour in *The Wealth of Nations*, Bk 1, ch. 1.

and duly exercised, in order that all may not only exist, but enjoy their existence. And this enjoyment cannot be complete until every faculty, quality, and power of our nature shall be regularly exercised to the point of temperance.

6th. 'The temperate exercise, at the periods of life indicated by nature, of all the propensities which form an essential portion of human nature.'

The propensities which constitute man's nature, and which are necessary to his existence, may be said to be the desire for food, for exercising his faculties, for sleep and rest, and for sexual intercourse.

These are necessary to the permanent existence of the human race, and apparently are made to give pleasure in their exercise, when temperately used, that individual life may be sustained, and the race continued from generation to generation.

These propensities are all equally necessary and equally good; and were it not for man's ignorance and presumption in supposing that he knows his nature, and what is necessary and beneficial for it, better than the power which so wonderfully forms it, and, unconsciously of the means to the individual, continues its existence through every moment of life, they (the propensities) would be productive only of health and enjoyment to all of the human race.

If man were trained from his birth to become a rational creature, and were placed within those external circumstances that would enable him freely to exercise his natural powers of reasoning, after having been so trained and educated through infancy, childhood, and youth, he would never err in the exercise of any of his propensities. He would know, as a rational being, what would be necessary exercise of them, to insure to him the best state of health and the highest enjoyment, through the longest life that could be given to his individual organization.

He would know that to live, he must eat and drink; but to be healthy and happy, he must eat and drink temperately, according to his individual constitution.

He would know that to live, he must exercise his faculties; but that, to be healthy and enjoy his existence, he must exercise each of his faculties temperately, according to his individual organization.

He would know that to live, he must rest from this exercise of his faculties, and sleep; but, to be healthy and enjoy life, he must rest and sleep temperately for his individual nature.

He would know that for the human race to live, the sexes must have the intercourse which nature requires; but, to be healthy and happy, each individual should have, at the proper period of life designed by nature, the temperate exercise of this propensity, according to the constitution of the individual.

Now, the ignorance of our ancestors respecting their own nature, when their imaginations were unrestrained by attention to facts, and their reasoning powers undeveloped, was so gross that they conjectured the most wild and incongruous notions to be truths, and acted upon them as such.

Among millions of random conjectures made at this period, they supposed that some of the human propensities were created good, and some bad; that some of them might be left to the natural instinct of the individual, but that they could regulate others better than nature, by their crude laws and absurd notions of right and wrong.

These errors of the infant mind of humanity have been transmitted from that period through succeeding generations to the present; and have filled the world, in their progress, with increasing crime and misery, which will continue to advance until these errors shall be arrested in their course, and a rational direction shall be given to the feelings, thoughts, and conduct of men.

The human race has yet to learn the foundations of right and wrong, of virtue and vice; and until these shall be understood by them, they will have no sure guide to direct the formation of character, or the construction of society to accomplish the object of their existence.

Until it shall be known and publicly acknowledged that virtue consists in promoting the general permanent happiness of the human race, and vice in opposing it, that that which promotes the permanent happiness of man is *right*, and that that which opposes it is *wrong*, there can be no wise or good legislation, or consistent and steady conduct, among any of the nations of the earth.

The happiness of the human race cannot be attained, unless the propensities can be temperately exercised, as nature directs. It is virtue thus to keep them in action; and it is vice to oppose this exercise. It is *right* to admit and to encourage this use of them; it is *wrong* to prevent or discourage this use of them.

Man has most egregiously erred upon this subject, through all past ages; and, in consequence, he has entailed disappointment, disease, vice, crime, misery, and insanity, to a frightful extent, upon all of his race. Until this error of attempting by ignorant laws and absurd ceremonies to direct, in opposition to nature, the due and healthy exercise of the propensities or natural instincts which all are forced to have, shall be removed, there can be no health, virtue, or happiness, in human society.

All men, women, and children, to be healthy, virtuous, and happy, require to exercise their propensities temperately, according to their individual nature. And the only mode by which they can know how to exercise their propensities temperately, to be beneficial for themselves and society, is to form decisive and efficient arrangements to train each infant from birth to become a rational being in mind and conduct, and to permanently surround all, throughout their lives, with institutions and all other external circumstances in accordance with their nature; taking care that none shall be permitted to remain that are opposed to the known and ascertained laws of humanity.

Were these principles adopted, and the institutions of society made in accordance with them, it is probable that in two or three generations, disease, vice, and misery, would be little, if at all, known.

It is the insane conduct of man, supposing that it is right and virtuous to oppose his own nature, and wrong and vicious to act in accordance with it, that now creates most, if not all, of the diseases, vices, crimes, and miseries, of the human race.

But man has been taught to shut his eyes to, or to cover in darkness or mystery, the vices, diseases, and miseries, of his own hourly creation, through endless institutions, customs, and practices, which have been formed by man to oppose his nature.

This error must be abandoned, before man can become intelligent, healthy, charitable, or happy; and arrangements must be formed to admit of each individual enjoying his natural right to the due and proper exercise of his faculties, powers, and propensities, at the times and seasons indicated by his nature, and in accordance with all the previously explained fundamental laws of human nature.

Until man shall discover that his propensities are as important a part of his nature as his senses, and to be stimulated to action in a similar manner, impelled by the instincts of his nature, and until the natural actions of each shall be known to be, and considered to be, equally necessary for the health, well-being, and happiness, of the individual, and in all respects equally virtuous, he will remain a mystified, irrational made animal.

Little do men of the present generation know to what extent they are imposed upon by the inexperience of our ancestors, and especially by the errors of the ancient Priesthood of the world.

It was these men, many of whom were wild enthusiasts, and some of them strongly insane, who introduced the impious notion, if any notion can be impious, that they know better than nature how to regulate the instincts of humanity. And by this impiety, they introduced sin and misery among the human race. When man deemed himself a better judge than nature of the regulation of the instincts of other men, and called some of these instincts virtues, and others vices, then crime and disease were introduced, fostered, encouraged, and made to pervade all the nations of the earth, as they became under the despotic sway of the mysticism of the Priesthood. The artificial and unnatural restrictions – invented by the Priesthood at different times, in different countries – on the necessary exercise, for health of body and mind, of some of the propensities of humanity, are at this day afflicting the human race with more division of mind, disease, crime, and misery, than any other cause, except the artificial restraints which they have introduced and made to be enforced on the expression of the convictions and feelings which individuals are compelled by their nature and external circumstances to receive and experience, independently of any internal power which they are supposed, by the uniformed respecting the unchanging laws of human nature, to possess.

Until this gross error shall be generally discovered, and seen in all its horrible consequences, and the evil practices which it produces shall be altogether abandoned, truth, full health of body and mind, and virtue, will be unknown among the human race. The due or temperate exercise of all the organs, faculties, senses, and propensities, of humanity, is essential to the production of health, virtue, satisfied feelings, and the permanent enjoyment of happiness.

Upon this division of our subject, the public have more to unlearn and more to learn, than upon any other connected with the general well-being and happiness of our race; and until they unlearn their errors, and acquire a correct knowledge of their nature, and of how to exercise it in accordance with their nature, there will be a stumbling block in their path to knowledge, health, and happiness; one so stubborn that it will prevent their advance to become rational beings, and will retain them in the low condition of beings ignorant of the value of their own faculties and qualities, and who, in consequence, will continually murder their own happiness and the happiness of their fellow-men, hourly giving abundant proofs that they are yet irrational.

While this misconception of the use of the propensities, of the necessity for their regular temperate exercise according to the constitution of each individual, of the misery which they create when unexercised or over exercised, shall continue, there will be no truthful, consistent conduct, in the laws, customs, manners, or language, of men – nothing but hypocrisy in the intercourse between the sexes – physical and mental disease – inferior organizations at birth – general dissatisfaction with society – unsatisfied feelings – disappointment of the affections – with the innumerable and horrible hidden miseries, arising from prostitution in those, generally speaking, the finest and best by nature among both sexes, but expecially in the most confiding of the female sex, who, under the strange circumstances now prevalent in Great Britain, are used and treated more cruelly and far worse than any brutes; and the whole conduct of legislators and of men generally, to allow of these proceedings, unchecked and unremedied, is the most certain proof of the low, inferior, and degraded condition of the human intellect, and of the very small progress which has yet been made in the institution of laws, customs, manners, and public opinion, towards a state of society deserving the name of civilization.

Civilization! how has this term been misapplied! how is it now misapplied!

A state of society based on ignorance, deranging the faculties of all!

The affairs of the world carried on solely by force and fraud, through massacres, legal murders, robberies, and devastations; – superstitions, bigotry, and senseless mysteries!

By sacrificing common sense and the improvement and happiness of the human race in contending about a Power that is yet a mystery to all, and that cannot be affected in any manner by the absurd forms, ceremonies, and opposing mad opinions of yet but half-formed animals, who are always most actively, but, as they imagine, most wisely, engaged, in preventing each other from acquiring real knowledge, or obtaining happiness!

By disputing and contending about wealth, to be grasped and hoarded by individuals who know not how, when obtained, to use it advantageously for themselves or others!

By contending like savages for this wealth, which is greatly diminished in value by such contentions; while, by the most simple yet beautiful arrangements, more wealth of superior qualities could be annually created, than would saturate the desires of all; and the highest pleasures would be attained and permanently enjoyed by the measures that might be adopted to create this wealth!

By supposing that the most degrading and injurious vices are the highest virtues; and that those virtues which would, if practised with knowledge of our nature and society, produce permanent health and happiness, are vices to be always cried down and avoided!

By living a continued life of hypocrisy, and private and public deception!

By continually sacrificing all that is known, substantial, and beneficial to the human race, for that which is unknown, unreal, and most pernicious!

By continually doing that which, for the well-being and interest of all, should be left undone; and not doing that which, for the permanent happiness of all, should be done!

By all being actively engaged in endeavouring to counteract the happiness of all; while it is the best and highest interest of all to endeavour heartily, cordially, and in all good faith, that all should be actively engaged in promoting the well-being and happiness of all!

And yet this conduct of gross ignorance and rank insanity is now called civilization! It may be the civilization of half-formed animals, pretending to be reasonable, or the embryo state of beings who may hereafter become rational, and, at some future period, attain to the condition of civilization.

When the world shall be governed in peace, without force or fraud – when truth shall be the universal language of man – when charity shall pervade every thought and feeling of all – when wealth shall superabound, and be uncoveted except for immediate use, and when to produce it in abundance shall be a constant source of active enjoyment to all – when all shall be carefully trained from birth to acquire none but the most lovely physical and mental qualities, with the most attractive manners and superior habits, and when, in consequence, all will be beloved by all – when prostitution and all injustice of man to the other sex shall be unknown, and when man and woman shall have full confidence in each other, and society shall know how to train and educate all from birth to become superior, rational, well-informed beings; – then, and not till then, shall man have a foretaste of what civilization will effect for the human race.

And it is only in this state that man can know the full advantages to be derived from the regular and temperate exercise of all the powers, faculties, and propensities, of his nature; – it is only when this state can be attained, that man can become rational, healthy, and happy. When society shall openly adopt true first principles, and shall act consistently in accordance with them, then will this superior civilization be easily attained, and a terrestrial paradise will be the natural consequence.

To preserve the organization through life, physically, mentally, and morally, in the best state of health, during its longest natural existence, it is necessary there should be.

7th. 'Healthy alternate occupation of body and mind, in proportion to the strength and capacity of both.'

Man is a highly complicated, complex, living machine; mechanically and chemically formed and united, to work, under wise arrangements, most efficiently and harmoniously, to produce excellence and happiness in each individual. But when some parts of this machine are continually brought into action, and other parts remain unexercised, the individual machine of human life is but partially formed, it cannot work efficiently, it is deteriorated in its powers and capacities, and man remains an imperfectly formed or irrational animal.

The principles on which society has been hitherto based, and under which the character of all human beings has been formed, have not admitted of this temperate exercise of all the faculties, powers, senses, and propensities, of our common nature; and at this day, the greatest possible waste is made of these invaluable faculties, because they are misunderstood, unexercised, or over-exercised; and the greatest injury is done to all by the wretchedly ignorant manner in which these several parts of our nature are now trained from birth, and used through the life of all that are born and live to maturity.

The governing powers of society appear ever to have been ignorant of the nature of man, of his faculties and powers, and, of course, of how to cultivate or to employ them.

They have been occupied with mysteries, or engaged in perfecting the means of coercing their fellow-men by force and fraud, and of maintaining a system of error to create tyrants and slaves, with insane, violent, or imbecile minds, and, thus, to render all unfit to comprehend or enjoy a rational mode of existence. Some have been thus doomed to exert one portion of their physical powers through life in one way, some in another; and these much varied according to the strange occupation in which they have been employed to gain the means of a confined and scanty subsistence. While others have had various small portions of their mental faculties constantly over-exerted, and, as well as the physical powers in the former case, often to affect the most useless, injurious, or vicious results, as is the practice with the greatest majority of mankind at the present hour, but, more especially, with respect to the mental faculties, which are made to suffer, under the present system of human affairs, by all manner of irrational proceedings.

Of what use or benefit to themselves, or to the human race, can those defectively formed beings be, or ever become, who are trained from birth to have all their mental faculties compressed to the study of what is called theology, or, properly speaking, of mystery; – of that which to man is unexplainable and incomprehensible?

The universe exists; some power effects all the changes in the universe, let them be called by men wise or foolish, good or bad.

Man knows not what this power is, what is the nature of the qualities by which the changes are made, or the present or ultimate object of these endless new individual or general forms of animate and inanimate existence, or of the changes which appear to be eternal. Man gives a name, in the varied languages of the earth, to this power, which we in our language call God.

Man, being ignorant of this power, cannot, by forms, ceremonies, or words, do this power any good or harm; and it is only while he remains in a most ignorant and grossly irrational state of mind and feeling, that he can attempt in any manner to address it, in the language of gross inconsistency, not to say insanity.

This is all that is known among men of what they irrationally call theology or religion; and all the faculty of the human race which has been, or that now is, employed on this subject, is not only wasted, lost for the benefit of the individuals and of mankind, but it is daily and hourly effecting the greatest evils throughout society, inflicting the most excruciating agonies upon the minds and bodies of many, under all the varied names and forms by which theology is known in every part of the earth. The mere theological made mind is not only the most useless and irrational, but it is also the most injurious upon earth; and the sooner it can be made to cease altogether, the sooner will mankind become wise, virtuous, rational, healthy, and happy.

Theology is a disease – a grievous malady of the human faculties. When man shall be made sane, it will be unknown.

Other portions of the human race, in those districts which are now called civilized, have a small part only of their mental faculties directed to what is called *law*; and which, like theology, has been made to differ in detail, at various times, in different countries, and often in the same country.

It is thus, like theology, uncertain and a mystery; being, like theology, an abortion of the imagination, in opposition to reason and common sense; and, like theology, it creates a disease in the mind, giving a false and most injurious direction to many of the mental faculties.

Law, like theology, is based on falsehood, or errors of the imagination respecting the natural qualities of human nature, and therefore are all its proceedings far worse than useless.

It imagines that man, by his original constitution, possesses the power, at his own controul, to believe and disbelieve, to love and hate, at the command of others. It serves, therefore, like theology, to confound and puzzle and perplex the human faculties, and to make man the most inconsistent and irrational of all terrestrial animals.

Examine now, guided by nature's unchanging laws, all the laws of man, given to him by man, through all the gradations of his experience, to the present hour – and what do we find? A mass of confusion, of utter contradictions, of gross absurdities, even in those codes deemed the most wise. And men are systematically trained to be doomed to spend their time and exert their mental faculties to comprehend that which no man has ever yet discovered – that which no man ever can discover; that is, to understand or make common sense of laws which are opposed to nature – of laws which continually contradict each other; and to find truth and justice in that which is based on falsehood and injustice.

The errors and evils hourly arising from theology and law are beyond human calculation; and those doomed by society to be occupied in them, are sacrificed to a false civilization, pretending to increase, while it diminishes, the happiness of the human race.

But, grievous as these two errors are, their ramifications in the whole business of life are so multitudinous and extensive, that it would be most unwise to attempt at once to abolish them, as society is now constituted. They cannot be at once abolished without great injury to individuals and to society; but they may be gradually superseded, advantageously for the world, for priests, and lawyers, and all connected with theology and law. They have ever been, they are now, and, while continued, they ever will be, substantive motives and causes of division and deadly hatred acting upon the populations of all countries.

Both professions, as they are called, train the individuals doomed to live by their study and practice, to become small and imperfect portions of what man might now with ease be made to become.

The medical profession is another of the present modes by which human beings have a small part of their faculties cultivated to little purpose. The individuals of this profession are so trained, like the unfortunate individuals who are trained in the mysteries of theology and law, as to have it made to appear to be their interest to deceive all those who are not of their own profession. Society is so erroneously constituted, owing to the errors on which it has ever been based, that were the most advanced members of any of these professions to declare openly and honestly the knowledge which they are obliged to acquire in prosecuting the study of their individual profession, they could not live by it – they could not earn sufficient for the support of their families. The business of life, as this false civilization has advanced, has become more and more a general system of falsehood and deception. Profession deceives profession; each trade deceives all others; and competition now has become so severe, by individuals opposing each other, that life is nothing better than a system of scrambling, gambling, and swindling; because it is now impossible for men to be honest and succeed, either in the professions or in business – a sure sign that some great change is at hand. The advanced members of the medical profession know that the health of society is not to be obtained or maintained by medicines; – that it is far better, far more easy, and far wiser, to adopt substantive measures to prevent disease of body or mind, than to allow substantive measures to remain continually to generate causes to produce physical and mental disorders.

When society shall be based on true principles, it will not permit any of its members to be thus made small and imperfect parts of what man might be more easily made to become. It will perceive the great importance of training infants from birth, to become full-formed men or women, having every portion of their nature duly cultivated and regularly exercised.

It will discover that man has not been created to attain the full excellence and happiness of his nature, until all his faculties, senses, and propensities, shall be well cultivated, and society shall be so constructed that all of them, in each individual, shall be temperately exercised, and their powers continued and increased by such exercise, until arrested by natural old age.

The naval and military professions are other instances of the great injustice done by the old system of the world to the human race – of the extent of mere physical training for limited and most injurious purposes – of a portion of mankind being set apart and especially well trained dexterously to murder their equally ignorant fellow-men, or to avoid being murdered by them, both acting under the command of other ignorant parties who know not what they do or wherefore they thus insanely act. Insanely act; because they all desire to be happy, and they thus adopt the most effectual mode to prevent themselves and others from even an approach to any such state of existence.

It is the highest interest of all of the human race, to which there cannot be a single exception, –

1st. That the entire faculties, senses, and propensities, should be well cultivated, and at all times duly or temperately exercised, according to the physical and mental strength and capacity of the individual; in order that whatever may be done by each, should be performed in the best manner for the general advantage of all: –

2nd. That there should be the greatest amount of wealth produced, consistent with the health and happiness of the producers: –

3rd. That the wealth thus produced should be preserved in the best manner for the use of all: –

4th. That it should be distributed the most beneficially and justly for all: –

5th. That it should be used and consumed the most wisely, to produce, to the consumers, the distributors, preservers, and producers, the greatest amount of permanent happiness.

But by training a portion of the human race purposely to murder or to be murdered; – to rob, plunder, and burn property, all are directly or indirectly most grievously injured; institutions are established, and laws and customs made, which are all calculated to continue the human race in ignorance, poverty, division, oppression of the strong and cunning over the weaker and more honest, and to perpetuate the most incongrous and insane thoughts and proceedings among all nations and people.

While war shall be encouraged, or deemed other than wholesale murder and plunder, arising from ignorance and gross insanity in the human race, what folly it must be to talk of virtue, of justice, of kindness, of charity, or of common sense or rationality, among men!

The military and naval professions, therefore, can never be introduced into a society in which there shall be 'healthy alternate occupation of body and mind, temperate in proportion to the strength and capacity of the individual.' No! nor into any society that is to be made rational and happy.

8th.[a] 'Extensive real knowledge of ourselves, society, and nature, in accordance with facts and external nature, and without mysteries to confound the understanding and judgment, or any of the other faculties of the mind.'

Without an extensive knowledge of our nature, of society generally, and of external nature, it is impossible that man can attain the happiness that he may, with this knowledge, permanently secure.

Until we shall know ourselves – a knowledge of which society appears to be profoundly ignorant – it is utterly impossible that man can think, speak, or act, rationally. While we remain ignorant of our nature, and especially while we are taught and made to believe that we possess powers which belong not to humanity, we shall in vain expect to discover the road to happiness.

While we are taught to suppose that we possess powers and capacities which do not constitute a part of our nature, we must continue to grope in the dark, and always mistake the path to happiness. While we remain under the impression that we are born with power to enable us to believe or disbelieve, to love or hate, contrary to the overwhelming instincts of human nature – who can expect man to acquire wisdom or happiness? While we quarrel and fight about our opinions and feelings, or convictions and affections – where can there be any bond of union? or on what foundation can charity and kindness be based?

While these errors shall be impressed on the infant and tender mind, it cannot be expected that religious animosities and political divisions should cease, or that religious massacres and political wars should not, as heretofore, occur again and again, and thus keep nations and people in a high state of irritation, anger, vice, and irrationality.

And it is in vain to attempt to take one step now in a right course to improve the general condition of society, until man shall be taught to know what powers or qualities he possesses. While ignorant upon this vital subject he cannot think a correct thought respecting virtue or vice – know what is good or bad for society – or see anthing around him, except through a glass, darkly;[b]

[a] 6th and 7th were omitted in the original.
[b] See 1 Corinthians 13:14.

neither can he discover any one just principle of action, or know in what manner to constitute society to produce excellence and happiness.

Until a correct knowledge of ourselves can be attained, it is futile in the extreme to imagine that we can acquire any knowledge of what should be. We know what society has become through ignorance of our nature; that this, the most advanced of old civilized society, has progressed until life itself is unbearable to many, and suicides are numerous and daily increasing; – that poverty, vice, and misery, are advancing by fearful and alarming strides; – and that oppression and injustice and imbecility are rapidly spreading throughout the length and breadth of the land.

The knowledge of facts is increasing, and so far a progress is making in a knowledge of external nature; but without a knowledge of ourselves and of society, an acquaintance with these facts may open new or an extension of the old sciences to us, but while we are ignorant of human nature and thence necessarily of society, the sciences, instead of being made to contribute to human happiness, will continue to be so misdirected that they will increase the errors and miseries which even now threaten to force society into confusion, through the dissatisfaction of so large a majority who are deeply suffering from these lamentable mistakes.

In fact, without a correct knowledge of what manner of beings we are, it will remain impossible for us to discover the only true path to knowledge, virtue, and happiness; and it is in consequence of the ignorance which has hitherto universally prevailed on this, the most important of all subjects, that man has nowhere yet advanced beyond the condition of an irrational animal, who knows not the use of his instincts, and who therefore deems it a virtue to counteract them; and thus is he taught to commit every kind of vice, and to be made so stupid as to believe that he is really practising virtue.

Until lately the educated minds throughout society were, with very few exceptions, chiefly occupied with the study and contemplation of mysteries and nonentities; and the imagination was the most favoured faculty of our ancestors. It was therefore universally cultivated, but on no solid foundation. Some ignorant learned individuals adopted some whim or fancy without any regard to facts or science, and then their imaginations ran for a time wild upon these irrational notions, until they formed a sect, or a mass of most incongruous, hetrogeneous, absurd contradictions, and after a time these were dignified with the name of a religion. Others pursued a similar course; and thus came many religions, all equally said to be divine and true; and in defence of these senseless imaginations – all productive of vice, crime, and misery, and all opposed to the progress of real knowledge based on the unchanging laws of nature – men have been trained to become ferocious animals, contending, fighting, and in cold blood massacring each other, for they know not what, or because their opponents would not do that which to them, trained as they were, was utterly impossible. And in this manner, at this day, is the population of the world chiefly occupied – producing as much crime and misery, and as little virtue and happiness, as gross ignorance enables them to effect.

Now, while there is so little knowledge of ourselves, of society, and of nature, it is vain to expect that there can be sound health, either of body or mind. Innumerable bodily diseases must be engendered while the laws and customs of the world enforce continual opposition to nature's instincts; endless mental maladies must arise while the mind is occupied, and often overwhelmed, with mysteries which it cannot understand, because they are opposed to all we know of nature, and are to us incomprehensible. These errors must be abandoned before there can be any chance for man to acquire the power 'to procure at pleasure whatever is necessary to preserve the organization in the best state of health.'

9th. 'Full, genuine, and pure CHARITY, alone derivable from an accurate knowledge of human nature.'

Without true charity there can be no real virtue, nor anything deserving the name of happiness, in the society of men.

Charity, derived from an accurate knowledge of our own nature, has been hitherto unknown among the nations of the earth; it is unknown even now in the laws, customs, manners, and conduct, of the people of these islands, said to be the most advanced nation in the, so called, civilized world.

Insane persecutions for conscientious opinions are general throughout the empire, over Christendom, and in all the nations of the earth. The phraseology of the languages of all these people is direct indication that hitherto they have not known what genuine charity means; and the history of all their practical proceedings confirms what their phraseology indicates.

These evince a total want of the knowledge of those facts respecting human nature, on which alone true or intelligent charity can be based.

The necessity for charity to form the spirit of man has been felt by many, and some few have had glimmerings of the beauty of this spirit, whenever it should become the directing spirit of the human race.

All who have deeply reflected upon what man has been, what he now is, and what he may be made to become, have ascertained that, hitherto, charity in its full extent of principle and practice has been a mere name with which to deceive the mass of mankind; and that the world will not have any correct conception of what charity is, until this feeling shall have been made to pervade the spirit, mind, manner, and conduct, of the human race. And this cannot be attained until arrangements shall be formed to train each infant from birth to imbibe this spirit, through every step of his progress to maturity, by giving him, through the instruction of facts – of living evidences – a thorough knowledge of his own nature, and of what manner of being he is. When he shall be thus taught, the seeds of anger, of ill-will, of jealousies, of revenge, of contentious ambition, of wars and fightings, of injurious competition, of ignorant selfishness, of all crimes, and of almost all, if not of all, misery, except that small amount which may arise from the conflicts of the elements of nature will no longer exist. The life of man will then be a delightful existence to promote the continually increasing knowledge and happiness of man; while, without this charity, derived from knowing what humanity is, man is opposed to the happiness of man, wherever he is now found upon the earth.

It is this charity which produces all the virtues and destroys all the vices of the human race, and this charity cannot be understood without the previous knowledge of the mode by which the character of each individual is formed, and how it is commenced before birth, and made up during life, until its decomposition at death.

This knowledge will lay a solid foundation for all other knowledge, and without it all other knowledge will fail to produce happiness.

This knowledge, by producing genuine charity, creates self-possession, inward satisfaction, and a serenity and superiority of mind and feeling, which no other knowledge can generate; and the attainment of it is necessary to preserve the organization in the best state of health.

10th. 'The esteem and affection of all our neighbours, friends, and the human race.'

The good opinion, esteem, and affection, of our fellow-creatures, are essential to preserve our organization in the best state of health.

Unless our feelings are in a good or pleasant state towards our fellow-men, the organization is not in a natural condition to attain the best state of health. We must be dissatisfied; and dissatisfaction diminishes health.

Now we cannot possess the most pleasant feelings for our fellow-men, if we do not also feel conscious that they have a good opinion, esteem, and kind feelings, for us.

But as we know, under the Rational System, the causes which produce these varied feelings for us in our fellow-men, and as we also know that these feelings for us are necessary to our health and happiness, we shall of course adopt that course of conduct through our lives which we know must generate, in all around us, those qualities of esteem, love, and affection, which we desire that our fellow-men should entertain of us. We shall be fully conscious that if we do not receive those feelings from the association of our fellow-men and their intercourse with us, we do not yet possess in ourselves the qualities competent to create them, and this knowledge will be a perpetual excitement to endeavour to acquire those qualities.

As truth, also, will be the universal language under the Rational System of Society, the feelings possessed by each will be known to all upon inquiry, and as correctly as nature compels the individual to have them; and, in consequence, the inferior, injurious, or disagreeable qualities of all, will, under this system, be more effectually removed in one month, than they could be in a life-time under the present system of falsehood and deception. In fact, it is a system of truth in the look, word, and manner of each, on all occasions, that can alone regenerate mankind, and make man intelligent, good, and happy; and truth can never exist in purity, or in useful practice, under the present system of society; because the system is based on falsehood, and will not admit of the plain, straightforward, and simple language of truth.

It is only upon a correct knowledge of what human nature is, and how its convictions and feelings are formed, that a systematic practice of undisguised truth can arise and become universal throughout society.

And this knowledge, preparing the way for the universal language of truth, will prepare all to acquire qualities to be esteemed and loved by human nature; and, thus, will all, ultimately, through this process, receive the esteem and affection of all; the qualities generating these feelings, under the enlightened and innocent language of truth, will pervade society, and none other feelings will, ere long, be known among men.

With this knowledge, these qualities, and these feelings, the organization of all will be kept, at all times, in the best state of health.

CHAPTER V

The best education, from infancy to maturity, of the physical, intellectual, and moral power of all the population.

THE *known* difference between uneducated and educated man, is the difference now existing between the lowest tribes of human beings, who have but the mere animal education, and those portions of our fellow-men whose physical and mental faculties have been the best educated among the most civilized nations of a most irrational and immoral world, the principles of which are based on falsehood. The *unknown* difference between the highly educated of the old world, and those who shall be educated from birth to become rational in their feelings, thoughts, and actions, who acquire a knowledge of facts, and who are placed under circumstances always to speak the truth, and to be deeply imbued with charity for the thoughts, feelings, and conduct, of all other human beings, is a difference far greater than the known difference now existing between the worst and the best educated portions of the human race.

The difference between the *known* most inferior of the human race, formed under the mere animal education, and the unknown excellence and superiority to which man may be educated to attain, physically, mentally, morally, and practically, is the difference to be obtained by the influence of external circumstances in forming the character of the human race. Or – to descend to the familiar language of commerce, the ideas and manners of which now pervade so large a portion of our population – it is the difference between the *material* of *humanity*, as exhibited in each individual of the human race, being *manufactured* in the worst, or in the best manner.

Man will remain blind to his interest and opposed to his own happiness, until he shall know how to well-form his offspring, and shall put that knowledge into practice.

Hitherto man has been kept ignorant of humanity; even now he knows not himself. He imagines the material of which he is formed to be what it never was, what it never can become. In consequence, he has remained ignorant of the principles and process by which humanity can be manufactured to become rational in feelings, thoughts, and actions; and nowhere, at any time, in any part of the earth, have external circumstances been formed to rationalize humanity, or to educate man to become at maturity a rational being. Even now there is not any country in the world in which an establishment exists to well-form the human character, physically, mentally, morally, and practically.

Hence the disordered state of men and nations at the present hour, exhibiting in all their conduct not more, at best, than the germs of future reasonable creatures.

The present chaos of society admits not of the means to form a reasonable human being.

The divisions of society into sects, parties, and classes, into different languages and nations, will, as long as they shall be permitted to remain, hold man in the bonds of ignorance, and keep him in the depths of irrationality. They will continue to train generation after generation in mysteries not to be understood – in divisions of feelings and of interests – in all the inferior passions – and in the same conflicts and random conduct that have marked with blood and folly every page of the past history of man.

If the human race shall ever be well educated – if man shall be made a rational creature, this change can be effected only by the nations of the world being induced, through their sufferings, to consent to supersede all the existing external circumstances of human creation, and all the institutions which have emanated from their erroneous imaginary notions respecting their own nature, and from a want of knowledge of what man, when made rational, may do to secure the happiness of man.

To educate man to become a rational creature, a new combination of external circumstances must be created; each circumstance devised to effect an especial good, in promoting the object to be obtained.

It is a vain anticipation to expect a rational being to be formed in any of the existing establishments for education, in this or in any other country. These are now admirably adapted to force humanity to become insane, and to train all individuals to act the parts of fools or knaves, or both, and to oppose their own happiness and the happiness of their fellow-beings, throughout the whole extent of animal life. By this education the germs of reason are destroyed or misdirected – the feelings are diverted from their natural channels – and the whole man is, in consequence, made a diseased animal, physically, mentally, and morally, and a being whose language, thoughts, and conduct, are at continual variance, opposing and perplexing each other, until man becomes at maturity the most inconsistent of all living existences, and the most deceptive of all earthly animals.

And this is the result now produced from that material of humanity which contains within itself the germs of every kind of human excellence and of high attainments; – germs which, when they shall be rationally cultivated, will insure high intellectual, healthy, and joyous happiness to each individual, and to every association of men.

Shall this grossly ignorant and irrational condition of humanity continue through other generations? Must man remain for ever the most inconsistent, and, in consequence, the most miserable being upon earth, when, at the same time, he possesses powers within himself, which, when rightly directed, are competent to insure to him the command of the earth, the happiness of himself, and, to a great extent, the means to make happy all that shall remain upon it?

Nature, through the discoveries made in this generation, emphatically says – 'No. The irrational period of human existence shall now cease. I have commenced to open my stores of knowledge and of true wisdom to man, to enable the present generation to start into new life, and break the hitherto hard and impenetrable shell of ignorance which has shut out every ray of rational light from their mental vision. They shall now soon perceive, without the shadow of a doubt, the causes of their mental blindness and their consequent physical and mental afflictions; they shall no longer grope in the dark, but shall distinctly see how to work out their own salvation from ignorance and its consequent errors, producing endless sin and misery. By these discoveries I have given man power to create wealth beyond his wants or desires, to *new*-form the character of all coming generations, and materially, as a preliminary, to *re*form the existing generation, in order that wealth, and knowledge, and excellence, may everywhere abound, and that man may at length enjoy the continually progressively increasing happiness, which, from the beginning, he has been formed at this period to attain.'

Such is evidently now the language of NATURE.

She thus speaks aloud through her modern discoveries; her political shaking of the nations, and the agitations throughout the earth, arising from the rancorous contests of the opposing Priesthoods of the world.

It is by EDUCATION, rightly understood and wisely applied to practice, that this greatest of all changes in the condition of humanity is now to be effected, to regenerate the human race from its gross irrationalities.

But how is THIS EDUCATION to be obtained, seeing that there are now none but external circumstances which are all calculated to force man to become an inconsistent and irrational being?

By one mode only. Not by hastily and with violence destroying these irrational arrangements of the old worn-out ignorant, immoral, and miserable, world; and treating unkindly those whose characters have been, of necessity, formed by and under these lamentable circumstances; but by gradually, peaceably, and with the kindest feelings to all, introducing a new, scientific, and very superior combination of external arrangements, which shall possess the essence of all that is of real use to man in these old random combinations, leaving out all their inconsistencies and absurdities, and uniting all that can be applied beneficially of the late discoveries, inventions, and improvements, to form around man, from his birth, those rational and consistent external circumstances, within which, alone, man can ever be made to become a rational and consistent, and therefore an intelligent, good, and happy, being.

These arrangements are in some degree shadowed forth in the plans described in the 'Development of the Principles and Plans on which to Establish Self-supporting Home Colonies,'[a] published by the Home Colonization Society, at their office, 57, Pall Mall, London, in the year 1841.

But this publication can give but an imperfect notion of the society that will be formed when there shall be a combination of such nuclei of society, near to and aiding each other, making their whole neighbourhood a portion of an earthly paradise, which, from the excellence and happiness which must be produced and reign throughout the district, will be the cause of the rapid extension of such nuclei over this country, and into other nations, until, by their irresistible advantages, they will extend over every part of the earth.

It is not in any of the old schools, or what are called establishments for education, that a rational character can be formed for man. His powers of mind, his capacity for knowledge, his manners, his spirit, and his conduct, must be formed in the great school, academy, college, and university, of actual life, amidst men and things; with whom and with which, to become eminently useful and happy, he must be early familiarized, and never so placed as to feel it necessary, as at present, to unlearn all that he had been uselessly or mischievously taught amidst conventional errors and absurdities.

It is only amidst the actual active operations of society, when, through all life's departments, the infant, child, and youth, shall be surrounded alone by rational beings, possessing charity and kindness, who will assist wisely to instruct, through every step of this progress, that full-formed rational and superior men and women can ever be produced; but by these means they may as certainly be made, as any superior fabrics are now manufactured from superior arrangements and managements intended to produce them.

---

[a] See *infra*, vol. 2, pp. 339–415.

Man ever has been, is, and ever must be, the creature, to a very great extent, of the external circumstances surrounding him. Put him now permanently within inferior and vicious circumstances only, and he must, with certain limited variations, become inferior and vicious. Place him within superior and really good circumstances, and, in like manner, with certain variations, arising from native individuality of character, he must become superior and good.

It is futile to talk about the details of education, until the great outline of external rational circumstances shall be created, in which rational details can be introduced and daily practised. And to educate aright, men and women must first be trained in normal establishments, to acquire the look, language, manners, and conduct, and especially the spirit, requisite to form and train youth to become rational at maturity. These must be taught, before they can teach others, the *cause* of falsehood, in the look, word, and manner of every individual, and how it is to be removed for ever; the cause of ignorance, of poverty, of division, of all uncharitableness, of crime, of all the inferior passions, and of the want of kindness for all the human race, and the certain mode by which these causes may be removed from human society. These teachers of a rising generation, to make them rational, must themselves be previously instructed how to fill the mind of each pupil with pure unadulterated charity and genuine kindness for the human race, overlooking the present endless ignorances and errors of the poor deluded sects, parties, and classes, into which a want of knowledge of humanity or the eternal laws of human nature, has now divided mankind, and thereby made them inveterate enemies to each other, to the lasting injury of each.

These teachers must be taught the hitherto unknown language of truth without disguise, and how to make it the undeviating habit with all their pupils, and to withdraw all motives from each, ever to desire to express a falsehood by look, word, or action. These instructors must acquire an accurate knowledge of the cause of all anger, to perceive its injustice and irrationality, and to enable their pupils, at an early period, to understand this cause and overcome its effects in their daily intercourse with each other. The same with the causes of pride, vanity, and individual conceit, which they will easily be taught to discover are the necessary results of ignorance of human nature, with the deteriorating influences of praise and blame, rewards and punishments, and all the irrational feelings and notions thence produced.

But it may be asked, where are these rational practices to be taught and acquired? Not within the four walls of a bare building, in which formality predominates, and nature is outraged; but in the nursery, play-ground, fields, gardens, workshops, manufactures, museums, and class-rooms, in which these feelings will pervade teachers and taught, and in which the facts collected from all these sources will be concentrated, explained, discussed, made obvious to all, and shown in their direct application to practice in all the business of life;

in order that each male and female, before the age of twelve, may have a distinct knowledge of the outline of human acquirements, and their existing limits; also of the departments of production and distribution of wealth; and not only of the general principles and practices of the means to produce and distribute wealth in the best manner, but of the necessity for both, and *why* it is to be produced and distributed in the manner that will be adopted in the rational state of society, by all its members at the proper period of life, for producing and distributing wealth advantageously for the whole of society. That they will also know the science or manufacture of human character, how their own had been so far formed in principle and practice, and how they should during their future lives assist to well form the physical, mental, moral, and practical, character of their younger friends and companions, to make them the best and most superior men and women that their natural faculties would admit; that, in addition, they shall have a distinct knowledge, also, of the principles and practices of rational governing, and understand the causes for and the uses of such form of governing.

In short, as soon as the science of forming the human character shall be taught to the instructors, so that they shall truly understand it, and it shall be properly applied by them in practice, from birth, under all the external circumstances which will be arranged for a rational state of existence, the children so treated, taught, and placed, must become well acquainted with the outline, and much of the detail, of the whole affairs of society, know the past history of their fellow-men, the outline of natural history, and what they have to do in the progressive scale of creation, to promote their own happiness, the happiness of their race, and the happiness, as far as practicable, of all that have life upon the earth.

And this now apparently extended education will be imperceptibly instilled into the minds and practice of all, without any overstrained physical or mental exertion, but with great and joyous pleasure to the instructors and the taught; and these results will be produced because all will be done *in accordance with nature*, while heretofore and now *all is done in opposition to nature*.

The acquisition of true principles, of real knowledge, of the spirit of charity and love, and of the natural manners thence ensuing, will be a progress of unmixed pleasure, which will lay a solid foundation for health of body and mind, and active happiness through a long life of satisfied existence.

This is the education which can alone fit man to attain a rational state of existence, to know himself and humanity, to acquire useful and valuable knowledge, to be advanced from being the slave of inferior and vicious circumstances, to a condition in which he will comprehend what are inferior and vicious circumstances, and what are superior and virtuous, how to remove the former, and to replace them with the latter, and to enjoy the necessary results of such a change. In fact, this is the education that will elevate man to a permanently rational and superior state of existence.

From that which has been now written, those who have had minds formed to comprehend the difference between that which is and that which is to be, will readily come to the conclusion that hitherto man has not known what education is, and that no establishment now exists or ever has existed to train any portion of the human race to become at maturity rational beings.

It is the education which has been now described which will prepare the world for the long-promised Millennium; with this difference, that the happiness which it will produce in all will continue and increase with the increase of knowledge, as long as the present earth and its elements shall remain undestroyed.

CHAPTER VI

The inclination and means of promoting continually the happiness of our fellow-beings.

A MOMENT'S reflection must make it evident that man cannot be happy unless he shall be made to possess a continued inclination to make all his fellow-men happy, and without the means shall be given him by which he can assist to produce this result. For the knowledge that there are portions of the human race, or that there is one indidivual, suffering physically or mentally, must deduct from the happiness of a rational formed mind, and stimulate it to exertion, until the cause of that suffering shall be detected and removed.

In a rational state of existence, progressing towards happiness, the business of life will be to attain and secure the happiness of every human being. And when the general happiness of all shall have been secured according to the best knowledge known, the active exertions of all will be continued to increase knowledge, that happiness may be proportionably increased, and continually better secured.

For the attainment of this condition of human happiness, the arrangements of society must be formed with the view of creating this inclination in all; and there are peculiar arrangements, which may be easily introduced into practice, which will be certain to produce this effect.

Could this inclination be given to the few only, and not to all, the happiness of none could be complete. In a rational state of human existence the defects or deficiencies of any would be a source of regret and a diminution of the happiness of all. Every one, therefore, would be strongly desirous that all should be well formed, physically, mentally, and morally, and that all should be superior in practice in every deparment through which they would have to pass. Great but pleasing energies of body and mind will be, therefore, called into continual action, to train all to be as perfect as their natural organization and the knowledge of forming character at the time will admit; and in forming this character the creation of the inclination, or the spirit of real desire to promote the happiness of all our fellow-beings, will not be forgotten, but will, on the contrary, become an essential part of such education. Under right circumstances, that is, in a rational state of society, there will be no difficulty in creating this spirit, or in giving full life to the principle, and giving it permanent existence. For it will not be sufficient merely to create the inclination, and give it a temporary existence; but it must be made permanent, not even to be stationary, but to increase as our experience of its practical benefits and our general knowledge shall be made to increase.

Nor will the inclination, when created, be of much service to society, whatever benefit may be felt by the individual possessor, unless the MEANS shall also be created by which the inclination can be gratified and effect its purpose.

Now the Rational System is devised, in part, purposely to secure to each one the means to be daily actively engaged in measures eminently calculated to promote the happiness of all, and measures, too, from which the individuals, so engaged, will derive continual pleasure, and, in consequence, continual encouragement to proceed in their most useful and good works.

It is in this manner that the condition contained in this chapter will be obtained, as far as it refers to our fellow-men; but it is also requisite that the inclination and the means of promoting the happiness of all that have life, as far as it is compatible with the general well-being of man, should be given and secured to all.

To minds rationally trained, it will be always a deduction from their happiness to inflict unnecessary pain, or to see it inflicted, or to know that it is inflicted, on anything that has life.

The object of a rational state of human existence will be to create the inclination and to obtain the means to extend happiness to its utmost bounds to all endowed with sensations to enable them to feel or be conscious of pleasure and pain.

To carry this principle and practice to its limit of utility, much more knowledge of animal and vegetable life, than is now possessed, must be yet acquird, and it must be left to future more rational generations of men to ascertain how far man can proceed, beyond promoting the happiness of his race, to promote the happiness of other sentient beings which are now placed, or which hereafter may be more placed, under his controul and government.

It is, however, certain that in proportion as man shall become intelligent and rational, his disinclination to produce pain, and his inclination to produce happiness, will increase; and it is extremely probable that all the sentient creation upon the earth, that can be trained to live in harmony with the human race, may, by man's kind and rational treatment of them, be made much more rational beings, and much happier, than the human race have been hitherto, or than it can be made to become, while trained and educated under irrational first principles, and subjected to all the practices which of necessity proceed from these erroneous first principles.

In the Millennium, to the speedy commencement of which we may now rationally look forward, there will be no inclination created to desire to hurt or destroy. To injure life, in any manner, will never be practised, unless dire necessity shall render it unavoidable for the attainment of some great permanent benefit in the government of society.

Man, in all his conduct, when made to be a rational being, will produce happiness to all that have life, to the extent of his knowledge and power; and, as real wisdom shall be increased by experience, the knowledge, power, and inclination, to produce happiness to all that have life upon earth, will also increase.

CHAPTER VII

The inclination and means of increasing continually our stock of knowledge.

It is knowledge alone that can extend and perpetuate happiness among the human race.

It is knowledge alone that can enable man accurately to trace the causes of evil to his race, to perceive how to remove those causes, and to acquire the power to effect their removal.

It is by an increase to our knowledge, alone, that man can know himself and the universal nature of humanity.

It is by an increase of knowledge, that the general mind of humanity can alone be made to discover the wretched state in which the human race has hitherto existed, in consequence of being born in ignorance, and of the necessity which has existed to acquire all useful practical knowledge by slow experience.

It is by an increase of knowledge, that man is yet to learn, for all practical purposes, that he is a being formed without his own consent – that he comes into existence amidst circumstances of which he is ignorant – and that he is, through life, a being compounded of his original individual organization, and of the influences of those circumstances which perpetually act upon his original individual organization.

It is by an increase of knowledge, that man is yet to discover the evil of division, the cause of it, and its remedy.

It is by an increase of knowledge, that man can learn to estimate the powers which he may possess to produce universal union and harmony in the general affairs of mankind.

It is by an increase of knowledge, that the causes of disease, and the means of removing those causes, can be discovered.

It is, also, by an increase of knowledge, alone, that the cause of poverty, with its endless evils and crimes, can be ascertained and overcome; and that money, hitherto the source of so much evil, can be made not only innocuous, but most beneficial.

It is alone by an increase of knowledge, that man can be made to understand what pure and undefiled charity means, how alone it can be obtained individually, and made to pervade the human race, or to know that until this can be accomplished, man must remain little, if at all, superior to an ignorant, competitive, vicious, and insane, animal, fond of contention, war, and plunder, and blinded to his own interest, or well-being and happiness.

In short, without an increase of knowledge, man must remain the priest-ridden miserable being which he has been hitherto.

It is therefore essentially necessary to the happiness of man that means be adopted to create a continual desire to increase our stock of knowledge in all directions whence facts can be acquired, to assure us that our new acquisitions are real knowledge, and consequently in unison with all our previously acquired real knowledge.

It is, however, fortunate for the future happiness of the human race, that real knowledge gives not immediate satisfaction, but that it also creates a desire, continually increasing in an increasing ratio, to advance in it, from stage to stage, without the disposition to rest and to say 'enough, we wish for no more.'

All real knowledge is satisfactory; but instead of satisfying the mental appetite, it creates a delightful hunger, ever desirous of more; and while it is not mysterious or inconsistent, but in accordance with all previous known facts, it will afford pleasure added to pleasure without retrogression or limit.

In a rational state of society all the arrangements for the business of life will be so formed as to produce the inclination for a perpetual increase to knowledge, and to secure the means to obtain it, as well as to discover whether the new knowledge is real or imaginary.

Every facility will be given to every individual by these arrangements, to acquire, in the best manner, and in the shortest time, the greatest amount of the most useful knowledge, with the most health and the greatest pleasure to all parties while acquiring it. And thus will this condition of human happiness be secured to all.

CHAPTER VIII

The power of enjoying the best society; and more particularly of associating at pleasure with those for whom we feel the most regard and the greatest affection.

MAN has hitherto grievously erred in all his endeavours to produce happiness for his race. He has commenced his proceedings without any solid foundation, and pursued his onward course at random, until, at length, he has advanced so far in error that he has become conscious he has never yet been in the right path – for he has always obtained, by his measures, sin and misery, instead of virtue and happiness.

And in no one condition, for the attainment of happiness, has so much error been committed, as in the artificial and most unnatural arrangements which have been formed under the insane notions and customs created by the Priesthood of the world, respecting who should and who should not associate together.

Nature has made certain qualities in individuals which are attractive to other qualities in other individuals; these qualities are more permanent in some constitutions than in others; and in the insane manner in which society has been hitherto constituted, the attractive qualities in all individuals have been fewer, less developed, and less durable, than they will become when men and women shall be trained and educated to attain the character of rational beings, and made to understand their own nature.

Before man can be placed in a condition to *enjoy* good society, good society must be first formed. Where is it now to be found? To what country, and to what district, must men now travel to find any association of men who constitute good society? It is not yet to be discovered among men. The Priesthood of the world have rendered it impossible that good society could be created, or exist, under their dominion of darkness. That which constitutes 'good society' is knowledge, charity, kindness, love, and the language of truth.

How could these exist under a Priesthood which continually inculcates the necessity to believe and love according to their whimsical dictates? and in a state in which to speak or write the truth is made to be the greatest crime that man can commit?

Good society can be created only by men and women being trained to become rational in their feelings, thoughts, and actions, without motives to deception or crime, and with the simple but dignified language of truth.

The errors which have created the Priesthood, and the errors which the Priesthood have created, through their long reign of mystery, falsehood, and absurdities, have made the human race so artificial and irrational, that they now imagine it will be impossible that man can ever become truthful, virtuous, and happy. And they say these evils must ever exist, because 'man is bad by nature.'

The Priesthood first adopt most effective measures to create vice, and to force men to become bad, and then they turn round, after having effectually excuted their purpose, and say, that 'men are bad by nature.'

These errors and these practices have continued so long, that the Priesthood of the present generation are trained sincerely to believe that they are the best men living, and that all that they have been taught is not only truth, but what they call *divine* truth, which may be supposed to be something more or less than real truth, and, consequently, all which they teach as *divine* truth is most generally in opposition to real truth. When any men pretend to have or suppose they have any knowledge or supernatural things or supernatural beings, they have been made to become irrational; whether they have been made so insane as sincerely to believe these things past man's finding out, or to act the hypocrite by saying and teaching what their common sense, or their necessary convictions from palpable facts, compel them to disbelieve.

Horrible injurious to the human race, and utterly destructive of human happiness, as the Priesthood of the world ever have been and now are, yet are the individual priests themselves great sufferers by the system of Priesthood which now prevails in all countries wherever a Priesthood is known. They are made to become artificial and unnatural beings, with their minds full of unreal ideas and useless or rather most injurious associations of sounds, meaning nothing but to be deceived by, and with which to deceive others.

All the theology ever taught – all the theology now known throughout the world, is far worse than useless; and the first step towards the attainment of a rational state of mind among the human race, will be to adopt efficient measures to provide, and, as they have been created by society, to provide well, for the Priesthood of all sects; the second, to abolish them; and the third, to destroy all the irrationalizing works of theology which now torment the world in all its various languages.

This, the greatest service that man can perform for future men, the growing charity, wealth, and knowledge of the age will some day, at no distant period, decide upon and execute; but not with violence or any feelings of revenge for past miseries inflicted, but from the most pure and genuine love of our immediate offspring, and of all the future generations of men.

When the Priesthood shall have been thus made to cease from troubling the human race and disordering the intellects of man, there will be no difficulty in forming those rational arrangements which will enable all to be so trained and placed that, most advantageously for all, each shall 'enjoy the best society, and more particularly shall possess the power to associate at pleasure with those for whom they shall be compelled to have the most regard and the greatest affection.'

This is the supreme pleasure of human nature; because it is strongly felt that a cottage or few things with those we are made cordially and ardently to love, produce far more satisfaction of mind and permanent happiness than a palace with all wealth, when we are obliged to live and associate with those we cannot esteem or love, and especially when, owing to their opposite qualities to those which are agreeable to us, we are compelled to dislike their society and association.

It is the Priesthood of the world, who, by their errors of instruction, create, or do not adopt the right method to prevent the creation of, these disagreeable and repulsive qualities in man; and who, after they have created them, or have neglected to adopt the most easy natural measures to prevent their creation, make arrangements to compel the poor creatures who have been made their slaves, to associate intimately and continually together, in defiance of all nature's created feeling between the parties. If this be not the essence of insanity, it is difficult to know what insanity means.

When the good, the superior, and lovely qualities only of human nature shall be carefully cultivated from birth in each individual, according to his individual compound of human qualities, and the language of man shall be made to become the language of truth, from highly cultivated minds and superior manners, then will men forego the forced associations maintained by the Priesthood, or proceeding from any of the present unnatural and artificial causes, or from any other notice except pure esteem and affection.

When the arrangements of society shall be so formed, as now they easily might, that each individual shall be trained to possess a superior mind and superior manners, and to have lovely qualities only – and when other arrangements, as may now be easily effected, shall be united with the former, to enable society to produce with pleasure abundant wealth for each individual, all the associations of mankind will be alone with good society, and with those whom they are compelled to love. But this state of human existence, this kind of association, of this character of society, will be so totally different from the vulgar, ignorant, hypocritical, absurd, and irrational, associations which the present wretched system has gradually produced, that our children will be astonished that such a degraded and miserable condition of life could have been so long submitted to; or that the ignorance of their ancestors could have been maintained through so many thousands of years.

How complicated, through a want of real knowledge, has human society become! That which to our children of the next generation will be so simplified that *all* will easily be made readily to understand the whole, is not now distinctly perceived or fully understood in any one of its parts or general divisions. Hence, instead of the human race being trained to have charity for one another, and to have qualities commanding love, and therefore to love one another, they have been trained by the priesthood of the world, not only not to have charity one for another, but not to know what the feelings of real charity are; and not only not to acquire lovely qualitites, but even not to know how alone lovely qualities can be given to any, and much less to the whole of the human race.

In the new moral world – in the world to come – in the world about to come – in the regenerated world, when man shall have been born again, and shall have had given to him a new mind, new feelings, a new spirit, a new language of truth, new morals, manners, and conduct, all will, of necessity love one another, and each will know, without duplicity, the love which each is compelled to receive from all, and for whom each is compelled to have the greatest affection.

Affection, the humanizer of humanity, the soother and diminisher of all calamities, the source of the purest pleasures and highest enjoyments in human society, will not be reduced to the degradation of prostitution, or to be purchased by aught save equally pure affection. It will not be forced, by the sole ignorance of the priesthood, and so forced solely for their intended gain and power, to descend in all directions, to all manner of vice and crime, public and private, to produce only deception, falsehood, and misery, to the human race, and a most inferior progeny to man, filled, thus, with the germs of physical and mental disease, and made much inferior to many, if not most, other animals, except in the invention of destructive machinery and instruments, by which, guided by animal cunning, he alone keeps them now in subjection.

Affection – that feeling which is often now the most degraded and degrading, through the mistaken arts of the priesthood to insure to themselves permanent wealth and power at the expense of all other classes – will become, in the rational state of society, the feeling which will the most elevate and dignify the character of all, blending with these characteristics a feeling that will make elevation and dignity also lovely, so as to create a combined impression of admiration and love, without fear or apprehension of aught repulsive or unkind.

When rational arrangements shall be formed to produce and distribute superior wealth abundantly for all, as wealth might now be produced and distributed – when the character of each individual shall be formed as the character of all now might be formed – and when man shall be governed as man might now be governed – then will the affection which is to make the human race happy, be universally created, and produce perfect love which will cast out all dread, or fear, or doubt, from man to man; and jealousy and revenge will be unknown among the human race; for man will be thus made to become, for the first time in his history, a rational being, whose feelings, thoughts, and conduct, will ever be in harmony; a perfect contrast to the feelings, thoughts, and conduct, of the irrational beings now inhabiting the habitable part of the earth, making each other as miserable as misdirected natural faculties can make them.

The time has arrived for this great change in the progress of humanity to be effected; and when it has been made, this earth will become the terrestrial paradise that has been so often in the imagination of individuals, through so many of the past ages of our ancestors.

Thus will that condition of human happiness be fulfilled, in which arrangements will be made for all to associate with those for whom they have the most regard and the greatest affection.

CHAPTER IX

The means of travelling at pleasure.

THE liberty and power of action, to the greatest extent practicable, under the best arrangements that can be formed for society, are essential to the highest happiness of the human race.

The idea that we are confined against our inclinations within any limits which others may pass, would of necessity be a deduction from our happiness.

And when all shall be, at an early age, made familiar with the past history of nations, and with their present religion, government, laws, institutions, customs, productions, etc, a desire will naturally arise to visit and examine the result upon the formation of character and the happiness of those who live under these varied external circumstances, and especially to compare these varied results produced by erroneous first principles, with the results which they shall have witnessed and experienced under a system founded on true first principles.

When the population of the world shall be enabled to enjoy the full benefit of the Rational System of Society, there will be no difficulty whatever in all, in regular rotation, visiting every part of the world, acquiring personal knowledge of climate, productions, and all things peculiar to every general locality.

Houses, or rather establishments, of rest, entertainment, and occupation, will be everywhere within one or two, or, at the most, three miles of each other, except when the seas are to be navigated to go from one part of the world to another. And as there will be frequent periodical communications between all the countries divided by these waters, there will be every facility for travelling without loss, expense, or inconvenience to any parties. And these changes from establishment to establishment, and these voyages, may always be made parties of instruction and of general benefit, as well as parties of pleasure, to insure high rational enjoyment.

These society establishments or family residences and domains, each for from two to three thousand persons of all ages, will equally belong to all; and when all shall be trained and educated from infancy to be fit inhabitants of these superior domains, any individual will be admitted on arrival, and will find apartments unoccupied, but prepared to receive any brothers or sisters who may arrive, their approach being generally made known by conspicuous telegraphs seen from a distance, or by the new electro-galvanic or the hydraulic telegraph, that parties may not be disappointed when the establishments happen to be full. And in these establishments every brother and sister will find all they may require after they have taken up their residence in them, and entered upon their avocation according to their age. For all will be so trained and educated from birth, as to be most useful in any one of these establishments, as sailors are now immediately at home in any new ship into which they enter.

In the transition state from this old worn-out system to the new, as the services of the comparatively few at first will be all required in preparing these establishments over the country, travelling will be chiefly confined to those who have business to transact in the old world, and to collect facts for useful practical application.

Travelling is now so inconvenient and expensive to the great mass of the people, that few can ever think of taking a long journey; and when, upon some extraordinary occasions, they do venture from home, they too frequently find themselves amidst strangers who feel no interest in promoting their happiness, but who make them conscious of the difference between being at home and with strangers.

The numbers of those who now can leave their homes or business, and who can travel for pleasure, compared with those who are compelled to stay at home from necessity, are few indeed; while, under the Rational System, as soon as it shall be established throughout society, all may conveniently travel without expense, and most beneficially for themselves and for the whole of society. For every member will be everywhere at home, and always, at each establishment, beneficially and pleasantly employed.

The roads of communication from establishment to establishment will be always kept in the best state for occupation, whatever may be the mode of travelling upon them: for the principle of having everything of the best, and always kept in the best condition, will be universally acted upon through every department and ramification of the new world. In short, one of the least difficulties in making the practical arrangements for the new world, will be to make them to enable all its inhabitants 'to travel at pleasure with pleasure,' and without being troubled with luggage of any description.

CHAPTER X

The absence of superstition, supernatural fears, and the fear of death.

WHAT mind is there that can contemplate the horrific miseries which, through all past ages, have been inflicted upon the human race, by superstition, supernatural fears, and the fear of death? These have been the horrors of human existence, the degradation of the human intellects, the powers of the Priesthood of the world, and the secondary cause of the irrationality of the human race.

Superstition, supernatural fears, and the fear of death, are created in the early stages of ignorance and inexperience, and create a dark mental night for man to pass through, before he can perceive the first rays of demonstrable knowledge, which can alone dispel the darkness of that dreadful night, during which men slaughter, plunder, massacre, and murder, each other, like madmen, for they know not what; and during which their language is a language of falsehood, and their whole conduct that of beings who have been made to be passing through a period of the most gross irrationality.

Until man shall be enabled to advance beyond this period of mental infancy, there will be no chance for him to become a reasonable or rational being. By these fears he is now kept the most abject mental slave in every part of the world. Even in Great Britain, said to possess more civil and religious liberty than any other country, its inhabitants, in small towns and villages especially, dare not express their opinions, when they are opposed to the superstitions of the Priesthood, without suffering loss of business or employment, which, to the working classes, is only another mode of depriving them of life. It is time that this period of mental degradation should cease, and that a party should come forward to claim and support the rights of conscience, which are the natural and unalienable rights of the human race, and to assert his mental liberty, that he may become a rational being, and, at length, attain the physical and mental enjoyments of his nature.

The world is even now overrun with superstition, supernatural fears, and the fear of death. The seeds of these, carefully sown in childhood, gradually ripen into a golden harvest of wealth and power for the Priesthood, under all its various names and insane forms and ceremonies.

What has man to do with that which he cannot comprehend, which is incomprehensible to him, and which weakens all the rational powers of his mind?

While man shall remain under the influence of superstition, supernatural fears, or the fear of death, it will be impossible to make him intelligent or good, or for him to have any just pretensions to be considered a rational creature, or otherwise than an ignorant irrational animal, full of vain pretensions to more wisdom than other animals, while, as the great object of all that have life is to be happy, his whole conduct evinces that he is the least rational of any of these existences.

The Jews believe the Christians to speak the language of insanity – the Christians believe the Hindoos to talk this language – the Hindoos believe the Mahomedans to be insane – and, thus, each superstition blinds the mental faculties of its victims, only permitting them to perceive the gross irrationality of all other superstitions.

O man! made blind to the past, present, and future – when will the time arrive that your mad career shall be stayed, and when you will ask yourselves what possible benefit could God or the active powers of nature ever experience from the religious wars, massacres, and murders, of past ages or present times? And what spark of rationality, or grain of common sense, can be discovered in human conflicts about supernatural affairs, impossible for human nature to fathom or comprehend? And why – when we see all organized existences begin to live, then grow, and die – should any be trained to have fears, which make them miserable through life, of their own death? The operations of nature are, from, apparently, a few in number of original elements, to compose unnumbered organized living existences; for these to increase for a longer or shorter period, and then to be decomposed or disorganized, to be again reorganized or composed into other living existences. This appears to be the universal law or order of nature; and why should man be kept ignorant of it, or made in any way to have fears or alarms respecting it? Such proceedings can only tend to make him physically and mentally weak and miserable, and such has hitherto been the effect which has been produced on the human race by the delusions or insane ravings of the Priesthood of the world.

And now – who gains by this system of delusion, insanity, and madness? Not one human being or animal of any kind. Man is made by it cruel to himself, to his own species, and to other animals; when, without it, he might speedily be made a God-like being, of knowledge, benevolence, kindness, and love for the whole creation, and one whose whole delight would arise from making all that have life as happy as the elements of their nature would allow; insuring to all the greatest extent of happiness that our knowledge of nature would admit.

Instead of training man to be afraid of death (for it is altogether a matter of early training), all might be instructed to view it, as it is, as a universal law of nature, unavoidable, and, in all probability, not only thus necessary, but, it may be, highly beneficial in its ultimate consequences to all that have life. Man should, therefore, from early life, be well informed respecting the known laws of nature, made familiar with those immediately influencing himself and his race, and educated to have no fears of that which is unavoidable, but rather to rejoice that, after experiencing one life of rational happiness, he shall, by his decomposition, receive an endless renewal of apparent improved existences. And thus, instead of most uselessly and irrationally embittering one life, and destroying its chance of rational enjoyment, each of these lives may be made highly intellectual, extremely interesting, and full of superior enjoyment.

A sure indication that humanity is approaching the confines of rationality, will be when superstition, supernatural fears, and the fear of death, shall form no part of the education of the human race; and when all these absurdities shall have given place to a direct instruction in the laws of nature, derived, not from the wild imaginations of our ignorant and less experienced ancestors, but from demonstrable, never-changing facts, which remain to-day and for ever the same as hitherto.

And until this change shall be effected, and man shall be thus made rational, he cannot obtain this condition of happiness, or be otherwise than a weak and miserable being.

CHAPTER XI

Full liberty of expressing our thoughts upon all subjects.

No real happiness can be experienced by any individual while he is under mental bondage. The ignorance of our ancestors has placed all men, from the highest to the lowest, under this state of humiliation and degradation. Majesty itself, the highest aristocracy, the most wealthy, the middle, and the lower classes, are all now under the infliction of this degradation. Nor can they escape from this condition of mental bondage until human nature shall be understood, and the causes of our convictions and feelings shall be known, acknowledged, consistently acted upon, and the language of truth, in the simple expressions of our convictions and feelings, shall become the universal language of man. 'Full liberty of expressing our thoughts upon all subjects' is a portion of human happiness to be enjoyed only by our more fortunate descendants, after the human race shall have been rationalized – when man shall be taught to know himself – when all his thoughts and feelings shall be known to be the result of the power which creates organization and life and mind, propensities, and senses, and all that appertain to man and other animals – when it shall be known that our thoughts and feelings have been made vices and virtues solely at the will and under the influence of the Priesthood of the world. Their power, influence, and existence, have arisen from their inventing vices, virtues, and crimes, and making men obedient to these artificial notions which they have promulgated.

In consequence of the Priesthood of the world having made some convictions and some feelings extremely sinful, and others highly meritorious, and as men and women could not avoid having those convictions and feelings which the Priesthood chose to designate as vices and most sinful, and being afraid, on account of the power which the priests gradually acquired over the more ignorant portion of the society, to acknowledge their natural and necessary convictions and feelings, they felt the necessity, that they might not appear to be sinful in the estimation of their neighbours, or be called so by the priests, to begin to falsify their language, which is quite contrary to the natural feelings of humanity, and to say that their feelings and convictions were different from those which nature compelled them to experience. And it is thus that the Priesthood of the world became the father of lies, and have made falsehood and deception universal wherever they have existed; and falsehood and deception prevail now over the world in proportion to the more or less influence and power of the Priesthood. Where they are all-powerful, as they yet are in many small towns and villages, even in England, said to be the land of freedom, there is not one individual among such populations who dares to speak his thoughts when they differ from those taught by the Priesthood, and the whole conversation of these parties is a conventional falsehood, as is, indeed, almost all the verbal intercourse of society. The real thoughts and feelings of men and women are at present unknown, and must remain so as long as merit and demerit, praise and blame, rewards and punishments, shall be awarded by man to any set or kind of thoughts and feelings whatever.

To talk of liberty of mind existing now in any part of the world, is only to exhibit the want of knowledge in those who imagine that such practice could obtain under the errors which pervade the world respecting our power to create our own thoughts and feelings. This most melancholy error meets us at every turn, in all places, and under all circumstances. It has created endless vice, crime, falsehood, and misery, and for the real benefit of no parties, not even for the Priesthood, except in appearance. It is true these latter have obtained wealth, power, and influence, by the invention and support of this error; but all the wealth, power, and influence, which they have obtained at any time in any country, have not secured for them the substantial, steadily increasing happiness which truth, if permitted to be spoken upon all subjects and upon all occasions, would insure in a short period, even to the Priesthood, as well as to all others; – a healthy, joyous happiness which never has been, which never can be, experienced under a system of falsehood.

Man, cowed, and mentally enslaved, under this insane system of falsehood and universal deception, knows not what manner of being he is destined to become. When he shall be relieved from this degrading mental bondage, freed from the fear of man for expressing his unavoidable natural thoughts and feelings, unrestrained by fear of giving offence or producing evil of any kind, and conscious of his rectitude while expressing the simple instincts of his nature, he will be a being almost altogether – in mind, expression of countenance, and even in physical form and action – different from any past or present tribe of human animals.

He will then stand forth a reasonable, rational, truth-speaking, creature, knowing the object of his existence, and how to obtain it; expressing, on all occasions, his pure, unadulterated-with-falsehood thoughts and feelings, as nature makes them to arise. He will thus acquire more real knowledge of man, in one month, from man, than he can now obtain in many years. Men and women know not now the real thoughts and feelings of each other, and are, in consequence, continually committing error upon error, and destroying, often without knowing it, each other's happiness, to an incalculable extent; when, if the practice of truth had been established, a few words of it would prevent the misery and secure the desired happiness.

The population of the world, in its present most irrational state, can form no adequate idea of the extent of evil created, and the loss of happiness sustained, through the system of falsehood now so generally practised by all classes in all countries, and especially among the higher and wealthier portion of the most civilized parts of the world. Or of the increased expense required to lessen but a small part of the many evils which the practice of falsehood hourly produces. The habit of always expressing our thoughts and feelings as our instincts compel us to have them, would create new attitudes and expressions for all, and so superior to those now created by the depreciating influences of mental bondage, and the life-and-death necessity for hiding our thoughts and feelings, that man will appear altogether a different being from the animal whose language is used to hide the natural impressions made on him, physically and mentally, by the instincts of his nature; – instincts which can alone direct him to health of body, ease of mind, and satisfaction with his own existence.

Some nations, such as the British, and their descendants the population of the United States of North America, imagine they now possess what they term civil and religious liberty; while both nations are in the very bondage of mental slavery, both civil and religious. These nominally liberty-loving men and women in the east and west, have so little mental liberty, that they dare not speak to any one what they are obliged to think and feel, and their civil and religious liberty consists in expressing within a small circle, such thoughts and feelings as they know by experience will pass current within that circle. If they infringe these bounds, they are likely to have Lynch law[a] in one country, and fine and imprisonment in the other. And yet they have laws in both countries giving to all, what they call, civil and religious liberty.

Thus is the whole world a farce and a tragedy, in which innumerable parts are acted, and the only character which no one has the hardihood to learn and

[a] Generally, rough popular justice; named after an obscure American judge.

practise is that of a man who will speak the truth, and inform the world what, by the instincts of his nature, he is compelled to think and feels although he cannot have merit or demerit for the one or the other.

Let it, however, be remembered that human happiness is not to be attained, or indeed approached, until such changes shall be made in society as shall not only enable, but shall induce, all, at all times, to speak that which they are obliged, by the unavoidable instincts of their nature, to think and to feel. This is, and must remain, an unchanging condition of human happiness.

When man shall be permitted by man to speak freely and openly to all, that which, alone, is true to him, namely, that which he is compelled to believe and feel while he speaks, then may the human race look forward to and rationally expect the coming of the period described as the Millennium. Truth in look, word, and action, must be the harbinger of this glorious change; but as long as the Priesthood of the word shall have power over the minds of men and women, truth can never become the language of mankind. But let it never be forgotten, that the creation of the Priesthood of the world has been the necessary result of previous circumstances; that they are now formed by society; and that, in the changes to be made for their abolition, society should adopt measures to prevent even a single priest from being injured, if possible, either in mind, body, or estate.

CHAPTER XII

The utmost individual freedom of action, compatible with the permanent good of society.

FREEDOM of action is essential to health and to the full enjoyment of animal and mental existence. It is the natural right of all animals, limited only by their action not being injurious to others.

Human laws have been framed to restrain, and thus to limit, individual and national action; but these have been conceived in ignorance and practised in error of human nature; in consequence they have not, in any country, at any period, attained the object required. And for this obvious reason, that all lawgivers have been ignorant of human nature, and unacquainted with the science of forming society in order to produce abundance of wealth, and with the principles of truth and justice, so as to form beneficial arrangements for its distribution and enjoyment.

Human laws, by every kind of artifice, and on false principles, have been attempted to be made to restrain men who have been deprived of their natural freedom, from injuring those who have deprived them of it, or continue to prevent their regaining it.

As all past and present codes of human laws have been based on false principles, and gross ignorance of human nature, and are opposed to nature's unchanging and unchangeable laws, it is not probable that as long as these laws shall be so based they can produce aught but evil. So long as man shall insanely make laws on the imagined notions that man can believe and feel as he pleases, so long will those laws produce falsehood, vice, crime, and misery, and retain the population of the world in a state of universal deception. With such notions for the foundation of society, and laws made in accordance with them for its government, man must always be formed into an irrational animal, unconscious how to create happiness for himself or others. Where is there now a code of laws in accordance with nature? Where an educational establishment that is not opposed to nature? And is it possible that man can be made to think and act rationally while so educated and governed?

Man can never acquire general freedom of action without injuring others, until he shall be trained from his birth to become a rational being. And when he shall be so trained, there will be no necessity for ill-imagined human laws, which, as no two cases can ever be alike, as no individuals or general circumstances acting upon them can ever be the same, it will ever be impossible to make either just to individuals or beneficial to society.[a]

Full freedom of action cannot with safety be given to man while he shall be trained, as at present, to become an irrational animal, and be governed by laws which pre-suppose him to be such, and which are calculated to keep him in that melancholy condition.

When, on the contrary, he shall be trained from birth to be rational in the use of all his powers and faculties – and, human nature being understood, this would be an easy and pleasant task to perform – and when, also, he shall be governed, through life, in accordance with the laws of human nature, then may man be left by man in full freedom of individual action; for he would be most careful at all times through his life to injure no one; for his continued pleasure and highest enjoyment would arise from his constant practice of doing all the good in his power to others and to society. When men shall be trained to be rational, and society shall be alone governed by the rational laws of nature – the only laws that ever can be rational – then will man become and continue a rational being, and all his actions, unrestrained by human laws, will always be rational, and consequently tend continually to promote the well-being and happiness of himself and of all society.

Until this education and these laws shall be established, man cannot be

[a] This line of reasoning probably owes something to Godwin. See *An Enquiry Concerning Political Justice* (3rd edn, 1798), Bk 7, ch. 4.

permitted to have full freedom of action, without creating constant collisions and injurious contests; and while he must be debarred – on account of being made, through ignorance, to grow up into an irrational animal – of his natural freedom of action, which he will ever ardently desire, he cannot acquire the happiness which human nature may be made to attain; and without this freedom of action, one of the conditions of human happiness will be deficient. But the wisdom that will open the book of nature to enable man to read and to understand it, will remove this cause of error, and prepare the way for man to enjoy his natural freedom of action, not only without injury to others, but most beneficially for all individuals, and, of course, for society.

From what has been written it must become evident that this full freedom of action can be advantageously obtained for the first generation that shall be made to become rational beings.

CHAPTER XIII

To have the chartacter formed for us to express the truth only upon all occasions, and to have pure charity for the feelings, thoughts and conduct, of all mankind, and a sincere good-will for every individual of the human race.

UNTIL this change in the condition of the human race can be accomplished, it will be impossible for man to be made happy. And this change can be made only by the abandonment of the errors in the principles and practices which have arisen from the supposition that man possesses the power to believe and feel as he likes, and that there is merit or demerit in either belief or feeling, any more than there is merit or demerit in the instincts of any other animal. We are made as they are made from the elements of nature; we are governed by the laws of these elements as they are governed by them. We are organized or composed, disorganized or decomposed, and reorganized or recomposed, in like manner as all other animals and material things are composed, decomposed, and recomposed, apparently eternally, without beginning or termination. And for being thus composed, decomposed, or recomposed, with the qualities possessed by or given to each compound, there can be neither merit nor demerit; – each must act, of necessity, according to the qualities received by each, and the circumstances which are made to act upon them. But all existences upon earth, with conscious sensation, desire to be happy; and such feeling, it is probable, pervades the universe of life.

Man, then, desires universally to be happy, and his organization has been made, by some cause or causes, at present undiscovered by him, to require certain conditions to secure the greatest amount of happiness to each individual, and to the race, through succeeding generations.

These conditions are those which have been described in this part of 'The Book,' and those which will be explained in the succeeding chapters; but without the attainment of the condition stated at the head of this chapter, the other conditions will for ever remain unattainable.

Until circumstances shall arise to form our characters in such a manner that, under every and all circumstances in which we can be placed, we shall have no motive to express, by look, word, or action, a falsehood, or anything approaching to it, happiness will be unattainable. Truth, the pure and simple expression of the convictions and feelings which we are compelled to have, by the nature which the operations of nature force us to receive, is alone competent to give us knowledge of ourselves and of humanity; – to give us health of body and mind; – to produce permanent inward satisfaction; – to withdraw all anger, ill-will, jealousies, and revenge; – to create genuine charity for the thoughts, feelings and conduct, of each; – and to implant and nourish the feeling of sincere good-will for every individual of the human race.

It is the unmixed language of truth alone that can create these individual and universal feelings and conduct; and it is a correct knowledge of our own individual nature, of human nature, and of the general laws of nature applicable to man, which can alone create minds with power sufficient to live in a perpetual atmosphere of truth. It is the qualities which simple genuine truth can alone create, that will form in us a knowledge of what is necessary to our happiness, and the moral courage to act uniformly on that knowledge.

But if human happiness depends upon this character being formed for all individuals, the question arises – 'Can it be formed? are the means in our power to effect this great good for mankind?'

It is perhaps the most gratifying of all reflections to know that the science has been discovered by which, without failure or mistake, this character may be insured to all that shall be born after the science shall have been made familiar to the public and the practice understood.

Yes, it is true that man may be trained from infancy to know no other language than that of truth; – to have no other feelings for all of his race than pure genuine charity for the thoughts, feelings, and conduct of all, of every clime and colour; – and to acquire a spirit of good-will and sincere kindness for his fellow-man, in whatever quarter or district of the world he may be found. This is the spirit which can alone insure peace upon earth, make man a rational being, and secure him prosperity and happiness.

But the character of truth, charity, and kindness, has never yet been formed for man; it is not now known in any part of the earth. The Priesthood of the world have prevented its formation, and they have made it unavoidable that the opposite character – that of falsehood, uncharitableness, and unkindness – should universally prevail, as it does at present over the whole earth. The

Priesthood and the world will now soon become conscious of the great error which has been committed and the evil of continuing it. They will now discover that they are all individually most severe sufferers in consequence, and they will become ready to effect the change for their own benefit and for the permanent advantage of their children and descendants. It is a law of human nature that man desires to be happy; as soon, therefore, as the Priesthood of the world shall be enabled to understand how much their profession is destructive of their own happiness, of that of their children, as well as of the whole population of the world, they will abandon it, as being productive only of imbecility in some, arrogant presumption and violent passions in others, and error, falsehood, and uncharitableness in all; besides being a total stop to the improvement and happiness of the human race. And certain it is, that until the character of truth, charity, and kindness, can be made the universal character of man, full and complete happiness cannot be experienced by any; for the knowledge that any of our fellow-creatures are inferior or less perfect than they can be made by man, will prevent the full enjoyment of the happiness of men made to become rational beings.

CHAPTER XIV

To reside in a society whose laws, institutions, and arrangements, well organized and well governed, are all in unison with the laws of human nature.

THE misery of the human race has been increased to an incalculable extent by the laws, institutions, and arrangements of society having been based on principles opposed to the laws of human nature.

They have all arisen from errors which have introduced falsehood and insincerity through all the intercourse of society. Man now knows not what man is, by reason of the universal system of deception which has been generated by laws, institutions, and arrangements, directly opposed to man's nature.

Where can we find a code of laws, ancient or modern, not based on the supposition that man is a totally different being from that which facts now demonstrate him to be?

In what part of the world can we find institutions based on a knowledge of what humanity is now proved to be?

In what country, at any period, have national arrangements been formed, except on the belief that man forms his own convictions and feelings and his own character, so as to make it right and just that he should be praised or blamed, rewarded or punished, have merit or demerit, for what he thinks and feels, and for what he is, physically, mentally, morally and practically?

Had it been known to our early ancestors that the universe is governed by instinct – that man, as well as all that have life, is governed by instinct – that he believes and feels, of necessity, by the instinct of his nature – and that his whole character is formed through the operation of these instincts, we should long since have had a state of society the reverse of that which has been alone known up to the present moment. We should now have a language of simplicity and truth – a spirit of charity – a conduct of kindness – and a cordial union throughout the family of man.

There would have been no religious differences – no party politics – no rancorous divisions – no wars or contests – no poverty or the fear of it – no jealousy or revenge – no one desirous to take from others; but all would have been anxious to contribute to the general well-being and prosperity of society, without knowing limits of kindred, country, or clime.

Instead of our ideas and feelings and knowledge being individualized, and regularly trained to become ignorantly selfish, universal ideas, feelings, and knowledge, would have been created, and man would have made an unit of the family of man, each cordially united to the others, through the whole extent of its members. The poverty, divisions, vices, and crimes, now so prevalent through society, would have been unknown; and the past history of man, instead of being a regular narrative of opposing parties, murdering, plundering, and making each other as miserable as nature would admit, would have been the history of rational beings, whose sole object would have been to produce the most happiness and the least misery to each other, through the whole extent of the population of the earth.

Until men shall understand how to make the laws, institutions, and arrangements by which the future generations shall have their characters well formed, physically, mentally, morally, and practically, and shall be enabled to understand human nature, its instincts, and its powers, and how to acquire the spirit of charity and kindness, the human race cannot be made to enjoy happiness; it will be deficient of one of the important ingredients requisite to insure its happiness; and until the laws, institutions, and arrangements of man, shall be made in accordance with the now ascertained laws of human nature, it will be a vain hope to expect that man can be made happy.

Such being the case, we have to consider what are the laws, institutions, and arrangements which men can make for their government, that will be in accordance with the laws of their nature.

These laws will be few, simple, and easy to be understood; and of a general character, yet sufficient for all practical purposes. The following may comprise all that is necessary for A RATIONAL CODE OF LAWS: –

1st. That, seeing that each child is born ignorant and without experience, every human being, male and female, shall be as well trained and educated from birth, physically, mentally, morally, and practically, as the knowledge of well-forming the human character possessed at the time will admit.

2nd. That all shall be actively well-employed, physically and mentally, according to age and capacity, through life; idleness being injurious to the individual, and unjust to society.

3rd. That all shall be well lodged, fed, clothed, and surrounded from birth to death by superior circumstances only, so far as society unitedly can create superior circumstances.

4th. That, in addition to the language of its parents, every child shall be well instructed in one general language, that this may become the language of truth and of the world.

5th. That, if it should ever occur among beings so trained, educated, employed and placed, that differences of opinion or feelings could arise to require interference of others to adjust, such differences – which are deemed almost impossible to occur after one generation shall be thus formed and placed to become rational in their thoughts, feelings, and conduct – shall be adjusted by arbitrators previously chosen, who will render all magistrates, lawyers, and courts of law, wholly unnecessary.

And 6th. That, as any parties thus trained, educated employed, and placed, who should act in opposition to the happiness of society, individually or generally, could do so only by being afflicted with mental disease, individuals so acting shall be placed within a house of recovery, treated as mildly as the case will permit, and kept no longer within the house and its immediate external inclosures, than is necessary to reproduce a sound state of health.

These are the only laws that will ever be required in a rational state of society.

The institutions will all be in accordance with these laws, and emanate from them, as the arrangements of society will emanate from the institutions.

The institutions will be to well educate and employ one and all, according to their physical and mental powers, so as temperately to exercise both, to keep body and mind in the best state of health and cheerful good spirits; in order that life may be extended and happiness enjoyed to the latest period that humanity will admit.

The arrangements will comprise the means to produce the greatest amount of the most valuable wealth, in the shortest period, consistent with the health and rational enjoyment of the producers; – to distribute this wealth most beneficially for all; – to assist, in connection with the previous institutions, to form the best character, physical, mental, moral and practical, for each individual, from birth; – to well govern all, locally and generally, without force or fraud, and solely by reason and kindness, based on an accurate knowledge of human nature and of the science of society.

These are the only institutions and arrangements which the world will require, to be formed into a terrestrial paradise, and its inhabitants into rational and superior beings.

And these institutions and arrangements may be formed and conducted so as to insure an incalculable increase of happiness to the human race, at a greatly reduced cost of materials and labour, compared with the random waste, misapplication of means, and misdirection of the most valuable and enormous powers, under the present most immoral, chaotic, and miserable system.

The laws, institutions, and arrangements, will all be in accordance with the laws of human nature and of nature generally. They will always aid nature, while the present system always opposes nature.

Under this change those who, for the time, govern, and those who are governed, will be the same in knowledge, in feeling, in interest, and in the objects to be obtained. There will be no open or secret opposition or contests of any description; there will be but one will between the governed and those who govern for the time being. Neither will anything be hidden by the one party from the other; for secrecy will be unknown throughout the whole transactions of beings thus united by knowledge, interest, and the desire to increase the happiness of all. The human race in this respect will become as little children, whose thoughts and feelings are freely and simply and innocently expressed to all who ask, or indeed, are unhidden to all who see them.

The happiness to be experienced by society when it shall be governed by laws, institutions, and arrangements, in accordance with human nature, and well administered, will produce a state of existence upon earth, of which few, if any, are competent to form a true conception. When these shall be united in practice, everything will proceed from a solid foundation, so systematically, regularly, and easily, that all will, after a time, believe that these proceedings are so natural that they could never have been otherwise. But experience has convinced the present race of man that all first discoveries are rude, complicated, expensive, and imperfect; while subsequent experience improves by simplifying the operations, reducing the expense, and making the results more perfect.

This is the process now in progress from the crude, complex, extravagant, and miserable system in which the world has been hitherto involved, to the more simple, economical, effective, and happiness-producing system, about to supersede the former.

When the two systems can be contrasted, the difference will be so striking – indeed so far beyond all comparison between the old and the new – that all must gradually abandon the old, while the great majority will be most eager to obtain and secure all the advantages of the new.

And assuredly man cannot be placed in a position to enjoy all the happiness of which human nature is susceptible, until he shall be enabled to reside in a society whose laws, institutions, and arrangements, well organized and well governed, shall be all in unison with the laws of human nature.

CHAPTER XV

The happiness of all that have life.

AFTER man shall have attained all the requisites to insure the health, unity, knowledge, charity, kindness, and general prosperity of his race, seeing or knowing that all that man can do for man has been done over the extent of the globe, his mind will be expanded, his sympathies will be increased, his knowledge of nature will be enlarged, and his desire to promote happiness will be unlimited as long as means shall offer to add to it among all that have life or conscious sensation.

Man will not then wantonly destroy the life of any animal, or give unnecessary pain to any conscious being that Nature has produced by her, at present, mysterious means, and for her, at present mysterious purposes.

By the previous appliances explained in this book man must become intelligent, charitable, and kind to man; and when he shall have been made intelligent, charitable, and kind, to all of his own species, he will become truly good, and he will not merely ardently desire to remove pain and suffering from all that have life, but he will earnestly exert himself to secure for all animal creation as much enjoyment as his existence and theirs will at the same time admit.

Man does not yet know how much of his ill-formed habits contribute to create animal misery and produce suffering to beings as sensitive to pain as himself, or in some cases, perhaps, more so, while in others it may be less. He has been trained in principles and practices which have made him cruel to his own species and to the animal creation generally. To be made rational he will be trained in principles and practices so different that he will be always kind and charitable to his own species, and, so far as is consistent with the progress and well-being of the human race, to all that has conscious existence. His desire will be made to be to withdraw the causes of misery from all that is conscious of pain, and to be an active agent upon earth to produce the most happiness to all that have life.

A rational being can never have pleasure in seeing or knowing that any other being is unhappy, and much less can such a being be a willing agent to cause the misery. Nor can man, while he knows there is pain experienced which he can remove or assist in removing, or pleasure unenjoyed which he can give or assist in giving, ever enjoy the full extent of the pleasurable sensations which he is capable of receiving.

Man has been especially formed with powers, when he shall be made rational, capable of giving and receiving, on a most extended scale, compared with his present position and proceedings, a high degree of happiness and enjoyment to his own and to other species; as in his irrational state of existence he has been equally well adapted to create and inflict misery on his own and other species.

The difference between man being an active agent to produce misery or to produce happiness, is the difference between a most inferior and a most superior being, or, in the language of superstition, between a terrestrial demon and an angel.

As soon as man shall be made rational, his pleasures, his happiness, his highest and most exquisite enjoyments, will arise from his active agency to produce happiness upon earth, not only without considering of what class, sect, party, country, or colour, his own species may be, but without considering of what species the living existences may be, so that the greatest amount of earthly enjoyment may be obtained for all that have life.

To effect this result, high intelligence and sound judgment will be required, as well as a spirit of universal benevolence. But the training and education to accomplish all that can be expected upon our globe will be secured to all by the superior acquirements and rational minds that will be given to every infant from birth. 'There shall be none to hurt or destroy throughout the whole earth.'[a]

And assuredly man cannot enjoy the full extent of the happiness of which human nature is susceptible, until he shall be so trained, educated, and placed, that he shall both desire, and be actively engaged in promoting, the happiness of all that have life.

END OF THIRD PART

[a] See for example Daniel 7:14.

THE BOOK

OF THE

NEW MORAL WORLD,

EXPLANATORY OF

THE RATIONAL RELIGION.

BY ROBERT OWEN.

TRUTH WITHOUT MYSTERY, MIXTURE OF ERROR, OR FEAR OF MAN, CAN ALONE EMANCIPATE THE HUMAN RACE FROM SIN AND MISERY.

PART FOURTH.

London:
PUBLISHED FOR THE SOCIETY, BY
J. WATSON, 5, PAUL'S ALLEY, PATERNOSTER ROW;
AND ALL BOOKSELLERS.

1844.

THE BOOK

OF THE

NEW MORAL WORLD

FOURTH PART

THE PRINCIPLES AND PRACTICE OF THE RATIONAL RELIGION

1st. That all facts yet known to man indicate that there is an external or an internal cause of all existences, by the fact of their existence; that this all-pervading cause of motion and change in the universe, is that Incomprehensible Power, which the nations of the world have called God, Jehovah, Lord, etc, etc, etc; but that the facts are yet unknown to man which define what that hitherto Incomprehensible Power is.

2nd. That it is a law of Nature obvious to our senses, that the internal and external character of all that have life upon the earth, if formed for them and not by them; that in accordance with this law, the internal and external character of man is formed FOR him, and not BT him; and that the knowledge of this fact, with its all-important consequences, will necessarily create in every one a new, sublime, and pure spirit of charity for the convictions, feelings, and conduct of the human race, and dispose them to be kind to all that have life – seeing that this varied life is formed by the same Incomprehensible Power that has created human nature, and given man his peculiar faculties.

3rd. That it is man's highest interest to acquire an accurate knowledge of those circumstances which produce EVIL to the human race, and those which produce GOOD; and to exert all his powers to remove the former from society, and to create around it the latter only.

4th. That this invaluable practical knowledge can be acquired solely through an extensive search after *truth*, by an accurate, patient, and unprejudiced inquiry into *facts* as developed by Nature.

5th. That man can never attain to a state of superior and permanent happiness, until he shall be surrounded by those external circumstances which will train him, from birth, to feel pure charity and sincere affection towards the whole of his species, – to speak the truth only, on all occasions, – and to regard with a merciful and kind disposition all that has life.

6th. That such superior knowledge and feelings can never be given to man under those institutions of society which have been founded on the mistaken supposition that man forms his *feelings* and *convictions* by his *will*, and, therefore, has merit or demerit, or deserves praise or blame, or reward or punishment for them.

7th. That under the institutions formed in accordance with the Rational System of Society, this superior knowledge, and these superior dispositions, may be given to the whole of the human race, without chance of failure, except in case of organic disease.

8th. That in consequence of this superior knowledge, and these superior dispositions, the contemplation of Nature will create in every mind, feelings of high adoration, too sublime and pure to be expressed in forms or words, for that Incomprehensible Power which acts in and through all Nature, everlastingly composing, decomposing, and recomposing the material of the universe, producing the endless variety of life, of mind, and of organized form.

9th. That the Practice of the National Religion will therefore consist in promoting, to the utmost of our power, the well-being and happiness of every man, woman, and child, without regard to their class, sect, party, country, or colour; and its Worship, in those inexpressible feelings of wonder, admiration, and delight, which, when man is surrounded by superior circumstances only, will naturally arise from the contemplation of the Infinity of space, of the Eternity of duration, of the Order of the universe, and of that Incomprehensible Power, by which the atom is moved, and the aggregate of Nature is governed.

CHAPTER I

'The religions, so called, of the world, have divided nation from nation, and man from man, from the earliest known period of history to the present. True religion must, on the contrary, unite man to man, and nation to nation, until the human race shall become as one family, united in feeling and interest, equal in education and condition according to age, and governed solely by charity and love, based on a knowledge of the sciences of human nature and of society, as explained in the first and second parts of this book.'

It may be here stated, as the subject is so important to all who are interested in the permanent happiness of the human race, that hitherto, the subject of which man knows the least, and which remains beyond the comprehension of his faculties, has been made, through ignorance, the chief study and business of his existence. In consequence, he has ever been in the path of gross error, and has gone astray from the beginning, consuming his time in doing that which he ought not to have done for his health, peace, and happiness, and leaving undone that which would have insured him health, wealth, peace, and a continued advance in knowledge and rational enjoyment. The religions of the world have confused the mind, destroyed the understanding, and given a false direction to the feelings of the human race. They have taught men to call good evil, and evil good, changed the natural healthy propensities of humanity into vile and ferocious passions, and misdirected all the faculties of man, making him an enemy to himself and to his race. Until the eyes of the world can be opened to enable men to see the errors, absurdities, and follies of all these religions, so called, it will be vain to expect any rational conduct from any people or government, or that either of them can become wise, good, and happy.

When once the public mind of the world can be disabused on this subject, so as to enable it to reason calmly and justly respecting the past and the present, and to see facts as they exist in nature, and not distorted by the misdirected imaginations of any of the varied and opposing religions of the world; there will be no real difficulty in introducing truth, knowledge, charity, kindness, among all ranks and descriptions of men. These religions stand in the way of making one step towards truth, knowledge, superior conduct, and happiness. They guard the road to these virtues, armed with the weapons of ignorance and superstition, and threaten vengeance to all who attempt to enter upon it. In fact, they ever have been, now are, and while they shall be allowed to influence and direct human affairs, they ever will be, engines of power to make men fools or hypocrites, and will remain the bane and curse of humanity.

But how are these hydras of mischief to be destroyed without a renewal of all the crimes and sufferings produced by the crusades of one system of madness to oppose another; by which hosts of human beings have slaughtered each other and inflicted all the crimes and miseries of the most ferocious warfare, in order that the superstitions of the cross or the crescent might be victorious over all the rational faculties of humanity? And all this rancour of the most fiendish vengeance, created and maintained by myriads to the death, for the honour and glory of a Being said to be a God of love, of justice, of charity, and of mercy, and the essence of all wisdom, power, and goodness!!! And yet this Being, Power, Essence, or whatever name may be given to the cause of all that has been, is, or may be caused – remains to this day as incomprehensible to man as when the first man was murdered, with the impious imagination that the deed was done to support the honour and add to the glory of that Power which no man possessing the slightest approach to common sense will now say he can comprehend.

While man shall have his faculties so destroyed as to be made conscientiously to believe that by anything he can do, *he* can honour or glorify a Power unknown and incomprehensible to him, or by leaving anything undone, he can anger or in any manner affect such Power, it is proof to demonstration that he has not been made a rational creature, and that he has yet to acquire the rudiments of the knowledge of his own nature, before he can learn what manner of being *he* is, or what is the true character of all humanity.

CHAPTER II

'That all facts yet known to man indicate that there is an external or an internal cause of all existences, by the fact of their existence; that this all-pervading cause of motion and change in the Universe, is that Incomprehensible Power which the nations of the world have called God, Jehovah, Lord, etc, etc, etc: but that the facts are yet unknown to man which define what that hitherto Incomprehensible Power is.'

FROM facts which no experienced and unprejudiced mind will deny, it appears to our senses, that there is an unceasing composition, decomposition, and recomposition, always in progress upon the earth; and we naturally infer, without, however, having more than plausible conjecture to guide our supposition, that a similar process obtains throughout the universe.

This knowledge, limited as it is, has been derived by very slow degrees, through ages of wild imaginations, and most random conjectures.

Upon all subjects connected with universal causes, effects, and operations, the human faculties have been hitherto unable to acquire such knowledge of facts, as can give any satisfactory results to their most extended investigations. The wisest course, therefore, for man to adopt, is at once to admit the extent of his ignorance as to the *cause* of all things, and its qualities, or motives, or intentions; if, indeed, motives and intentions as they are found to exist in human nature, exist in such cause. By admitting our ignorance, the ground is cleared from the wild and random imaginations of our poor deluded ancestors, before they had been trained to observe and carefully to investigate facts, and to draw only self-evident deductions from well-ascertained facts. And if we are now to make any progress in real knowledge, we must abandon all imaginations *unsupported* by facts, and especially all those which are *opposed* to facts unknown to change during the past history of our race.

When the wild conjectures and now evident prejudices, derived from the false education of our more remote as well as immediate ancestors, can be abandoned, and the mind left free to make the most of the best authenticated facts, obtained through the past period of human existence, the probability, even amounting to the approach of certainty, appears to be:

1st. That the Universe, the materials it contains, and the Power, whence proceed motion, life, and knowledge – composition, decomposition, and recomposition, with all the action within the Universe (if the term *within* can be applied to that which can have no bounds,) are ETERNAL, or could not have had a commencement, and can have no termination.

2nd. That the Universe, these materials, this Power, how these actions arise, are continued, and their future results, are all alike hidden from the human faculties; and that, until new facts shall be discovered, it is no more than an amusing exercise of those faculties to imagine or conjecture, or to predicate anything respecting either the one or the other.

3rd. That for any human beings to pretend to know, correctly, anything respecting the Universe, the materials it contains, the power that directs and controls them, the will, intention, motives, objects, or qualities of that Power, or why this apparent eternal composition, decomposition, and recomposition proceed, is a proof of their utter ignorance of these matters, respecting which they have been made to become insane or hypocrites.

4th. That this insanity and hypocrisy have created miseries to the past generations of men, beyond all human calculation and conception, and that at this day they are the only obstacles to the progress of knowledge, to the advance of all the superior qualities of humanity, to the attainment by all individuals of high virtues, and to the progressive happiness of our race.

5th. That this gross insanity and hypocrisy, which our ancestors have unwittingly transmitted to the present generation, must, by some means or other, be stayed and overcome, or there will be no chance for improvement and happiness to man.

Experiencing this misery, and now plainly perceiving the immediate cause of it, the question for the consideration of all the nations of the world now is; – How is this gross insanity and hypocrisy to be stayed and overcome with the least evil to those poor creatures thus made insane or hypocrites? Or, how can the change from insanity and hypocrisy, which have been made so general, be effected in the shortest period, with the least evil to all nations and people?

Surely, by stating in clear and distinct, yet in mild terms, the whole truth, as far as it is known, upon these matters; and by avoiding all personal blame to the poor deceived individuals who have been, by the laws of their nature, compelled to become insane or hypocrites upon these subjects; subjects so far beyond their capacities to comprehend.

It is with this view that we give the simple statement which appears to the head of this chapter, 'That all facts yet known to man indicate that there is an external or an internal cause of all existences, by the fact of their existence; that this all-pervading cause of motion and change in the universe, is that Incomprehensible Power which the nations of the world' call by some name which they hold in reverence, and to which all the actions of the universe are referred.

Now it is evident that this Power, whatever it may ultimately be discovered to be, either foresees and determines all things – past, present, and to come, in the wisest and best manner, from universal knowledge, or that all the changes in the universe are the results of necessary chains of events, one link succeeding another in endless succession; and in either of these cases, for man to concern himself about this Power, hitherto totally incomprehensible to him, and to make himself and all his fellow-creatures miserable by such proceedings, is the very essence of irrationality, and exhibits, in the most glaring point of view, a total absence of all approach to the first indications of common sense, or sound judgment that can lead to a superior and a rational state of society.

Of what possible importance can it be to this Incomprehensible Power what man thinks or does in reference to it? He either acts in accordance with its laws, or in opposition to them, if such an absurdity can be for one moment admitted. If in accordance with its laws, then why make ourselves responsible and miserable for that which is unavoidable and beyond our control? If we do not act in accordance with the laws of this Power – whence our power of action, and from what source is it derived? It is evident we do not make ourselves, understand ourselves, or create our own motives to action. Why, then, lay any stress on any imaginary notions respecting a Power which is yet wholly unknown to us? Why, in the name of the first approach to the elements of reason, should we make ourselves and others miserable about that of which, hitherto, men have had no knowledge, no not even the slightest rational conception? We are conscious that those things around us, palpable to our senses, exist – but how they are made to exist, or why exist, or why so many living things having the faculty of feeling pleasure or pain, should exist, and experience, during their lives, so much suffering of body and mind, we are yet totally ignorant; and it is a proof of the irrational state in which our ancestors and ourselves have lived, that we and they should have spent so much valuable time, and so many means of happiness in endeavouring to find out and fathom that which, so far, has been made incomprehensible to our faculties, and from which efforts misery only has been the result. It is now evident that this course of action must be altogether abandoned before there can be any chance of the human race becoming rational, or that it should enjoy anything approaching to the happiness which it desires, and which appears within reach as soon as this ignorance can be overcome.

What advance in real knowledge is made by men giving to this Power any name, or all the names that nations have given to it? – or by multiplying and extolling its fanciful attributes? Have these multiplied terms, or these aggregates of imaginary attributes, added one iota to human knowledge or happiness? Are not the most superstitious men and women over the whole world at this moment the most ignorant, imbecile, or furious of all the animal creation? Are they not the most inconsistent and irrational of all living creatures? Is there anything too absurd for them to imagine, or too ridiculous for them to say or do? While under these unfortunate impressions – most horrible if they were true – that a Being should make other beings when and how he liked, and then, having made them to please himself, and having placed them where he liked, and given them a will to think and act as they liked, and yet that they could not do anything contrary to his pre-ordained decrees; and then for thinking and acting in accordance with eternal fore-known knowledge, they are, after a temporary existence of a few years, to be tortured without hope of cessation for a moment of time, or future relief from this torment after millions of ages of never-ceasing suffering, is a notion so degrading to all power, and so destructive of every idea of justice, mercy, wisdom, or goodness, that it is not possible for any, except beings whose faculties have been deranged to the utmost extent of derangement, to entertain such gross and horrible notions of any existence; but to attribute infinite wisdom and goodness to any such existence, exceeds any degree of madness that can enter into a mind not totally deranged in all its reasoning functions. And that which is still more extraordinary is, that these most insane and horrible conceptions should be gravely taught by men called learned, reasonable, and sensible, when all that they all know, when all their knowledge is united, consists in the simple fact, that a Power, to them unknown, and altogether incomprehensible to man, causes all the effects and changes which have been known and unknown to man and throughout the universe.

All who possess powers of reflection, and who can reason in the most ordinary manner, admit that the Power which acts throughout the universe is to them incomprehensible, – they know not its form, or mode of existence, or means of action. They only know that its power must be in all places at the same time; but what the universe is, what are the elements, their qualities, powers, and extent, within or composing it, no man knows: facts have not yet been discovered by man to give him more than wild conjecture upon these matters, about which those with deranged intellect speak as fluently as though they knew these matters familiarly, and the causes of all things, while they are totally blind to the cause of everything. From the past history of the human race, from the present condition of man over the world, it is evident 'that the facts are yet unknown to man which define what that Incomprehensible Power is,' which is the primary cause of all motion, life, mind, and their consequences, throughout the universe.

CHAPTER III

'That it is a law of nature obvious to our senses, that the internal and external character of all that have life upon the earth, is formed *for* them, and not *by* them; that, in accordance with this law, the internal and external character of man is formed *for* him, and not *by* him; and that the knowledge of this fact, with its all-important consequences, will necessarily create in every one a new, sublime, and pure spirit of charity for the convictions, feelings, and conduct of the human race, and dispose them to be kind to all that have life – seeing that this varied life is formed by the same Incomprehensible Power that has created human nature, and given man his peculiar faculties.'

As soon as the human mind shall be delivered from the ignorance of the infancy of humanity, during which it is filled with the monstrosities of a wild, crude, inexperienced imagination, uncorrected and undirected by any accurately known facts or laws of that nature of which humanity forms a part, or one link of an eternal chain, the beginning and termination of which exist not, – it will be obvious, by the examination of facts, that the organizations of all that have life upon the earth are formed *for* them, by a Power unknown to the individual organizations thus formed. That this process is yet a secret of nature hidden from the human race, and that all the knowledge yet acquired on the subject is some acquaintance with the processes by which these, to man, extraordinary effects are produced. These processes appear to the human faculties to commence, proceed, and terminate in the full-formed organizations, by uniform changes, which men have called laws of nature. These laws have now been discovered to some extent, and men can so far act upon them as to interfere with their original or first known processes, and thus produce a material change in the combinations of the several qualities composing some of these, to man, wonderful compounds of nature; yet not such a change as to alter the general character, but only the individual character of the organization. Thus men, by studying the general laws of animal life among those animals domesticated and submitted to their continual observation and inspection, have acquired a knowledge of the modes by which a material change can be made in the qualities of the dog, sheep, cattle, horses, asses, etc, etc; and there can be no doubt that an attention to human nature, like that which has been given to other animal nature in this respect, would open a wide field for the improvement of the infant and matured organization of the human race; for such a change in this respect, with regard to the internal and external man, that all the inferior or misery-producing qualities of the human race may be gradually made to cease to exist in humanity, and all the superior ones combined and carried to a much higher elevation, so as to form man into a rational and greatly superior being, compared to his past and present existence; to become far superior, physically, mentally, morally, and practically, and most likely to attain such powers of improved combination as should extend the life of each individual organization greatly beyond its present general duration.

But whatever the organizations of men may have been hitherto, or whatever they may be made to become, still each organization has been formed at its birth *for* each one, without its knowledge, consent, or control; and to talk of its being bad or good by nature, or to make human laws to punish or reward artificially individuals so formed, are acts of pure insanity, and could never have been thought of and introduced into practice, except by beings who were in a state of infant process, slowly passing from an irrational mental condition towards another state, in which the seeds of rationality might be received and allowed by degrees to germinate and grow into full rationality.

The rudiments of the most valuable knowledge that man can acquire are those respecting the laws of his own formation, as far as they can be traced with accuracy and certainty. And to know that the internal organization and external character of each individual are formed *for* him, and that adult man, and especially men formed into a society, united to produce all practical excellence and happiness to the human race, can most materially influence the qualities of the internal organization and external character of every one, is an attainment of inestimable value to the human race; and which knowledge, when it shall be farther increased by the acquirements of the sciences, to enable the adults accurately to understand all the best means by which to improve each internal organization and external character, will place the human race in the most enviable of sublunary conditions; for then man will be advanced to that state in which the adults of the race will be enabled to ensure the happiness of the rising or succeeding generations, to the termination of human existence upon the earth.

This knowledge will new-form the human race, regenerate man, give him a new mind, dissolve all his old false associations of ideas, extract them from the existing old erroneously-formed and filled minds, and open a new world to the human faculties; a new world, which shall change their thoughts, feelings, and conduct, withdraw all notions of force or fraud, and make truth alone the universal language of man, and justice, charity, and love the sole conduct of the human race.

Has a slight glimpse been yet obtained of the never-ending, all-important consequences that will arise to the eternal family of man, from the knowledge that the character of each is formed *for*, and not *by* the individual?

No! Not a human being has ever yet been competent to receive the idea, and follow it, step by step, to all its legitimate and most certain consequences. The discovery of the general law of gravity has been considered a most important addition to human knowledge, and so undoubtedly it is, as are the discoveries of all previously unknown general laws of nature; but what is the importance of this material law, in comparison with the mental law of the principle, by which the internal organization, and external character of man *are* formed, and the means by which both may hereafter be *well*-formed, and thereby the permanent progressive happiness of humanity be secured, as long as humanity itself shall exist?

What is the rule, and where are the figures, by which this difference can be calculated, and its full value be estimated?

Man is irrational and miserable without this knowledge; rational, progressively improving, and always happy, with it.

In what words, or by what means, shall this difference be expressed?

It is the difference between an earthly pandemonium, inhabited by insane demons, whose delight has been to oppose, traduce, vilify, rob, and murder each other, for the love of God; and an earthly paradise, in which no one of those insanities will exist, but in which all will earnestly and affectionately endeavour to increase the well-being, and promote the happiness of each; and in which, charity, kindness, love, and truth, will be alone known, and be ever united actively to advance all in every kind of excellence and knowledge, until the earth shall be filled with goodness and wisdom, and man shall truly rejoice in his lengthened existence. Here, then, in this new course, will the path be opened in which will be found the germs of 'that sublime and pure charity for the convictions, feelings, and conduct of the human race, which will dispose them' – nay, compel them, through the laws of necessity, – 'to be kind to all that have life, seeing that this varied life is formed by the same Incomprehensible Power that has organized human nature, and given man his peculiar faculties.'

With the knowledge accurately ascertained, and received without doubt into the mind, that the internal organization of man is created for him, without his consent, knowledge, or control, and that his external character is formed for him by the society and external circumstances which surround him from birth – that he is compelled to entertain the impressions which force upon him his convictions and his feelings, and that his conduct necessarily emanates from his convictions or his feelings, when opposed to each other, or from both when united, – how could motives to falsehood, the bane of human existence, ever arise, or anger, ill-will, violence, wars, plunder and murder, jealousy, revenge, contest, or competition, avarice, or any desire for individual possessions, privileges, or advantages?

These, as well as all the other unenumerated evils of past and present society, have, one and all, arisen immediately or more remotely from the insane idea, that man formed his own character, and was responsible to the causes which created and formed it, for what these causes irresistibly compelled it to become. Hence the endless and senseless superstitions of the human race in its infancy of ignorance, as to all the fixed laws of its nature; hence the reign of insanity for so many thousand years over the earth; hence the bloodshed of man by man, and the worse than childish contention of nation against nation, and the universal deception and falsehood by which each nation now strives to obtain advantages over other nations.

Hence the rank insanity at this day, of England and America, and other nations, contending for territory and wealth and power, when they know not how, advantageously, to use the enormous territory and wealth and power which they possess, while unconscious that they possess the most ample, nay, illimitable means, to increase wealth and power beyond the utmost limits of all rational desires.

Let men but renounce the ignorant notion that they form themselves, and are responsible for that formation, and the world will immediately become religious in the only sense in which the word can have any rational signification; for by this sane conduct all would speedily become good, wise, and happy, and to become so would be the essence of all true religion; when all would speak the language of truth only, and act, in every instance, in accordance with the principles of the most extended, most enlightened, and purest charity.

CHAPTER IV

'That the knowledge of this fact, with all its important consequences, will necessarily create, in every one, a now, sublime, and pure spirit of charity, for the convictions, feelings, and conduct of the human race, and dispose them to be kind to all that have life, seeing that this varied life is formed by the same Incomprehensible Power that has created human nature and given man his peculiar faculties.'

THE knowledge of the fact that man does not make himself or any of the qualities of humanity, will – when it shall be understood in the full import of this expression, and when its innumerable links in the chain of consequences shall be foreseen, and systematically pursued step by step to their ultimate results, – be discovered to be one of the most sublime truths that man has been unabled yet to elicit from thought and reflection for the happiness of his race. It is the turning point between ignorance and knowledge; between vice and virtue; between irrationality and a sound state of mind; between division and union; between all manner of unkind and uncharitable feelings and thoughts, and the most unlimited kindness and charity for man and all that has life, as far as the latter is practicable with a superior state of human existence; in fact, between universal strife, degradation and misery, and cordial union, elevation of character and happiness.

While man is forced to receive the insane notion that he formed his own qualities of humanity, and especially his own individual qualities, differing, as they are found to do, from every other individual, he cannot be made to understand what real charity means; he has no power within him to grasp either its source or its inevitable consequences. If he had been trained to comprehend this subject, he would know that charity could no more be commanded than love or hatred; that charity is alone the result of an accurate knowledge of the mode by which humanity is so wondrously combined in man and woman, and how the character of each individual is formed before and after birth to the extent that the facts known to man allow him to investigate them. While, on the contrary, the imaginary notion, that man forms himself, can believe, disbelieve, and love and hate at his pleasure, shall be forced from birth into the minds of all, and man shall form his religion, laws, governments and all other institutions upon these errors of the imagination, all real charity must be destroyed; and to command, or advise human beings to be charitable, under such instruction and institutions, is as useless as to command or advise them to fly, without first giving them wings with sufficient power to enable them to fly. And when such wings shall be given to them, they will have too much pleasure in the exercise of the power of flight to require either command or advice to use it. So will it be when the human race shall be taught the eternal laws of humanity, when the religion, laws, governments, and institutions shall be devised in accordance with those laws, and when the character of each individual shall be in unison with them; *for then no necessity will exist* to command or advise any one to be charitable; they will be, *of necessity*, compelled to have the feelings of charity for all, in its highest and most pure state, and sympathy and kindness for all, will become a permanent instinct of their constitution.

When society shall be based on true principles, and every character formed in accordance with them, precepts will be useless; one feeling or instinct of action will alone pervade all; the impulse formed within them will be to be actively engaged in promoting the happiness of the human race, without having any suspicions about the feelings, thoughts, or local prejudices, or any supposed errors of others; knowing how all these have been formed to become blind instincts of humanity, for which the parties trained in error have the greater cause for our sympathy and kindness, in proportion to the local or general errors with which they have been afflicted.

By the character of individuals being based on true principles, and society formed in accordance with them, all the inferior qualities hitherto exhibited in human conduct will be overcome, and in future prevented; there will be no cause existing to create pride, ambition, anger, revenge, jealousy, envy, hatred, or malice; or any unkind or uncharitable feeling for the physical, mental, moral, or practical character of any individual. The *causes* generating these evils, in past and present humanity, will cease to exist, and their removal will destroy the effects which hitherto they have so abundantly produced. By these *natural* means being adopted to remove the causes generating error in all individuals and throughout society, a new spirit, totally unknown in the human character up to this period, will be created and diffused through the whole of society by each one being thoroughly imbued with it.

Nor will there be any uncertainty in the character of this new spirit, or in the conduct of individuals; their feelings and convictions having been formed in accordance with human nature, it will be known how they will think and act under all the changing circumstances as they may arise. There will be as much certainty in human proceedings, individually and generally, as there has been and is in the general laws of nature, and they will be calculated upon with as much accuracy. It will be known that all will, of necessity, act under every variety of new circumstances in such manner as will the most effectually promote the permanent general benefit, and the happiness of all individuals.

And not only will all, influenced by this new spirit, act in this manner to their fellow men, but to all that have life, that happiness may be extended among the animal creation as far as it is practicable with the well-being of the human race; – that race being possessed of the most superior organization; for it is natural and best that that which is the inferior and least useful should be subservient to the more useful and superior.

It is most desirable that there should be the greatest amount of happiness throughout the universe; and why all things constituting the universe, possessing sensation, or the capacity to feel pleasure and pain, are not eternally happy, it is most difficult to answer, except under the conviction that the greatest amount of happiness has ever been experienced that the elements composing the universe is capable of producing; for no intelligent and good power would put limits to the greatest amount of happiness that is attainable. If any power should act otherwise, it cannot be kind, charitable, or benevolent in its qualities. And as pain and misery exist to a great extent upon this earth, the only rational conclusion – with the facts known – is, that the best that can be done, by the eternal laws of necessity, ever has been, and is now, effected, with the elements of which the earth is composed. When this new character of knowledge, charity, and love shall be given to man – and it may be now more easily formed for him than the present character of ignorance, want of charity and love – he will have no inclination to ill-use, maltreat, or be cruel to anything having life and conscious sensation; and, in consequence, the animal creation will also become different in character. It will have no fear of man, or suspicion that it will ever be harshly or unkindly dealt by, except when absolutely necessary in self-defence. There will be no cruelty in man's nature; real knowledge of himself, and of the general laws of nature, will, of necessity, create a spirit of universal charity and good feeling for all that has life, and no desire will ever arise to inflict avoidable pain, even upon what appears to our senses the most insignificant of living existences.

Those fierce and untameable animals which cannot be subdued into friendship for man, or into a condition in which they shall not be injurious to him and his most helpless progeny, must have their races destroyed, in order that the earth may be safely and happily enjoyed by the most superior mental and moral existences which have been produced from it.[a] Thus will a terrestrial paradise be formed, in which harmony will pervade all that will exist upon the earth, and there will be none to hurt or destroy throughout the whole extent of its boundaries. And thus will that varied life, formed by the same Incomprehensible Power that has created man, be made to enjoy existence to the extent of the capacity given it to enjoy.

[a] Owen's views on taming animals may have been indebted to the German-American socialist John Adolphus Etzler, with whose works he was well acquainted. See Etzler's *The Paradise Within the Reach of All Men* (1833).

CHAPTER V

That it is man's highest interest to acquire an accurate knowledge of those circumstances which produce *evil* to the human race, and of those which produce *good*; and to exert all his powers to remove the former from society, and to create around it the latter only.

WITHOUT a knowledge of the immediate causes which create evil and good, individually and generally, throughout society, man may be said to be moved to action, by ordinary animal instincts, and by instinctive reason.

Hitherto, through the natural ignorance of man, arising from the infancy of humanity, – an infancy which is only now progressing towards childhood, – the human race has been forbidden to investigate the causes of *good* and *evil*, yet without an accurate knowledge of which it can never attain wisdom and happiness. A distinct perception of the *causes* of good and evil, is the next step for humanity to attain, to advance it from its present infant state, in which all has been mystery, imagination, and wild conjecture, towards a state of certainty and rationality, or to a clear conception of those unchanging facts, which man, as he progresses in age and experience, becomes competent to investigate, and by accumulating and arranging a multiplicity of them to form fixed sciences, and thus to attain a knowledge of general truths, which will disclose the past and present causes of good and evil to mankind, and the means of securing future happiness.

As true religion consists, only, in the acquisition of *the knowledge of truth, and its consistent application to practice, according to the ascertained facts or laws of human nature, which knowledge and application will ensure the permanent happiness of humanity*, the attainment of a distinct perception of the immediate *causes* of *good* and *evil* among men will be the first step to a knowledge of true religion. The second will be the application of this knowledge to remove, wisely and peaceably, the *causes* which now immediately produce evil, and which have had this effect through all preceding generations. The third step will be to introduce those causes which shall permanently create *good* to all of the human race, without distinction of class, sect, party, country, or colour.

The knowledge of the facts connected with humanity which disclose the causes of good and evil to man, and the application of that knowledge to *remove* the immediate causes of all human evils, and *introduce* the causes of permanent good to all of the human race, will constitute the basis of true religion among all people and nations to the end of time.

There can be no religion in preaching and talking about vice and virtue, goodness and wickedness, while there is no substantive knowledge either in the preaching or talking. True religion consists not in *words*, but in *actions*; not in words that make no substantive impressions of permanent improvement on mankind through thousands of successive ages, but in *deeds* which produce immediate progressive improvement and happiness among all people and nations; *uniting*, instead of *dividing*, all of the family of man; an improvement and happiness constantly advancing without any retrogression, until great knowledge shall be acquired and universally diffused, – endless discoveries in the arts and sciences made and universally applied to practice, – the earth highly cultivated and made a paradise, – man everywhere trained from his birth, physically, mentally, morally, and practically, to become, compared with his present low and degraded existence, a superior being, in knowledge, excellence, and happiness.

Thus the religion of an old immoral world, – immoral because based on false principles, – has been a religion of forms, ceremonies, and unmeaning mysteries, and of much useless preaching and talking, having no soul or substance within it; a religion of baseless imagination, from which, as the whole past experience of the human race, as narrated in history, confirms, divisions, contests, wars, and hypocrisy, with all that is artificial in mind, feeling, manner, and conduct, could alone emanate. While the religion of the new moral world is based on facts never yet known to change; thus forming universal truths, which no one can successfully dispute; a religion devoid of forms, ceremonies, and mysteries, – a religion from infancy implanted in the heart and mind of every one, and which will require afterwards neither preaching nor talking: it will in every individual become part of his nature, ever present in his spirit, mind, and conduct, ensuring a perpetual sunshine of life, and ever expressive in the countenance and evident in the conduct. When this religion shall become universal, there will be no disease, vice, crime, or misery, from the period when the children of an improved generation, well born, shall have been consistently trained in its principles and practices.

Those trained in the old world of error, can form no adequate conception of a state of human existence, when the change shall be effected from the inferior circumstances which man has created for man even from the beginning, to those new and superior circumstances which the experience of all the past, and the progress of modern science, will enable man now to create for man. When the physical form, the mental power, the moral faculties, and the facilities of practice, shall be carefully attended to and highly cultivated in all from birth, – when real knowledge of the most valuable description shall be given with all plainness and simplicity to each, – and when the language, in look, manner, and word, shall be, alone, the language of truth. This state of society, in which there will be but one interest and one object, no one remaining within the selfish and limited circle of the old world's ideas and practices can in any degree understand; how men and women will speak the truth only to each other, have but one interest and one object, and that without disguise of any kind, being to promote the best, the highest, and most permanent happiness of each other, is to them at present a mystery, a miracle altogether beyond the utmost stretch of their mole-like comprehension. A germ of this new state of human existence must be patiently worked out by a few determined minds, by men and women who shall devote themselves to this godlike purpose, to give, as far as they can, amidst an ignorant and prejudiced world, an approximate example to a now unbelieving people; unbelieving, because it is only through sight that the multitude can receive full faith in that which without an actual perception of the change in practice by having it before their eyes, they cannot in their present state of mind, ever imagine, but through a mist of confusion.

It is only when an approximate example to this new condition of the human race shall be seen in practice, that the governments of the world can become conscious of their present blindness and folly; that they can perceive the misery which they now inflict upon the multitude, and understand the extent of excellence and happiness of which this old worn-out system deprives themselves, their children, and their class.

It is only then that the men of influence in all countries will be enabled to discover that true religion is a religion of practice, and not of preaching; and that the practice consists, not in useless unmeaning forms, ceremonies and childish mysteries and miracles, but in proceeding, in a straightforward common-sense manner, to remove all those causes removeable by the unity of men, which continually, generation after generation, produce *evil* to the human race; and by man uniting all his power with his fellows to create a new existence of superior external circumstances, as far as existing means and knowledge will admit; so superior, that each shall produce positive good, while their combination shall ensure a high degree of excellence and rational enjoyment to all.

Seeing the all-importance of this mode of action, knowing the causes and consequences of this system of human life, all, trained from their infancy to become rational beings, will adopt this practice, persevere in it, bring society to a high state of comparative perfection, and carry it onward without retrogression as long as human time shall last. This conduct will be one essential part of true religion.

CHAPTER VI

That this invaluable practical knowledge can be acquired solely through an extensive search after truth, by an accurate, patient, and unprejudiced inquiry into facts, as developed by nature.

IT will be now asked by the most inquiring minds of the world – 'How can men acquire an accurate knowledge of those circumstances which produce *evil* and those which produce *good*, that we may immediately abandon the one, and set about the creation of the other?' This is an important inquiry; it is one which it would have been well for the world, if circumstances could have existed a century past to have induced the human race then to have entered upon the investigation of this long-neglected, yet now obvious question.

The answer involves considerations of the last importance to the well-being and happiness of all future generations. It contemplates the acquisition of a new science; of a science far more important to the well-being and happiness of man than all previously known sciences; a science which shall make the causes of good and evil obvious to all of the human race – which shall advance man in the scale of creation, from a most irrational creature, ever acting in direct opposition to his own happiness and to that of all his fellows, making the earth a pandemonium, and his offspring, prejudiced in favour of all that is inconsistent, unnatural, untrue, opposed to each other, and therefore miserable; – to a rational being, who wisely seeks the happiness of himself, of all his fellows, and, as far as to him is practicable, of all that have life.

When man shall acquire a full knowledge of this new and all-important science, *the science of the influence of external circumstances over human nature, and how wisely to apply it to practice*, the miseries of the human race, black, red, and white, and of all intermediate shades, will speedily terminate for ever.

Man ever has been, is, and ever will be, the creature of the external circumstances which are made to surround him; while these are inferior or bad, such as those of St Giles, Wapping, or similar – man will be inferior and bad; while mixed – as now among the middle and upper classes, – man will be mixed in the qualities of mind and body; but when he shall be alone surrounded from his birth with superior circumstances, such as shall be developed through an accurate knowledge of the 'Science of the influence of external circumstances over human nature,' then will humanity take its evidently natural position among the animals of the earth, and become, indeed, their lord and master, for his own and their happiness, as far as this union can be made; at all events to the extent of an incalculable increase to the comfort and well-being of all that the earth, highly cultivated by the most extended scientific operations, can be made so to support.

When this science shall be known and shall be universally applied to practice, as it will be the highest and obvious interest of all that it should be so applied, it will be impossible that one human being should then be allowed to grow up in ignorance – to be in poverty or the fear of it – to be opposed to his fellows – to have inferior habits, manners, or conduct – to have any but a kind and charitable spirit for all of his race, and for all that have life; knowing how life is given to, and character formed for, each, according to its nature. Men will then learn the absurdity and folly of calling anything good or bad by nature; – that before they thus pronounce an opinion of that which now they do not comprehend, they must know what the universe is, and the spirit, power, or agencies which give motion and progress to the elements which exist, and form the universe. Of this knowledge, man has been profoundly ignorant, and is as little informed accurately to-day, as our ancestors were when their histories commenced. The universe exists; how it exists – why it exists – what has been the distant past – or what will be the distant future, are unknown to man. His first step towards any substantial progress in real knowledge, or in that knowledge which can make man wise, good, and happy, is to become conscious how little he really knows with any accuracy or approach to certainty, of the universe, its designs, the nature of its elements, the power which regulates or governs the union, and separation, and reunion of these elements, or the remote causes of anything; in fact, nothing more than the apparent immediate cause of a few things acting in, upon, and around us, being made to live upon the surface of a globe, itself an atom in the illimitable expanse of the universe, necessarily infinite in extent and duration.

For creatures thus existing – formed without their knowledge – thinking, feeling, and acting, by an impulse, to them incomprehensible – to pretend to know the origin or ultimate cause or causes of these mysteries, the will and intentions of these mysteries, and to have the power to anger, displease, or glorify, these hitherto unconceived causes of universal action and organization of body or mind, is the very essence, not only of ignorant presumption, but of the most gross irrationality and rank insanity.

Man yet is ignorant of himself – his second step towards any substantial progress in that knowledge which can make him wise, good, and happy, is to know himself, and especially how very little he knows accurately of himself at this day.

In opposition to every fact known through the history of the human race, men even now think that they possess within themselves, and of themselves, powers which they never have had, or according to their nature ascertained by unerring facts, they never can have, because they are contrary to his nature: and while this ignorance remains, he can make no advance to sanity or to happiness.

Owing to this most lamentable ignorance of his own nature, man, surrounded by every desirable means to ensure health and long life, to be enabled to acquire comparatively a vast amount of invaluable knowledge for all the purposes of human existence, the most desirable qualities of body and mind, unity of interest and design, universal charity and love, and to make the earth an abode for highly intelligent, superior rational beings, remains blind to all these powers and advantages, appears unconscious of their existence, and instead of organizing them to produce these results, he actually, at this day, applies these illimitable sources of all good to inflict the greatest amount of evil upon himself and his race.

Man has not yet been taught, or put in the right path to discover the causes of *good* and *evil*. It appears that humanity, in its infancy, has been doomed to be mentally blind for a certain period; that hitherto they have remained, and are yet passing through this state of intellectual darkness, but that there are slight indications that the time approaches when their eyes will gradually open, and when they will be permitted to see things as they really are, and become astonished and confounded with the extent of the errors which have been committed, before they were allowed to see, through the light of truth, how truly their whole conduct has been irrational and insane.

As soon as this period of mental blindness shall cease, they will plainly perceive that the only path to real knowledge is through patient and unprejudiced search after truth, by the investigation of facts, as developed by nature, and thus bringing out consistent results, through every branch of investigation, until every division of human knowledge shall be united in one harmonious whole, in which no one fact shall be left in opposition to, or inconsistent with, every other fact throughout the extent of human acquirements. It being certain that truth can never be opposed to itself, or any two facts in discordance. The universe, according to our limited notions of universality, must be ONE GREAT TRUTH, composed of all facts, past, present, and future, if there can be past, present, and future in infinite duration, and that each of these facts must not only be unopposed to, but in perfect unity with every other fact, and that this conformity alone constitutes truth.

To acquire this accurate knowledge of facts, it becomes necessary to abandon all the old absurd imaginations of our poor, blind, and deluded ancestors, respecting the mysteries, forms, ceremonies, and downright insanities of what they were taught to call *religion*, and all the superstitions which these irrational proceedings engendered in the perplexed mind of humanity.

While these errors of mental blindness remain, they effectually block up the entrance to all knowledge which can lead to charity, affection, and happiness, and turn all into the road of ignorance, violence, contest, and misery.

'An extensive search after truth, by an accurate, patient, and unprejudiced inquiry into facts, as developed by nature,' can alone now lead to any satisfactory results – too many facts are already known and secured in perpetuity for the use of man, to permit much longer the continuance of superstition, or the denial of unchanging facts. The notions, so wild and incongrous as they all are, which the nations of the earth have hitherto dignified with the names of religions, derived from inexperienced imagination, must, ere long, give place to the religion emanating from unchanging facts; to the religion of, and for practice, which shall make, and permanently keep, man wise, good, and happy, and for the first time in the history of our race, make him a rational being. It is truth only that can set him free to act in accordance with his nature. While he is opposed, through the errors of superstition, to his nature, he will remain an ignorant, superstitious, and irrational being, whose thoughts, feelings, and actions have been made to be opposed to truth, and consequently to his progress to happiness. And, as it has been previously stated, truth can be discovered only by its uniform consistency with itself and with all nature.

When the human race shall earnestly, and with single mindedness, 'search after truth, by an accurate, patient, and unprejudiced inquiry into facts, as developed by nature,' it will be found pure, simple, and unadulterated with useless mysteries, vain superstitions, or senseless inconsistencies. Men will then cease from the childish mental slavery of inquiring after the truth, as it is in Moses, or Confucius, or Jesus, or Mahomet, or Robert Owen, or in any other name than as it eternally exists in nature; for truth, as it exists in nature, is and must be eternal.

How simple, beautiful, and advantageous is the truth which is derived from the unchanging facts of nature! How naturally step succeeds step to produce the most valuable knowledge, the largest amount of the highest qualities of humanity, and the greatest degree of permanently progressive happiness, that man, in his onward course, is capable of enjoying! These steps shall be now marked, that all may perceive their simplicity, wisdom, and goodness, to eternally secure the well-being and happiness of the future man; of man as soon as he shall be trained, educated, and placed to become a consistent rational being in his feelings, thoughts, and actions.

1st. Man, by the powers in nature, is organized, without his knowledge, to possess the united qualities of humanity.

2nd. These qualities, although the same generally in all of the race, are beautifully and most advantageously varied in their compound in each individual.

3rd. These natural qualities of humanity, at birth, are capable of being now cultivated and improved, throughout the animal creation, by the experience which man acquires, generation after generation, to an indefinite extent; and man may perhaps, in this respect, be more improved by man, than he can improve the organization, at birth, of any other animal now under his control.

4th. These natural or improved organizations, at birth, are capable of indefinite change, by the varied changes of the external circumstances, made to exist around them. And man admits of more varied changes than perhaps any other animal; those changes to be effected by the union of adult men over the infant and growing man.

5th. The sciences thus open, by which the organization of man may be indefinitely improved by man, as well as his adult character, by acting simply upon the combination of external circumstances with which the adult man may surround the infant man.

6th. The adult man and woman as parents are made, by nature, to have a greater amount of happiness in the well-being and happiness of their offspring than of themselves, and thus is the desire created in the parents, to improve the condition or external circumstances which surround the infant man and woman.

7th. It being ascertained, through long experience, that man is to an indefinite extent, the creature of the external circumstances made to exist by man, before and after the birth of each individual, and as the adults of the animal race are made generally, and man especially, to endeavour to secure the safety and happiness of the young before their own, here is a permanent security created in humanity, that, as soon as the science of the influence of circumstances over our nature shall be known, it will be universally acted upon, and thus will the progressive improvement and happiness of man be for ever established.

8th. Adult man thus, generation after generation, will create and improve the circumstances of infant man, and thus will the individual and general character of the human race hereafter rapidly, and, in an increasing ratio, progress towards high, illimitable excellence and happiness.

And, from a knowledge of these facts, perceived in their regular connection and whole extent, man acquires a knowledge of the principles and practices of the formation of individual character, he ceases to blame the individual, or any parties, anger dies within him, he learns the causes of good and evil, how the first can be ensured and secured, and the last prevented from coming into existence. Charity for all, and pity for each, where excellence and happiness have not been made to exist, pervade every character; all contest, except who shall discover and introduce the most favourable circumstances, will cease, and universal happiness will gradually reign throughout all nations and people, and the art of war, having served its purpose and its day, will die its natural death, and be heard of no more, except as part of the history of the irrational period of human existence.

Man will thus speedily learn to create the circumstances by which the formation of character, the production and distribution of wealth, and governing, without force or fraud, by charity, wisdom, and affection, will proceed unchecked; all will be at all times secured in abundance of the best and most valued wealth, with knowledge to expend it beneficially and enjoy it rationally, with all his fellows equally wealthy and well informed and superior in conduct.

These, and many other most beneficial results not yet enumerated, will assuredly arise through 'an extensive search after truth, by an accurate, patient, and unprejudiced inquiry into facts, as developed by nature.'

CHAPTER VII

'That man can never attain to a state of superior and permanent happiness, until he shall be surrounded by those external circumstances which will train him from birth to feel pure charity and sincere affection towards the whole of his species, – to speak the truth only on all occasions, – and to regard with a merciful and kind disposition all that have life.'

UNTIL man shall be placed under circumstances to have no motive to speak aught but the truth from his birth to his death, he cannot attain, or even know what happiness is. He will be incompetent to know himself or humanity – he will be unable to feel charity for the human race – to have sincere affection for his species, or to have the slightest pretension to a knowledge of TRUE RELIGION. But man will not be in a position to speak the truth, without motive to falsehood, while the system of falsehood governs the world, and it is filled by man with external circumstances in accordance with that system. While this universal system of error, falsehood, and fraud, pervades and penetrates into every part of society, it is vain and useless to attempt to introduce truth, charity, and affection into the practice of the human race, or to talk or preach about an unmeaning word called religion. This change can be effected only by an entire change in forming the character of man from his birth, and by the complete reconstruction of society based on those principles which are directly opposed to the wild and random notions on which the system of error and falsehood has been founded, and on which mysteries and superstition, called religion, have been engrafted, and thus destroyed the value of the human faculties. True religion will be known by its simple, plain, and straightforward language of truth, 'without mystery, mixture of error, or fear of man;' and by the undeviating feelings of charity which it will produce for all, and its consequent practice of kindness, not only to man, but to all that have life, so far as it is consistent with the safety and happiness of humanity.

True religion cannot exist without the universal language of truth, nor with the language of truth can vice, crime, or misery of any kind afflict the human race, except by the effects arising from the overwhelming war of the elements of nature, beyond the present control of man to regulate or prevent. The consequences that will necessarily follow from the universal adoption of the language of truth, no human mind has yet encompassed; the substantial permanent benefits that will arise, are far beyond all present estimate. To this part of our subject, and of its ever-lasting importance to the human race, the mind of man does not appear yet to have been opened, although, until its overwhelming influence in giving excellence and happiness to humanity shall be well understood, and measures shall be adopted to prepare the means to withdraw all motives to falsehood, and truth shall become the universal language of man, it will be useless to talk of justice or virtue, or of man being a rational animal.

At present there is no groundwork for truth in society. Under the present system, it is said, 'that children and fools alone speak the truth;' and so true is this saying, that if a man, and more especially a woman, were to commence the practice of really speaking the truth in their common every-day proceedings in life, neither the one nor the other could proceed in this path of savage and of the most enlightened and highest cultivated nature, for one week, without being generally considered insane, and deemed fit subjects for a lunatic asylum.

Here is the striking evidence of the lunacy of the present system. The preaching is, that all should at all times speak the truth; – the practice is, that any one who would honestly and fully do so would, in a very short period, be considered not safe to be at large in society, but a madman or madwoman, and only suffered to live as the inmate of a madhouse. Are not the sufferings now created by the system which has hitherto prevailed among the human race, sufficient in extent and suffering to open the mental faculties of man to the enormity of its errors, and to perceive that it is totally incompetent to produce TRUTH OR CHARITY in human society? Before this knowledge can be attained, how much more falsehood must be introduced, and force and violence to support that falsehood? How much more injustice and oppression? How much more division, ignorance, and poverty? How much more crime, prostitution, degradation, and starvation? Or how long is it necessary that man should continue to be the greatest enemy to man, and the most formidable obstacle to each other's progress towards excellence and happiness?

Are these evils yet not of sufficient magnitude to open the eyes of some, that they may become actively employed in opening the eyes of others? Without the universal language of truth man must be what hitherto he has ever been, a vicious, presumptuous, and irrational animal, and, until he attains a true and full knowledge of his present low and degraded condition, a vicious, presumptuous, and irrational animal he most assuredly must remain. The first step to real knowledge, on the part of the human race, will be, to become fully conscious of their present ignorance, folly, and degradation, and that they are continually talking one way and acting another. This irrational and truly insane mode of thinking and acting must be abandoned before the human race can even understand what religion is, much less to act upon it; for it must be understood before it can be acted upon. But, before it can be understood and acted upon, the public must be prepared for this great change, from a universal system of falsehood to a universal system of truth. It must be enabled to comprehend that of which it now appears to be totally ignorant, that *true* religion consists in universal truth; that truth is religion and religion is truth. When all motive to the expression of falsehood shall be removed, when truth, without reservation, shall become the universal language of man, then will mankind know themselves, become virtuous, intelligent, affluent, united, and happy; then will they indeed become truly religious, – when all men shall know each other even as they know themselves, – then will human intercourse become a divine intercourse, for truth alone is divine, and any system that cannot admit of the innocence of truth is false in its foundation, and must be governed solely by force and fraud. The religion of truth will not admit of force or fraud; but this result, the mind formed in the old world cannot comprehend, – it cannot imagine human existence without falsehood in look, word, or action. It understands not how the world can be governed without force and fraud, much less how it can be far better governed by knowledge, justice, charity, and love than it has ever yet been governed by falsehood and violence, or by human laws, based on the principle that man forms himself to be what he is.

At this moment, to the men of the old world, nothing appears more visionary than to suppose the existence in practice of truth, charity, and love, and yet they continue, generation after generation, to talk about religion, and practise falsehood, force, and fraud, while they admit, with their lips, that religion consists in the practice of truth, charity, and love. Herein is to be found the ignorance, inconsistency, irrationality, and insanity of the old immoral world. Of what inestimable value would truth be now to the world, under its accumulated and accumulating difficulties, dangers, and miseries produced solely by this old system of ignorance and falsehood? It would at once open the eyes of all to perceive the immediate causes of human evils, to know that until these causes shall be removed, the evils must continue, to ascertain how, with the least evils, those causes may be removed, and be replaced with others which shall produce knowledge, justice, truth, charity, and love, and thus make this globe an earthly paradise, far superior in reality than any imaginary paradise ever described by man. But, how is this religion of truth to be introduced into a world most opposed to it, by reason of its ignorance and falsehood, and necessarily of vice and misery? Falsehood is now triumphant, truth despised, and force and fraud govern the masses in all the nations of the earth. Who, then, shall dare to encounter these united enemies to man's progress to knowledge and happiness? Who will now take up the cause of truth in its most despised state, oppose it to falsehood, while the latter is in its plenitude of pomp and power, ruling the nations of the earth with a rod of iron,[a] and making all tremble under its sway? Those only are prepared for this great and glorious conflict who are willing to put their life in their hand and to go forth determined to conquer or to die. The great question, then, now is – Is the world in a condition to warrant the commencement of such a conflict with

[a] See for example Psalms 2:9.

any the slightest prospect of success? And if the ignorance, vice, crime, and misery, which have accumulated to an almost unbearable extent, have sufficiently divided this old world, and weakened its powers of resistance, to offer a reasonable hope that the time has arrived for the destruction of all that is erroneous and misery-producing in human existence, and for the reign of truth, charity, and love, to commence? These are now considerations for the men of progress; for those who are imbued with the sincere desire to improve the condition of the human race, and who are prepared to make personal sacrifices to attain so great, so good, so glorious an object; to attain the emancipation of the world from falsehood, and to establish the universal reign of truth; because truth alone can make all the nations of the earth free from mental bondage, and all the evils thence ensuing.

It is this spirit and language of truth which must pervade the whole mass and the entire of society, before man can conceive what man can achieve, or society united can accomplish. It is said by uninformed, or, it may be, uninspired minds, who have not been enabled to grasp the past, the present, and the future, within human limits, that these great and glorious truths, and these approaches towards perfection of action, are hundreds of years before the confined and degraded minds and conduct of the existing generations; but it is not so – the words of truth have gone forth, they are hourly extending from mind to mind, and from country to country, until ere long they will become familiar to the leading and most inquisitive minds in all parts of the earth.

Unlike the mysteries and superstitions of the old worn-out world, none of which could be ever comprehended by the human faculties, and if persevered in would confound the human intellects, and divide man from man to the end of time; truth is simple, and when placed in plain language, and consecutively before the mind, commands conviction. The powers of the world being ignorant, immoral, and oppressive, in consequence of those wielding it having been trained and nurtured in falsehood, have ever been opposed to the development of truth. Those, therefore, who were enabled to perceive it, who were made to love it and to desire to spread it among the human race, speedily lost their lives, or they were under the necessity of expressing their thoughts in parables, or in such a covert manner that it was not obvious to the multitude, and when even thus given, it was in such small portions, that it was of little or no practical utility. It is now discovered that truth upon the general affairs of mankind could not be made practicable in such portions intermixed with the old falsehoods, mysteries, and superstitions of the world; they could be no more united than oil and water, or any two of the most repulsive elements of nature. Falsehood is one, and must be supported by falsehoods added to falsehoods. Truth is one, and can be made of practical utility, by its unity only, uncontaminated with falsehood. Hence the necessity for the maintenance of the existing system of falsehood, with all its artificial props and support; or for the entire new system of truth, with all things in accordance with it. It is most useless to halt between the two systems; the world must be governed by the one or the other. It must continue a pandemonium inhabited by demons of falsehood and violence, forming the oppressor and the oppressed; or it must become a highly cultivated paradise, inhabited by superior beings of truth, knowledge, charity, and love.

The earth must remain kingdoms of falsehood, force, and fraud, opposed to falsehood, force, and fraud; or it must be an united empire of truth, devoid of falsehood, force, or fraud. It must remain the one or become the other.

Until man can be trained to hear the truth, to learn the truth, and to act the truth, he will continue to be the miserable child of falsehood, and of all manner of inconsistencies and of evils.

Before knowledge, charity, and goodness can be united, and be made to become the uniform governing powers throughout society, truth alone must become the language of the human race, and falsehood and fear must cease to exist; and then man will become merciful and kind to all that have life.

And when men shall speak the language of truth, not only without fear, but with pleasure to each other, over the whole surface of the earth, and shall be kind to each other, and merciful to all that have life, then will they understand the character of true religion, and that it consists not in words, but in actions.

CHAPTER VIII

'That such superior knowledge and feelings can never be given to man under those institutions of society which have been founded on the mistaken supposition that man forms his *feelings* and *convictions* by his *will*, and therefore has merit or demerit, or deserves praise or blame, or reward or punishment for them.'

Superior knowledge, and superior feelings, have never yet been attained by the human race; they never can be obtained so long as the institutions of society are founded on error, and upon errors too the most opposed to truth, and the most lamentable in their consequences to all of human kind.

Superior knowledge and superior feelings can arise only from truth without mystery or mixture of error. There must be not only mystery and mixture of error, but utter confusion of mind, and every inferior feeling generated under institutions based upon the undoubting belief that humanity has been created with an independent internal power of believing and feeling according to a will possessed by each individual; and that consequently each has merit or demerit, deserves praise or blame, reward or punishment, for them, according to the notions of some of these individuals themselves, and in fact that some of the human race must be responsible to others for that which they think, and feel, and do.

These notions, conceived in ignorance, nurtured in presumption, and carried into execution under all manner of injustice, cruelty, and oppression, have filled the earth with insanity, and made it, as it is at this day, a perfect pandemonium. Man has not yet staid in his course to inquire what am I? What powers have been given to me? Do I yet know myself? Am I compelled to feel, think, and act from the instincts of my nature; or have I internal power of my own to feel, think, and act according to my own will and pleasure? No: he has been made, for purposes hitherto incomprehensible to humanity, unconscious of his powers, and to hurry forward in a course which has led him onward to a stage of error so glaring that he can no longer continue blind to the incongruities of his position, or to the evils which these errors now inflict upon his race. Nature, – or that power which everlastingly acts throughout the universe – now, in its mysterious course, says to man, 'Stop, you must proceed thus no longer, it will lead you to evils unbearable by humanity; you must now learn what manner of beings you are, what internal qualities you possess, what you have not, and how you can make the best use of those which you have. The time is come when you must learn that you have no choice in what you are made to feel or to believe, for if you had, you would always determine to feel happy, and to believe only that which is eternally true: had you the power of choice, there would be no misery, no error; the world would be wise and happy. You must now be undeceived on all these matters, which are so essential to the future well-being and happiness of the human race. And it is only by your being undeceived that you ever can become truly intelligent, charitable, and kind to all, or know what real virtue is.'

This is now the language of nature in progress to ulterior results yet hidden from man; but all the indications of the past and present are, that this progress will lead to universal knowledge, unity, and happiness, physical and intellectual.

When man shall know of a certainty that his belief and his feelings are formed for him by the unavoidable instincts of humanity, then will he cease to be unkind or uncharitable to any one of his race; then will anger cease from the earth, being known to be irrational, and temporary insanity; – then will the eyes of humanity be for the first time opened to see truth in its native fulness, simplicity, and efficiency, without the intervention of any false or darkening medium; – man shall then know himself even as he is known, and understand the causes of good and evil, and be made to adopt, from choice, the good, and to abandon for ever the evil. It is this ignorance of man of the natural qualities of humanity, which now inflicts almost, if not all, the ills which the human race suffer. It is the sole cause of disunion among men; it will, while continued, prevent union between men and nations; and without union, based on knowledge, there can be no virtue or happiness, no peace and good will among mankind. The causes which produce belief will be now readily known; when those causes exist, belief must be received; when absent, belief can never be forced, however strong may be the worldly motive to desire it; blame or praise for it will be perceived to be irrational, and reward or punishment to be most unjust. A new language will arise consonant with this new knowledge; 'you ought to believe as I believe, or as I wish you to believe,' will no longer be used by any one; – as belief is the natural instinct produced by conviction, the only question will be, 'Is the evidence sufficiently strong to call forth your instinct of conviction? for if not, more evidence must be brought, even until conviction shall be made to remove all doubt, and to establish full belief?' But no praise or blame, reward or punishment, will ever follow, in a rational state of society, from belief or disbelief; for whether any statement be true or false, the individual must receive the impressions in accordance with the convictions made upon his mind.

The causes which produce feeling will be equally well known, and known also to be instincts of humanity, by which all liking and disliking are forced upon each individual. Before tasting of food, seeing of objects, hearing sounds, smelling scents, or knowing persons, no one can say whether these will be liked, indifferent, or be disliked; and no merit or demerit, praise or blame, reward or punishment, will ever be given for one or the other, from the period when man shall become a rational being. Praise or blame, reward or punishment, will be no more given for these things than are now given when individuals possess inferior or superior features or persons, which are effects equally the results of the instincts of human nature; instincts cultivated by the adults, with greater or less care, to produce these effects upon the young of one generation, as are intended by the older of the preceding generation.

It is fortunate for the future happiness of the human race, that although these instincts cannot be created by the individual, yet as soon as this new knowledge of ourselves shall become generally known, as well as the best mode of applying it to practice, the adults of one generation may most materially assist the young of the succeeding generation to pursue a course by which the convictions and feelings of the young may be directed into the paths of truth and of happiness. But as these convictions and feelings are created *for* the individuals, by nature, and the adults and objects around them, the irrational language of individual praise and blame, and the insane practice of rewards and punishments, will entirely cease, and the language of common sense and of truth, and the practice of justice to all, will supersede them.

High knowledge, great simplicity, and unvarying truth, will be the necessary consequences which will arise from the abandonment of the long and most lamentable misconceptions respecting our convictions and feelings, and from the adoption of the truth, as demonstrated by facts, on these most important parts of our nature.

It is now only that facts have demonstrated the truth upon this all-important subject; all-important, because the permanent misery or happiness of man are involved in its solution. If the will of man is an independent power within him, and by which he can believe and feel whatever he wishes or desires, then, judging by past proceedings, there can be no hope for the future; for hitherto man has felt, thought, and acted most irrationally, and there is no foundation on which to rest better hope for the future; but if the convictions and feelings of humanity are created for the individual, and these again, either separately or united, create the will or decision to act, then, by the acquisition of the knowledge of the science of the influence of circumstances over human nature, or of the causes which produce convictions and direct the feelings, and thus create the will to act, a new power will be given to humanity, by which, ere long, those circumstances which create evil may be removed, while those which produce good may be made permanent throughout the future existence of the human race. All the irrational notions of merit and demerit, praise and blame, reward and punishment of individuals, will then for ever cease, and with them all the irrational thoughts, feelings, and actions consequent upon those erroneous notions.

And these errors removed, the path by which all the causes of sin and misery may be removed will be opened and easy to pursue, and thus all that has heretofore kept man ignorant, poor, and divided, will be removed, and by the creation of another and superior arrangement of circumstances, a new existence will be prepared for him. Truth and Charity will be triumphant, reign universally unopposed, and the practice of both will become the true, useful, and most efficient religion of man; the earth will gradually, by this change of circumstances, as population increases, be made a paradise, and be occupied by new-formed men and women, associated in a society newly constructed on rational principles. In a society in which its natural elements will be united in their due proportions, to produce always a surplus of superior wealth; – to distribute this wealth most beneficially for every one; – to ensure the most useful and best character for each individual; – to govern all well, wisely, and harmoniously, and, (as soon as the rational character can be given to the individuals comprising this society) without elections or selections of persons; because both these practices are calculated to destroy all unity and harmony among men.

But it will be some time before the men and women of this old world can be made to comprehend these principles, and yet longer before they can be instructed to apply them consistently to their every day practice.

CHAPTER IX

'That under institutions, formed in accordance with the Rational System of Society, this superior knowledge and these superior dispositions may be given to the whole of the human race, without chance of failure, except in case of organic disease.'

Now, as all the institutions of society have been based on the supposition that man forms his character, that by his will he believes and feels as he likes, and acts independently of his instinct, convictions and feelings, and as these notions have been demonstrated to be opposed to all known facts, and therefore erroneous, it follows, that the condition of the human race can be permanently improved only by the change of the fundamental principles from which these institutions have arisen, and by the creation of other institutions based on the now ascertained principles of human nature; – institutions totally different from those now existing, whether compared with the principles of which they are based, or the practices which have necessarily emanated from them. The great question for the most grave consideration of the human race is now – 'What are the institutions and alterations in society, which, under the proposed change of fundamental principles, are to be superseded and abandoned; and what are the new institutions and changes by which they are intended to be replaced?'

The institutions and practices which are based on error are:-

1st. The religions, so called, of the world.

2nd. The governments of the world, under every form and name.

3rd. The professions, civil and military, of all countries.

4th. The monetary systems of all nations.

5th. The practice of buying and selling for a monied profit.

6th. The practices which produce contests, civil and miliary, individual and national.

7th. The present practice of producing and distributing wealth.

8th. The present practice of forming the character of man.

9th. The practice of force and fraud, as now prevalent in every department of life, in all countries.

10th. The practice of separate interests, and consequent universal disunion.

11th. The practice of isolated families, and separate family interests.

12th. The practice of educating women to be family slaves, instead of superior companions.

13th. The practice of artificial and indissoluble marriages of the priesthood, varied as they are in principle and practice over the world, and often forcing the society of the sexes in opposition to the feelings of nature, when not to be overcome.

14th. The practice of falsehood and deception, now prevalent over the world.

15th. The practice of unequal education, employment, and condition.

16th. The practice of the strong oppressing the weak.

17th. The practice of levying unequal taxes, and in expending them upon inefficient measures for good, when they might be applied, most efficiently, to produce wealth, knowledge, and permanent prosperity to all the people.

18th. The practice of producing inferior wealth of all kinds, when the most superior would be more economical, and far more to be desired.

Instead of these unwise, complicated, and opposing institutions and practices, all emanating from a few false fundamental crude imaginations respecting humanity, producing evil continually, the following simple arrangements and practices are recommended:-

1st. That the knowledge and experience of the human race should be collected and concentrated, in order that a right and beneficial direction should be given to all the powers, manual and scientific, which have been accumulated through the past ages.

2nd. That mere locality of feeling and acting, whether sectarian or national, be abandoned for universality of mind, spirit, interest, and conduct.

3rd. That these powers shall be, in every locality, concentrated to produce the greatest amount of the most valuable wealth, with the least unhealthy, or disagreeable manual labour, in the shortest period, with the least waste of capital, and most beneficially for all parties.

4th. That artificial or scientific power be introduced, to the greatest extent, in the domestic arrangements of society, as well as in every other department of life.

5th. That everything inferior, throughout all the divisions and ramifications of society, shall be abandoned for that which is the most superior, according to the existing knowledge and means of society.

6th. That thus there shall be no inferior arrangements for the cultivation of the soil, for dwelling accommodation, or for producing and preparing food and clothes; that there shall be no inferior mode of education, or of forming the character from birth, of men and women, to become superior rational beings in their feelings, thoughts, spirit and conduct.

7th. That the wealth produced shall be preserved under superior arrangements, and distributed the most advantageously for all.

8th. That the local and general government shall be in accordance with this new and superior state of existence, in which there will be little to govern beyond preserving the unity of the respective parts of society, so as to ensure full justice to each, according to age, that the progressive happiness of all may be permanently secured.

9th. That the education and condition of each shall be as complete as the united knowledge and means of all will admit, and that the only division throughout society will be that of age, – serving in childhood and youth – producing, preserving, and distributing in manhood – governing, and enjoying more leisure in advanced age.

10th. That all be thus at all times actively and pleasantly engaged in promoting the universal improvement and happiness of society, without immediate reference to self. By this superior mode of life and conduct, the happiness of each individual will be permanently secured without contest, and increased *much more* than a thousand-fold.

11th. That this mode of educating and employing all, and conducting society on principles of justice and kindness, will supersede the necessity for artificial religion, laws, and governments, and render merit and demerit, praise and blame, rewards and punishments, unnecessary, and far worse than useless.

12th. That the sexes shall be equal in education, rights, and privileges, and the women formed to become superior companions for the men. The associations of the sexes to be formed according to their affections, in the manner that beings made rational, and placed within, or under, circumstances rationally formed and combined, would rationally unite under wise arrangements; the effects of which no one can foresee or know without actual experience. The children to be all educated as the children of one family, – the great family of man, united in interest and affection, devoid of all repulsive influences.

13th. That the only language spoken, or expressed by word, look, or action, will be the language of truth, without mystery, mixture of error, or fear of man, and by which all human knowledge will speedily become general, and rapidly increase without retrogression; and man will become a far superior being to any that could be formed under the old errors of humanity.

14th. That peace will become universal, by the most advanced and influential discovering the incalculable advantages of unity over division, and therefore using their power to prevent war.

15th. That no taxes be levied; but that all, at all times, shall be well supported from the superabundance of the common stock. Such injurious exactions will be no longer necessary.

Thus will the turmoil, and inexplicable confusion and counteraction of a false condition of humanity be unravelled, and formed into a simple, yet beautiful arrangement of society, – into a society which will consist of establishments uniting in their due proportions the natural elements of society – each establishment producing, preserving, distributing, and consuming wealth, the most advantageously for the attainment of these objects in perfection, and for educating and locally governing the members most beneficially for all, while each establishment, under a general arrangement, will be united in interest and feeling, and in the constant exchange of products and kind offices, to the mutual lasting prosperity of all these establishments.

Instead, therefore, of the present artificial and now most injurious division into the upper and lower classes, as in some countries, or into the upper, middle, and lower, as in other countries, there will be but one highly superior class, divided into sections according to age, under the arrangements that will permanently insure to each individual, from birth to death, the greatest amount of advantages that the original organization of the individual will admit. In fact, by this change, society will become one beautiful scientific arrangement, connected throughout the whole of its ramifications, *to produce, preserve, distribute, and consume wealth the most advantageously for every individual and for the entire of society*; and to this result there will be no exception: also, *to well form, from birth, the physical, intellectual, moral, and practical character of each, and to govern the whole, without either force or fraud, in such a manner that there will be a continual progress made in the attainment of higher excellence in every department of life, in all kinds of knowledge, and in the enjoyment of purer and more substantial happiness.*

And to pursue this course, without turning to the right or left, will be the essence of true religion, and the only means to establish universal truth, peace, charity, and love among the human race. And thus will be secured for all, superior knowledge and superior dispositions, whence alone superior and permanent happiness can emanate and become general throughout society.

To these high and delightful results there will be no chance of failure, except in case of organic disease in the individual. And let it not be forgotten that this change in the general system of society will continually diminish the chance of such organic disease being produced, until, in two or three generations, it will, like all moral evils, entirely cease to arise, and all organizations will be born complete and healthy.

CHAPTER X

'That in consequence of this superior knowledge, and these superior dispositions, the contemplation of nature will create in every mind, feelings of high adoration, too sublime and pure to be expressed in forms or words, for that Incomprehensible Power which acts in and through all nature, everlastingly composing, decomposing, and recomposing the material of the universe; – producing the endless variety of life, of mind, and of organized form.'

ALTHOUGH it is obvious to our senses that this Power never has been discovered by man, it cannot be said, with any degree of certainty, that it may not at some future period be made known to us. It is true, it is now, it ever has been, incomprehensible to the human race, and man must act under this defect of knowledge, until it shall be expanded, if it ever shall be so expanded, to make him comprehend the moving Power of the Universe; – the composing and decomposing Power. Man, by the evidence of his senses, knows that a Power to effect these and all other changes which are made, exists; but of the real qualities or attributes of it, the human race are yet ignorant; and for any one to pretend that he knows what it is, or its designs, or will, or language, is too grossly absurd for a rational made mind to entertain for a moment. Until all such notions shall be abandoned, man must remain, as heretofore, irrational. To become sane on this subject, it is necessary to recollect that man is a mere atom on an atom of a globe, itself a satellite, or child to its parent globe, which again, with all its revolving globes, is comparatively less than an atom in a universe which can have no limits. How, then, can such a being as man, so situated, have the presumption to suppose that he can act contrary to the Great Cause of all motion, life, and mind, throughout infinite space and eternal duration; or that he can in any way whatever glorify or benefit such Power, especially while it remains to him and his race incomprehensible. But when this Power is reflected upon and its results considered, so far as the limited capacity of man can comprehend them, he must view it with feelings of wonder and awe, too sublime for any human words to express by any sound, or form, or ceremony; for any words or ceremony must diminish the purity of the feelings, and bring back the flight of thought attempting to reach illimitable space, and to grasp eternity of time, in which, composition, decomposition, and recomposition, universally proceed, without ceasing, producing never ending variety of movements, life, and mind. Vain and impotent man, to talk of adoring, defending, or glorifying such incomprehensible attributes!

Were we not now acquainted with some of the more obvious laws of humanity, it would appear incredible that beings possessing any power of observing, comparing, and deducing results from these capabilities, could have opposed each other so violently, and sacrificed unnumbered masses through so many thousand years, for the supposed honour and glory of that which even now is utterly incomprehensible to all their faculties, and respecting which, they are a mere atom to infinitude in space, and eternity in duration. A greater error or folly it is impossible for insanity to commit. Humanity has no other means by which so much misery could be inflicted upon itself; by which happiness could be so much retarded; by which the human faculties could be so long kept in a state of almost hopeless mental derangement. Instead of wasting wealth and time on a subject, admitted by all, ignorant and learned, to be beyond man's present comprehension; the time and talent, hitherto so unwisely devoted to the far worse than useless profession of the priesthood over the world, will be most beneficially applied to make man a reasonable and rational being, and to train him to have the greatest pleasure in devising plans and putting them into execution, to promote the substantial and permanent happiness, as far as his capacity will admit, of all that have life upon the earth; because the varied organized forms of life and mind are evidently the result of the same laws of nature, or Power Incomprehensible to the present state of the human faculties. The sooner, therefore, that the profession of the priesthood over the world shall be abolished, the sooner will man be made humane, intelligent, rational, prosperous, and happy. While the priesthood shall continue to instil the wild contradictory notions into the minds of the young, which they have hitherto done in all ages and countries, it will be waste of time and intellect to attempt to unite these senseless mysteries with facts, or common sense; or consistent reasoning from those facts which the world is compelled to learn through the progress of science, which is daily on the advance. Another mode to form the human mind than that hitherto adopted by the priesthood of all religions, must now be introduced and acted upon, if sublime and pure ideas respecting Eternal Power are to be acquired by the human race; or a consistent mind, or sane conduct given to them. Every one made to become a priest of any religion, is thereby prevented from being useful to himself or others; and no greater evil can befal any one than to have his mind and conduct so perverted from all that is beneficial for himself or his race. All thus injured are objects of compassion, and call for perpetual commiseration: they are made either too weak in intellect to discover the injury done them, and they remain evil-doers, conscientiously believing they are continually doing good; or they are made hypocrites, and to become insincere in all their conduct, and thus made more miserable than the others. There is no necessity for, or real utility in, the office of priesthood, nor will one be made in a rational state of human existence. Every one should be so trained and educated as to become his own best priest; and, of course, in the classification of society in the new moral world, there is no profession of the priesthood, or arrangement to perpetuate ignorance of human nature and of nature generally, nor any one so placed that it shall appear to him to be his interest to keep any of his fellow men in a state of physical or mental slavery or degradation. Knowing, as he will, that he and his fellows have been formed by the same Power, and that by due arrangements in society all may be made equal in education and condition, most advantageously for all, none of the old inferior feelings, cultivated hitherto through error, will be brought into action; and man will rejoice in his existence, delight in all his fellows, and have the most pure and sublime aspirations and exalted feelings for that mysterious Power which sustains the endless variety of motion, life, mind, and organized form. But man will not be so irrational as to interfere with man upon a subject which can alone concern or interest the individual; much less will any one condemn or find fault with another because there may be a difference of feeling respecting that Power which is yet mysterious to all, which none can comprehend, and the most advanced in intellectual attainments can only contemplate through the most uncertain and unsatisfactory conjectures. Let man, therefore, cease to dispute – to be angry, much less to enter into violent and deadly contentions respecting the unknown Power of the universe, the attributes of which have been hitherto hidden in mystery from the human race; but let each in kindness declare to his brother the impressions which he is compelled to have on this subject.

CHAPTER XI

'That the practice of the Rational Religion will therefore consist in promoting, to the utmost of our power, the well-being and happiness of every man, woman, and child, without regard to their class, sect, sex, party, country, or colour; and its worship in those inexpressible feelings of wonder, admiration, and delight which, when man shall be surrounded by superior circumstances only, will naturally arise from the contemplation of the infinity of space, of the eternity of duration, of the order of the universe, and of that great and Incomprehensible Power by which the atom is moved and the aggregate of nature is governed.'

ANY *theory* not reducible to *practice*, can be of little or no service to mankind; but theories of religion which are impracticable, and which create contests between man and man, and nation and nation, are far worse than useless: they disturb and distract, to a most injurious extent, the thoughts and feelings, and give a false and most lamentable direction to the mind and conduct of all, and create a state of society the least calculated to produce peace and happiness among mankind. On the contrary, such theories must, of necessity, lead to evil added to evil, until the excess of grave folly shall become too absurd to be longer supported, and too glaring for any rational-made being to countenance.

Religion, to be of any real utility to the human race, must be *practical*. It must have for its object the well-being and happiness of all in *this life*; and that which does not tend to this all-important result, can be of no benefit to man. That alone is true religion which will effect a continued improvement in the physical, mental, moral, and practical character of all, without exception; and those who torment themselves and others about what we shall be hereafter, may rest assured that the best preparation for any future state of existence, will be the highest improvement and cultivation of all our faculties, as they are formed for us in our present mode of existence; and that no time can be more uselessly expended than by wasting it upon conjectures, founded on no reality, of what we shall be hereafter. Let man do all in his power to make this earth a paradise – to cultivate and beautify it to the extent of the enormous means now at his disposal – to well educate, from birth, physically, mentally, morally, and practically, every infant – to surround each with the most superior external circumstances, which may be now so easily created and combined around all;

and in these arrangements to make due provision to well cultivate and regularly exercise, at the proper period of life, all the human faculties, organs, propensities, and powers, and so to regulate their action that they shall not be over or under exercised, but stimulated to their natural use up to the point of temperance, and none need fear to attain the enjoyment of a pure and happy existence upon earth; and they may also banish the absurd notions and alarms which have hitherto tormented mankind about the mode of their existence in another state – a life of which they can know nothing that can be of any practical utility to them.

The primary and necessary object of all existence is to be happy; the desire to be so has been evidently given to stimulate all to action, and ultimately, to right action. But happiness cannot be obtained individually; it is useless to expect isolated happiness; all must partake of it, or the few can never enjoy it: man can, therefore, have but one real and genuine interest, which is, to make all of his race as perfect in character and happy in feeling as the original nature or organization of each will admit. When all shall be cordially engaged in promoting the happiness of all around them to this extent, then will they have entered upon the real business of life – then will they be occupied in promoting, to the greatest limit, their own individual happiness, which has been made permanently to consist in the happiness of the race; and the only contest among men will then be, who shall the most succeed in extending happiness to his fellows. Herein will consist true religion, and the pure and genuine adoration of all that is great, good, beautiful, and magnificent throughout the universe.

CHAPTER XII

'That the practice of Rational Religion will therefore consist in promoting, to the utmost of our power, the well-being and happiness of every man, woman, and child, without regard to their class, sect, sex, party, country, or colour; and its worship in those inexpressible feelings of wonder, admiration, and delight, which, when man shall be surrounded with superior circumstances only, will naturally arise from the contemplation of the infinity of space; of the eternity of duration; of the laws of nature; and of that Incomprehensible Power, which everlastingly composes, decomposes, and recomposes the elements of all existences, and by which the atom is moved, and the aggregate of nature is eternally governed.'

The object of all that have life is to attain the happiness which can be enjoyed by each individual organization. This is the stimulus to all action, and every movement is made instinctively to promote this result. This, in fact, appears to be the universal law of all that have conscious sensation, and for this end, life appears to the individuals of all species alone to exist.

All animals, except man, pursue this object from birth to death, in accordance with their respective organizations, and appear to deviate only when man interferes and compels some of them to live an artificial life to suit his convenience or pleasure. By acting always in accordance with their nature, all animals appear to enjoy their respective existences; but man, from some cause or other, has disowned his nature, made all his laws, customs, and habits, opposed to it, taken a notion that he can make it better by opposing its instincts and natural propensities, and thus has he created disorder throughout the physical, mental, moral, and practical character of the human race, to an incalculable extent, substituting falsehood for truth, and deception for sincerity, making human society, in the most civilized state to which it has yet attained, a mass of gross absurdities and of grave follies. All the knowledge which man has yet acquired of the Universe, is, that it exists, but why, or wherefore, he knows not. He is conscious that there must be some cause which gives action to the elements which it contains, but what that is, no man has, or combination of men have, any knowledge whatever.

And the strongest proof of the irrationality of our forefathers, and their ignorance of themselves, of nature, and its laws, may be derived from all their past gross absurdities, and grave follies respecting this Power in nature, of the qualities or attributes of which they are, and ever have been, totally ignorant. At this day, the cause of motion, life and mind, throughout the universe, is an enigma to man; a dark mystery hidden from his faculties, and totally incomprehensible to him; and yet man's life, through all preceding generations, has been a strife, contest, war, and massacre, respecting that which has been continually incomprehensible to every individual of his race. It continues to be thus, even at this day. He wastes his time, destroys his wealth, and deranges all his rational faculties about this Power, of which he knows nothing, and man continues to be divided against man, and nation against nation, to the extent of destroying or preventing the happiness which otherwise all might enjoy, in contending about that which all, in their calm moments, upon the slightest reflection, must admit is as much a mystery and as incomprehensible to them now as it was to our most ignorant, crude, and unenlightened ancestors. The only difference between them and us, in this respect, being, that we are perhaps more conscious of our mental infirmities regarding first causes than they were; for we are beginning to learn how totally ignorant of them the human race are at this day. But herein is cause for rejoicing, for the first true step towards knowledge, is the discovery of our ignorance.

Our religion; the only rational religion that ever will be upon the earth, is, to promote the happiness of the living existences upon it to the utmost extent practicable, with all the means in our power. This practice of religion is in accordance with common sense, or plain understanding of ordinary minds, and with, at the same time, the highest attainments of the human faculties. There is no mystery, no superstition, and no doubt about its beneficial results. It will never grow too old for the human race, never as all religions, so called, have, or will soon, become obsolete; but, on the contrary, as man advances in knowledge, and his faculties shall become more and more highly cultivated and improved, the more will this inestimable practical religion appear to be useful and necessary, and then, also, as the human intellect shall be made gradually to expand, will it the more and more be discovered, that it is the only religion that is in accordance with nature, or a rational state of human existence; – the only one that can ever make men wise, good, and happy, or the world permanently and progressively prosperous.

It is a religion to which no sane mind can object; there is nothing in it but unmixed good for all of the human race, now and through all futurity. There is nothing complicated in its whole extent; children, at an early period, as well as the most advanced in intellect and age, may easily be made to comprehend and to act upon it; – without much effort, it may be placed distinctly and indelibly upon the memory of every one, and the oftener it shall be repeated, with understanding, by young and old, the more valuable will it appear to every one, and the more benefit from its practice will be experienced by all.

It is true, that the world, as soon as efficient measures shall be adopted to make it rational, will have but one religion, language, and interest, and is there any other religion ever likely to become universal than this rational religion? All may believe in its truth; all may adopt its practice, even while they retain some of the impressions made on their minds by their respective local or geographical religions, – religions which, without any contest with them, will be gradually discovered by all, to be devoid of any other foundation, than the crude imaginations of the early generations of men, when they know little of this globe and less of themselves; when they were infants in real knowledge, and were without the light of science upon any subject; in fact, while the human faculties were incompetent to investigate, without superstitious fears and fancies, the laws of nature, so as to form a science based on well ascertained facts.

These varied local and geographical religions of the imaginations of our early ancestors have been the causes of disunion among mankind from the earliest period. They are so at this day; and while the professors of them preach or recommend the practice of charity for the feelings and opinions of those who differ from them, these religions destroy the very germs of charity in all who are taught conscientiously to believe in any one of them. And, at this day, there is no real charity to be found upon the earth among any of these spurious religions.

No! all these crude notions of our early ancestors will now, gradually, without violence of any kind, or ill-will on the part of those made too rational to entertain any of them, die the natural death of all error, when truth has been discovered.

And this change over the globe cannot occur too soon for the happiness of the human race; for while these deranging superstitions are forced into and retained by devotees to them, there will be no chance for man to be made rational in his feelings, thoughts, or actions.

What is now the great obstacle to an immediate happy state of existence in the British Empire? The superstitions which are called religion. This terrible monster of every kind of depravity now makes a pandemonium of England, Ireland, Scotland, and Wales; and makes it so by destroying every vestige of charity in those influenced by one kind of superstition, for those who by the ignorance of their education, are forced to believe some other of these most irrational imaginations by which their mental faculties are so lamentably deranged.

Were it not for this monster, which guards every avenue to common understanding, or simple rationality, the inhabitants of these islands, whom it now disunites to the greatest extent of hatred and contempt for each other, would speedily become charitable, kind, united, prosperous, and happy. The materials to effect this change exist in the utmost superfluity in Great Britain, and Ireland, and throughout the empire, – and it is the individual and general permanent interest of the whole population, that all should be now made charitable, kind, united in interest and feeling, prosperous and happy. It is, consequently, the first and highest interest of every one, that this monster of ignorant superstition should be now destroyed; and it can be destroyed only by the introduction of real knowledge, derived from well ascertained facts, to supersede the false learning of an irrational period in the history of the human race, when men were taught to *believe*, and not to *reason*, but to *condemn reason*, and instead thereof to receive the crude notions of the most *wild imaginations*. It is so even at this day; for proof of which, see the so called learned Presbyterians of Scotland, with their numerous insane divisions; – the population of Ireland, with the insanity of Catholic and Protestant contentions; – the innumerable opposing sects in England and Wales; – making together an heterogeneous mass of contending absurdities under the name of an enlightened people – absurdities such as the world in its first stages of ignorance and inexperience seldom if ever witnessed.

The period for effecting this great mental revolution appears to be at hand, and to be more ready to commence in the British Islands than in any other part of the world. Here the old formed mind is now at sea, without rudder or compass; the population is sailing in all directions, but at random, in search of truth, charity, kindness, and unity; which, however, owing to the dense fogs arising in all directions from the exhalations of various opposing superstitions, it cannot discover. The disappointment, however, which has been hitherto experienced, and the misery arising from the evils continually increasing from these contending superstitions, have, at length, given an earnestness to the search, that bids fair to enable men, ere long, to steer in the right course, to leave these fogs of superstition, and to enter the clear, smooth, and brilliant sea of truth and rationality; and then will men soon forget the dangers with which, on all sides, they have been so long surrounded.

But it is said, that man requires some being, or power, or principle to worship, and that the faculty of veneration,[a] implanted in his organization, previous to birth, must have some object, real or imaginary, to worship, to believe in, and to be submissive to, as a mental slave.

When man shall know himself, shall understand the general laws of humanity, and what human nature really is, he will know that *he* is not more, compared to the universe, and to the Power eternally giving motion, life, and mind, by endless changes throughout endless space, than a mere speck or atom, amidst innumerable systems of suns and planets which, to imagine, calls for the utmost stretch of the most enlarged minds; and these, when so expanded, must be lost in wonder, admiration, and delight, while contemplating the infinity of space, the eternity of duration, the mysterious laws of nature, and that Incomprehensible Power which everlastingly composes, decomposes, and recomposes the elements of all existences; and which Power excites the atom to action, and eternally governs the aggregate of nature.

But will man, when he shall acquire only the rudiments of rationality, imagine that he can ever do anything to honour or glorify such being, power, or principle? That any of his genuflections, forms, or ceremonies, acted upon this insignificant earth, of which man individually forms so insignificant a part, can be of any service whatever to that Power which to the human faculties is utterly incomprehensible; or that anything which man may say or do, himself being always an effect proceeding from this Incomprehensible Power, could, by possibility, be of use, benefit, or gratification, to such Power, or change the eternal laws of nature emanating from, or which may be, this Incomprehensible Power; but of which man knows nothing, except that which he sees around him, and the impressions which these make upon him to give him experience or knowledge.

All the time, money and faculty expended upon all the varied superstitions, popular at different periods of the world, in different countries, have been, in reality, applied to derange the human intellect, and keep it in a state of mental bondage and degradation. It has been an enormous waste of the most valuable materials, to produce an enormous amount of irrationality and wretchedness to man; keeping him, even to this day, in all the blindness of mental ignorance.

If it be reasonable to regret that which has passed, and cannot be recalled, surely it is to be lamented that such invaluable means, if wisely applied, should have been wasted in a futile attempt to do honour, (the honour by man!) to an infinite, eternal, and Incomprehensible Power, of which man knows not yet how to imagine anything approaching to rationality.

---

[a] A reference to phrenological categories of mental organisation and analysis.

Worship, veneration or exercise of the higher mental faculties will be called forth in the worship of truth, in the admiration of nature, when it shall be better understood, and when man shall be filled with the spirit of charity and love of nature; but of nature, cultivated to the full extent that man's faculties will admit; and then the earth will be beautiful. The first duty of man will appear to consist in the highest cultivation of the earth, and the animal creation upon it; but specially as a ground-work, the highest cultivation of the animal man, through whose improved faculties and increased powers this high cultivation of the earth and other animals is to be effected. Thus will man become, in the fulness of time, according to his nature, a rational being; and wisdom, order, peace, and happiness, will gradually extend over the world. Superstition will be unknown, contests will cease, the causes of division will be removed, and vice, crime, and misery, will be remembered only as effects produced during the past irrational period of human existence.

Thus will the direct consequences of religions, so called – or rather the madness of man, produced by an over excitement of his faculty of imagination, cease from the face of the earth, and the uncharitableness, unkindness, and all division of feeling, created by man's ignorance respecting his own nature, of the faculties with which he is endowed, and the manner in which his opinions and feelings are formed, will for ever terminate; and this pandemonium, produced by error, will be transformed, by truth, into a terrestrial paradise.

CONCLUDING CHAPTER

THE subjects under the name of Religion have hitherto occupied more of the time, attention, and, directly or indirectly, absorbed more of the capital of the world, than all other subjects, united, except war; and religions, so called, have been, mediately or more remotely, the cause of most wars, as well as of the universal division, unkindness, and uncharitableness, among the human race.

It is now ascertained, that the religions of the world have all originated in the vain imaginations of our ancestors, before they know how to investigate facts, to deduce accurate conclusions from them, and long before they had a knowledge of their own nature, or of the laws which govern humanity.

As the universe appears to be a system of necessary effects succeeding certain causes, through a chain mysterious to man, whose faculties cannot encompass the infinite and eternal, it follows that these opposing and deranging imaginations, called religions, have been necessary links in this endless chain; but it is equally certain that they cannot be much longer maintained in the mind of man, now that it has been discovered that these imaginations are directly opposed to the laws of nature, and tend only to perpetuate ignorance, imbecility, mental slavery, and hypocrisy.

There must be now a mighty effort made by the most mentally advanced, to throw off this incubus to the happiness of all in every country. Men, for the permanent well-being of their race, must now acquire moral courage to meet this monster of evil, openly encounter it, follow it even to its strongest holds and last retreat, and destroy it root and branch from the earth for ever. It has hitherto made mental cowards of mankind; made them, in all countries, and at all times, abject slaves to fears, conjured up by interested parties to keep man submissive to a class, trained to be the most wily, and, as a class, the most dishonest and injurious to their fellows of all the injurious classes into which society has ever been divided. Yet, as the characters of all these individuals have been formed for them, they are not more to be blamed than those trained in other classes. They have been the creatures of their peculiar circumstances.

The time for rationally blaming individuals for what they have been made by nature, and the education of localities, is fast passing away; it is useless, it is unjust and irrational, to blame or punish the individual priests of any religion; it is *the system* which forms all these priests that requires to be abandoned, and the principles on which the system is based, to be abrogated.

This is that great thing which is required now to be done, to prepare the way to make the human race wise, rational, united, permanently prosperous and happy, and always substantially increasing in knowledge of the laws of nature, and to increase in this knowledge, generation after generation, without limit.

When mankind shall become so rational as to terminate for ever an order of men, to teach that which is, to all men, incomprehensible, and therefore unteachable, then will the cause of disunion among the nations of the world cease for ever; then will charity and love supersede uncharitableness and unkindness; real knowledge will cover the earth, peace will universally prevail and be permanent; the evil and inferior passions and feelings, the necessary results of ignorance, will be unkown. The lovely qualities, only, of humanity will be carefully cultivated in each; and consequently all will be beloved; nature's laws, well understood, will become the sole laws of man, force and fraud will be no longer required to govern nations or individuals; the earth will be highly cultivated, all will be beneficially and pleasantly occupied; none, no not one, will be idle; man will be regenerated, and have a new mind, producing a new conduct, and each one will be secure in the enjoyment of a terrestrial paradise.

These delightful results will rapidly follow the abandonment of mysteries, miracles, superstitions, and the irrationality of wasting capital, time, and invaluable faculties, in vain attempts to explain that which is incomprehensible to the human mind; or in the yet greater absurdity, not to say ignorant impiety, of vain attempts by man, to honour Incomprehensible Power, or to do any manner of good to a power or being imagined to be omniscient, infinite, eternal and all-powerful, knowing and directing all things throughout the universe, past, present, and to come; a Power, the attributes of which are past man's finding out; but in the action or dispensation of which it is man's highest wisdom to acquiesce, making the best use of the faculties given to him, to promote, to the utmost extent of those faculties, the well-being, well-doing, and happiness of all that live upon the earth, but especially of his fellow men, whose nature, through a knowledge of himself, he will best comprehend.

The happiness described awaits the human race; but to obtain it and secure its permanence, or rather its never ending increase, through all succeeding generations, the source of past and present miseries must be abandoned, and society must be firmly based on those everlasting principles of truth, which are in accordance with all nature's known laws.

This change will terminate the language of falsehood, introduce the language of truth, open human nature like a map easily to be inspected and known, without deception of any kind, in the character, as formed for every individual. And it will be then discovered, that it will be for the permanent interest or happiness of every one to promote, to the utmost extent, the happiness of all.

END OF THE FOURTH PART

THE BOOK

OF THE

NEW MORAL WORLD,

EXPLANATORY OF

THE ELEMENTS OF THE SCIENCE OF SOCIETY,
OR OF THE SOCIAL STATE OF MAN.

BY ROBERT OWEN.

TRUTH WITHOUT MYSTERY, MIXTURE OF ERROR, OR FEAR OF MAN, CAN ALONE EMANCIPATE THE HUMAN RACE FROM SIN AND MISERY.

PART FIFTH.

London:
PUBLISHED FOR THE SOCIETY, BY
J. WATSON, 5, PAUL'S ALLEY, PATERNOSTER ROW;
AND ALL BOOKSELLERS.

1844.

THE BOOK
OF THE
NEW MORAL WORLD

FIFTH PART

THE ELEMENTS OF THE SCIENCE OF SOCIETY, OR OF THE SOCIAL STATE OF MAN

CHAPTER I

Having explained, in the four first parts of this work, the five fundamental facts, on which the science of the Rational System is based; the fundamental laws of human nature, or first principles of the science of man; the conditions requisite for human happiness; with the principles and practices of the Rational Religion; it is next in order now to explain the 'Elements of the Science of Society, or of the Social State of Man.'

Hitherto society has been a chaos in the minds of all, in every country, and in all ages. It never has been received as a science; the materials had never been collected in any mind, to form it into anything approaching even to a crude attempt at order or system in a general arrangement, for uniting men in society to produce for all, knowledge, unity, wealth, charity, kindness, progression, prosperity, and happiness, continually increasing as real knowledge extended from generation to generation. No such expanded view of society has been yet taken, by any parties in any age or country. The latest opportunity presented to the human mind, to evince the progress made towards a knowledge of the science of society, was that offered to the inhabitants of the thirteen United States in North America, when they obtained their freedom from their mother country.

Upon this subject, the highest advance made was evinced in the constitution formed by the most experienced men of that day, who took an active part in preparing and making it as perfect as their knowledge would admit.

With some of those individuals, and their immediate descendants, the Founder of the Rational System had most interesting personal confidential communication.[a] Especially with John Adams, the second President of the United States, Thomas Jefferson third, James Madison fourth, James Munroe fifth, John Quincey Adams sixth, General Jackson seventh, and Van Buren the eighth President of the United States, with Messrs Henry Clay, Calhoun, Crawford, and other aspirants to be candidates for that office.[b] Also with many of the leading statesmen of Europe, and many deemed highly experienced men of this country.

Yet, among all these eminent men, there was not one who had dived to the foundations of society, or ever suspected that it had a false base, and that all the efforts of man building upon that base, could never succeed in raising a superstructure of order, wisdom, and happiness. The men most active in promoting the adoption of the New American Constitution, and who wrote and perfected their 'Declaration of Rights,' acknowledged to the Founder of the Rational System, that they were, in 1825, after a trial of half a century, greatly disappointed in the result of the work, to accomplish which, they had exerted all their energies and ran the risk of the sacrifice of their lives. They were severely disappointed in the new character, growing up for the Americans under the new constitution, from which they had anticipated results far different. This sentiment was strongly expressed, and apparently deeply and keenly felt, especially by John Adams, Thomas Jefferson, James Madison, and James Munroe, all of whom, it was evident, desired to attain the most perfect society, and to introduce the best combination of it, both in principle and practice.

But not one of these experienced men ever imagined that it was necessary to change the fundamental principles on which society itself had been based from the beginning, and to found it anew upon the most opposite principles, before man could be formed into a rational being, and society made into a science, that would, in practice, ensure the permanent happiness of the human race.

When this idea was mentioned to Thomas Jefferson, who was perhaps the

---

[a] Owen addressed a joint meeting of the Senate and House of Representatives in Washington D.C. in February 1825, prior to commencing at New Harmony. See *infra*, vol. 2, p. 3–37.

[b] John Adams (1735–1826): 2nd President of the United States.
James Monroe (1758–1831): 5th President of the United States.
John Quincy Adams (1767–1848): 6th President of the United States.
Andrew Jackson (1767–1845): 7th President of the United States.
Martin Van Buren (1782–1862): 8th President of the United States.
Henry Clay (1777–1852): U.S. Senator.
John Calhoun (1806–59): Illinois politician.
William Harris Crawford (1772–1834): U.S. Senator.

most alive, of any of the parties previously named, to the errors of the existing system,[a] his mind recoiled at the very supposition of a new base for society; a base totally opposed to the only one he had ever previously considered; but after two or three days in close conversation, and steady consideration of the subject he became conscious of the necessity for a great change, which, sooner or later, he discovered must take place; but he confessed that he was unequal to the task of a new creation of the human character, or reorganization of society.

In the earlier days of these men, the progress of knowledge had not advanced so far in the best of minds, as to lead them to suspect that the very foundation of society was unsound, and that nothing stable, or permanently beneficial to the human race, could ever be erected upon it. The priesthood of the world had so effectually guarded all the avenues to real knowledge, and especially to the investigation of the human causes of human evil, that the strongest mind, trained under the circumstances which the superstitious had been instructed to create, never dared to approach these cunningly denominated sacred and divine subjects. The causes of incessant and perpetual evil to the human race, were, by the priests of all the varied superstitions which deranged the human faculties, tabooed from the touch or slightest inspection of the laity, under pain of excommunication or death.

Thus it was, that in the days of George Washington, John Adams, Thomas Jefferson, Patrick Henry, James Madison, James Munroe, Andrew Jackson, etc, etc, not one of them ever imagined that the countless evils suffered by humanity, emanated from a few fundamental errors, upon which society had ever alone been based. They therefore, in mental blindness, built their new, and, as they supposed, most perfect republic, upon sand, and it soon exhibited symptoms of the same unsound foundation on which all former governments, whether despotic or democratic, had been based. Upon such a foundation, the only one hitherto acted upon or known, trials to create a superior character, government, or society, will be sure to fail, should they be continued to all eternity. To continue to build upon sand, now that it is discovered to be sand only to the lowest depth, would be worse than past folly and irrationality.

The last new-formed government, the North American United States Constitution, formed with so much care, anxiety, and deliberation, by so many men whose minds had been gradually worked up, and aroused to a high state of disinterested enthusiasm, is itself the most decisive proof, by its signal failure, by good men, desirous of forming a rational and prosperous state of society, that the old systems of the world, based on the most lamentable errors, are dying their natural death, and that a new mode of existence must be given to man, and a new form to the society in which he must in future live.

[a] Jefferson was a deist, though he was circumspect about advertising his religious views publicly.

This is that change which an increase of knowledge in some, united with great suffering inflicted by this old system upon many, will now force upon the world.

And this will be a change from chaotic confusion, to order, system, and correct proportions; in fact, to a new state of human existence, based on unchanging laws of nature, and scientifically built up to ensure the superiority and happiness of mankind, not for the year or the century, but through all human futurity.

It is now necessary to inquire, what are the elements which compose society? Are they fixed, unchanging, or are they coeval with society itself? What then is society, when disrobed of the multiplied mysticisms which have been heaped upon it, and which have made it a perfect chaos in the minds of all men?

Society, when thus relieved from the ignorance of past times, may now be made a simple and beautiful arrangement to make man wise, good, and happy; the earth into a terrestrial paradise, and men united to produce harmony of thought and action, through all future generations. Society will then become an arrangement to enable man, when united with his fellows, – 1stly, To create the greatest amount of the most valuable wealth, in the shortest time, with the least labour or capital, and with the most pleasure to the producers of it. 2ndly, To distribute the wealth, thus produced, the most beneficially for the whole number who may have to partake of it. 3rdly, To form the best and happiest character for all that the individual organization of each will admit. 4thly, To govern all, locally and generally, to ensure the harmony and happiness of every member of the society in which he may happen to reside. And 5thly, To unite each separate nucleus of society, to form one harmonious whole, with all other nuclei in every part of the world.

A superior rational society will then be formed of the elements of production, distribution, formation of character, and governing; these elements being scientifically combined in their due proportions in every nucleus, or small division of society; each division being thus made, to a great extent, independent and complete within itself; that is, having all the means of self-support within its own boundaries, as far as the necessaries and ordinary comforts of existence are required, with a superior arrangement for the formation of character, and for local governing, with power to aid in the government of general society.

These elements of production, distribution, formation of character, and governing, exist in all stages and states of society, from the savage to the most civilized, and ever must exist, however in other respects the human race may increase in knowledge and power; for this progress will only enable future generations to benefit by a superior application of these same elements to practice. Society must always remain a combination of arrangements to produce and distribute wealth, to form individual and general character, and to govern locally and generally.

It may be said, that there is a *science* of production, a *science* of distribution, a *science* of forming character, and a *science* of governing, and that the essential progress of society will be in perfecting each of these sciences, and in uniting them in their due proportions, in each nucleus of society, in order to give the greatest advantage, and highest happiness, to each and to all individuals; the attainment of this result being the end and object of all human efforts.

But to produce and distribute wealth, form character, and govern in the best manner for the happiness of the human race, it will be, on reflection, evident that society, in its outline, detail, and entire ramification, must be reorganized and changed from its foundation, through every part of its superstructure; that it must be not only newly organized, but newly based and classified, and the character of all, from birth, newly formed in accordance with the new organization, base, and classification; and this entire change must be effected, in order that society may be consistent throughout, in principle and practice, in word, deed, and spirit.

Society must be thus changed before production, distribution, the formation of character, and governing, can be scientifically arranged and organized, so as to obtain the most beneficial results from each element of society separately, and from the whole united; – before the due proportion of each can be combined to form that which alone can be called a consistent, scientific, and rational arrangement of society.

When this arrangement shall be formed, and made familiar to the world in practice, the cause for competition and contest will no longer exist; individual possessions will cease, from the superabundance of wealth that will be annually created and produced, and always waiting the consumption of those who require it.

The scientific power of production, properly applied, under health and pleasurable direction, will enable the few to over-supply the wants and wishes of all consumers, however many they may be, leaving always a surplus to be destroyed annually, to make room for the new and superior production of the current year, to supersede the old stock. When society shall be thus constructed, with scientific power universally introduced and wisely directed, *money* will become useless, unsought for, and will be for ever abandoned, and gold and silver will then find their intrinsic value; a value below iron and steel. To effect this change, all required will be, that efficient and suitable stores and warehouses shall be erected, convenient for each nucleus of society, or community, of from 2,000 to 3,000 persons; – such stores and warehouses to be efficient to contain all the wealth that can be required for the permanent demand of the numbers in each nucleus; and that these stores and warehouses should be kept supplied, as the various articles are taken out for consumption. To keep up the supply equal to the wants of a rational-made society, will be all that will be required, physically from the population, and with the enormous aid that can now, without additional discoveries, be derived from former and modern scientific inventions, discoveries, and improvements, to furnish this supply, will be no more than healthy and pleasant exercise to the younger members, under thirty years of age, in every association or community, and a continual source of rational occupation, for amusement to the older members.

It is sufficient to know that society possesses powers the most ample, when they shall be understood by the public, and wisely directed, to over-supply itself with all that can be rationally desired by the population of the habitable parts of the earth, or at least of any part that ever need to be inhabited. And also, to form a superior character for all these individuals, by surrounding them, from birth, with circumstances so arranged as to effect this result.

The knowledge that these powers do exist throughout society, or may easily be made to do so, is the true foundation for an enlightened equality, and, when followed to all their legitimate and natural consequences, will open wide the door to an amount of permanent happiness for the human race upon earth, under the government of knowledge, charity, and love, of which the present faculties of man, mistrained and directed as they have been, can form only imperfect imaginations, far short of what the reality may be made to become.

The more extended detail of these measures will be found in the next and succeeding chapters.

CHAPTER II

'On the practical knowledge of the best mode of producing, in abundance, the most beneficial necessaries and comforts, for the support and enjoyment of human life.'

The element of production is, in one sense, the most important of all the elements of society, Without it, the human race could not exist, except in small numbers, and in a savage state. This element increases in importance as the population of the earth multiplies; but such has been the progress of society, that the powers of production have continually kept in advance of this increase of the numbers of the earth. In the last century, this element has increased in power, within the British Isles, beyond the increase of population, much more than twenty to one, and it is now capable of illimitable increase for the benefit of the human race; and a monopoly of this power within any country, if it could be so restrained, would be an injury to every country, and to all individuals.

The increase of mechanical inventions and chemical discoveries, with the means of illimitable additions to both, in proportion as science shall advance and experience extend, have secured to mankind the most ample sources of maintenance, in a superfluity of comfort, and, if found to be permanently desirable, in splendid magnificence.

But this element or power of production is, at present, a chaos in the human mind, and a mass of absurdity in practice. In consequence, the productive powers of society are everywhere misapplied and most extravagantly wasted, even when the greatest economy is intended to be worked out by individuals, companies, or nations.

The practice of the world, with respect to this element, has been erroneous, in the same proportion that the means to obtain real power has been augmented. And now, when it is far more powerful than it has been at any former period in the history of the world, it is the most uselessly and injuriously directed. Instead of this power being made efficient, as it now easily might be made, to remove poverty, or the possible fear of it, and to create wealth to overflowing for the people of all nations, and for endless centuries, it is applied, 1st, To create and maintain enormous warlike powers to waste and destroy daily more wealth than, if wisely directed, would ensure abundance of all the necessaries and comforts which man could or would require. 2ndly, To waste and destroy the second large amount of it in support of the insanity of theology; indeed, it may be doubted whether, in the present most irrational state of human existence, the warrior or the priest destroy most of the faculty and wealth of the world; but it is certain that both annually either waste, destroy, or prevent the production of more wealth than, wisely applied, would maintain the population of the world permanently in great comfort, harmony, and happiness.

This element of happiness is not at all yet understood by any portion of mankind; it is under the direction of localized individual ignorance, and it is scarcely possible to conceive how this element could be worse applied, for all rational purposes, than it is now in Great Britain. To produce the greatest amount of the most valuable wealth, in the best manner, is yet a science now to be learned, for the first time, by the population of the world.

It is a science deserving the best application of the faculties of the human race – it is the groundwork of all practical sciences. To live, is the first call upon man's exertions: without the means of existence being secured, he can make little progress in any higher pursuits; and the second is, to live in rational comfort, or under such circumstances as will allow the beneficial exercise of all his faculties for the happiness of his race, and consequently of himself.

The first proper business of society is to secure these two results permanently for the human race. There must be enough annually produced for all, before justice, virtue, or happiness can exist among men. – The means to produce enough, and with pleasure, are now at the control of the governments of the world.

It is the proper business of all governments to apply these means, and to call the natural and scientific powers of production into action, *until the existence of every individual under their government shall be permanently secured in comfort, and with full security for its continuance during their lives.*

This result, through a scientific or superior arrangement of society, may be now easily effected; but to accomplish this first step in practice of a rational state of human existence, the production of the wealth to enable all to live in comfort must be learned as a science, in connexion with the science of its distribution, the science of the formation of character, and the science of governing locally and generally; but of these additional sciences, an explanation, in considerable detail, will be given in subsequent chapters in this part of the book.

To produce wealth abundantly, under these arrangements, will be a pleasurable exercise for the young, healthy, and active portion of the population, and under such combined scientific arrangement, *there need not be, throughout the world, one individual in poverty, or even in the fear of it.* It is a sure proof that, while one individual is in poverty, or the fear of it, with the enormous powers of production of all kinds of wealth at the control of society, that governments and people are yet unacquainted with the sciences of production, distribution, the formation of character, and of governing. Yet all, from the highest to the lowest, in one way or another, for want of this knowledge, are grievous sufferers, and in consequence are deprived of knowing what the happiness of a state of rational existence upon earth would be, if once fairly introduced into practice.

But how are the powers of production now wielded and employed over the world?

The reply to this question, in truthful accordance with existing facts, will open a field of error to investigation such as must astonish all who have not reflected upon the subject.

The misdirection of this power, and its most extravagent waste in all direction, under the old, worn-out system of individual and national competition, exceeds all means of correct estimate, and a loss to all individuals far beyond the present limited comprehension of the public mind.

The probable annual production of wealth now created in the British empire, may be stated, without being too far from the truth to affect the following calculations and reasoning, to be between three and four hundred millions of pounds sterling, at the present value of money.

But with the powers of production, natural and artificial, *now* at the control of the British government and people, were they cordially united, this amount of annual creation might be with ease increased from so many hundreds of millions to at least an equal number of thousands of millions; indeed, increased to an illimitable extent – to an extent far beyond all possible wants of the population; and the like result may be effected by all nations over the globe.

To effect these results, an entirely new view of society must be taken, and extensive new arrangements foreseen and gradually adopted; but the prize beyond all estimate now to be acquired will prove well worthy the effort necessary for its attainment.

That this subject may be understood by those who are unacquainted with the statements which have been given elsewhere, some important facts will require to be shortly restated here.

About a century since, the population of Great Britain and Ireland was about fifteen millions. The productive power, in round numbers, consisted of three millions of manual power, and equal, in round numbers, to about twelve millions of old established mechanical and other scientific power; – of such old crude mechanical powers as existed just previous to the introduction into practice of the great mechanical and chemical improvements emanating from the minds of Watt[a] and Arkwright.[b] With the discoveries and inventions of these two extraordinary men commenced the reign of a century of a new manufacturing system in Great Britain, a system which, in its unforeseen progress, has produced, and in its further unavoidable advance will produce, changes in human affairs, which, until now, no mind ever contemplated. *Through great and innumerable sufferings, and much error in principle and practice, it will in its due time secure an earthly paradise to the human race*; but in its progress, it has been the means of creating more inferior and injurious circumstances around a large portion of those engaged in its active operations than have ever been produced by the savage, hunting, pastoral, or agricultural and commercial stages of human progress. These inferior and injurious circumstances have, to a great extent, in vast numbers, deteriorated their physical powers and mental capacities, and have made them most abject and miserable beings. But this new manufacturing system has also greatly enlarged the power and capacity of another portion of those under its immediate influence, – of those who had to invent, to arrange, to superintend in various departments, and to direct multiplied combined operations upon a large scale. These faculties of human nature, through a desire to amass large amounts of individual wealth, were called and stimulated onward to an activity far surpassing any previously known, in a similar direction, for individual gain. It may be termed *the war of wealth*, in which each is trained to scramble for the most he can, in any way, by his individual powers obtain.

There can be no doubt that this system has created stimuli to exertion for individual gain, similar to the stimuli for war to obtain national plunder and fame. But very different will be the results when superior peaceful faculties and powers shall be brought into full activity; for it is now evident that the inventive faculty will ere long terminate the activity of the powers and propensities for war. *Invention, wisely directed*, will obtain an incalculable

[a] James Watt (1736–1819): inventor of the steam engine.
[b] Sir Richard Arkwright (1732–92): inventor of textile machinery.

greater amount of advantages in peace for humanity, than *the most successful warlike operations* ever did or can. *Invention*, wisely directed, will increase and preserve the most valuable wealth, *while war*, now, will *prevent* its increase, and *destroy*, to a great extent, that which has been already created. Any rational cause for war no longer exists; man requires for his well-being and happiness now, other faculties to be brought into action than those of war, contest, and competition. These preliminary powers of humanity have performed their task, and they are destined now to give place to inventions and discoveries, to create, preserve, and unite. The period for the evils of disunion is rapidly passing, and the time for one language to be acquired, one interest to be understood, and one heart and mind to be formed for the human race, as rapidly approaches. The steam paths by land and water, in all directions, are making for these new powers a facility to travel along with railway speed to the uttermost parts of the earth. The time comes when man will be too wise to destroy, when it is his permanent highest interest to create; or to waste, when it is his true interest to preserve; or divide and oppose, when it is his best interest to unite and aid.

The advances already made towards this change, would, a short period past, have been pronounced by all, impossibilities never to be realized. But impossibilities are now daily vanishing, one after another, until man will ere long hesitate to say again what *is* impossible. Already, in one century, he has increased the wealth-making productive powers at his control, from an amount, in the British Islands, equal to the labour of fifteen millions, to an amount exceeding the labour of eight hundred millions, with the most ample means to effect a rapid and extensive increase; an increase illimitable by man in his present state of little more than local knowledge, and isolated opposing exertions.

With this enormous amount of new scientific power in aid of manual labour, which it may soon be made greatly to supersede, there is no necessity for man being longer deceived by what are called the civil professions, however long-established and venerable; they are devices arising necessarily from the fundamental errors of the old system of the world, and have been applied to mystify, confound, and derange the intellects of, and extract most unjustly the wealth from, those who produce the wealth, giving them in return only the poison of human happiness.

The waste of wealth in the support of these, now far worse than merely useless professions, enormous as that waste is, will not represent anything approaching to the extent of the direct and indirect injury which they inflict upon society. They are the real instruments used by the landed aristocracy and wealthy members of society, to oppress, and mentally and physically to degrade the mass; the most usefully industrious mass of society in all countries. The members of these professions have not, most evidently, the slightest notion of the grievous evils which they are made the immediate instruments to inflict upon themselves and society.

Upon themselves and their families as well as all society; for they are themselves great and severe sufferers by the deception first practised upon them when young and inexperienced, and by the deceptions which the various professions practise on each other and upon the public, by which the character and condition of all are reduced to a very low standard of virtue and of happiness.

The civil and military professions are the combined power of force and fraud, directed by the governments of the world to keep the great mass of its population in poverty, disunited, criminal, degraded, irrational, and miserable; while these results reach, with an influence little suspected by the aristocracy of the most powerful nations, upon those who have the governing influence in each state under their control.

None under this system can be virtuous, rational, or safe, even with the highest of the very limited advantages which this wretchedly imagined system can give to the most favoured class of individuals.

These civil and military professions not only waste most injuriously, as previously stated, a very large amount of the limited wealth which is annually created under the most inferior and worst circumstances in which it is produced; but, by the efficient physical members of society, seduced through ignorance into the armies and navies of the world, and the more efficient intellectual members of society who are seduced into the civil professions, and unitedly trained and placed to deteriorate society to an incalculable extent, prevent by these means the creation of new wealth, far more, by many times multiplied, than all the riches produced under the present system over the world, in addition to these professions being the most powerful demoralizers of the human race, making real virtue to be disesteemed and degraded as if it were vice, and vice and crime to be esteemed and exalted as though they were the highest virtues.

In fact, they destroy, or prevent the creation of more wealth than could secure the highest permanent prosperity to the population of the world; while, at the same time, they irrationalize and demoralize it to an extent beyond the utmost bounds of the present public mind even to imagine. The riches wasted, deteriorated, or prevented from being created, directly or indirectly, by these professions, under the direction of the aristocracy of the so-called civilized nations, will amount, in the empire of Great Britain alone, to probably more than a thousand millions sterling annually. The earth teems with all the materials to create illimitable wealth; science now offers illimitable powers to apply those materials to obtain wealth from the surface and depths of both land and water, more abundantly than if society had discovered the long vainly sought for, and when found useless, philosopher's stone.

In short, let men be enabled to open their eyes to real existences, and to their now acquired power to act most beneficially upon those existences, and it will be discovered that already the time has arrived when, by the most simple and beautiful arrangements, with no more exercise of body and mind than will be found requisite to keep men and women in the best state of health, to enjoy the highest physical and mental happiness, far more of the most desirable wealth may be annually created than it is possible for the population of the world rationally to consume; each one being permitted to use it freely, without any other restraint than that which would necessarily exist in the mind of every one, as all would be trained to feel, think, and act rationally from birth, through life to attend.

Added to the incalculable deterioration of character and loss of wealth arising from the introduction and continuance of the military and civil professions, are the deterioration of character and loss of wealth under the existing system throughout society, of buying and selling for a monied profit. The loss of both exceeds all present imaginations upon the subject: but as the more extended detail of this division of loss of character and loss of wealth will be given in the succeeding chapter, on the science of the distribution of wealth, it may suffice now to say, that the direct and indirect loss of wealth by the present practice of buying and selling for a monied profit, is equal to a large portion of the wealth now annually created.

Another most enormous loss of wealth arises from the most unwise practice of allowing, by the rich, so large a portion of the now only industrious class to grow up in ignorance, when so much valuable knowledge in principle and practice might be given to them; and in allowing them to be surrounded, from their birth, with inferior external circumstances, and then to apply their ill-trained powers without being aided by the invaluable experience of the most experienced, or with the capital necessary to give full efficiency to their active exertions of body and mind.

The amount of physical and mental power to create superior wealth, which is thus lost or wasted, far exceeds all other losses united. The ignorant, isolated condition of nine-tenths of the population of the world, thus, through neglect, rendered comparatively useless, and often in great numbers most injurious, creates a loss of wealth not to be estimated by any ordinary powers of calculation; and as to the loss arising from the neglect of cultivating the superior faculties of this mass, so as to form them into rational instead of irrational beings, no one is now prepared with sufficient experience to estimate, or to enter, with any chance of success, upon the calculation; – suffice it to say, that here is a mine of wealth almost unopened, certainly never rationally viewed, of far more value than all the mines of silver and gold and precious stones ever discovered, or that ever will be found within the bowels of the earth. The power of turning all things into gold would be of infinitely less value than the power, properly applied, to well cultivate and draw into active application all the good qualities that could be created in each individual of the human race. And yet each individual of the human race is deeply interested in the superior formation of the character, and in the actual good conduct of every other individual.

No gain to man individually, or to nations generally, can be compared with that which will arise from each one at birth, and through life being made as perfect as the natural, physical, mental, moral, and practical powers of every one will admit. This will indeed be a gain of illimitable amount, far beyond all present human calculation.

Another enormous amount of loss of wealth and of happiness arises from the ignorance of the population of the world respecting the science of the influence of circumstances over individuals, nations, and the human race.

When a knowledge of this science shall be acquired in principle, and its best mode of application to practice, a new and very superior world will be made manifest to the human faculties.

Although it has been said and thought, by those who have been trained to reflect upon the causes whence effects uniformly proceed, or follow so certainly that hitherto the one has always succeeded the other, that 'man is the creature of circumstances;' yet who has acquired the knowledge to make the knowledge of this circumstance to be itself the means of giving the future man the power to know what circumstances are injurious to the human race – what beneficial? and yet more to know how to remove the former, and to make a new combination of circumstances around mankind, in every part of the world, which shall consist altogether of the latter; or, in other words, to abolish all the inferior circumstances of man's creation during the state of his irrational existence, and to replace them by the most superior circumstances that man, with this knowledge, will possess the power to create?

Is the human mind yet open to appreciate the value of this knowledge and this power? Can it comprehend the change which this practice will some time hence make in the general condition of the human race? Is it prepared to calculate the annual increase of wealth which will be produced, for the use and enjoyment of all, when it shall be brought forth under the most superior, instead of the most inferior circumstances? And are there yet any who understand the extent of the existing inferior circumstances for the creation of wealth, formed by man during the past irrational state of his existence, and the evils thence arising? Are there any who have yet considered the extent of the new, most inferior, and degrading circumstances created within the last half century by the competitive increase of the new manufacturing system of Great Britain? No: this knowledge, so valuable for man to acquire, has hitherto been hidden from him – it is yet unknown to him. But the dawn of the day of this knowledge approaches, – the destruction of the causes of man's misery, and the advent of his happiness, draw nigh; the inferior shall soon give place to the superior, and man shall exist in the midst of those circumstances alone which shall ensure health, wealth, knowledge, unity, goodness, and happiness?

In enumerating the many great causes which create a loss of enormous masses of wealth to the population of the British empire, the want of superior knowledge, in principle and practice, of those elected to make its laws and direct its government, is one of the greatest, if not the greatest of all.

In fact, the want of knowledge in those who direct the government of the civilized world, is the one great cause which allows the existence of all the other causes that keep any portion of the human race now in ignorance or poverty, or in any degree in the fear of poverty, for themselves or descendants, through future ages.

With the surface of the earth, capable as it is now known to be – with its mines and minerals below the surface – with the all-powerful aid to work both from the discoveries in chemistry and inventions in mechanics – with the skill and industry brought into action in the new and scientific manufactures of Europe and America – and with the annual increase of a population which may be made, by a wise formation of the character of each individual from birth, invaluable for directing the new scientific improvements already introduced, and in the discovery of others which, without assignable limits, may be made; – with these incalculable advantages superadded to the newly-acquired knowledge, how, by a superior arrangement of circumstances, formed on the newly-discovered laws of human nature for the formation of a rational character for man, now and throughout futurity; – were the governing influences of the civilized nations experienced in these matters, real wealth, of substantial value to man, might be annually created, with pleasure to all parties, far exceeding any wants that could arise among a people once made rational.

But examine the proceedings of the British parliament for the last century, an assembly admitted to be the most advanced in political and general knowledge of any public assembly in the world, and the directors of those who govern the greatest combination of worldly power that has ever existed in the known history of man; and yet, with all these advantages, there will not be found recorded in the speeches of these men a single paragraph indicative of a knowledge of themselves, of the laws of humanity, as they have ever existed, or of society, as it should be constituted for the happiness of their race. Every law which they have made, has been an ignorant law of inexperienced man, in opposition to the eternal laws of man's nature – to that nature which contains, at birth, the germs of the same qualities at this day as existed in our ancestors at the earliest period known.

The laws promulgated from this august assembly, as it is often called, have been, and are, the bane of British society: when it was first established, men were ignorant and irrational, and although they have acquired experience in many matters, and made much progress in a knowledge of the arts and sciences, they are still ignorant and irrational, – they have made but slow advances in a knowledge of themselves, the laws of their own nature, or of the means necessary to constitute a rational and happy society, or to produce peace on earth and good will to man.

The errors of the British parliament are at this day most grievously experienced throughout the empire, and, by its influence and example, in all the nations of the world. It has permitted, it yet permits, the most false and injurious direction to be given to the newly-acquired powers derived from the discoveries in the various sciences. It permits a power equal to the productive capacity of nearly a thousand millions of well-trained, active, adult human beings, to be so miserably directed as to produce far less prosperity and happiness for a population not exceeding twenty-eight millions, than was attained a century ago by a power of production not exceeding fifteen millions.

It is then probable that this assembly must discover the means peaceably to re-organize society, or that society will, by some other mode, be re-organized; for it cannot much longer proceed under the present errors, in principle and practice, which influence and direct the whole proceedings of the British parliament. The errors in principle and practice of this assembly, which so materially influence, directly or indirectly, the affairs of the civilized parts of the world, create a loss of wealth to the nations forming this part, far beyond any estimate that the limited mind of any persons, trained under the deteriorating influences of the old system of society, have the capacity to comprehend; the amount far exceeds many hundred thousand millions of pounds sterling annually, or a value of wealth far exceeding the whole amount now produced by this, so called, enlightened part of the earth. When the difference between the results ensuing from the principles of error hitherto alone acted upon by the human race, and the principles of truth emanating directly from the laws of nature, unknown to change, shall be made manifest to those who rule the nations of the world, they, as well as those over whom they rule, will be confounded with the extent of the evils for which they now contend, as though evil, in its very worst form, was the chief object to be attained by man's utmost exertions.

The imperial parliament of the British empire, the most advanced concentrated mental power now in existence, is, during its sittings in session, daily inflicting, unconsciously, the greatest injustice on its own members, their posterity, and upon the human race. It encourages, and defends, and engenders, under the names of religion, justice, and virtue, every kind of vice and crime that can, through error, be implanted and cultivated in human nature, when aided by powers derived from scientific discoveries which overwhelm all individual opposition. It is a terrific power for evil; it may be made to become an irresistible power for good; it must be the former while influenced by fundamental principles of error; it will become the latter when all its proceedings shall be based on fundamental principles derived solely from nature, or, in other words, on principles which, by their unchanging consistency and undeviating accordance with all known facts, demonstrate themselves to be true, and the only principles, when applied to practice, that can ever make man good, rational, and happy, and form society to be universally charitable, by uniting the human race in one language, one interest, and in one general feeling of vivid desire, carried into strong, unceasing, active, practice, to promote cordially and earnestly the improvement and happiness of every one.

The imperial British parliament, properly constituted, is, by far, the best existing power to effect peaceably, and most beneficially for the human race, this great change in the constitution of society over the world. It may now commence, with great advantage, at the opening of the next session of the present parliament, to prepare the minds of the public to abandon, in due time, upon a magnificent scale, the errors of our inexperienced ancestors, and to adopt, upon a scale yet more magnificent, the fundamental principles of truth in accordance with all nature, and the glorious practices which will necessarily emanate from this true source of knowledge and happiness.

See how beautifully the agitations of the Irish repealers,[a] of the corn-law repealers,[b] of the free-church advocates,[c] of the Puseyites,[d] the extended church builders,[e] the O'Connor and Sturgite chartists,[f] the contending educators, and no-education-for-the-poor advocates; with the friends of emigration, of the repeal of all monopoly, of all indirect taxes, of an extended paper currency, of fixity of landed tenures, of united interest in opposition to competition; and, last, of a change from the present irrational, to a full and complete rational state of society. Yes, see how beautifully and powerfully one and all of these active parties, with many other contending schemes and plans, are preparing to make it easy of practice for the Imperial Parliament to silence all, stay the proceedings of all, allay the national ferment, and satisfy all, by abandoning openly and boldy all its proved errors in principle and practice, and by throwing itself, with the necessary moral courage, firmness, and perseverance, upon the public opinion of the world, adopt the great and glorious fundamental principles of nature for the future formation of the human character from the birth of each infant, and for the foundation of a rational construction of society which shall benefit all, and therefore be universally extended throughout all the nations of the earth.

Let the Imperial Parliament of Great Britain thus act at the opening of the ensuing session, and by its measures save itself, the British empire, and the

---

[a] Irish repealers sought to end the union of England with Ireland.

[b] The Corn Laws supported domestic wheat production by preventing foreign corn from entering before domestic prices had reached a certain level. They were renewed in 1815 and abolished in 1846.

[c] The Free Church of Scotland was formed in 1843 in opposition to patronage and state interference in the Church of Scotland.

[d] Puseyites were followers of Edward Pusey (1800–82), Regius Professor of Hebrew at Oxford and supporter of Anglican revival.

[e] Advocates of a new church building programme in the late 1830s.

[f] Among the radical political reformers, Feargus O'Connor (1794–1855) was the most popular Chartist leader. Joseph Sturge (1793–1859) was an anti-slavery and Anti-Corn Law League reformer.

civilized world, from the horrors of revolution after revolution, until its population shall be overwhelmed with contention, murder, and plunder, and the sacrifice of its best and most valuable members, who will attempt to stay this madness of blind, ignorant selfishness.

CHAPTER III

'On the practical knowledge of the best mode of distributing these productions most advantageously for all.'

THE second great and permanent element of all society is the *distribution* of the wealth after it has been produced, that it may sustain life and increase happiness. All nations and people must have some mode of distribution, and this has varied at different periods in all countries.

It has been the most justly effected by the North American Indians, before their characters were deteriorated by the white men and their superstitions. Many, if not all, the tribes of these savages, as the Christians have called and treated them, divided to them the most essential portion of their wealth – their food, – according to the natural wants of the members of the tribe, giving it when they had suffered want, first to the children, then to the women, and last to the men who had procured it.

But the general mode adopted by our early ancestors was not this simple and most honest practice of the Indians upon the principle of public property, but that of individual barter, exchanging commodity for commodity, until money was invented, and became the general custom with most nations. Money offered many conveniences, at its introduction into practice, and for some centuries afterwards; but latterly it has introduced evils far exceeding its advantages. It is now made the instrument of the grossest injustice and oppression, and espcially in those nations calling themselves the most enlightened. It is now made to be an instrument for swindling upon the largest scale, and it is used by the wealthy at this day to extract, in a manner mysterious to the ignorant, the most valuable wealth from those who labour hard to produce it, and to give the accumulation and enjoyment of it to the most useless, if not the most injurious, members of society.

The money thus used and applied is artificial, and possesses little or no intrinsic worth. It is paper, or gold, or silver, or copper; the first having no intrinsic worth, while gold, silver, and copper are not equal as metals to iron, steel, and some other metals.

In Great Britain and the United States of North America, the two most commercial nations in the world, this artifical money is highly advantageous to sharpers and swindlers having wealth and consequent power; but most injurious to the industrious classes of all countries, and by its artificial influence upon society, is the cause of preventing the creation of more wealth annually than is now produced. It is an artificial cause to perpetuate ignorance and poverty and disunion among mankind. It isolates man's interests in the midst of millions whom he could serve, and who would in return amply compensate him. Although this foreign and artificial money is not the root of *all* evil,[a] for it is ignorance alone which is that root, yet it is now the cause of incalculable error and misery to the human race, and a main cause of creating and maintaining the ignorant selfishness which in modern times so generally pervades the population of most countries, but especially those nations who are commercially the most wealthy. It is the artificial medium which enables some few to become enormously rich at the expense of the many, dooming masses of them to the lowest stage of poverty and degradation; those who produce the real wealth suffering the latter, while those who make the artificial wealth, or money from paper, gold, silver, or copper, enjoy all the advantages at present derivable from real wealth, which they obtain for their artificial wealth.

In a rational state of society, this irrational mode of distributing wealth will be abandoned, and full justice will be done to every one, and every one will act justly to every one.

Wealth, under the present system of society throughout all civilized countries, is distributed in the most extravagant and worst manner that could be adopted for the benefit of the producers, distributors, and consumers of it.

This distribution of wealth has arisen gradually from the errors of the fundamental principles on which all society hitherto has been based; it is a necessary result of the complicated, confused, and chaotic state of social life which those errors have produced in all countries. Those errors have isolated man, his feelings, and his interest, and made him a most ignorant, selfish being; desirous thus made, to grasp all for the benefit of himself and family, he loses wealth, knowledge, and happiness, of which, in his isolated state, he can form no conception; – a tithe of the advantages thus lost would be now deemed visionary to expect in this life. Those who now distribute the wealth of society are the retail and wholesale dealers throughout the cities, towns, and villages; the merchants, bankers, and brokers, and agents in the home and foreign trade, with the receivers of rents, taxes, salaries, and interest for capital. The professions are also distributors of the wealth which they extract from the public for their supposed necessary and valuable services, like the legislators and other members of the aristocracy.

Yet, in a rational state of society, these, one and all, would have no

[a] See 1 Timothy 6:10.

existence; there would be no necessity for one of them, but, on the contrary, they would be discovered, with some very partial exceptions, to be very much worse than useless.

To produce wealth, to educate in real knowledge, to remove the inferior and substitute superior circumstances, will be, in a rational state of society, the substantial business of all, until abundance of all that is good for man shall be produced, a superior character formed for all, and the existing injurious circumstances shall be replaced by those calculated to benefit all from their birth to their death.

To effect this change is the first and highest interest of man; it is his individual and universal interest, and all will be well instructed thus to act.

When this first stage of a rational existence shall be attained, and when all men shall have, without anxiety or fear, as much of the necessaries of life as health requires, and shall also receive from birth a good education, physical, mental, moral, and practical, and when the inferior circumstances shall have been exchanged for superior, then may men justly and rationally advance another stage in civilization, and employ surplus time and capital to decorate, ornament, and improve the condition of all, without limit, as far as the capital and knowlege of society will admit.[a]

But to accomplish this result in high perfection, no arrangement admitting of retail or wholesale dealers, professions, bankers, or merchants, trading for individual profit, agents, brokers, or idlers of any kind will be necessary.

These parties, who, were they well-trained and placed, might easily be made, in a properly constituted and well-organized society, to create, with greatly increased advantages to themselves and society, three or four hundred millions annually of the most valuable wealth, are now so unfortunately placed, that they cost the present actual producers of the wealth which they consume, much more than two hundred millions sterling every year.

And for what services is this direct expense, on one hand, and the loss of wealth that they might create, on the other, sustained by society? For none that is of any real value to any portion of the human race – for none that might not very speedily be dispensed with, as not only useless, but very injurious to the best and highest interests of the population; injurious to the minds and bodies of all, to their own as well as to others.

None of those parties create one particle of wealth during their lives, but aid in deteriorating much that has been previously good and wholesome. No such classes will be required in a rational state of existence. The training to be good wholesale or retail dealers, or to be of any of the professions, deteriorates, to an incalculable extent, the character of every one so trained and placed. To

[a] This emphasis on the decorative and ornamental contrasts with the more spartan or puritanical ideas of self-restraint Owen sometimes appeared to promote in the 1820s. See the general introduction, *infra*, vol. 1, p. xxxvii.

endeavour to buy cheap and sell dear, or to mystify knowledge, is destruction of superior mental powers. Under arrangements to effect a rational state of human existence, there will be no necessity for these consumers and non-producers. All in this new state of life will be trained to be essentially valuable producers of wealth and teachers of knowledge, and then they may advantageously be consumers of the best wealth of every kind, and the enjoyers of superior knowledge under the most favourable circumstances to perpetuate health and happiness to the most advanced period to which these advantages will enable life to be extended.

The distribution of wealth in the rational state of society will be the most simple of all the departments into which the business of life will be divided.

The wealth, as produced, will be lodged in stores or warehouses, suitable to its qualities for keeping it in the best condition for use; and in each nucleus of society, that is, in each association of from one to three thousand persons of all ages, parties of the proper age for this occupation, will be distributors of such wealth as will be required daily for those numbers. By this simple arrangement, the carriage first to one place and then to another will be avoided – the deterioration by being divided and subdivided will be prevented, the injury arising from placing various articles of food especially, in unfavourable temperatures, will not take place: the waste of time waiting for customers will never occur, risk of sale will be unknown; spoiling stock and wasting time in choosing and bargaining will be done away with; the inferior character which the retail trade creates by its immediate dependence for profit upon customers, will cease to be formed; and above all, the depreciation and misapplication of the human faculties by being trained as tradesmen, merchants, bankers, professional characters, or idlers, to endeavour to buy cheap and sell dear, will be put an end to for ever. Its extremely injurious effects will become so obvious, that it will never again be resumed in practice.

Distribution will, therefore, become merely the giving out of those things daily wanted for use and consumption. It will be, in the rational state of society, a healthy, pleasant, light employment for those members of the new proposed associations or communities, who may be from twenty-five to thirty years of age, after they shall have passed through the previous periods for *producing* wealth. They will, at that age, after their previous training and experience, know the qualities and value of the wealth which they will have under their care to preserve and to distribute; and they will be thus well prepared to effect both, economically and in the best manner, for all the members of their society and for themselves.

CHAPTER IV

'On the knowledge of the principles and practices by which to form the new combinations for training the infant to become, at maturity, the most rational being.'

To have this knowledge, it is necessary to be well versed in a science yet unknown to the world; it may be called the 'science of the overwhelming influence of circumstances over human nature.'

This knowledge is new to the world; all must be taught to acquire and apply it beneficially for all.

To know the causes which have hitherto retained the human race in ignorance of their own nature and of humanity; which have kept them, unto this day, in a most irrational state of society, and made them vicious and miserable; and also to know the causes which are competent to remove this ignorance, irrationality, vice, and misery, and how to introduce and apply these causes for the general benefit of mankind; is an advance in mental science which has been until now hidden from men.

Yet it is knowledge the most important for man to attain; his future well-being and his attainment of rationality and prospect of permanent happiness depend upon it.

This science can alone resolve the great question, 'What are the circumstances which keep the human race in an irrational state, and what are those which can transform them into rational beings?' Until now, no answer could be given to this question, although upon its solution depends the permanent misery or happiness of mankind.

The cause of the irrationality of man through past ages, has been his *born* ignorance of himself, and the incapacity of his mental faculties to discover through a correct and patient investigation of facts, what are the unchanging laws of humanity; and having, through an inexperienced imagination, supposed, in opposition to all facts, that these laws of humanity were the reverse of those, which the most matured past experience of the world now demonstrates them to be.

Hence man has hitherto made all his external circumstances in accordance with his erroneous imagination of the laws of his own nature; and these external circumstances, which have been devised by a few leading individuals, have acted powerfully upon the mass of mankind, educated and trained all in the most irrational thoughts and conduct, and given a false and most injurious direction to their feelings. It is under this malady of ignorance that the human race are suffering at this day ; and suffering from it in proportion to the extent of knowledge which they have discovered in the exact sciences.

They thus suffer by the increase of knowledge, because their crude imaginations respecting the laws of humanity, and the practical arrangements which they have made for the government of society, being in conformity with those crude imaginations, the exact sciences and those imaginations do not assimilate; they are opposed and cannot be made to act beneficially or harmoniously together. Thus arises an universal conflict throughout the world; – nation being opposed to nation, and man to man; when, if men were trained to be rational, they would never be opposed one to another individually or nationally. IT IS THE ONE GREAT AND UNIVERSAL INTEREST OF THE HUMAN RACE TO BE CORDIALLY UNITED, AND TO AID EACH OTHER TO THE FULL EXTENT OF THEIR CAPACITIES.

When they shall be made rational beings, they will be thus united, they will have charity for each other, and love one another, without reference to the distinctions of class, sect, party, country, or colour; there will be no limit to the one or the other. It will be discovered by all that they have but one interest, and in consequence they will be cordially united.

Between this state of society and that which has been and is, there will be a difference in the condition of each individual far beyond all present human estimate. But it is a waste of words, of time, and of faculty, to say to human beings, and to reiterate the saying, generation after generation, 'You should have charity for and love each other.' Charity and love will never be created at the bidding of any one, whatever character he may possess or assume.

Charity and love for the human race can emanate alone from knowledge, – from a knowledge of the laws of humanity, which laws are unknown to change, and from all the circumstances of human creation being made in accordance with those laws. Man must be made, not commanded, 'to have charity for all men, and to love them as himself;'[a] and made to acquire these feelings through an accurate knowledge of the laws of his nature, and by being surrounded with human-made circumstances, all formed in accordance with those laws.

To make man rational in his feelings, thoughts, and actions, he must be taught real knowledge derived from facts, – from facts which disclose the laws of humanity and of nature generally. He must not be forced to receive, in infancy, childhood, and youth, any of the errors of the imaginations of our ancestors. To make a human being rational, there must be no mixture of truth and falsehood, – no crude imaginations or suppositions blended with such facts as are unknown to change. Whenever suppositions, conjectures, or imaginations are brought forward, they must be stated and received as such, – as possibilities or probabilities, as the case may be, and accepted as such, and for no more.

It is then seen that erroneous first principles, – such as, that man forms

[a] See Mark 12:33.

himself, his feelings and opinions, and their necessary consequences in practice, – will, of necessity, make men and women irrational, as these circumstances have done up to the present period. That the existing superstitions, laws, government, institutions, and classifications of society are irrational circumstances, emanating from most erroneous first principles, and tend continually to keep man irrational.

That to make man rational, his mind must be based on true first principles; all his subsequent instruction must be in accordance with these true fundamental principles, and all circumstances of human creation, to be rational, must be also in accordance with them. Here is now a solid foundation on which to build up a knowledge of the principles and practices, by which to form the infant into a rational being at maturity. To effect this great change in man, the infant must be surrounded from his birth with rational external circumstances only.

This much-to-be-desired result cannot be obtained in the present generation, because the old irrational circumstances yet exist in considerable power, and because those who are to instruct, are yet but novices in the application of rational principles to practice, having themselves been trained in the midst of the most irrational circumstances of the passing generation.

But if the infant cannot yet be surrounded by the whole extent desirable of rational circumstances, an attempt must now be made, by beginning with the greatest number of the most favourable circumstances that can be combined around the infant, in order that an approximation to a superior character may be attained, – and attained in the expectation, that such improved beings will more effectually assist in greatly extending the formation of a still superior character in the next generation.

The most important external circumstance to commence with, is to have properly qualified nurses and persons around the infant from birth: those who shall be previously instructed in the laws of humanity, and who will, in every case, apply those laws to practice. They should have a natural love for children, and know how to teach them early, cleanly, and good healthy physical habits; they should also have patience and kindness without limit, to enable them to make full allowance for individual differences of organization; and their tempers should be the creation of a new mind, formed from the knowledge that the character of every individual is a compound, created before and at birth by nature, and from birth by external circumstances, chiefly devised and introduced by society, and under its control. This knowledge will destroy all the hitherto prevailing notions that children are to be made what is called good, by individual rewards and punishments, or individual praise or blame. It will naturally train the mind to become familiarly and constantly in the habit of tracing effects to their causes, and if the former are injurious, not to waste time and faculty in blaming them, but at once to apply the acquired knowledge of the laws of human nature, to remove the cause or causes which produce the objectionable effects. This knowledge of human nature will fill the mind with illimitable charity for the human race; there will be no exceptions in this charity on account of colour, country, party, sect, sex, class, or individual character; it will be pure and genuine as the source whence derived: in its nature it can be no respecter of persons; the feelings which it will create will be heartfelt, cordial desire that all may be beloved; while the knowledge derived from the laws of humanity will make it evident that this love can be produced only from the lovely qualities evidenced in the individual. The individual cannot give himself these lovely qualities, nature has laid the foundation for them in the organization of every human being; the material is there in the universal natural qualities of humanity. These qualities, although the same in number and kind, are given apparently in illimitable unchanging combinations, in order that no two human beings should have precisely the same individual character. It is a wonderfully compounded material, given at birth for experienced man to form, as he manufactures other materials into inferior, medium, or superior qualities of fabrics, in proportion as he may have acquired a knowledge of the qualities of the materials, and skill in applying the proper machinery and other appliances to perfect the object intended to be attained. Human character is, then, a manufacture from a natural material, as decidedly as any other fabric from its natural material, and is capable of being well or ill formed, according to the skill which shall be brought to bear in the cultivation, training, or manufacture of it. There is a distinctive difference in the qualities of different materials, as between iron, silk, copper, flax, timber, lead, wool, etc, etc, all of which require different appliances to change into finished fabrics. So differ the inanimate materials from the animate, and the animate one from the other. There is, however, not only the great and decisive difference between one material and another, both animate and inanimate, but a difference in the qualities of the same kind of material, known technically by the terms good, medium, or bad, in endless shades of difference, as they appear to the experienced fabricator of the peculiar fabric desired to be formed by him.

So it is with human nature; there are endless differing combinations and qualities in the material composing each infant at his birth, called by irrational-made man, good, medium, or bad, according to his crude notions of what man ought to become at maturity, or of the qualities which, in his ignorance of what man and society should be, he should be trained to possess. It is very probable that the organization which can be the most easily trained to become a mere automaton in feeling, thought, and conduct, has been hitherto deemed the best; while, in future, those qualities in the infant which can the soonest be formed into an intelligent rational being, to act in accordance with his nature, will be ascertained to be the best natural material.

This ground-work of knowledge will be required in all who are to be around children from their birth ; and this knowledge will destroy the seeds of all the inferior passions and of all prejudices; expand the mind to enable it, at once, to discover the causes of evil effects as they arise, and quietly and calmly, but most decisively, to remove those causes, and to replace them with others, if necessary, to produce the superior effects which may be desired. These trainers and instructors of the young, if previously instructed, as it is most desirable they should be, to be rational themselves in feeling, thought, and conduct, will never exhibit anger, ill-will, or bad temper of any kind in their own conduct; and especially will they be guarded in this respect before the children who will be trained by their example far more than by their precepts. Their language should be good in all respects, in order that the children who hear it may not have to *un*learn that which is inferior or detrimental to the superior consistent character which should be formed for them. These parties should possess the outline, at least, of much of the most useful knowledge for children to acquire, and of the order in which it should be placed on their mind; for the mind is built up like a dwelling, and ought to have its proper foundation, and regular layer upon layer, until the whole shall become complete in all its proportions, and well sustained in every part. In fact, there is as much an inward or mental science of architecture now to be acquired as there has been an outward or material one already attained; with this difference, that the science of mental architecture will prove immensely more valuable to the human race than the material science of architecture; inasmuch as MAN, rationally trained and built up, physically, mentally, morally, and practically, will be of inestimably more value than any building of stone, brick, or other inanimate material. But these rational mental architects have yet to be trained, and 'this book,' through all its parts, is written to aid to form these new architects. When they shall be formed, it will be difficult to estimate their value. The foundation of this new mental architecture must be laid in the proper formation of the health, habits, and manners of the children so as to create, at an early period, in each child, the temper, conscience, and spirit which belong alone to the Rational System of society. These constitute the essential parts of a rational character for the human race. It is not what is usually called learning that is of much value now to the world; the greater part of it is useless, or, rather, highly injurious superstition; or that which is little less injurious to the temper, spirit, and conduct of those who are so unfortunate as to be made irrational in their feelings, thoughts, and actions by a long instruction in what is called the classics; an instruction which forms those so instructed, to become anything in human shape and figure but rational beings, or to possess faculties at all equal to the naturally directed instincts of many other animals; for most of these would not destroy each other's lives and properties, or prevent their fellows from obtaining, by their own industry, food and shelter, or those other requisites for their existence, as these men-animals of classic formation of character have been always, unfortunately for themselves and others, trained most unwisely to do, and often, apparently, as pastime to relieve the idleness arising from their taught dislike to every kind of useful or rational occupation. These human animals of classic instruction are, most lamentably for themselves, mankind, and many other tribes of animals, made the most misery-producing and mischievous of all terrestrial existences, and are greatly to be pitied for having such noble natural qualities inherited by them at their birth, thus so vilely misdirected as to become the active instruments to cause so much misery to man and many other animals; when they might, by another training, under other and far better circumstances, be made to become really useful and rational beings, whose business and pleasure it would be to contribute daily to promote the happiness of others, and thus the most effectually promote the permanent happiness of themselves.

The erroneous feelings, thoughts, and actions which instruction in the classics creates, make the mind familiar with blood, murder, and every kind of violence, injustice, and oppression. It teaches the parties to call these most ignorant, vindictive, and cruel proceedings by the false terms of *victories: magnificent* slaughters of their fellows, and *glorious* destruction of their property, and also of the best and most rational means to create, with pleasure, the power and wealth for which these parties insanely thus contend, while they know not what they do,[a] or what manner of beings they are. Nor yet do they possess any useful knowledge of their own nature, while without that knowledge they must continue to be what they have evidently, by the past history of our race, always been, that is, mere mischievous, irrational animals, destroying one another and the wealth which was useful and required so much labour to create, and which so many needed for their animal existence. Had they been made rational animals during this period, they would have been taught through each generation to improve each succeeding generation, and to have preserved the wealth that had been created, that it might be applied to its proper use. The invaluable wealth that the fighting men, wisely employed by the fighting capital, might have been made to produce, would have created an enormous addition to it, and another increase in proportion to the number of efficient human beings which they so irrationally butchered, and to the amount of capital which they so irrationally destroyed.

Real knowledge, in opposition to the learning, so called, of the old world, will, when properly arranged in its due order of layer upon layer, according to the age of the infants and children even to maturity, be most easily given – under proper arrangements it will be competent for almost any educated person to give; society is now full of those persons who could, with little trouble or cost, teach this knowledge. But the parties to form the proper dispositions, habits, conscience, and conduct in children, are so scarce, that educated as men and women have been hitherto, it is most difficult to find any one well

[a] Mark 10:38.

prepared for the task, even in the best cultivated society, among those trained to practice; while those inexperienced in practice, cannot effect much immediate benefit to any cause. The best instructors, however, that can be obtained must be procured, and the most judicious means be adopted to enable them to acquire the character which is so valuable to form a rational character in others. But to form this character in individuals, to enable them to create a continually advancing, prosperous, and permanently happy society, each from an early age should be taught, according to their strength and capacity, to practise daily some useful work, in which, whatever it may be, they should be well instructed from the commencement of their attempts, in order that they may do whatever they are employed about in a superior manner. Children to be well educated should never be idle; nature urges them to continual physical and mental activity, both may be easily directed rightly or wrongly. They should, of course, be always rightly directed, and arrangements, properly devised and well executed, should be made in every establishment in which it is intended that a superior character should be formed for the rising generation, thus to occupy the time in giving due, but not over exercise to the physical and mental powers of the young; that is, in such proportion as will always keep them in the best state of health and spirits; for by keeping human beings in that condition of body and mind, the greatest amount of physical and mental power can be obtained, with the greatest economy to society. The children should, however, be trained from their earliest working age in the most useful occupations, varied as they advance in age and knowledge.

Now any occupation may be made, by education and public opinion, to be esteemed the most honourable, or the reverse; so much so, that the most savage, unjust, and degrading operations may be taught to be esteemed by men, while in an irrational state of existence, to be the most valued, honoured, and to be the highest rewarded: while the most essential to procure the necessaries of life, without which man could not live, may be made to be deemed the lowest in estimation, the least rewarded, and the practisers of it to be looked upon as serfs and slaves, to be treated with neglect or contempt. For example: now, in the irrational condition of man, those who are trained to become the most successful in the savage practice of butchering their neighbours or fellow men, and robbing or devastating their property to the greatest extent, are the most honoured, and are the most extensively rewarded, often receiving the hurras of the ignorantly trained multitude when they appear in public; while the operative practical gardener, or general cultivator of the soil, is disregarded, looked down upon, and so little rewarded as often to end his days wretchedly in a workhouse.

In a rational state of society this character of human proceedings will become too obviously unjust, oppressive, cruel, and barbarous, ever to be admitted into it. Employment will be always highly esteemed, and the most useful the most highly; and all will be occupied so as to ensure the greatest amount of health, wealth, rational amusement, and happiness for all. And each will be thus employed, physically and mentally, according to age, in such manner as to produce the most efficient services for the public, with the highest gratification to the individual; and this result will be effected through every period of their lives.

It is the interest of each one, that the best, the most rational character that can be created should be formed for himself, and for every other individual of the human race. This is the mode by which the greatest amount of individual and combined power may be acquired and safely applied, to secure the permanent happiness of every one without contest, competition, or opposing or repulsive feelings or conduct of any kind.

All society is therefore deeply interested in having arrangements made in every district of the world to ensure the best, most useful, and valuable character to be formed for each individual that his organization or natural faculties at birth will admit.

But so opposed to these arrangements is society, as it has been constituted, that there is not one educational establishment in this, or in any other country, based on principles, or conducted in a manner calculated to form a rational character for one individual of the human race.

To understand the causes which have, from the beginning, produced this state of irrationality over the world, and which have prevented one establishment from being yet devised to train and educate one individual to become a rational being, is the first step towards the formation of a rational state of human existence.

The causes are, as frequently stated, in various parts of this book, that man is born without knowledge, and from his birth has to acquire it from others, and by his own experience, according as he may be formed with more or less organic capacity for the attainment of knowledge, and as he may be more or less favourably placed within circumstances to act beneficially or otherwise on his natural powers, physical and mental. That the faculty of imagination is the most early mental faculty in strong activity, and that its quality is immediately to adopt first impressions as permanent realities; which first impressions, with few exceptions, require to be afterwards corrected by slow experience, derived from a patient investigation of facts. That by this experience and investigation of facts, and comparing facts with facts, it is now discovered that the imaginations of our early ancestors, from whom the foundation of the existing system has been derived, were as erroneous respecting their own nature individually and human nature generally, as they were respecting the form of the earth, its motions, and the rising and setting of the sun. And that they vainly imagined each individual possessed the power to make himself what he liked, to believe or disbelieve what he liked, and to love and hate or be indifferent to persons and things as he liked; while a slow, patient, and accurate perseverance in the investigation of facts, demonstrates that man cannot make one of his natural faculties or one of the external circumstances which exist at his birth; and that these faculties and external circumstances determine the foundation and early part of the character of every one, which is continually increased by the new circumstances which daily and hourly impress their influences upon the previously-formed part of his character; and thus is the whole man formed at every moment of his existence, and thus is he compelled to feel, to think, and to act irrationally or rationally according to the kind and quality of the external circumstances by which he may be surrounded from his birth, and not, as many suppose, according to the original qualities of the organization at birth; for these in each one are capable, by the influence of external animate and inanimate objects or circumstances, to be directed to force the individual, except in case of organic malformation, to become either irrational or rational.

It has been seen how all organizations hitherto have been made irrational from their birth; but a patient and accurate investigation of facts, and a comparison of the present facts with the past, have at length discovered, not only the causes which have hitherto made all men irrational, but the causes which, when brought into action, will force all, individually, and nationally, to become rational in feeling, thought, and conduct. The facts that have been thus discovered, which, when brought to bear on the formation of a rational state of human existence, are, that man has not been created with power to form himself physically, mentally, morally, or practically, – to believe or disbelieve, – or to love, hate, or be indifferent as he likes. It is this discovery that now renders it necessary that the character of man should be newly formed, and society newly constructed on this new base. Hence the necessity for the new organization of society into manageable masses of such extent, that each one, according to age, should have full justice done to him, that he may do full justice to society.

It is only by such a new organization of society, that the circumstances can be combined to act efficiently on the individual from birth, to make him become a rational being; or that an establishment can be obtained, in which justice shall be done to human nature, to relieve it from the hitherto overwhelming influence of the most powerful injurious circumstances, to force all to become irrational from birth to death. In this new organization all must be educated and systematically trained to understand the principles, and be well versed and expert in the practice, of the whole business of life in each association; each performing that which is to be done at the period of life most suitable to effect the work well, that is to be executed. There is great difference between doing anything in an inferior or superior manner, it is the difference between misery and rational happiness. There can be no happiness, except that of the mere animal, where ignorance directs, and that which is practised is inferior, or inefficiently performed. The difference nationally between having everything as well done as the existing capital, skill, and industry of British and Irish population could be now directed to do, and the manner in which these powers are at this day applied, is the difference between chaos and beautiful systematic order, between all manner of discomfort, disgusting to a well-ordered mind, and all that is calculated to ensure health of body and mind, gratified feelings, and as much permanent happiness as human life can experience. But the difference in point of economy between the chaotic and inferior condition of society, as it is now misgoverned, and having the existing powers at the control of the government and population, arranged to produce the best that can be produced of everything, in their due order, under the direction of minds trained to be rational, would be, in the British dominions alone, several thousands of millions sterling annually.

In fact, by the *government* and *church*, unitedly, adopting a system to govern by force and fraud, through the ignorance of the people and mystification of all classes, from the highest to the lowest; the loss of health, wealth, security, comfort, and happiness to all, far exceeds any estimate that any parties, in the shackled and confined state of mind in which all are kept, have the capacity to make, or powers fairly to investigate.

The individual members of the government and church, are great sufferers in their own persons and those of their descendants, by this most ignorant and irrational mode of proceeding, and the sooner another mode of governing society can be decided upon and practised, the better; for better will it be for every member of every government and church, that they should have better health, greater security, and far more and higher permanent enjoyment than can be derived from their present course.

And if such advantages will arise nationally from everything being done in the best manner, so also in a degree similar to its extent, will be the benefits which will arise from such superiority in every separate association, community, or nucleus of persons, under the new organization of society.

No parties need be alarmed at the term new, or re-organization of society; for, one and all will be immensely benefited by the change, and the sooner it is made, the better for the individuals of every class and sect, in every country and of all colours; the change, such as is in contemplation, will prove to be an unmixed good for all.

But the rational character will be of value only in a world made rational for its reception; a rational character placed in an irrational world, would be most miserable, except it should be cordially, nay, enthusiastically occupied in measures to terminate the irrationality of the system; – occupied as intelligent, philanthropic physicians are, when they live in a lunatic asylum, solely to assist in effecting a cure of its insane inmates. Therefore, at the same time that measures shall be introduced to form individuals to become rational in their thoughts, feelings, and actions; measures must be also adopted to create a rational world in which they may live happily in accordance with the new knowledge given to, and character formed for them.

No condition can be more pitiable than that of either man or woman, whose character has been made rational, in being compelled to live among irrational beings, without being engaged in active measures to cure them of their malady.

From what has been written, it is evident that the first thing now necessary in society, is a Normal School, in which to form the characters of those who are intended to train others: that this School should be based on the principles of nature for the formation of a rational character, and that the practice should be made as speedily as possible in accordance with those principles. The principles are those so often stated in this book – 1st. That man does not form any part of his individual nature: 2nd, that he has not the power to believe or disbelieve; or 3rd, to love or hate at his will.

And the formation of character for each individual must be based, and made to be consistent throughout, on these great and all-important facts. When the character of man, and the constitution of society shall be formed in accordance with these fundamental principles of nature, man will be made wise, his conduct rational, society prosperous, and the earth will become a substantial paradise.

CHAPTER V

'On a knowledge of the principles and practices by which to govern man under these new arrangements, in the best manner, as a member of the great family of mankind.'

Man, under the new arrangements or constitution of a rational society, must be governed by knowledge and kindness, instead of force and fraud, as he has been alone hitherto governed in all nations from the earliest known period.

Physical force and mental cunning devising superstitions, and holding them in terror over the more ignorant in all countries, have been the only instruments used for governing mankind.

This system of government has regularly forced man to become more and more irrational, through every succeeding generation, until, now when he is in possession of more ample means to ensure permanent progressive prosperity and happiness to every one, he is so mistrained and misgoverned, that these wondrous powers to create wealth, knowledge, and unity, are most actively and extensively directed to destroy wealth, limit knowledge, and encourage division and contest of the most irrational character.

The fact must not for a moment be lost sight of, that all the inferiority of character, all the contests individual and national, and all the vices, crimes, and miseries suffered or inflicted by the governed, are the immediate results of the governments and churches in all countries.

The *governments* and *churches* of the world should sustain all the responsibility that belongs to humanity, for all the crime and misery produced by and inflicted upon the human race. They are the sole immediate cause now of all ignorance, poverty, division, crime, and misery among all people and nations.

It is true they are yet ignorant, how universally to produce knowledge, wealth, union, virtue and happiness among men. It is not their fault, but their deep misfortune, that they have been thus trained without the most useful of all knowledge; – a knowledge of human nature and of society, with the inexhaustible powers for good possessed by both, if they were judiciously cultivated and brought into full action.

This knowledge must be now given to all governments and churches, for the substantial permanent benefit of every member of both in all the nations of the world. It is for the interest of all that it should be now given to them for their own immediate benefit, for the advantage of their children, and for the permanent happiness of the human race.

The great change now required in the principles and practices of society, and in its entire organization, will be more easily effected through the present framework of the existing governments and churches in all countries, the people being habituated to them, than by any sudden changes effected by violence, which must be the case if governments and churches are to be remodelled against the power which they at present possess.

It is acknowledged that this mode of meliorating the wretched condition of mankind, when the wretchedness has been created and maintained by these governments and churches, may appear at first sight to be difficult or impossible.

No such thing; the government and churches of Great Britain are the most wealthy and powerful in the world, yet both may easily be directed by public opinion, once formed on true principles and sure grounds, to adopt measures founded on true principles, and the practice of which shall be proved to be for the general benefit.

And such are the measures recommended in every part of 'This Book;' all of them are based on ascertained principles of nature, the practice of which will produce unmixed good to all. When, therefore, the principles are demonstrably true, and the practice proceeding from them highly advantageous for the human race; patience and perseverence, united with moral courage, under the guidance of charity and love for man in every clime, of every colour, and of every creed, however insanely superstitious, will be sure, in opposition to all obstacles, ultimately to succeed. It is for the individual and united interest of man, that now true principles should prevail over the false hitherto triumphant, and that beneficial practices should supersede those hitherto most injurious to every member of the family of man.

The experience of all the past declares that it is the most useless of all attempts to well-govern man on any principles opposed to his nature; nature always forbids it, and everlastingly proclaims to the world, 'My laws shall prevail over man's laws, for all the laws of men are in direct opposition to my laws. Man's laws ever have, and while maintained, ever must produce crime and misery and all manner of disorder throughout the world. They have made, and they will keep it a pandemonium, as long as men shall submit to be governed by ignorant man's most ignorant laws, and while they reject and contemn my most righteous, wise, and beneficent laws. Man's laws obstruct the entrance into the human mind and heart of charity and love for his race, while my laws would make both universal, and to form an essential part of the matured constitution of every individual. Adopt my laws, and live in peace and harmony unbroken through endless future ages – maintain man's opposing laws, and exist in never-ending discord, contest, crime, and violence. Obey man's laws, and continue in sin and misery – the sin of disobeying my laws and the certain misery thence ensuing; or obey my laws, and be wise and happy through all human existence.'

Such has been the language of unerring nature, and hitherto, by inexperienced and irrational-made man neglected or rejected; – such is now her language to all the sons of men, will they still neglect and continue to reject it? Has time given them experience to discern the difference between laws leading direct to falsehood, crime, and misery, and those which lead direct to truth, knowledge, goodness, and happiness?

Surely the time is at hand when ignorance must give place to knowledge; falsehood to truth; division to cordial union; poverty, and partial enormous individual riches, to universal wealth without fear of poverty; and crime and misery to goodness and happiness.

The materials to effect this change are in abundance in the British dominions, where man's laws and customs are producing, among the most industrious of the people, the most degrading and heartless misery; but these materials abound in almost all places; – certainly in all in which man needs to live, and why should they be longer misapplied anywhere? but why should they be longer misapplied by the government and people of the British empire, the most advanced in wealth and scientific power, and the most miserable of all nations?

The British government, according to its own statements, has not acquired the knowledge how to govern her millions in progressive prosperity. It has been taught to think that it can do little for the population to relieve it from poverty, disunion, contest, and crime: while it has the power and possesses all the means, except knowledge or moral courage, to terminate those evils in a very short period. And all circumstances conspire to render it more essential that the British government should now set the example of this great and truly glorious change to the governments and nations of the world.

The world is in misery – its cup is brim-full, running over;[a] all nature,

[a] See for example Psalms 23:5.

through the suffering of human nature, cries aloud for change. All things are prepared for it; – misery has had full time to grow, to expand in every direction, until it is full ripe, and requires to be plucked from the tree of evil,[a] the tree itself to be cut down and destroyed root and branch, never again to be planted, or allowed to seed, in the soil of humanity.

What a rational government for the human race will be, when measures can be introduced to make man sufficiently rational to be so governed, shall be explained in the succeeding or sixth part of this book.

It is sufficient here to state that the human race, or any portion of it, can never be well governed, unless all the laws, institutions, classification, and public opinion, shall be in undeviating accordance with the laws of nature, and the entire practices of the governed shall be consistent with those laws; but to effect this change, society must be re-organized in principle and practice, and all its existing arrangements and institutions must be gradually, by wisdom and foresight, superseded by those in accordance with the eternal laws of humanity.

The present is the most extraordinary period in the progress of human affairs. Circumstances unforeseen and uncontrolled by man have arisen, and lately most rapidly, to expose the unsoundness of all human devised institutions, and the immediate and more remote causes of ignorance, poverty, crime, and misery, and to render it unavoidable that a re-organization of society over the world must take place for the benefit of the present generation, and for the permanent superior happiness of all future generations. Man's laws and institutions must be abandoned, and nature's laws alone adopted and systematically applied to practice.

CHAPTER VI

'On the knowledge of the principles and practices for uniting in one general system, in their due proportions, these separate parts of the science of society; to effect and secure, in the best manner for all, the greatest amount of permanent benefits and enjoyments, with the fewest disadvantages.'

THE last chapter concluded with stating that 'man's laws must be abandoned, and nature's alone adopted.' Man's laws have been separate and detached efforts of mental powers in slow progress towards a rational state of human

[a] See for example Genesis 2:9, 17.

existence. These laws have had no beginning, middle, or end in view; they have been chiefly devised by those in power, to increase it, and keep those without power in greater subjection to the authority of those in power. Nature has been consulted in making these forms, only apparently that it may be the more effectually opposed. The mind of man has been hitherto unequal to the discovery of true first principles of man's nature, and to form an unbroken chain of consequences proceeding rationally, link by link, without disconnection from those principles, to ultimate true and great and glorious results; in other words, to ensure the permanent progressive happiness of the human race. All man's feelings, thoughts, views, and interest have been until now individualized; his world has been a little local circle of his own, centred in self. This period of ignorant selfishness and irrationality is terminating; the errors which it has accumulated cannot be made longer to work, without throwing society into confusion bordering upon chaos. Individualism has had its period of existence in human progress, and its reign is of necessity drawing towards a close.

Individual short associations of ideas, based on a false foundation, or on unsound mere imaginary notions, must now give way to a new construction of the human mind, – to mind based on ascertained facts or eternal truths, – and every idea, and every association of ideas, will be of necessity in perfect accordance with those fundamental truths; and of course, every separate association of ideas will be entirely consistent, and in perfect union with every other association of ideas.

There will be, consequently, no clashing of one idea with another, of one association of ideas with another, or unhealthy or irrational friction in any mind thus founded and built up, by those who have acquired a knowledge of human nature, and of a rational formation of human society.

By this change, in giving a new mind, – a rational instead of one always made to become irrational, – man may be truly said to have his mind born again; his ideas, feelings, and views will become universal instead of individual and local. It will be no longer, '*What is best for* ME?' regardless of the family of man, of which the individual must always be but a unit; but it will always be, 'What is best for the human race?' for it will be clearly perceived that that which is best for the family of man must be the very best for every individual of that family.

The question will no longer be, 'What shall I do to support myself and my family?' or 'What shall I do to aggrandise myself and my family?' the family being in this case the immediate children of two helpless irrational-made beings. On the contrary, it will be in every case, 'What can I be made to do the most effectually to permanently benefit the family of man, and to promote the happiness of every child of man?'

The difference between these two minds in their consequences to the individuals during their lives will be far beyond the powers of irrational-made man to estimate. It is now sufficient to state that it will be the difference between a low state of the existence of a mere animal, whose natural instincts have been always opposed and his nature continually thwarted, and a being acting rationally, in accordance with his instincts and consistent with his nature; that nature, too, highly cultivated, physically and mentally, and the being filled with a large store of the most valuable knowledge to ensure the permanent happiness of his race. The individual will no longer have his mind confined within the circle of mere local ideas formed into false associations, and with feelings of petty individual interests; thereby forcing each one to become an irrational localized animal, – a being whose faculties have been so trained and erroneously directed, that while desiring to be happy, he is perpetually engaged in measures to thwart his own happiness and destroy that of his fellows.

Instead, therefore, of each one in setting out in life asking, 'What shall I do to support or aggrandise myself and immediate offspring and relatives?' it will be, 'What can society do to produce, in the best manner, the greatest amount annually of the most valuable wealth for use and enjoyment? How can this wealth be the most beneficially preserved from injury, and distributed when required for consumption? How can infants be formed into the best men and women? And how are they to be governed, to ensure the most happiness to every individual, young and old, through the life of each?'

These are the important questions now to ask, – this is the important knowledge now to be acquired; – for until this knowledge can be attained, and these questions can be rightly answered, society must remain, as hitherto, a confused chaotic mass of indescribable absurdities, and man a most inconsistent irrational nondescript; a being opposed to his own happiness, to the general well-being of his race, and regardless of the comfort or happiness of all other animals, except in so far as they contribute to his supposed benefit.

Circumstances have arisen, and are daily arising, to make it imperative upon man, in the present generation, to acquire the knowledge to enable him well and wisely to answer these all-important questions.

And the first consideration which presents itself is, Can wealth be better created, preserved, and distributed, the character of all individuals better formed, and society better governed, by men separately and opposed to each other in interest; or by the human race being united, trained to act cordially together, and having but one clearly perceived and well understood interest?

To a mind liberated from local impressions and prejudices, the reply would be, at once, that the advantages of union, compared with isolation and disunion to each individual, will be millions to one; in fact, not yet to be estimated by the crude, chaotic-made mind of the present generation.

Who, trained as men have yet been, are prepared to reply to the question – the great practical question which events require to be solved – 'What is the best mode to produce, preserve, and distribute wealth, form the character of all, and govern society?' Who? the priest, the lawyer, the soldier, the physician, the theoretic stateman, or political economist, the banker, the merchant, the trader, the agriculturist, the manufacturer, or the country squire or great landlords of the world? Or shall the question be asked of the philosopher or mere man of literature? Can any of these answer the question? Are any of these yet advanced beyond their class, the bounds of individualism, or limited local knowledge? Are not all these, of necessity, mere small portions of humanity, or mere animals of some class, sect, or party, not yet formed into men, but very limited parts of what full-formed men should be?

Will not rational full-formed men and women be trained and educated to know what society is, how in the best manner to produce, preserve, and distribute wealth, manufacture a superior character from the invaluable human material at birth, and in due time, at the proper age, to aid in governing society well and wisely?

Until all shall be trained, educated, and placed to know and to do all these first duties of man in the best manner, as all, under proper arrangements, may be made to know and to do, man will be only growing from childhood towards maturity.

Why should not these arrangements to form full men and women be now made? It is the interest of every human being, without one exception, that they should be now so formed, and the other arrangements carried fully into execution: all the materials are ready to be applied for this great and godlike purpose.

Let the faculties of the human race be aroused and man advanced to his destiny! May these considerations become new circumstances to stimulate the minds of all to new exertions, to endeavour to attain the knowledge, the power, and the happiness which human nature, properly trained and placed from birth, may be made to acquire!

It is not only necessary, then, for men to acquire a knowledge of the science or best mode of producing wealth, of preserving it, of distributing it, of forming the character, and of governing; but also to know how to unite these various parts in such proportions and in such a manner as to form one scientific nucleus of society. A nucleus, to a certain extent, complete within itself, but so combined as to unite cordially with other similar nuclei, so as that each shall aid the others, until nothing shall be wanting in each; and thus to unite man to man, and nucleus to nucleus throughout all nations, making the whole earth, as soon as there shall be numbers to occupy and cultivate it, truly a terrestrial paradise in which man will have but one interest, and all will perceive the advantages of, and will desire to have but one language. As there will be but one interest there will be but one object, that is, to increase the happiness of all to the greatest extent that the materials of the earth when applied, under the combined knowledge of the human race will admit; – applied too, when all shall have their physical, mental, moral, and practical powers trained to the extent of the existing united knowledge acquired by man.

And under this change, from universal individual isolation and repulsion, to universal union and attraction, the arrangements of society may be so made that the use and enjoyment, through life, of the earth, and all which it may, under the highest improvements, be made to contain, shall be the undisturbed and unenvied inheritance of every one, in return for the healthy and pleasurable exercise of body and mind rationally directed.

On what principles, then, is the scientific nucleus of society to be combined, so as to unite within it the elements of all society in their due or most beneficial proportions? This is the important practical question to be solved. To understand and properly reply to it, much previous knowledge in principle and practice is necessary. The elements of society must be understood, and a knowledge of their relative importance, the order of their arrangement, and a general familiarity with the practice of each.

There must be united in one well combined arrangement to work harmoniously, agriculture, gardening, manufactures, trades, in certain cases mines, minerals, and fisheries, for production; – stores, warehouses, and other places to preserve the productions; modes of distribution convenient for consumption; with arrangements to form the character for all ages, or from birth to death, and additional arrangements for local and general government.

To accomplish this measure, society must be re-organized from its foundation through its whole superstructure. It is useless now to think of attempting any minor change by uniting any portion of false principles and practice with true principles and practice; – they cannot be made to assimilate; by any attempt to unite them, they would only the more expose the error of the unnatural union.

To benefit the human race, the re-organization of society must be complete in all its parts; so much so, that 'old things must pass away, and all become new'[a] in this re-organization.

The religions, laws, governments, classifications, institutions, and all commercial arrangements for the old world, must be given up and abandoned as speedily as the new organization can be introduced into practice, and made to supersede these long established causes of human misery: but introduced without violence or disorder of any kind. In this change, wisdom and foresight will be required through every step of its progress, and required to prevent the evil of contending feelings and interest, and, as far as it may be practicable, to avoid giving offence, or creating injury to any one.

It may naturally be now asked, Are all the materials to be obtained, and is society ripe for this change?

[a] See for example Psalms 58:8.

Is the population of the world prepared to abandon individualism, opposing interest, disunion of mind and feeling, and all their evil effects, and adopt the principle of union of feeling and interest? Or, in other words, Are the people of this country, who suffer now the most grievously from the existing organization of society, prepared to set an example to the world by the introduction of an organization, new, but true in principle and practice, and, of course, directly opposed to the old?

The reply is, that the world *is* prepared, and *especially* the empire of Great Britain; and prepared through the sufferings produced solely by the old organization of society; – of sufferings become unbearable, and now crying aloud for immediate change throughout the whole industrial population of Great Britain and Ireland. The change from the one organization to the other, is the work of dire necessity; – of necessity which has produced pain sufficient to stimulate to seek relief, and to endeavour to attain the happiness which all that has life desires.

For this re-organization, land, capital, skill, labour, and other materials are required; these all superabound in the British Islands, and railways are formed, and forming, to convey the heaviest of them from where they are in excess, to where they are deficient and will be useful.

To effect this organization with wisdom and foresight, or in the best manner for the permanent benefit of all, the government should purchase from the present proprietors, at a fair full price, the railways already completed, and also the land on each side of them, to the breadth of from three to six miles. These lands should be then laid out by the best engineers and most practical men that the government could engage in its service, for the formation of a new nuclei of society, and for the re-organization of society without prematurely disturbing the old organization; – but to commence the new arrangements gradually, peaceably, and most beneficially for all, and thus to supersede it, in the order which nature, in her matured wisdom, directs.

But, it will be asked, by what principles and practice, are these engineers, architects, and other practical men, to be guided and assisted in laying out the arrangements for these nuclei of society, to form the new organization to supersede the old?

The plan for one nucleus, to form a part of this new organization, has been given in an outline, with considerable detail, by the writer of 'The Book,' in a work published under the title of 'A Development of the Principles and Plans on which to establish Home-Colonies,'[a] etc, to which the public is referred for more particulars of the detailed information mentioned.

But as a further guide to these supposed agents of government, it may be stated, that to each nucleus there must belong the due proportion of land and

[a] See *infra*, vol. 2, pp. 339–415.

of manufactures for the production required for its population, when at its maximum, and for ever; – arrangements sufficient to store these productions, to preserve them in the best manner, and to be the most convenient to distribute for consumption; other arrangements to be the most advantageously united to train the young, and form the matured character of all, to make it consistent with nature, and rational in feeling, thought, and action; and these arrangements to be so combined as to be the most easily locally governed, in order that no one individual shall be unknown, uncared for, or in any manner neglected by society. And until this result shall be attained, and every individual of the human race shall be cared for, and well done to, from birth to death, society will not be in a rational state.

Hitherto the happiness of the race has been disregarded, the aggrandisement or local interest of the individual and his family have almost wholly absorbed the thoughts of men, and all human arrangements have been made with this view, by the accumulation of wealth and power; wealth being the chief means by which power is maintained.

In the new organization now to be proposed for society, over the world, every part of it is formed to create and secure the happiness of the race, and to carry forward improvements in all things appertaining to human existence, with continually accelerating power arising from the progressive increase of knowledge and capital which will be obtained through every succeeding generation.

Each nucleus of society will be founded and entirely constructed on this principle. THE HAPPINESS OF ALL will be the end and object of every portion of this re-organization, through the whole extent of society.

These general principles being explained, the combination of the various parts of each nucleus, and their union with every other nucleus, will be more easily understood.

To secure the happiness of all, permanent comfortable existence must be secured for all, and a superior character ensured to all.

This is what society has to do, and as it possesses all the materials requisite to effect it over the world, and as it is the interest of every individual of the human race that it should be done; as soon as this interest can be made evident, it will be done.

To make this interest so evident that it cannot be misunderstood – one nucleus of a scientific arrangements of society, in which its four natural elements shall be combined in their due proportions, has to be seen in full action; its contrast with the present chaotic confusion of all things, will be too striking upon the common sense of all classes, and of all individuals, to admit of any doubt which of the two systems of society shall have the preference. Man desires to be happy; when he clearly perceives the right road, he will pursue it.

In forming this nucleus, or practical example of a scientific arrangement of society, it should be made as complete as the knowledge to be collected from the experience of the past, and from all other sources, will now admit.

The arrangements, be it remembered, of this new nucleus, on which to found another, and altogether a new mode of human existence, is to combine the materials of society in such a manner that the greatest amount of the most valuable wealth shall be produced in the shortest time, with the least labour and capital consistent with the best health and highest happiness of the producers of it, and that it shall be preserved and distributed in the best manner for the consumers, who will have been the producers, in their threefold capacity of producers, educators, and governors; or the lower, middle, and upper classes in the old world, but in the proposed new order of society, the young, middle-aged, and experienced in age and knowledge; and this threefold character will be given, in considerable perfection, compared with the past and present, to all of the human race.

Each one will receive from birth sufficient knowledge to make him through life charitable, in its fullest meaning, to all of his race; and each one will be trained to acquire so many good, superior, and lovely qualities, that he must be beloved by, and love all his neighbours as himself. And all will know *that it is by this practice alone*, that charity and love can be introduced and permanently maintained among mankind.

To obtain these results in the shortest and best manner, the scientific nucleus of society, or foundation for universal union and cordial aid and co-operation, has been devised.

This nucleus, then, is to consist of as much land as, when well cultivated, shall produce sufficient, for ever, to provide its population, when at its maximum, with an abundant supply, annually, of the necessaries and comforts of life, to prevent poverty, or the fear of it, to any one. It must be of such extent as to be conveniently well cultivated *in cumulo*, or under one arrangement, when divided into four divisions, equi-distant on each side from the centre of the dwellings in which the population will reside. The site of these buildings should be as near to the centre of the land, as its local circumstances will advantageously admit.

These dwellings should be arranged with reference to health, convenience, and pleasureable scenery. They should be in these respects well adapted for the minimum, progress, and maximum of the population as it increases from the first to the last in number. There should be a due proportion of manufactures, mining, fisheries, or useful navigation, according to the locality of the nucleus, in addition to the land, for its perpetual support, which every nucleus should possess. The nucleus must also contain the best devised establishment for training, educating, and forming the character of all its members from birth to death, for upon this part of the arrangement will depend the great moving power that will ensure value to all the operations of the nucleus; it will create the mind and spirit which are to direct and pervade every portion of it, and it is therefore essential that this division of the nucleus should be at all times in the highest order, and conducted under first-rate abilities. The success anticipated to be obtained under this new oganization of society will mainly depend upon this part of it being well understood in principle, and in the application of the principle to practice.

Although to produce a full supply of the necessaries of life is the first duty of man to himself and fellows, the second is not inferior to it; the one supplies that which is necessary for the sustenance and health of the body, the other that which is equally necessary for the sustenance of health of the mind, and for the creation of the all-pervading spirit of charity and love, without which human society must be a pandemonium, while, directed by them, the earth may soon be made a terrestrial paradise.

Then, united with the production, preservation, and distribution of wealth and the formation of character, must be other arrangements to facilitate the superintendence or governing of the nucleus and its population.

With practical arrangements thus formed to produce, preserve, and distribute wealth, and to form character, the superintendence of the operations and government of the population, so that each one shall be well cared for, and justice done to him, will be the most simple and easy to apply to practice of all the elements of which each nucleus will be formed.

To govern advantageously a population whose characters shall be well-formed from birth; who shall be always well employed according to the age, capacity, and experience of each; who shall be placed within the most favourable circumstances to produce, preserve, distribute, and enjoy wealth; who will comprehend the principles and be familiar with the practice of a society, whose instruction has given its members the desire and power, cordially, to promote the permanent happiness of each other; from whom all motive to anger, jealousy, revenge, and all the inferior and evil passions, has been withdrawn; who through the knowledge of their nature which they have received, are filled with the spirit of charity and love for their race, and who will be, according to age, upon a perfect equality of education and condition through life, will be not difficult, but an exercise of utility, pleasure, and high satisfaction.

It is now necessary to state the numbers of men, women, and children which will be the most advantageous to unite at a minimum and maximum in each nucleus, as these numbers will influence the arrangements of the dwellings and public buildings of the establishment.

These numbers will be regulated by the consideration of the most convenient amount to be well educated together, and to be employed in producing, preserving, and distributing wealth, in educating the young, in local and in general governing in accordance with the principles and practices of the Rational System of society.

To effect these purposes, when aided by every improvement in all the sciences, which will be always cultivated and encouraged to the extent of human attainments, the minimum of men, women, and children, in the usual proportions should be about five hundred, and the maximum about four times that number, or two thousand.

These numbers could be easily made to form good family parties for all the purposes of a nucleus in a rational state of society; and as each nucleus would be encompassed by other nuclei at, upon an average, about a mile and half distant east, west, north, and south, there would be, when at the maximum, a population of neighbours in the first circle around each nucleus, of eight thousand, and its own population of two thousand, making ten thousand of well-educated, highly-informed, beneficially occupied friends, according to the age of the parties, and in the next extended circle, of three miles' distance, about sixteen thousand more, and so on, according as these circles extended, and thus, by these arrangements, properly carried out, will every square mile be made, with ease, to maintain in comfort, under greatly superior circumstances to any existing, at least four times the number that it could, under the average of the best constituted society as it is, but ten times at least the number which the land in Great Britain is now made to maintain.

And this change for the happiness of all will be effected without resorting to any of the unfavourable circumstances which now inflict so much misery upon those kept ignorant and forced to be poor; such inferior circumstances as streets, lanes, courts, and alleys in towns, and wretched hovels in the country; places in which these outcasts, who are kept ignorant and forced to be poor, are compelled to live out a wretched existence, proving at once the gross irrationality of the system which has hitherto governed the human race, – a system in direct opposition to common sense or right reason.

Thus by analyzing society, discovering its original elements, ascertaining their past and present chaotic state and gross perversion, by learning how to unite them in their due proportions, in every nucleus of society, and to unite these again to form the great family of man, shall the human race be relieved of its irrationality and its consequent miseries; and full-formed men and women shall be created and placed under such improved circumstances that they shall enjoy an extended superior existence, – an existence in which health, knowledge, wealth, and united interest and feeling will combine to ensure the well-being and happiness of one and all over the world.

Under this change there will be no contests between individuals or nations about that which is mysterious, and of course not found out; about human laws, when nature's defined, fixed, and immutable laws are directly calculated to ensure man's well-being and greatest happiness; about governments, when all, at a proper age and duly experienced, will become a governor, and have his fair proportion of the government of the world; when all mere professions will be worse than useless; when the rational classification of each individual into the lower, middle, and upper class shall terminate all class interests, and when in consequence the world will become a paradise instead of a pandemonium.

CHAPTER VII

'On the new classification of society, according to age and experience, and the eternal laws of humanity.'

As all men are born ignorant and inexperienced, and must receive their knowledge either from the instincts of their nature, which are given to them at their birth, or from surrounding external objects, animate and inanimate, which they do not create; all, by nature, have equal rights. Neither can it be justly said, that anything formed without its knowledge can have more merit or demerit from being what it is, than another. All men partake of the same general qualities of human nature, in such proportions, and under such combinations as are given to them by the Power which gives to them, and all things, their existence.

The distinctions of class and station are artificial, and have been conceived and adopted by men, while they were ignorant, inexperienced, and irrational. The errors and evils of this classification have been stated in previous parts of this book, and it is now proposed to introduce measures, gradually to supersede them by the natural and rational divisions, into which, experience will prove, it will be greatly for the interest and happiness of all, that society should resolve itself. It may be stated as a first principle of justice, that, 'NO MAN HAS A RIGHT TO REQUIRE ANOTHER MAN TO DO FOR HIM, WHAT HE WILL NOT DO FOR THAT MAN; OR, IN OTHER WORDS ALL MEN, BY NATURE, HAVE EQUAL RIGHTS.'

The natural and rational classification of society, when adopted, will for ever preserve those rights inviolate; and it is, beyond all estimate, for the interest and happiness of the human race, that this classification should be universally adopted, for it will calm the evil passions, terminate every contest, private and public, individual and national, and introduce order and wisdom, instead of chaos and irrationality, into all the affairs of mankind.

The futile, petty disputes between men and nations, about matters of no real interest to the well-being of society, would cease; a new spirit of equity, justice, charity, and kindness, would be created, and pervade the population of the world; more, for the permanent well-doing and happiness of mankind, would be effected in one year, than can be accomplished, under the existing classification of society in a century, or, indeed, within any given period of time.

The natural and rational classification of the human race, is the classification of age – each division of age having the occupations to perform, for which each age is best adapted by nature.

By this classification, the causes of the evils with which the human race is now afflicted, will be permanently removed; and whatever is to be done, will be effected in a superior manner, willingly, cheerfully, and with high gratification to every one.

There will be no occupation requisite to be performed by one, which will not be equally performed by all; and by all under this system, far more willingly than any of the general affairs of life are now performed by any class, from the sovereign to the pauper. In the present irrational state of the human mind, and human affairs, no one can form a true conception of what individuals may be trained and educated to acquire and accomplish at their various periods of life.

Because it is yet unknown what are the capabilities of human nature when it shall not be forced to imbibe error and falsehood from its birth; – when it shall not be daily trained in most injurious habits and artificial manners; – when it shall be taught truth only, by every word, look, and action of all around it; – when it shall be educated to acquire the best habits for its own happiness, and the well-being of society; – when it shall attain the individual self-sustaining manners, which, by such training, will naturally arise, and ensure pleasure, by its variety, to all; – when it shall possess the valuable knowledge which by such training and education will be given to it; – and when it shall acquire the facilities in the practice of the operations of society, in which, as it advances in life, it will be instructed.

It may be, however, confidently stated, that each individual thus trained, educated, and placed, would acquire far more valuable knowledge and power, and accomplish more, and in a superior manner, than great numbers of the human race can acquire or accomplish, under the training, education, and classification of the existing system, founded on, and emanating from, the absurd notions of man's free-will in forming his own convictions, feelings, and general character.

It is, however, somewhat difficult, previous to additional experience, to decide, very accurately, what should be the precise permanent divisions of human life, to form the best classification. But there is now sufficient knowledge for present purposes; and experience will afford more, as soon as it shall be required.

Probably, periods of five years, up to thirty, will afford a useful classification, and each class to be occupied as follows: –

First class, – from birth, to the end of the fifth year. To be so placed, trained, and educated, as that they may be in a proper temperature for their age; fed with the most wholesome food; lightly and loosely clothed; regularly and duly exercised in a pure atmosphere; also that their dispositions may be formed to have their greatest pleasure in attending to, and promoting, the happiness of all who may be around them; that they may acquire an accurate knowledge, as far as their young capacities will easily admit, of the objects which they see and can handle, and that no false impression be made on any of their senses by those around them refusing a simple explanation to any of their questions; that they may have no knowledge of individual punishment or reward, nor be discouraged from always freely expressing their thoughts and feelings; that they may be taught, as early as their minds can receive it, that the thoughts and feelings of others are, like their own, instincts of human nature, which they are compelled to have; and thus, may acquire in infancy the rudiments of charity and affection for all; that they may have no fear, but full and implicit confidence in every one around them; and that the universal selfish or individual feeling of our animal existence may be so directed, as to derive its chief gratification from contributing to the pleasure and happiness of others.

By these measures a solid foundation will be laid for healthy and consistent minds, good habits, superior natural manners, fine dispositions, and some useful knowledge. By these means, they will be so well prepared before they leave this class, that, for their age, they will think, speak, and act rationally. They will be, therefore, at the end of this period, in many respects in advance of the average of human beings, as they are now taught and placed, at any time of their lives, for these are so instructed as to be prevented from becoming rational at any time of their lives.

It is true, that at this age they will not be equal to the men of the old world in physical strength, or in the number of sensations which they have experienced, or impressions received; they will, however, for their age, have more sound health, and be more active; they will have superior dispositions, habits, manners, and morals; they will have fewer *notions* and *fancies*, but they will have a greater number of *true* ideas. These true ideas being, of course, all consistent with each other, and in accordance with every known fact, will be of far more advantage to the individuals, than the matured minds of the old world, in the majority of which, there are but few true ideas, among many false notions. These false notions destroy the value of the few true ideas which the individuals may have acquired; for the few true ideas, thus mixed with many errors, tend only the more to perplex their reasoning faculties, and to confound their judgment.

The first class being prepared by this new rational nursing and infant training, will leave the nursery and infant school, to be removed into the appropriate arrangements for the second class; which class will consist of children from five to ten years complete. This class will be lodged, fed, and clothed, upon the same general principles as the first class, making only the difference which their age requires; but now, their exercises will consist in that which will be permanently useful. According to their strength and capacities they will acquire a practice in some of the lighter operations in the business of life; operations which may easily be made to afford them far more pleasure and gratification than can be derived from the useless toys of the old world. Their knowledge will be now chiefly acquired from personal inspection of objects, and familiar conversation with those more experienced than themselves. By this plan being judiciously pursued under rational arrangements properly adapted for the purpose, these children will, in two years, become willing, intelligent assistants in the domestic arrangements and gardens, for some hours in the day, according to their strength. Continuing this mode of education, these children from seven to ten will become efficient operators in whatever their physical strength will enable them easily to accomplish; and whatever they do they will perform as a matter of amusement and for exercise with their equally intelligent and delightful companions. These exercises they will pursue under the immediate directions of the juniors of the third class; for it is anticipated that the young persons twelve years of age, and under, will, with the greatest pleasure and advantage to themselves and society, when, thus rationally trained and placed, perform all the domestic operations of their own immediate association or family, and perform them in a very superior manner.

They will also assist to keep the gardens and pleasure-grounds of the family in the highest order, for the rational enjoyment of themselves, their own immediate association, and also of those numerous superior friends who will visit them from other similar family establishments.

When these children shall be advanced to the age for leaving the second class, they will have their characters so formed physically, intellectually, morally, and practically, that they can no longer be compared with any of the irrational characters which have been formed under the old system of man's free agency. At ten they will be well-trained rational beings, superior in mind, manner, dispositions, feelings, and conduct to any who have yet lived; and their deficiency in physical strength will be amply supplied by the superior mechanical and chemical powers which will be contrived and arranged to be ready for them to direct when they enter the next class. These new operations will be to them a continual source of instruction and amusement, and to which they will look forward with the delight experienced by the acquisition of new important attainments.

The members of the second class, when they shall have completed their tenth year, will enter the third class, which will consist of those from ten to fifteen years complete. This class will be engaged the first two years, that is, from ten to twelve, in directing and assisting those in the second class from seven to ten in their domestic exercises in the house, gardens, and pleasure-grounds, and from twelve to fifteen they will be engaged in acquiring a knowledge of the principles and practices of the more advanced useful arts of life, a knowledge by which they will be enabled to assist in producing the greatest amount of the most valuable wealth, in the shortest time, with the most pleasure to themselves and advantage to society. This will include all the productions required from the soil; from mines, from fisheries, the arts of manufacturing food, to keep and prepare it in the best manner for daily use; the art of working up materials to prepare them for garments, buildings, furniture, machinery, instruments, and implements for all purposes; and to produce, prepare, and execute whatever society requires, in the best manner that the concentrated wisdom and capital of society can direct. In all these operations the members of this class, from twelve to fifteen years, will daily assist for as many hours as will not injure their physical strength, mental powers, or moral feelings; and with their previous training, with the daily superior instruction and aid which they will receive from the members of the class immediately above them, they will perform all that will be necessary for them to do, with no more exercise than their physical and mental health will require to keep them in the best state of body and mind. In these five years, also, they will make a great advance in the knowledge of all the sciences, for they will be surrounded with every facility for acquiring accurately the most valuable knowledge in the shortest time; facilities such as will open more than a 'royal road' to the acquisition of all knowledge attainable by man, with the aid of all the facts yet discovered. This will be a period of great progress and consequent interest to this new race, thus trained to become, for the first time in human history, intelligent rational beings. They will now be well prepared to enter the fourth class, which will be formed of those from fifteen to twenty years complete.

This class will enter upon a most interesting period of human life. Within its duration its members will become men and women of a new race, physically, intellectually, and morally; beings far superior to any yet known to have lived upon the earth; their thoughts and feelings will have been formed in public without secrecy of any kind; for as they passed through the previous divisions, they would naturally make known to each other, in all simplicity, their undisguised thoughts and feelings. By this rational conduct, the particular feelings of affection or otherwise which they were obliged to entertain for each other will be accurately known to all. Thus will it be ascertained who by nature are compelled to have the strongest attachment for each other; and these will naturally unite and associate together, under such wise and well-prepared arrangements, made by the most experienced in the society, as shall be the best devised to insure to the individuals uniting the greatest amount of permanent happiness, with the least alloy to themselves and injury to society.

Under this classification and consequent arrangement of society, every individual will be trained and educated to have all his faculties and powers cultivated in the most superior manner known; cultivated, too, under a new combination of external objects, purposely formed to bring into constant exercise the best and most lovely qualities only of human nature. Each one will be, thus, well educated, physically, intellectually, morally, and practically. Under this classification and consequent arrangement of these associated families, wealth, unrestrained in its production by any of the artificial absurdities now so common in all countries, will be most easily produced in superfluity; and all will be secured in a full supply of the best of it, for all purposes that may be required. They will, therefore, all be equal in their education and condition, and no artificial distinction, or any distinction but that of age, will ever be known among them.

There will be, then, no motive or inducement for any parties to unite except from pure affection, arising from the most unreserved knowledge of each other's character, in all respects, as far as it can be known before the union takes place. There will be no artificial obstacles in the way of the permanent happy union of the sexes; for, under the arrangements of this new state of human existence, the affections will receive every aid which can be devised to induce them to be permanent; and under these arrangements, there can be no doubt that, as the parties will be placed as far as possible in the condition of lovers during their lives, the affections will be far more durable, and produce far more pleasure and enjoyment to the parties, and far less injury to society than has ever yet been experienced under any of the varied arrangements which have emanated from the imagined free-will agency of the human race.

If, however, these superior arrangements to produce happiness between the sexes should fail in some partial instances, which it is possible may yet occur, measures will be introduced, by which, without any severance of friendship between the parties, a separation may be made, the least injurious to them and the most beneficial to the interests of society.

No immorality can exceed that which is sure to arise from society interfering by human laws with natural affections, or from compelling individuals to live continually together, when they have been made, by the laws of their nature, to lose their affections for each other, and especially when they have been made to entertain them strongly for another. How much dreadful misery has been inflicted upon the human race, through all past ages, from this single error? How much demoralization! How many murders! How much secret unspeakable suffering, especially to the female sex! How many evils are experienced over the world at this moment, arising from this single error of the imaginary free-will system, by which men have been so long, so ignorantly, and so miserably governed!

This portion of the subject, to do it full justice, as it has been hitherto involved in so much error and mystery, would require a much more extended development; but this limited view must suffice, as this subject is more fully explained in other parts of this book.

This fourth class will be still more active and general producers of the various kinds of wealth required by society, as well as the kind and intelligent instructors of the senior members of the third class, to enable these senior members to acquire the knowledge which has been previously taught to themselves, when members of the third class. It is not improbable that these four classes, under such simplified arrangements in all the departments of life as may be made, will be sufficient, aided in all ways by the new powers derived from mechanism and chemistry, to produce a surplus of all the wealth which a rational and superior race of beings can require; but to remove all doubt respecting this part of the subject, and to make the business of life a pleasure to all, another class of producers of wealth and instructors in knowledge shall be added, and they will form the

Fifth Class, which class will consist of those from twenty to twenty-five years complete.

This will form the highest and most experienced class of producers and instructors; and beyond the age of this class, none need be required to produce or instruct, except for their own pleasure and gratification. This fifth class will be the superiors and directors in each branch of production and of education. They will perform in a very superior manner, that which is now most defectively done by the principle proprietors and active directing partners of large producing establishments, and by the professors of universities. The great business of human life is, first, to produce abundance of the most valuable wealth for the use and enjoyment of all; and secondly, to educate all to well use and properly enjoy their wealth after it has been produced.

We have now most amply provided for the production of the wealth, and also for the formation of a superior character, to use and enjoy it in the most advantageous or rational manner by the five classes of producers and instructors which have been described.

The *Sixth Class* will consist of those from twenty-five to thirty years of age complete.

The business of this class will be to preserve the wealth produced by the previous classes, in order that no waste may arise, and that all kinds of it may be kept in the best condition, and used, when in the most perfect state, for the beneficial enjoyment of all parties. They will also have to direct the distribution of it as it may be required from the stores, for the daily use of the family. Under the arrangements which may be, and no doubt will be, formed for these purposes, two hours each day will be more than sufficient to execute the regular business of this class in a very superior manner. Some part of the remainder of the day will most likely feel the greatest pleasure in occupying with visits to various parts of their beautiful and interesting establishment, to see how every process is advancing; with each of which, by their previous training, they will be familiar, and now, at their leisure, they may consider whether any improvement can be made in them for the general benefit.

Another portion of the day they will probably devote to their most favourite studies; whether in the fine arts, in the sciences, in trying experiments, in reading, or conversation, or in making excursions to the neighbouring establishments, to give or to receive information, or to make visits of friendship. This will be the prime period for the more active enjoyments of life, and all will be by this calculation most amply enabled to enjoy them. They will have high health, physical and mental; they will have a constant flow of good spirits; they will, by this period, have secured a greater breadth and depth of the most varied useful knowledge in principle and practice than any human beings have ever yet attained; they will also be familiar with those acquirements which, in addition to their attainments in that which is useful in principle and practice, will render them delightful companions to each other, and to all with whom they may come into communication. And they will be thus preparing themselves to become fit members of the class immediately in advance of them, that is, the

Seventh Class. This will consist of all the members of the family from thirty to forty years, inclusive.

The business of this class will be to govern the home department, in such manner as to preserve the establishment in peace, charity and affection; or, in other words, to prevent the existence of any causes which may disturb the harmony of the proceedings. And this result will be most easily effected for the following reasons:

First, because they will know what their own nature really is, and that the convictions and feelings of the individuals are not created by their will, but that they are instincts of their nature, which they must possess and retain, until some new motive or cause shall effect a change in them.

Secondly, because in consequence of this knowledge, all in the establishment will be rational in their thoughts, feelings, and conduct; there will, therefore, be no anger, ill-will, bad temper, inferior or evil passions, uncharitableness, or unkindness.

Thirdly, because no one will find fault with another for his physical, intellectual, or moral nature, or acquired character as all will know how these have been formed; but all will, of necessity, feel a deep interest in doing whatever may be in their power, by kindness directed by judgment, to improve these qualities in every individual.

Fourthly, because there will be no poverty, fear of poverty, or want of any kind.

Fifthly, because there will be no disagreeable objects within or around the establishment to annoy or to produce any injurious or unpleasant effect upon any one.

Sixthly, because according to age, there will be a perfect equality in their education, condition, occupations, and enjoyments.

Seventhly, because by their training, mode of life, and the superior arrangements, in accordance with and congenial to their nature, and by which they will be continually influenced and governed, they will very generally, if not always, enjoy sound health and good spirits.

Eighthly, because there will be no motive to engender ambition, jealousy, or revenge.

Ninthly, because there will be no secrecy or hypocrisy of any kind.

Tenthly, because there will be no buying or selling for a monied profit.

Eleventhly, because there will be no money, the cause now of so much oppression and injustice.

Twelfthly, because there will be no religious or injurious mental perplexities or estranged feelings, on account of religious or other differences of opinion.

Thirteenthly, because there will be no pecuniary anxieties, for wealth of superior qualities will everywhere superabound.

Fourteenthly, because there will be no disappointment of the affections, both sexes rationally and naturally enjoying the rights of their nature at the period designed by nature, and most beneficially to ensure to all virtue and happiness.

Fifteenthly, and lastly, because every one will know that permanent arrangements have been purposely devised and executed to ensure impartial justice to every one, by each being so placed, trained, and educated from birth to maturity, that he will be, as he advances in age, secure of experiencing all the advantages and enjoyments which the accumulated wisdom of his predecessors knows how to give to the faculties and powers which he derived from nature.

This class of domestic governors, will, naturally, for order and convenience, divide themselves into sub-committees, each of which sub-committees will more immediately superintend or govern some one of the departments, which will be divided between them, in the best manner their experience shall direct.

In this manner, the whole business and affairs of each association will be governed without jealousy or contest. And, as each establishment will always be kept in high order, and as no cause which can create disputes or differences will be permitted to remain, there can be little to govern in families thus made rational; every member of them being, from their birth, placed within rational arrangements, and surrounded solely by rational external objects.

By these arrangements and classifications, every one will know, at an early age, that, at the proper period of life, he will have, without contest, his fair, full share of the government of society.

But final decision upon every doubtful point of practice must rest somewhere, and it is, perhaps, most natural, that this power should be vested in the oldest member of this class, who will possess this precedence for a short time only, because he will soon be superseded by the next senior member of this class, and he will become a junior member of the

Eighth Class, which will consist of those from forty to sixty years complete.

After providing for the production of wealth, for its preservation and distribution; for the training, education, and formation of character from birth to maturity, and for the internal government of each establishment: it is necessary to make arrangements to connect each large family or nucleus establishment with all other family establishments founded on the same principles; or to form what may not be improperly called the external or foreign arrangements.

The eighth class will have charge of this department; a department so important to place under the direction of the best-informed and most experienced, yet active members of society. The individuals from forty to sixty years of age will be so informed and experienced as a class, after they shall regularly have passed through the seven previous classes. Their business will be to receive and attend to visitors from other establishments, to correspond with other establishments, to visit, and to arrange the general business of the public roads, conveyances, and exchanges of surplus produce; inventions, improvements, and discoveries, in order that the population of every district may freely partake of the benefits to be derived from the concentrated knowledge and acquirements of the world; and that no part may remain in an ignorant or barbarous state. For by these means a new power of invention and discovery will be opened to mankind, many millions of times more efficient than that which has ever yet been in action, and more will be accomplished by it for the advance of the improvement and happiness of the human race, in one year, than can be attained under this old, ignorant, wretched, and irrational system, in any given period.

The members of this class will circumscribe the world in their travels, giving and receiving in their course the most valuable knowledge, and continually interchanging acts of friendship and kindness with all with whom they come into communication. Their wants, wherever they may go, among these new family associations, will be most amply supplied, for there will be everywhere among them, a large superfluity of every kind of useful or desirable wealth. The most varied and delightful sensations appertaining to human nature, when the physical, intellectual, and moral powers and faculties shall be called forth in their due order and proportions, and cultivated in the superior manner previously described, will be continually called into action; and this period of human life will be one of high utility and enjoyment. For the earth will not be the wild, barren, waste, swamp, or forest, which, with some exceptions, it ever has been and yet is; the united effort of a well-trained world will speedily change it into a well-drained, highly-cultivated, and beautiful pleasure scene, which, by its endless variety, will afford health and enjoyment to all, to a degree such as the human mind in its present degraded and confined state, has not the capacity to imagine. For the human faculties have been cultivated to have a perception of regions of torment, but never of those of happiness; the hitherto fancied heaven of irrational man, would be a state of stupid, monotonous existence, most unsatisfactory to an intelligent, rational being.

By these arrangements, being carried out to the extent intended, the whole human race, from the age of forty, will be, in reality, more truly sovereigns of the world, than any one is now sovereign of an empire or kingdom. These superior rational beings will have all the productions of the earth, which they can use or enjoy much more effectually at their control than any sovereign can now command them. These men of the new classification will all be well trained, and properly prepared, to make the best use of wealth, and to obtain its highest permanent enjoyment, without making abuse of any part of it. And these high enjoyments will be yet enhanced to these men, by the knowledge that they are not depriving a single human being of similar privileges and advantages; but, on the contrary, that each one of their fellow-men will derive additional gratification from witnessing, or knowing, that this control over all the enjoyments which the world in its most highly cultivated or best state can afford, is thus possessed by so many of their fellow-men justly and advantageously for all other classes, and which privileges and advantages all these classes will also, at the proper period of life, equally enjoy.

There is, however, one apparently insurmountable difficulty to be overcome, before the great change in human affairs can be accomplished; one that appears too deep-rooted, too widely spread over all quarters of the world, and too gigantic in its power for mortal man to attempt to contend against. This is the power of PREJUDICE, forced into the minds and upon the habits of all men, by their local position; – a position which inflicts upon them their geographical language, religion, manners, habits, associations of ideas, and conduct, and thus compels all men, without exception, instead of being trained to become rational beings, to acquire the character of irrational animals, to the deep injury of all the inhabitants of the earth. How is this universal evil to be fairly met and overcome, without creating misery by the conflict, to all these localized animals? Mortal man, by any power which in ordinary language he can call his own, would never think of attempting that which now appears to all men of the old world most wild and visionary, nay, not to be exceeded in folly or insanity by any of the most extravagant or mad enterprises ever undertaken by man in his most rude and irrational state. Well, then, what earthly power can be brought to this mighty conflict against localized irrational man; to obtain the victory over him for intelligent rational man; that the human being may no longer remain, or his offspring be forced to become, the mere geographical creatures of local impressions, producing and reproducing continually, local errors and associations of ideas, destructive of real knowledge, of virtue, and of happiness? Evidently most vain would it be for any mere earthly power to enter upon this more than mortal conflict. A new and divine weapon must be obtained from that source whence man has derived his organization and his mental faculties; a weapon of such might and power as shall, when daily wielded, and with certain aim directed, sever the gordian knot of human ignorance and prejucide so effectually, that it shall never more be the cause of inflicting error and misery on man.

But where is this divine weapon to be found? or, when found, who will have the temerity to wield it, and commence the conflict to destroy the localized animal of prejudice, give victory to rational man, and place him, secure for ever, upon the throne of reason, supported by charity and affection, and thus sustained, enable him to govern the world in peace, with ever increasing prosperity?

Rejoice, all ye who have so long desired to see the period arrive, when all of the human race shall become wise, and good, and happy, for this weapon of mighty power has been discovered! – its name is TRUTH! Its sharpness and brilliancy, now that it is, *for the first time*, fully unsheathed to open view, no mortal can withstand. It is a weapon derived direct from the Supreme Power of the Universe – the source whence alone, Truth has ever been obtained, or can ever emanate. Yet who shall wield this divine weapon? who, among the sons of men, have been trained from their youth upwards, to practise with it? who will now dare firmly to grasp it, and boldly go forth to battle against the accumulated prejudices of ages, and cry 'VICTORY OR DEATH?'

My Friends, fear not. The appointed hour is come. The victory is near at hand. It is already secured – there is a little band – insignificant in number, but they have shielded themselves in impenetrable armour – have cast all worldly consequences far away; lovers and worshippers of Truth, without admixture of error, they have no fear of man, or of what man can do against them. Already have they practised with this divine weapon, and are familiar with its use. They have firmly grasped it; they have gone forth; they have entered upon the conflict; and they return not until ignorance, falsehood, superstition, sin, and misery, shall be banished from the abodes of the human race; and peace and charity, reason, truth and justice, love, and happiness, shall reign triumphant, and for ever, over the whole family of man, wherever man shall exist; and slavery, and servitude, and oppression, or evil of any kind, among the sons of men, shall be known no more!

END OF THE FIFTH PART

THE BOOK

OF THE

NEW MORAL WORLD,

ON

GOVERNMENT AND LAWS.

BY ROBERT OWEN.

TRUTH WITHOUT MYSTERY, MIXTURE OF ERROR, OR FEAR OF MAN, CAN ALONE EMANCIPATE THE HUMAN RACE FROM SIN AND MISERY.

PART SIXTH.

London:

PUBLISHED FOR THE SOCIETY, BY

J. WATSON, 5, PAUL'S ALLEY, PATERNOSTER ROW;

AND ALL BOOKSELLERS.

1841.

THE BOOK

OF THE

NEW MORAL WORLD

SIXTH PART

GENERAL CONSTITUTION OF GOVERNMENT AND UNIVERSAL CODE OF LAWS,

Derived from the Constitution and Laws of Human Nature, and which will ultimately be secured to all who shall have been born and trained within the arrangements of the Rational System of Society.

A rational government will attend solely to the happiness of the governed.

It will ascertain what human nature is; – what are the laws of its organization, and of its existence from birth to death; – what is necessary for the happiness of a being so formed and matured; – and what are the best means by which to attain those requisites, and to secure them permanently for all the governed.

It will devise and execute the arrangements by which the conditions essential to human happiness shall be fully and permanently obtained for all the governed; and its laws will be few, easily to be understood by all the governed, and perfectly in unison with the laws of human nature.

CHAPTER I

General Constitution of Government and Universal Code of Laws.

The proceedings of the human race from the earliest recorded time to the present, although they must have emanated from nature, are now discovered to have been based on error from the beginning, and that the whole organization of society has been in strict accordance with those fundamental errors of inexperienced imagination.

Thus has error been added to error through the known history of man, which history may truly be called, the life of man through the irrational period of his existence, or the opposing and repulsive period in the progress of humanity.

The error of this base has been discovered, its evils are apparent, the true base is unveiled, the road to knowledge, excellence, truth and happiness, is opened; and all are thereby invited to enter upon and continue in it during their lives. The abandonment of the base of error, and the adoption of the base of truth, will be the commencement of the attractive and happy period of human existence.

The erroneous base required an erroneous organization of society for its support and continuance so long in opposition to innumerable every-day facts.

The true base will require a true organization for its support and continuance.

A re-organization of society is therefore inevitable, if man is to be made intelligent and good, or rational and happy.

To re-organize society is to change all the institutions of the world, and give a new direction to the feelings, thoughts and actions of all men.

This re-creation of man and of society would be difficult, if not impossible, were it not that the change is FOUNDED ON PRINCIPLES EVERLASTINGLY TRUE, AND THAT THE PRACTICES EMANATING THEREFROM WILL BE HIGHLY BENEFICIAL TO EVERY CHILD OF MAN.

The evils now so universally experienced from the erroneous organization which has emanated from the false principles on which it has been based, are such that as millions will not, fortunately for all, longer submit to bear, and these evils cannot be overcome or avoided now, except by an entire re-organization of society; a re-organization based upon, and in accordance with, the true fundamental principles of humanity; that is, with first principles consistent with themselves, and in accordance with every well-ascertained fact; there being no other criterion of truth known to man.

A re-organization presupposes an entire change in the principles and practices of governing, educating, and of carrying on the entire business of life: and it should be distinctly known, that there is but one rational mode by which the business of the human race can be performed. *There is only one right way.*

There can be but one true system of forming the human character, of governing, of producing, preserving, and distributing wealth; one true code of laws, one true classification of society, and but one true mode of uniting the human race into one family, with one interest and one language; because these can be based only on true principles; and true principles are one, invariable, or without change through eternity.

Truth being one and always the same, those principles which were true at the earliest period known to man, are equally true now, and will remain so through all time. Truth is that which, under the same circumstances, is unknown to change. The time will come when man, over the world, shall be made an intelligent and rational animal; there will then be but one universal system of conducting the affairs of life, and that will be the only true mode to secure the happiness of all through all future ages.

To effect this change, those who have been well informed, who have been enabled to collect the knowledge of the past and present that they may discern the future, will agitate without ceasing. The happiness to be derived from this change is in store for man, and no change is now deserving the notice of the wise, except it be the one from wrong to right, from error to truth.

The true and the right consist of universal ideas; these are all beneficial for the race of man; the experienced will now attend alone to them, for universal ideas alone can direct man in the path to permanent happiness.

It is from true universal ideas that principles for governing the world aright can alone be elicited.

Some of the universal ideas to enable men to know how to govern aright, and how to be governed rightly, are the following:

1. Man is born helpless, ignorant, and inexperienced, but capable of being taught, by injurious or beneficial circumstances, to be irrational or rational.

2. He derives the continuance of his existence from the unceasing appliances of external circumstances acting upon his original organization at first, and afterwards, as it is thus continually changed, physically and mentally, by the additions of these appliances.

3. He derives his knowledge only through the influence of external circumstances, acting upon the individual qualities and instincts given to him by nature previous to his birth.

4. These qualities or instincts are of the same number and general character in all men, but compounded in different proportions in each.

5. The instincts or qualities of humanity, as compounded by nature in each individual, are capable, in the young, of indefinite direction; and of illimitable combination by society when it is united for the attainment of any practicable result.

6. That inferior external circumstances, when allowed to act from the birth of infants, have a most powerful tendency to make them inferior as long as such inferior influences are allowed to surround them.

7. That mixed or medium external circumstances will, in the same manner, tend to form medium characters, while

8. Superior external circumstances will have an equally powerful influence in forming infants to acquire superior characters at maturity.

9. It is the interest of the human race that none but superior circumstances should exist; and society united possesses illimitable power to remove the inferior, and replace them with superior.

10. To a *very great extent* the adult generation forms the character of the rising generation, and it is the interest of all of human kind, that not one

inferior character should ever be formed; but the superior character can only be formed by superior circumstances.

11. That without equality of education and condition among mankind, there can be no virtue or permanent peace and happiness; and mechanism and chemistry make this equality easy of attainment.

12. That all born with healthy natural qualities may be trained, educated, and placed to become useful, good, and valuable members of society, and the unhealthy born will require the sympathy and affectionate care of society to patiently overcome their defects.

13. That by all being thus trained, educated, and placed, wealth may be easily and pleasantly created in great superfluity for all, without contest, or any unpleasant feelings or conduct.

14. That the poverty, sin, and misery of the world, emanate alone from man's ignorance of himself, and of the powers at his control, now existing in society, to remove the *causes* which produce these evils.

15. That ignorance, poverty, disunion, injurious passions, vice, crime, and misery, may be now easily *prevented*, throughout all nations and people, by a re-organization of society on true fundamental principles.

16. That wars are become an unmixed evil; and the waste of life, of property, and labour, which it creates, is more than sufficient, rationally applied, to ensure perpetual prosperity to the human race.

17. That knowledge, justice, morality, or happiness, can never co-exist with war, violence, and destruction of property.

18. That disunion is the cause of the greatest evils that man can experience, and it is the most extravagant mode by which human affairs can be carried on and conducted.

19. That by the cordial union of men and nations, the most permanent benefits will be obtained for the human race, and through it the greatest economy will be attained in conducting the affairs of life.

20. That it is vain and useless to attempt to form this union among men while they they shall be forced to receive the notions opposed to all facts; 1, That man forms himself; 2nd, his opinions; and, 3d, his feelings; because, while these three gross absurdities are forced into the mind from birth, man can only become an irrational and violent animal, opposed to his fellows, and always acting in opposition to his own happiness, and to that of all around him.

21. That by training man in a knowledge of his own nature and of society, and creating circumstances to enable him to act in accordance with his nature, union may be attained among the human race, and for ever cordially maintained.

22. That, by a scientific arrangement of society, in accordance with the reorganization of it, as explained in the last chapter of the previous part of 'this Book,' wealth may be made, with pleasure, at all times to superabound.

23. That the world can never be well and peaceably governed so long as the governors shall be elected or selected, nor can union be maintained.

24. That the contests of men, in an irrational state of existence, are chiefly about the production, preservation, distribution, and enjoyment of wealth; religious and political opinions, some objects of ambition, and women.

25. That sufficient knowledge of human nature and of society, has now been discovered, which, when extended throughout society, and consistently applied to practice, will remove the causes of all these contests.

26. That the cause of contests about wealth will cease when arrangements shall be made to create it with ease and pleasure, to be always in superfluity for all.

27. That all contests about religious opinions will cease when it shall be known that all that man now knows on this subject is, THAT THERE IS A POWER IN THE UNIVERSE WHICH EFFECTS ALL THAT TAKES PLACE WITHIN IT; BUT WHAT THAT POWER IS, OR HOW IMPELLED TO ACT, ARE MYSTERIES UNKNOWN TO THE HUMAN RACE.

28. That all contests about political opinions will cease when the principles shall be known, and the practice adopted, by which each one will be secured through life in the full advantages that it is practicable or possible for human beings, constituted as they are at birth, to enjoy. Also, when it shall be known that it is not the will of man, but the strongest convictions made on the mind, which form his religious, political, and all other opinions for him.

29. That all contests about ambition will cease when it is known that no one forms himself, and that the height of the most ambitious views of a rational being will be secured from birth for everyone; even to make each individual, in reality, far superior in knowledge, wisdom, and power to any sovereign that has ever reigned.

30. That the cause of all contests of men about women, and of women about men, will cease, when both shall be trained from birth to become rational beings, to know their own nature and that love, indifference, and hatred are not acts of will, but unavoidable instincts of humanity; instincts which, well understood and rationally directed, will always be most beneficent for all individuals of both sexes. Knowledge of the causes of affection, when the human race shall be trained to become rational beings will destroy the germs of all jealousy, as well as of all deceptions respecting the feelings of affection, or the absence of them.

31. *The organization of society, and the government of it, will therefore be based on the knowledge that man does not form himself, his opinions, or his feelings.*

From these universal ideas governments may be everywhere instituted for the permanent benefit of the governed and governors, in accordance with the new classification of society, as given in detail in the last chapter of the fifth part of this Book.

'A rational government will attend solely to the happiness of the governed.'

Having ascertained that the fundamental laws of humanity are, that man cannot form himself, his feelings, or opinions, and that there can be no merit or demerit to the individual who is formed; whose feelings are created, and whose opinions are forced by the strongest convictions made on the mind, and that man is to a very great extent the creature of external circumstances; a clear, full, and most substantial foundation is thus laid for a true organization of society, a superior formation of character, and a rational government, each of which will be consistent with the others, and throughout with the laws of nature, and especially of human nature.

The organization of society will consist in arrangements to create wealth, to preserve it, and to distribute it the most beneficially for all; to ensure the best character for each individual, from birth to death; and to govern all the most advantageously for each, that the greatest happiness may be secured through life for all.

Thus will society be so simplified, that the human race, rationally trained, and properly placed from birth, will be, at the age of twelve, competent to understand its outline in principle, and be prepared to comprehend and to take an active part in its practice.

They will know that society must consist of arrangements to produce, preserve, and distribute superior wealth abundantly for all; to ensure a superior physical, mental, moral, and practical character for all, from, or before birth; to govern all locally and generally, well and wisely for the happiness of each; and to effect these results, which are simple and easy of attainment, when understood and scientifically combined, by creating around all of the human race superior external circumstances to supersede the inferior, which have necessarily emanated from an inferior, false, and chaotic state of human existence, by which all were forced to become irrational in thought and action.

Such is the outline of the organization of the new or rational state of human existence – a state in which all will be essentially benefited; in which not one, after the change shall have been effected, will ever be injured or made unhappy; for the whole business of the life of each will be, in the best spirit, and with great knowledge of men and things, to endeavour to promote the well-being, well-doing, and happiness of all.

By studying the new classification of society, it will be seen that all that is really beneficial now in the lower, middle, and upper classes will be secured and greatly improved, and all that is now inferior and injurious in each will be rejected; that by this classification each one will become, through the various stages of his life, a prototype of society; the individual will gradually, as the necessary experience to accomplish all well shall be acquired, become producer, distributor, educator, local or home governor, and general or foreign governor, so far as that can be called foreign which partakes of one and the same interest and feeling, without motive for opposition or contest, and when the use of all shall belong to all, through the life of each.

From what has been said, it will be seen that there cannot be the slightest necessity for attempting to retain any part of the existing classification of society; it is a compound of unmixed evil, and of the most gross irrationality. It continually injures all, it permanently benefits no one of the human race. Presently it will be a matter of surprise to all, how and for what reason that which is an unmixed evil should have been maintained for so many thousand years; and that, for so long a period, that which will produce unmixed good should have been undiscovered, and every approach towards it be forcibly opposed and violently rejected. A rational government, formed thus on the eternal laws of human nature, will ascertain what are the conditions necessary for the happiness of beings constituted as men are by nature.

Upon investigation, it will discover that to secure the highest degree of permanent happiness to all, according to the individual constitution or organization at birth of each, it is necessary that efficient permanent arrangements should be made by the government to ensure the following, as

CONDITIONS REQUISITE FOR HUMAN HAPPINESS.

1. A good organization, physical, mental, and moral.

2. The power of procuring at pleasure whatever is necessary to preserve the organization in the best state of health.

3. The best education from infancy to maturity of the physical, mental, moral, and practical power of all the population.

4. The inclination and means of promoting continually the happiness of our fellow-beings.

5. The inclination and means of increasing continually our stock of knowledge.

6. The power of enjoying the best society, and more particularly of associating at pleasure with those for whom we feel the most regard and greatest affection.

7. The means of travelling at pleasure.

8. The absence of superstition, supernatural fears, and the fear of death.

9. Full liberty of expressing our thoughts upon all subjects.

10. The utmost individual freedom of action, compatible with the permanent good of society.

11. To have the character formed for us to express the truth only upon all occasions, and to have pure charity for the feelings, thoughts, and conduct of all mankind; and a sincere good will for every individual of the human race.

12. To reside in a society whose laws, institutions, and arrangements, well organized and well governed, are all in unison with the laws of human nature.

The above conditions are to a great extent under the control of society. These conditions being the requisites for human happiness, a rational government will adopt the most efficient measures to obtain and secure them for all the governed. And it should never be forgotten that it will be much more easy to form arrangements to obtain and secure them permanently *for all*, than for any division of society less than the whole.

To secure these requisites there must be equal education and condition, and all must be surrounded with the best circumstances which man in the present advanced state of the sciences can create. Such arrangements may be now made, and each individual, thereby placed within these circumstances, will be much to be envied by the most favoured individual living, or that ever has lived.

All hitherto, from the beginning, have been placed within irrational arrangements, and their minds have been filled with irrational notions, opposed to their own nature, which as they understood it not, they called *bad*, and concluded that it never could be made good. This error has arisen from mistaking the first principles of human nature, and supposing them to be the reverse of those which facts now demonstrate them to be.

What government has ever yet attempted to make arrangements to obtain for the governed the requisites for happiness which have been stated? Or what government has not put innumerable obstacles in the way of their attainment?

But, as previously stated, to accomplish the great end of society – the happiness of all, the present principles on which all the institutions of man are based must be abandoned, and all the practices which have emanated from them; a new organization of society must be made to supersede the old, the new must be based on principles of nature, and all the arrangements for the government of the population of the world must be in accordance with them. Upon these principles a rational government will easily devise and execute those arrangements, and make the laws in undeviating accordance with them, in order that there shall be no counteraction or inconsistency in the whole business of life.

As the laws of nature will be the permanent governing laws of society, human laws will be few and simple, and always in accordance with nature's laws. They will also be temporary and local, and merely to assist to make the change more easy from the absurd and cruel laws of man based on error, to the wise and benevolent laws of human nature based on truth.

When all shall be trained from their birth within rational circumstances, and of course made rational in their feelings, thoughts, and actions, no human laws will be required; nature's laws, well understood and consistently applied to practice, will be sufficient to secure the well-being, well-doing, and the permanent happiness of the race, and then will all human laws be for ever abolished.

To govern the world on these principles and arrangements, under the new organization and classification of society, – and when each human being, from birth to death, shall be well seen to, and efficiently and affectionately well cared for – will become, not only easy, but a constant source of pleasure, a pastime to the more experienced and aged, assisted as they will be, cordially and heartily, by those of every age and qualification.

CHAPTER II

Transition Laws, to enable society to pass gradually from man's ignorant, unjust, and cruel laws, to the government of nature's wise, just, and kind laws.

LIBERTY OF MIND AND CONSCIENCE. – All laws, to be just or useful, must be based on the knowledge of the fact, that individual man cannot create himself, physically, mentally, or morally, and that his feelings and opinions are formed for him. Consequently it has been an error of past generations to make laws to attempt to make him accountable hereafter, or in this life, to his fellow man, for his feelings, thoughts, or actions, seeing that these ever have been, and ever must be, formed for the individual.

All laws therefore which prevent men expressing the full truth respecting their thoughts and feelings, and upon all subjects, are unjust and most irrational. Consequently the first law in the rational state of existence will be, 'That all will have liberty to express the truth, not only as respects their natural thoughts and feelings, but upon all subjects, civil and religious.' Without this law, the language of truth and practice of virtue, or right conduct, can never be known among the human race; for without the simple, pure, and genuine language of truth without mixture of or motive to falsehood, virtue or rational conduct will remain as heretofore unknown to man.

It is, then, of the first importance to the human race, that no obstacle should be placed in the way to prevent truth becoming the only language of man.

To supersede the universal practice of falsehood and deception which error has introduced, by the universal practice of truth and straight-forward honesty in word and action, will effect more for the well-doing, well-being, and happiness of man, in one year, than has been achieved by all the religions and governments of past and present time. Therefore must man not only have full liberty to speak the truth, but every encouragement must be given to him never to deviate from it.

No one man, nor any body of men, can have just right to interfere with, or control the opinions of others, except by fair argument maintained in the spirit of charity and kindness.

Who has any right whatever to control the thoughts and feelings of others when expressed in the language of truth and sincerity?

Any assumption to coerce the opinions of others, except by fair argument, evinces a gross ignorance of the laws of human nature, and that the assumers are totally incapable of directing the government of human affairs. Such assumption on the part of any is proof that they have been mistaught, and are fit only for the infant school of the Rational Society. For one man to say to another, 'You should not believe as you do,' is as rational as to say to those who are low in stature, 'You should not be so short, you ought to be tall. I am taller than you, and you ought to be as I am, and I therefore require you to add to your stature, of if you will not do so, I will have you punished in this world, and you shall be eternally, severely tormented in another life after this, and to which torments there will be no end.'

Or, for one human being to say to another, 'You ought not to feel the pleasure or pain, love or dislike, which you do; because I feel differently, and you ought to feel as I do, or as I desire you to do,' is about as wise or rational as if the dictator were to say, 'You have blue eyes, and see erroneously with them; you see I have black eyes, and always therefore see things as they are. You have no business to have those blue eyes to make you see differently from what I wish you to do; I demand of you to change them for black ones, that you may see as I do.'

Such have been, such are, the laws of man, – of man made to be irrational by such laws from his birth, and in consequence to be miserable himself, and to inflict misery on all around him. – Law second, 'Therefore, no one shall have any other power than fair argument to control the opinions or belief of another.' Opinions, or belief, being always forced on every individual by the strongest evidence made on the mind, there can be no merit or demerit to the individual for any opinion or belief which may thus be forced upon him.

No one by a supposed free and independent will can determine what he shall believe or disbelieve, or what opinions he will entertain upon any subject, nor how often these shall change during his life. The eternal law of humanity is, that man, whether he desires it or not, must believe according to the strongest evidence made to influence his mind. And it is as irrational to praise or blame men for their belief or opinions on any subject whatever as to praise or blame them for the size or form of the features of their countenance; they have just as much merit or demerit for the one as the other; they are as much compelled to have the one as the other.

The irrationality of the phraseology of the world in saying you *ought* to believe this, that, or the other, or you *ought not* to believe so and so, will now be evident to all taught to draw just conclusions from facts reasoned upon in accordance with common sense. But what can be said of our ancestors, who butchered each other by millions and for centuries, because one party had been trained conscientiously to believe in the cross and the other in the crescent, and each thought that the other could at pleasure, and therefore ought to change their own for the other's local superstition. This insane conduct of the human race, solely arising from the ignorance of man as to one of the first and most simple eternal laws of his nature, continues in full vigour of irrationality even to this day.

And such is the extent of this dreadful mental malady, that in the empire of Great Britain, claiming to be the first and most powerful in the world, the greatest evils are at this day inflicted upon its subjects, through the whole extent of its dominion, by this worst of maladies that has or can derange the human faculties.

The supposition that man possesses the power to believe or disbelieve anything by a free will at his command, and that there is merit or demerit due to the individual for some particular belief, is the true cause of this mental malady; and the real foundation of all the superstitions that have so often desolated countries and originated massacres, and which now insanely divide man from man over the earth; while it is his first and last interest to be cordially united as one being, possessing the qualities and qualifications of the aggregate when each shall be highly cultivated in accordance with all the ascertained laws of humanity.

The cure of this insanity, which has made, which makes, maniacs of so large a portion of each generation, is one of the first steps to be taken in preparing the human race to become rational in their feelings, thoughts, and actions. Therefore, law third will be, that 'no praise or blame, no merit and demerit, no reward or punishment, shall be awarded for any opinions or belief.'

But the great question is, how is this disease, fatal to man's rationality and happiness, to be cured and eradicated from the human constitution? Not by anger, violence, or punishment of any kind. The patient willed not the fatal malady under which he suffers; he is unconscious of its existence as a disease, dreadful as it is in its consequences to the individual and throughout the world; nay, he deems it a blessing, – a *divine* blessing, – being so taught to feel and think from his birth.

Punish or in any way persecute the poor diseased invalid, and the disease is thereby increased. The patient thus afflicted should be treated, as other lunatics are in the now best conducted lunatic asylums, with great kindness and forbearance, and seldom should they be openly opposed, for the reason previously stated, that they would by opposition become the more strongly attached to the cause of their disease.

The cause being now known, the remedy can be more advantageously applied.

The disease has been generated by a strong early impression, often repeated, being made on the mind.

It can be the most easily removed by other counteracting impressions being made in the spirit of kindness, candour, and charity, gently and skilfully applied as the patient can bear them. Much judgment and knowledge of human nature, as it has been made to feel, think, and act under this malady, are required to apply this curative process to be successful; but the application of the remedy must be made with reference to times and circumstances. Sometimes it will be well to apply the curative process to one or a few individuals being in a certain stage of the disorder; at other times to more numerous bodies, to whole nations, or to the world.

A curious effect is produced upon both small and large numbers by this disease. They may be easily made to perceive that others, innumerable others, are overrun with this mental plague, and they are made to wonder that those they see or know are infected with it, even in its worst stages, as they are taught to believe, are at the same time most unconscious that they are themselves equally, or perhaps more deeply, affected by another phase of the same disorder, while the former poor creatures, suffering grievously as they do, are unconscious of the cause acting upon them, but they are most clear and quick-sighted in perceiving how the evil affects the latter. Thus by all parties supposing that they are themselves free from this far worse than Egyptian plague,[a] and that all except their own party are deeply infected with it, each party becomes afraid of being infected by the others, and they almost always quarrel dreadfully on this account, go to war with one another, and often are aroused to such a state of frantic madness as to determine secretly to massacre in their fury great masses of their poor afflicted opponents.

This dreadful mental and moral plague has been of long standing almost all over the world, and it must even now be treated with great skill, kindness, and tact, or the poor afflicted invalids who are advancing towards a state of frantic madness, may, before the straight waistcoat of public opinion can be placed upon all of them, become so outrageous as to massacre their best friends, who would run great risks to effect their perfect cure, and to eradicate the disease for ever from the world.

This being the present state of matters in all countries, and as none of these helpless invalids were the cause of their own malady, and, of themselves, cannot effect their own cure, and as violence would only increase the disorder, the fourth law must be, 'That all, of every religion (or varied phase of this malady) shall have equal right to express their opinions or feelings respecting the cause of their peculiar aspect of this disease, or of that unknown mysterious Power which moves the atom and controls the aggregate of nature and of the universe, and to worship that unknown Power under any form, or in any manner, agreeable to any of the particular phases of the malady with which, in their infancy, childhood, and youth, they were, for themselves and the world, so unfortunately infected, provided that, by this liberty, they do not interfere with equal rights in others.'

This law is made to be the most just to all parties, and to be the best preparation for the change contemplated – from an insane to a sane state of the human intellects.

Many who have not thought or reflected on the causes which produce effects, whose minds have been kept localized, and whose feelings, thoughts, and actions are all merely geographic, will be, at first, irritated and angry with

[a] See for example Exodus 8:6.

those who, owing to favourable circumstances, not of their own creating, have been compelled to see this local disorder, and to discover the cause of its different phases, in all parts of the earth, and of the misery which it has produced, and is, at this day, producing, in all nations and among all people. But, upon more mature and calm reflection, aided by such works as are now being published in different parts of the civilized world, and new experiments making in Europe and American to introduce a better, and, if possible, a rational system of society into practice, their first fears, feelings, and opposition will gradually subside, and they will ultimately begin to perceive the advantages of the change.

CHAPTER III

Providing for and Educating the Population.

It is now ascertained, beyond all doubt, that the discoveries which have been made in modern times in the various arts and sciences, to give new, and, to many, inconceivable productive power to aid the labour of man, are already more than sufficient, under a rational arrangement, to saturate the population of the world with wealth, so as to make it abundant, without contest or competition, to supply the wants and wishes of the human race.

And to supply them, by beautiful scientific arrangements, with health, ease, pleasure, and high gratification to all, of every age, and in every country which it is necessary to inhabit over the globe; and yet this wondrous new power of production is but in its infancy. It may now be annually increased to an illimitable period – many times more than it is possible to increase population. During the last century, in Great Britain and Ireland it has been increased, under the most blind direction and profound ignorance, more than twenty to one. In a century more, it may be increased more than one hundred to one, compared with the increase of population. It may be so directed as to produce the like result in every population over the globe. Or if there could be any utility in doing so, this increase of productive power over the increase of population, may be annually extended to an amount that is present far beyond that which can be credited by the uninformed upon this, with the present starving millions around us, most important subject. Suffice it now to say, that whenever well-informed men of science shall enter upon the investigation, they will find that the means of creating new power to make wealth, at all times, more than abundant to satisfy all human wants and wishes, have been already discovered, and secured for the use of man, may now be increased to an illimitable extent, and that, by scientific arrangements, easy of execution, a termination may be put to poverty, or the fear of it, for ever over the world, and thus to lay the foundation for the cessation of all contests, and the endless evil consequences proceeding therefrom, respecting wealth among the human race, and be no more known among the family of man.

It will be necessary, to make these scientific arrangements to be the most useful, that they should be soon made to become national and general; for, in a rational state of society, there can be no local or exclusive interests, it will be soon discovered that there can be but one interest among men, if they are to be made superior in character, healthy, well-informed upon the most useful subjects, moral in spirit and conduct, – valuable men and women in the substantial business of life, and happy in their intercourse with each other.

No! machinery, chemistry, and other arts and sciences, have destroyed the possibility of much longer maintaining the individual and repulsive system of the world. Fortunately for the human race, machinery and chemistry, which have so far, under the influence of individualism, increased the poverty of the industrious, and the immorality and misery of all to a great extent, are ultimately destined to destroy poverty, the fear of it, immorality, and misery. Machinery and chemistry will yet be made to do all the unhealthy and disagreeable labour of society, leaving only healthy and pleasant occupation and employment for men, women, and children to perform.

As soon as men shall be made a little rational, they will discover the absurdity of poor laws,[a] or any provision for pauperism. They will soon perceive that pauperism can never exist in any country in which the inhabitants have been made to become intelligent and rational. The fifth law will be, 'That every one shall be equally provided through life with the best of everything for human nature, by public arrangements, which arrangements shall give the best known direction to the industry and talents of every individual.'

Under this law and these arrangements, all property will cease to have a saleable value: there will be, at all times, and in all places, as soon as society shall be scientifically arranged, a continual surplus of it to satisfy the demand of all, and then all will be allowed freely to use it; and the producers of it will be also the intelligent enjoyers of it. As wealth will have no saleable or exchangeable value, there will be no contest about it. As air, the most valuable of human wants, is freely used by all without contest, so will wealth be obtained, because, by the most simple order of society, it will everywhere be provided with pleasure in superfluity.

After providing abundantly for the physical wants of the human race, it

[a] System of parish relief by which rates were levied to provide work and support for the poor. Its cost rose from c. £1.9 million in 1785 to £6.9 million in 1817. A much harsher system was introduced with the Poor Law Amendment Act of 1834.

becomes necessary to make equal effective provision for their mental and moral wants and requirements.

To those experienced in a knowledge even of the present disordered state of society, the difference between a neglected human being, physically, mentally, morally and practically, and one well cared for, and the best trained and educated in all these respects, is very great; much more than a thousand to one; but the difference between the former, and a full formed man and woman made rational, will not be easy to calculate with accuracy, but it may without hesitation be estimated at many thousands to one; and were the minds of men more advanced in a knowledge of this subject, it might, with truth, be stated at millions to one.

Educating, or forming the character from birth to death becomes, therefore, next to providing the necessaries of life, the second great object of human existence. For the superior enjoyments and happiness of man will depend upon this task being well executed.

And it is most important that all should know, that the character of every infant with a sound or healthy constitution, may be manufactured by society to become, at maturity, a most useless and detrimental, or a most useful and valuable being.

That this subject has been so long neglected, misunderstood, and misapplied, has been owing to the ignorance created by the three fundamental errors on which society has ever been based. It might be supposed that the innumerable daily existing facts to show the power and importance of forming the character of each, and the advantage to all, from making it superior for all, would have long since induced the world to have directed its best energies and largest capital to have ensured the best training and cultivation of body and mind for every individual of the human race. When a fair and just comparison can be made between a human being born in misery, neglected from birth, placed amidst circumstances, the most inferior and injurious, trained to feel the injustice of the wealthy, aided by no one, and made, step by step, as he advances in years, an enemy to man and society; and placed beside a similarly organized being at birth, who shall be born amidst plenty, and well cared for from the hour of his existence, surrounded with superior circumstances only, his physical, mental and moral faculties and powers, judiciously and well cultivated, the mind being stored with the most useful and valuable ideas, efficiently trained and well occupied in the useful and important business of life, made a friend to mankind, and to have his greatest pleasure in promoting their happiness.

When this comparison shall be faithfully made and duly estimated, then will the world become conscious of the great error which it has committed through past time, that it now commits, especially that Great Britain nationally commits, by voting thirty thousand pounds to educate the people, and seventy thousand to build stables for royalty; while, a few years since, it expended one hundred and thirty millions sterling in one year to carry on war, to murder and plunder on a most magnificent scale.

Is not the difference between the neglected and the well trained, educated, and employed individual, a difference in mere wealth to the state during an average life of each, much – very much more, than one hundred a-year? But take it as this figure, which is so greatly below the truth, and supposing the average of life to be thirty years; while, under rational arrangements, its duration would probably reach sixty, and take the population of Great Britain and Ireland at twenty-eight millions, the result would be thirty years, multiplied by one hundred pounds for each year, would be three thousand pounds difference of money value in the life of the two individuals; then multiply twenty-eight millions of population at three thousand pounds each, and it gives eighty-four billions of pounds sterling difference in value of the whole population for thirty years; then divide this amount by thirty, and the result is two billions eight hundred millions, as the difference annually between the population of Great Britain and Ireland, when ill or well educated and employed. Extend this calculation to Europe, America, and to the population of the world, and then estimate, if present human faculties can encompass the amount, what is the sum total lost daily by the human race, through the neglect of well training and educating each individual from birth through life. Some idea may be obtained, by dividing the two billions eight hundred millions of pounds, the annual loss upon a population of twenty-eight millions, and the result is one hundred pounds a-year loss to every individual, young, middle aged, and old – as by the hypothesis. It is estimated at a low calculation that there are eight hundred millions living upon the earth, and under a rational system of society, scientifically arranged, it would be easy of practice to well train, educate, place, and employ the whole of this number, indeed, much more easy and economical than to conduct the world as its affairs are at present administered, and the difference upon the population of the globe would be eighty billions of wealth annually. Such, with regard to wealth alone, is the loss to the population of the world between the non, or ill education of each individual, and the physical, mental, moral, and practical superior formation of character for each.

But, if such is the loss of wealth, how is the loss arising from the deterioration of the human faculties, the encouragement of all the inferior, and suppression or depression of all the superior qualities which might be drawn forth and well cultivated in each one of the family of man? How, and by what rules of arithmetic shall the calculation be made to ascertain the difference between the health, knowledge, excellence, and happiness of this family, under the neglect in the one case, and the due care in the other?

That these calculations should be left to this period, and that man should be untrained or ill trained and educated over the world, is demonstration itself that the human race, in its feelings, thoughts, and conduct, has never yet been made rational. Therefore, the sixth law will be,

'That all shall be educated, from birth to death, physically, mentally, morally, and practically, in the best manner known.'

When this law shall be put into practice, and fully carried out, as it ought to be, for the benefit of all, in every country, tyranny, slavery, ignorance, poverty, division, crime, and misery will be unknown; for all be made to feel, think, and act rationally through life.

The principle of right and justice is, that 'no man has a right to require another, of the same age, to do for him what he will not do for that man; in other words, all men, by nature, have equal rights.'

To carry out this principle of justice most beneficially for the human race, the arrangements of society should be made to give equal advantages, from birth to death, to each male and female, to the extent that the difference of original conformation at birth will admit.

This is the only principle that will admit of the practice of virtue among men – virtue being equal justice between man and man, without reference to class, creed, country, or colour, and to the extent of the population of the world. It is only by the best education, domestic teaching, and the most useful employment being given to all, according to age, strength, and capacity, that the world can ever be governed in peace, order, and harmony.

Under this arrangement, there will be no rational cause for complaint of any kind, all trained, as they will be, seeing and fully comprehending the justice of this law, and its innumerable advantages to all, will be at all times so satisfied, that the mind and feelings will be in the best state for exertion, physical and mental, and the greatest progress will be thereby daily made in promoting the well-being and happiness of all through every succeeding generation.

Under these arrangements there will be no contest for wealth or station – no motive to any other ambition than who shall do the most to advance the knowledge, union, and happiness of man over the world.

It will be no longer be, 'How shall I the most benefit myself, or my family, or my neighbourhood, or my country? but how shall I the most contribute to the knowledge, union, and happiness of the human race?'

The advantages to be derived from the population of the world having equal education and employment, according to age, will far exceed all the present powers of man to estimate. Some of these will be a daily progress in knowledge charity, and love, – a continued increase of the most valuable wealth, – a more extended union of interest and feeling among the human race, and a perpetual growing prosperity in all ways that will ensure the advance of happiness as new knowledge shall be acquired.

But, as soon as the world can be disabused of the errors upon which all human affairs have been based, and from which all religions, laws, governments, institutions, and classifications of society have emanated, there will be no difficulty in the way of speedily abandoning all local notions, ideas, habits, and customs, and clearly perceiving the advantages and increased perfection to be acquired by exchanging them for universal ideas and motives of action, and especially for universal education and employment, according to age, strength, and capacity. The seventh law will therefore be,

'That all shall pass through the same general routine of education, domestic teaching, and employment.'

It has not now to be stated for the first time, that the immediate parents and grand parents, and private family residences, are not the proper persons and places to do justice to human nature in their training and educating from birth to maturity. The natural animal affections of parents for their immediate children or grand-children, render them, by all the experience of the past, the most unfit, especially under the circumstances of private family dwellings, to train and educate their own children, however qualified they may be to train and educate the children of other parents.

Experience proves that children, to have justice done to their nature, all their faculties brought out, in due order, and at the proper time indicated by nature, should be trained and educated in numbers in public, and all treated with uniform care, consideration, and kindness; they should not perceive partiality, nor should any be treated generally in any manner different from the mass of the same age.

Nor can any difference, under proper associative arrangements, ever be required or useful, because the extent of care and justice will be applied to one and all, regardless of who or what they may be, as they will be known only as the expected future members of a rational community of mutual interests and equal advantages, according to age. The whole adult members of these associations will be trained to consider all the children as the children of their family, and future heirs to their knowledge and possessions; and they will naturally acquire a parental affection for them in proportion to the good and lovely qualities which will be cultivated, even from birth, in all these children. Parents seeing this, and the daily improvement in their own children with the others, will gradually acquire the united affection for the children of the community, and be satisfied and gratified with seeing them and their proceedings as often as they desire.

It is a great mistake, which many make, in supposing that the parents will be more excluded during education and life in community arrangements, than they are and have generally been under the old chaotic no-arrangements of old society. The parents are often compelled, from various causes, to be much separated from their children in the old world; while in the new they will be always near them, and may see them daily, or as often as they could reasonably desire.

The eighth law will therefore be,

'That all children, from their birth, shall be under the especial care of the community in which they are born; but their parents shall have free access to them at all times.'

So long as children shall be trained in twos or threes, in private families, and in separate creeds, classes, and parties, they will continue to be made, as heretofore, not full-formed men and women, with all their faculties, physical, mental, moral, and practical, properly drawn out, well cultivated, and duly exercised at the proper period of life up to the point of temperance; but mere localized animals, ignorant of themselves and of the general laws of humanity, and in consequence, always tormenting themselves and others, while it is their highest interest to make themselves and all others happy.

It has been supposed, but most erroneously, that parents have a greater interest than society in the education of their children. Society may be made to suffer immensely by a single child being ill trained and wrongly educated; or it may be benefited to a like extent by one individual being well trained and educated. While in either case the parents and near relatives, who suffer or enjoy under these circumstances, form but a very small portion of the society who suffer or enjoy.

No mistake, therefore, can be greater than for society to entrust the formation of the character of its members to the private tuition, or no tuition, of the parents, who neither understand how to form superior men and women, nor are they in possession of the arrangements in private houses to surround the young with the circumstances which alone can form superior men and women.

By all the children of the same establishment being brought up together as the children of the same family, all treated alike, according to age, and devoid of all notions of or desire for individual advantages or private property, a very superior character may be given through the community, in public arrangements, to all, when compared to that which could be formed by their respective parents in private dwellings. In fact, to form a superior, virtuous, and rational population, the characters of all must be formed together on the same general principles, but devoid of all class, creed, and other local errors. The knowledge given to each should be universal truths, which will be ever consistent when compared one with another, and always in strict accordance with every ascertained fact.

The most important of these universal truths will be a knowledge of the facts which develop what human nature is, and of course how it ought to be treated, through every stage of the life of each individual. Above all, they should, at the earliest period that their judgments can be trained to understand facts, and draw accurate conclusions from comparing fact with fact, be called upon to consider the great facts on which a right or wrong system of society must be based. And to ascertain from their own investigation of facts, each for himself, whether he possesses the power to form his physical, mental, or moral faculties; whether he possesses the power to believe or disbelieve according to a free will at his command, and whether he has, within himself, the power to love and hate at his pleasure, or to change the one into the other, either for persons or things, at his will.

These are matters to each individual, and to the aggregate of society, of the very highest importance, and with which every one must be convinced in his own mind, before he can have any chance of becoming a rational being.

For should children be trained by all around them, as heretofore, to believe, without investigating facts, that they are responsible to men and spiritual beings for the qualities of their nature, which are forced upon them even before their birth, and for the influence of the surrounding circumstances, which they did not create, upon those qualities; that there is merit or demerit due to individuals for believing or disbelieving certain dogmas, notions, or opinions, and that the individuals have the power within themselves to believe or disbelieve whatever they like; and that they have also the power to like or love, be indifferent, or dislike or hate, who or what they please; then will they be forced, through life, with few exceptions, to become most irrational beings in feeling, thought, and action, and fit only to act as slaves to a few, under the present injurious and irrational system for conducting the affairs of mankind.

While, on the contrary, should children be trained from their birth to observe facts, to investigation them accurately, and to compare fact with fact, and thus gradually acquiring the power to draw just conclusions from those comparisons, and in this manner ascertain for themselves that it is contrary to facts that an individual could form his own bodily or mental powers; that he can, by a supposed free-will, believe or disbelieve any dogmas, doctrines, or opinions; or that he can like or dislike, love or hate, or be indifferent about persons and things by his own determination, then will they become rational beings, and always think and act accordingly.

Then will another and altogether new mind be formed within the individual; another and altogether new state of society will necessarily arise, and men and women will perceive all things as they are, without any false medium to derange and distort their feelings, thoughts, and actions. They will become rational individually and collectively, and society, for the first time in the history of man, will become sound in theory and practice.

Thus, and thus alone, can the incongruous and baneful system of human affairs, by which all are so grievously injured in body and mind, from birth to death, be, without convulsion or disorder, gradually and peaceably superseded; full-formed superior men and women be educated, and the world made the abode of a rational and happy race of intelligent beings.

Therefore the ninth law will be –

'That all children shall be trained and educated together, as children of the same family, and shall be early taught a knowledge of the laws of their own nature.'

In a state of society based on true first principles and its superstructure, in all its parts, in accordance with those principles, there will be no motive to falsehood or deception of any kind.

All falsehood and deception emanate from the false fundamental principles, upon which the old superstructure of society has been raised.

These erroneous principles instil falsehood and deception in the formation of character, of all individuals, through every step of its progress from birth to death.

'You ought not to feel as you do; you ought not to think as you do; you ought not to act as you do;' is the language of the old world, which, with the necessary consequences of such irrational expressions, stultify every mind, place a dark glass of error before every eye, and enforce a language of falsehood upon one and all, and a universal conduct of deception. As the world has been hitherto constituted, men and women cannot freely and honestly express their feelings and convictions upon the subjects most conducive to their misery or happiness; the parties who simply spoke the truth on all occasions, and expressed without deception the feelings and convictions which they were compelled by their nature to have, whether they desired to entertain them or not, would be subjected to every kind of inconvenience, annoyance, punishments, and death.

While the language dictated by nature, when nature, rationally cultivated, shall rule the destinies of man, will be the plain, straight forward, simple, and beautiful language of truth only; – a language which, to an extent which men and women trained as they have been in fundamental errors and all their baneful consequences, have no minds yet formed to enable them to comprehend or appreciate.

When society shall be reconstructed on true fundamental principles, newly organized, newly classified, and the character of all newly formed in accordance with those principles, the language of truth only will be spoken, and all motives to deception will be unknown. And by this change from the language of falsehood and practice of deception, to the *language* of truth and the *practice* of truth, *more knowledge of human nature and more virtue will be given to the human race in one year, than it has yet obtained during all the period that has past.*

Man does not yet appear to have caught the slightest glance of the immensity of the change for good that will be attained when society shall be organized to enable all to speak the truth only on all occasions, and upon every subject. Man will not know what man is until each shall speak to the other, freely and without the slightest disguise, the genuine feelings and thoughts which nature compels each to have; and when each shall be trained from birth to become rational, and shall be placed within those external circumstances in which alone rational beings will be placed, the advantage of truth, over disguise or falsehood of any kind, will become evident to all, and that evidence will destroy all motive to deception in look, word, or action. Truth alone is the language of virtue with falsehood; or of a knowledge of human nature and deception; or of man being rational with motive to mislead his brother upon any subject whatever. Therefore, the tenth law will be, –

'That every individual shall be encouraged to express his feelings and convictions as he is compelled by his nature to experience them; or, in other words, to speak the truth only upon all occasions.'

In consequence of the inexperienced imagination of our early ancestors, respecting the power of each individual, by a supposed internal free will, to like or dislike, be indifferent, or to love or hate persons and things at his pleasure, a false and most injurious character has been formed for man and woman over the world; the errors proceeding from which society has endeavoured to correct by the varied modes of marriage adopted in different countries, and in the same country at different periods. And yet at this day, in the most advanced nations towards a state of rational civilization, the greatest disorder, degradation, crimes and misery are produced without ceasing.

All lawgivers and legislators have endeavoured, to the utmost stretch of their faculties, to prevent these evils, and to overcome them by varying the forms and ceremonies of marriage without limit, yet no one has ever yet succeeded in this object. The cause of the ever-recurring disappointment has been the fundamental error on which all these changes have been made. One and all of these lawgivers have supposed, as taught by their predecessors, that man could love, hate, or be indifferent at his will and pleasure, and every change to remedy the evils previously created, has been based on this error. Now, whatever changes in the form and ceremony of marriage may be made, based on this supposition, they will produce only vice and misery, and never virtue and happiness. The supposition is contrary to the eternal law of nature, and nature will eternally assert her right, and therefore men and women do not love, or hate, or be indifferent to each other according to any human marriage, form, or ceremony ever yet invented. In defiance of all the puny attempts of man to contravene this law of nature, by fines, imprisonment, death, or promise of eternal reward or threats of eternal torment; men and women have been compelled to dislike that which was disagreeable to them, and to like that which was agreeable to them, and they will be compelled thus to feel as long as human nature shall exist. And no irrationality can be greater than for man, by his puny laws in opposition to nature, to imagine that he can overcome and successfully set aside her everlasting laws.

The experience of the past proves the fallacy of all such attempts, even from the beginning of known time. The existing state of the British dominions demonstrates the enormous amount of evil and misery daily and nightly produced, owing, solely, to this insane contest of ignorant man with the wisdom of nature to carry out her own designs to effect the happiness of the human race. For when man, through ignorance, opposes nature, she punishes him; and if he obeys not, by the smaller measure of it, she increases it until he is compelled through suffering to abandon his error. When man shall cease to be ignorant; when he shall perceive and clearly understand the laws of nature, he will no more rebel against them. His laws will be nature's laws; crime and all evil will then terminate for ever; for man will have passed the period of his irrational existence; he will have entered on that state which will make and for ever keep him a rational being; rational in all his feelings, thoughts and conduct.

In the rational state of society, men and women will be trained, from their birth, in the language of truth only, in a knowledge of their own nature, and of the laws which govern, influence, and direct it, under all circumstances. They will therefore know the causes which produce love, indifference, or dislike; and knowing the cause, they will never be surprised or unprepared to expect the natural effects from those causes.

Men and women, thus enlightened and made rational, will entertain no jealous feelings because they are not loved by some others. They will know that they do not possess the requisite qualities to create love in them. By the language of truth they will learn the exact state of the feelings and thoughts of others, and why they are compelled to have those thoughts and feelings. There will be no displeasure created on this account; anger or revenge will never exist in minds sufficiently intelligent to understand the laws of their own nature; the simple language of truth, regarding the feelings which each is compelled to receive and entertain, will speedily remove anger, ill will, jealousy, and revenge, as well as all sexual crime, disease, and suffering, now proceeding from ignorance, poverty, and the disappointment of the affections.

As soon, therefore, as man shall be enlightened respecting the laws of his nature, and thus made rational, and all shall be well educated and rightly placed, then will men and women unite according to their strongest affection, and union will never take place without mutual affection, nor will sexual crime be known, or any of its evils be experienced.

In a state of society thus made rational, there will be no human laws to counteract nature's all-wise laws. Man and woman, not united by nature's laws, will never be compelled, required, or expected to associate contrary to their feelings. All human laws made with a view to force affection, have produced disease, crime, and misery continually, and, while persevered in, will always produce crime and misery. When society can be made rational, no attempt so insane as to endeavour to force affection by human laws, in opposition to nature's laws, will ever be made or thought of, much less introduced into the practice of any country. As all will be well educated, physically, mentally, morally, and practically, and equal in condition; as all will know the feelings, through the language of truth, which each is compelled to have for all others, there will be no disguise or deception regarding affection between any parties. Those having the strongest affection for each other will naturally unite; there will be no artificial obstacle in their way, and all will speak of their affections with as much simplicity and truth as they now express themselves respecting their likes and dislikes of any object of their senses, whether in seeing, hearing, tasting, smelling, or feeling. And why should they not, except from their total ignorance of their nature, and of the laws which govern their senses? The affections of the human race, which, through the most gross ignorance, are now, by human laws, made to produce more dreadful crime and misery than any other single cause, are capable of being made the source of the greatest happiness to all. The crimes and misery thus inflicted upon the human race, and especially upon often the most deserving of the female sex, are clouded in the shades of night, hidden from the public eye and sympathy, by the darkness of impenetrable secrecy from those who, could they but see such misery, and know the cause whence arising, would never suffer it to exist. These human laws attempting to regulate affection in opposition to nature, produce now, in addition to the enormous crime and misery which they hourly inflict upon all, the most absurd and inconsistent language and conduct between the sexes, keeping up a system of deception destructive of virtue, truth, common sense, and happiness. Trained from their cradle to believe that they have the power to love or hate at their will, they often say or swear to each other, that they will most affectionately love one another through life to death; being at the time so totally ignorant of the laws of their own nature, that they may not have the power to love each other even for a week, or perhaps not for twenty-four hours longer; for a look, word, or action, may destroy it even in less than an hour. In a rational state of society, this blindness of the human intellect will be removed, and no such absurdities will exist.

Now, in this new state of society, the condition of the two sexes will be greatly changed. They will be trained, educated, employed, and placed to become through life, superior companions to each other. Women will be no longer made the slaves of, or dependent upon men, more than men will be made slaves of and dependent upon women.

In a society in which the business will be to produce wealth, to distribute it, to form character, and to govern locally and generally, women may be trained and educated to be equally useful and valuable as the men, and in all these operations to give their assistance with equal beneficial effect as the men.

The progress of the world in various sciences, but especially in mechanism and chemistry, has been such within the last century as to equalize, to a great extent, the physical powers of men, women, and children above a certain age; for now a single child of ten years of age, aided by machinery and chemistry, can effect as much as many men could do a few years previous to these inventions.

The position, therefore, of men and women will be altogether different in the new from what it has been in the old state of society. They will be equal in education, rights, privileges, and personal liberty; they will be made to become the enlightened and delightful companions of each other, each being, upon all convenient occasions, with those who, by their nature, they are the most compelled to love; the affections will be thus freed from the often unbearable influence of disappointment or jealousy; and the horrid overwhelming crimes and sufferings arising, under the present irrational and insane system, from unavoidable prostitution, will be entirely unknown.

Could the respectable and influential members of society be made conscious of the causes and consequences of prostitution – of the misery which it inflicts upon millions of the finest naturally organized and finest dispositions among the human race, they would never rest until the *causes* of this gross injustice and male cruelty were entirely removed from the earth.

But it never can be removed, so long as society shall continue to be based on the supposition that individuals can love or hate at their pleasure, and that man shall attempt, by his puny efforts, when opposed to nature, to bind in affection those whom nature disjoins. Vain, foolish, irrational man has made this attempt, under one form or another, for many thousand years, and to-day he is as far from success as the day he made the first insane effort to accomplish that which is impossible for man to perform.

Therefore the eleventh law will be, that

'Both sexes shall have equal education, rights, privileges, and personal liberty; their marriages will arise from the general sympathies of their nature, uninfluenced by artificial distinctions, and be maintained as long as rational-formed individuals can maintain them, when placed under the most favourable circumstances to foster and encourage their continuance; but no such parties, in the rational-made society, shall be forced to cohabit and live together, when it shall be ascertained, under properly devised proceedings, necessary and useful for all, that they have been compelled to lose their affections for each other, – it being an essential condition of human happiness that individuals should have the power to associate with those for whom they are compelled to feel the greatest regard and affection. And as the Rational System has been introduced solely to ensure the most permanent happiness of the human race, no attempt shall be made by man's inhuman laws to force the affection of man or woman against nature.'

This law is, perhaps, the most opposed to the ignorance and prejudice created among the human race by the error of opposing man's laws to those of nature.

It will be at first the most opposed by the most irrational-formed minds in Europe, Asia, Africa, and America, although the existing forms, ceremonies, customs, and public opinion differ so widely in these four quarters of the world. It will, therefore, be the most canvassed and fully investigated, and after a reasonable time, all parties will discover the errors made on this subject by their early, inexperienced ancestors, who were entirely ignorant of the unchanging laws of humanity, and how grossly they have themselves been deceived, to the destruction of all the best and finest feelings of their nature.

When man shall know himself, and understand the three great fundamental truths on which a Rational Society can alone be based, then will this law of the new world be understood in all its value, and will be always rationally applied to practice.

CHAPTER IV

GENERAL ARRANGEMENTS FOR THE POPULATION

As soon as society shall be re-organized upon the three fundamental principles of truth, and arrangements shall be formed in accordance with the science of society, to produce, preserve, and distribute wealth, form character, and govern in the best manner, it will be found that wealth will be created in great superfluity, preserved and distributed beneficially for all, as a pastime, and for pleasurable exercise; and that no necessity or motive will exist, upon the part of any, to be burdened with the cares and anxieties about private property, no more than individuals who live near a continually running stream have any desire or motive to trouble themselves to bottle or barrel it up for fear of future want; they would know it was an insane waste of bottles, barrels, time, and of space, to retain this useless surplus.

Society, by simple and beautiful arrangements, may now be made at all times to command a surplus of wealth wherever it can be necessary or required. With the last century of inventions and discoveries, society, scientifically arranged, and governed by simple common sense principles of equity and justice, may be saturated with wealth of superior qualities, with less than four hours necessary and pleasant-made exercise. There is, therefore, no longer any rational necessity for contest or competition about wealth. The time has arrived when, in the due course of nature, it must terminate. And when this period shall arrive – and it may be made to come over Europe and America in a very short time, if the governments would unite, as it is their highest interest now to do, cordially and heartily – in the work of reorganizing society, – a work which cannot be long put off or avoided, without forcing a universal revolution by violence, through the oppression and unbearable suffering of the industrious class, through an insane competition for individual wealth.

Private property has been, and is at this day, the cause of endless crime and misery to man, and he should hail the period when the progress of science, and the knowledge of the means to form a superior character for all the individuals of the human race, render its continuance not only unnecessary, but most injurious to all; injurious to an incalculable extent to the lower, middle and upper classes. The possession of private property tends to make the possessor ignorantly selfish; and selfish, very generally, in proportion to the extent of the property held by its claimant.

So selfish, that many possessing thousands a-year beyond all reasonable wants, calmly read or hear of thousands of their brother men daily starving for want of that employment which these wealthy withhold; and withhold often that they may preserve animals, first to destroy the wealth that the industrious create and require to support their existence, and then to consume their wealth, time, and mind in destroying these preserved wild animals in the most cruel manner, for the pastime of these most ignorantly selfish-made, wealthy, irrational creatures in human form. It may truly be said that private property has been so sadly injurious to the human race, that it trains those who possess the most of it to become, in very many instances, no better than two-legged animals, whose chief pleasure and delight, through their lives, is to destroy four-legged animals, or other two-legged of the feathered tribe. An evident proof how little society has yet advanced from the state of brutal barbarism.

Private property also deteriorates the character of its possessor in various ways; it is calculated to produce in him pride, vanity, injustice, and oppression, with a total disregard of the natural and inalienable rights of his fellow men. It limits his ideas within the little narrow circle of self, prevents the mind from expanding to perceive extended views beneficial for the human race, and understand great general interests that could be made most essentially to improve the character and condition of all. It confines the human mind to immediate self and its petty concerns; when the possessor, if he had been trained from birth without the deteriorating influence of the desire to obtain and retain private property, might have been educated to comprehend the advantages of general interests and universal ideas; to be familiar with the whole science and practice of society, instead of possessing some mere local ideas respecting a very small part of a mystified chaos called society.

Private property alienates mind from mind, is a perpetual cause of repulsive action throughout society, a never-failing source of deception and fraud between man and man, and a strong stimulus to prostitution among women. It has caused war through all the past ages of the world's known history, and been a stimulant to innumerable private murders.

It is now the sole cause of poverty, and its endless crimes and miseries over the world; and in principle it is as unjust as it is unwise in practice.

In a rational-made society it will never exist. Whatever may have been its necessity or utility, before the introduction of the supremacy of machinery and chemistry, it is now most unnecessary and an unmixed evil; for every one, from the highest to the lowest, may be ensured through life much more of all that is really beneficial for humanity, and the permanent happiness of the individual, through public scientific arrangements, than it is possible to obtain through the scramble and contest for procuring and maintaining private property.

Private property also continually interferes with or obstructs public measures which would greatly benefit all, and frequently to merely please the whim or caprice of an ill-trained individual.

When everything except mere personals shall be public property, and public property shall always be maintained in superfluity for all – and when artificial values shall cease, and intrinsic values shall be alone estimated – then will the incalculable superiority of a system of public property be duly appreciated over the evils arising from private property.

With a well-arranged scientific system of public property, equal education and condition, there will be no mercenary or unequal marriages; no spoiled children; and none of the evils which proceed from these errors in the present system, if crudities which pervade all the departments of life, and are thoroughly inconsistent, can be called a system of society.

In fact, as soon as individuals shall be educated and placed – as it is for the best and permanent interests of society that all should be educated and placed – the saving of time, labour, and capital, between public and private property, will be beyond any estimate the mind of man can form in favour of public property. In the British empire alone it may be made to be several thousand millions sterling annually. The present contest for individual wealth creates the greatest possible extravagance and waste through every department of society, and destroys the best and finest qualities of human nature, while it cultivates and encourages all the inferior feelings and passions.

Therefore the twelfth law will be, that –

'Under the Rational System of society – after the children shall have been trained to acquire new habits and new feelings, derived from a knowledge of the laws of human nature – there shall be no useless private property.'

The old system of the world has been created and governed on the assumed principle of man's responsibility to *man*, and by *man's* rewards and punishments.

And this principle has been assumed upon the original supposition, that man was born with power to form himself into any character he liked; to believe or disbelieve whatever he pleased; and that he could love, hate, or be indifferent as to all persons and things, according to an independent will which enabled him to do as he liked in all these respects.

The present system is, therefore, essentially a system supported and governed by laws of punishment and reward of man's creating, in opposition to nature's laws of punishing and rewarding. The former system is artificial, and always produces crime and misery, continually increasing, and therefore requiring new laws to correct the evils necessarily forced upon society by the old laws; thus laws are multiplied without limit by man to counteract nature's laws, and ever without success. While nature's beautiful and benevolent laws, if consistently acted upon in a system made throughout in accordance with them, would produce knowledge, goodness, and happiness, continually increasing, to the human race.

By man's laws being forced upon the population of all countries, in continual opposition to nature's laws; with law added to law, in the vain attempt to remedy endless previous laws, the world had been made and kept criminal, with crimes multiplying as human laws increased.

The laws of man are made to support injustice, and give additional power to the oppressor and to the man devoid of truth and honesty over the innocent and just. And such must be the result, as long as human laws, lawyers, and law paraphernalia shall be sanctioned by society.

But it is not sufficient that men should be trained in a knowledge of the laws of human nature; it is equally necessary that they should be educated from birth to act in obedience to that knowledge, and that all the circumstances of society should be made in unison with those laws, and not, as they have been hitherto, in accordance with man's laws.

Nature's laws carry with them the only just rewards and punishments that man should experience; and they are, in every case, efficient for nature's purposes, and to ensure the happiness of man in all countries and climes; and, differing from man's puny, short-sighted laws, they are always adequate to the end intended to be accomplished. And this end is evidently to increase human knowledge and happiness. It is through these laws of nature, that man has attained the knowledge which he has acquired. He has been continually urged onward to make discoveries, and to invent, through pain experienced, or pleasure enjoyed or anticipated.

But man has been trained to have his character formed, and to be governed by laws of his own making; his habits, manners, ideas, and associations of ideas have emanated, directly or indirectly, from this artificial and injurious source; and, in consequence, the mind, language, and practice of all individuals have become a chaos of confusion. And this chaos in the character and conduct of individuals has made a yet greater chaos in all the proceedings of society: and, in consequence, man is now opposing man, and nation opposing nation, all over the earth. Yet all nature declares, that it shall be by union of man with man, and nation with nation, that the human race can ever attain a high degree of permanent prosperity and happiness, or become rational.

Nevertheless, while this irrational individual and general character shall remain, those men and women who have been made to receive this character, and to be so injured, must continue for a time to be governed by these most injurious laws. The laws of nature being alone applicable to a society, whose laws are in accordance with the laws of nature.

When this rational society shall be formed, and men, individually and generally, shall be trained to act in accordance with it, then shall human punishments and rewards cease, and cease for ever.

The thirteenth law will therefore be, that –

'As soon as the members of these scientific associations shall have been educated, from infancy, in a knowledge of the laws of their nature, trained to act in obedience to them, and surrounded by circumstances all in unison with them, there shall be no individual reward or punishment.'

The Rational System of society is one and indivisible in its principles and practices; each part is essential to its formation. It is one unvarying consistent system for forming the character of all individuals, and for governing their affairs; and it is essentially a system to *prevent* evil, and render individual punishment and reward as unnecessary, as they are unjust and most injurious to all. While, on the contrary, the present system, based on error, could not be continued without individual rewards and punishments; and, while it shall be maintained, however unjust these individual rewards and punishments must be, when applied to beings who do not form any part of themselves, and who are kept ignorant of their own nature, these irrational rewards and punishments, of man's devising, must be continued.

Individual punishments and rewards, ignorance, the inferior feelings and passions, with all crimes and miseries, will go together when the irrational system shall be abolished. WHEN THE CAUSE OF EVIL SHALL BE REMOVED, THEN WILL THE EVIL CEASE, AND NOT BEFORE. The causes of human evil, as so frequently stated, are the three fundamental errors respecting man forming himself, having the power to believe or disbelieve whatever he pleases, and to love or hate, like or dislike, or be indifferent to persons and things, at his pleasure. While these errors, and the practices which necessarily emanate from them, continue to be the system of the world, the causes of evil will be always present, always active, and will produce misery continually. It is the great business of human existence to discover the *causes* of misery; and the *causes* of happiness; and to *remove* the one, and *introduce* and for every establish the other.

Individual rewards and punishments are, in themselves, perpetual sources of misery, the three errors render rewards and punishments necessary to the continuance of those errors; these fundamental errors must be therefore removed before the *causes* of evil can be prevented from acting.

It is not, then, by any partial changes in society, that evil can be removed, and man made to enjoy a rational and happy existence. The present system, with its organization, classification, and individual rewards and punishments, must be maintained, with its sufferings, miseries, contests, degradations, endless turmoils and confusion; or it must be altogether abandoned, to make room for a new system, true in principle and beneficial in practice; a system which, when fully introduced, will ensure the permanent happiness, not of a few individuals, or of one nation or quarter of the globe, but of the human race, through the life of every generation, and the happiness increasing, without retrogression, with every succeeding generation.

It is only now that the error and evil of individual rewards and punishments are beginning to dawn upon the members of old society. They are beginning to inquire, what portion of the physical, mental, or moral part of man is made or decided upon by himself; or which of the circumstances, existing at his birth, has he formed, controlled, or determined upon? Had he the slightest control in deciding at what age of the world he should come into existence? In what part of it? Whether he should be a child of Europe, Asia, Africa, or America? Or an islander in the pacific ocean? Or of what particular kingdom or district he should be a native? Or who should be his parents, or whether they should be of the prince, peasant, or any other class? What should be his language, superstition, habits, manners? Or what his ideas or association of ideas?

And then, if it has been impossible for the individual to have had any control in any one of these great and overwhelming causes, to form the foundation of his feelings, thoughts, and conduct how much power he has left beyond what these have given him, to form any part of the future circumstances which, acting upon this thus formed foundation, create all his subsequent character day by day, as one day and its circumstances precede the next and its circumstances?

These facts, when rationally considered, will terminate the system which has rendered, and which renders, individual rewards and punishments necessary; for, were it not for the influence of man's individual punishments and rewards, the system of error which, in opposition to nature, he has adopted, could not be maintained. Rewards and punishments are themselves circumstances created by man, to force his fellow men to feel, think, and act in opposition to their own nature or to their happiness; but yet these individual rewards and punishments must remain during the transition state from irrationality to rationality. But when all shall be trained from their infancy to understand the laws of their own nature, educated to act in uniform obedience to them, and surrounded by circumstances all in unison with those rational laws, the causes for individual rewards and punishments will be removed; and, from that period, their injustice and injurious effects will become so obvious to all, that they will be thenceforward for ever abandoned.

The thirteenth law will then be, that –

'As soon as the members of these rational scientific associations shall have been educated from infancy, in a knowledge of the laws of their nature, trained to act in obedience to them, and surrounded by circumstances all in unison with those laws, there shall be no other rewards and punishments than those which nature awards to all who obey or infringe her laws.'

While the human race shall be divided into single separate families, with private property, appropriated by or to individuals of those families, the laws of nature cannot be introduced. Individualism, with opposing interests between man and man and nation and nation, cannot co-exist with the laws of nature. These separate interests and individual family arrangements with private property are essential parts of the existing irrational system. They must be abandoned with the system. And instead thereof there must be scientific associations of men, women, and children, in their usual proportions, from about four or five hundred to about two thousand, arranged to be as one family, each member united with the others to aid one another to the extent of their knowledge, and these associations to be united with each other in a similar manner. The best present arrangement probably would be to commence with three, four, or five hundred, according to local circumstances, with arrangements so planned and devised, as, when complete, to be sufficient to provide for and to accommodate about two or three thousand of which number a full family will consist.

As this family will form a nucleus of an entirely new state of human existence, in which all will have given to them new mind, new feelings, new spirits, and a totally different conduct from the old man of the old world; the arrangements for the dwelling, employment, education, and amusement of this family, will be very different from any of the existing arrangements to carry forward the business of life.

By these arrangements, the evils arising from large cities and towns will be avoided, while they will concentrate within themselves all the advantages of the large cities and towns, without any of their disadvantages; and each member will be enabled to enjoy many more of the benefits to be derived from extensive possessions, than the largest landed proprietors can do under the present individualised system of society.

Thus trained, educated, and placed, each one will have his powers of body and mind multiplied, as it were, by the number of his associates in each family; and the benefits to be derived from thus enlarging the families with one undivided interest, will exceed belief by many until it shall be seen and experienced, in practice. The economy of time, labour, and capital, in producing and distributing wealth, in forming character, and in local government, by this new arrangement into large families will be found to partake of the difference between hand labour and superior machinery, between spinning for instance with one spindle by one adult, and the same directing the movement of machinery to spin two thousand threads in the same time; and now a thousand other such advances, the effects of extended well devised combinations may be instanced.

Society also by this arrangement will be beautifully and most beneficially simplified. Its outline and much of its detail will be grasped by every male and female mind, when they shall be trained to be rational from birth, before they shall attain maturity.

Each large family will be a prototype, in many respects, of every other in its outlined and general arrangements. To produce, preserve, and distribute wealth, to well educate all from birth, and to govern the family without force of fraud, yet with order and system, and to assist in the general government of many of these united families over a given district, will be all that will be required, with the addition of arrangements for rational amusements and recreation, if such can be sought for, when the whole business of life will be, according to age, healthy, pleasurable recreation. The life of these individuals may be, with ease, made one of continual interest, pleasure, and rational enjoyment.

Such must be the case, when all shall be trained from birth, in good habits, dispositions, manners, and conduct; to have a large fund of the most useful and superior knowledge; to be imbued with the pure spirit of universal charity; not in its mere name, but in its daily and hourly practice; when there shall be, through their own well directed industry, abundance and to spare for all, one clearly perceived interest among all, and when all shall be surrounded by superior external arrangements and objects wherever the eye can roam, and all trained and educated to have a sincere desire, and greatly extended faculty and knowledge, to promote the happiness of each.

Under these extended new family arrangements, the earth may be made, in conjunction with those other superior economical dispositions for producing, preserving, distributing and consuming, educating and governing; to maintain, at least, four times the number that it can under the present wasteful and most extravagant, individual, competitive, and repulsive system of society.

Therefore the fourteenth law will be, that –

'Society will not be composed, as at present, of single isolated families; but of men, women, and children, in the usual proportions, from about five hundred to two thousand, as local circumstances may make the most convenient.'

When simplified in language to the greatest extent, that which is proposed to be effected is, to abandon three now palpable errors, on which society appears to have been always based, and to adopt three truths, of which no sane mind can doubt, as soon as they shall be fairly and fully investigated; and to replace the three errors by the three truths.

What can appear more simple in words than the previous sentence? What mind is yet sufficiently enlightened and expanded to imagine the extent of the benefits, which the change will ensure for ever for the whole of the human race?

There is not one individual now benefited by the retention of these three errors, or of any one of them. There is not one individual who is not deeply injured by their retention as the base of society.

There is not one individual who would be injured by the adoption of the three truths, for the base of a new organization of society.

There is not one individual, who would not be essentially benefited by this change.

Yet such is the state of irrationality, produced by the character of all being formed from birth, in accordance with these three errors and their unavoidable consequences in practice, that, at this day, the human race, over the world, is strongly opposed to the abandonment of the principles or source of all evil, and to the adoption of the principles or source of all good in human society; the one being the cause of all falsehood and deception, the other the cause of truth and honesty.

This state of mind and of feeling among men, is the natural result of their characters having been formed on the three errors and their consequences.

It is therefore, that men thus trained in so much error as to make them of necessity, up to the present period, more irrational than any other tribe of animals in their conduct to each other, are opposed to the most simple truth, however important that truth is to their happiness. And therefore it is, that every kind of weak, and often most contradictory, objections are made to the change of false principles for true, of most injurious practices for the most beneficial.

It is now said by many, that the scientific associations of families of two thousand may be beneficial to the extent of a small population, or to a limited isolated district, but that such arrangements are not suited to large kingdoms and empires.

Now, on the contrary, these arrangements of scientific associations of large families, are admirably suited and especially devised, to be extended in unbroken united interests and feelings, and cordial good fellowship from parish to parish, until they comprise a county; then from county to county until they will constitute a province or principality, then by a union of these to form a kingdom, then empires, then the human race into its family of brothers and sisters, occupying in peace and harmony, as the undivided family estate, equally the property of all, the surface of the earth, including land and sea; leaving no motive for contest, envy, or competition; and each one, in fact, by his rational training and education from birth, a prince or princess of the earth, free to go and enjoy its superior made advantages in any clime, and in any local district. And with the full right, power and means of doing so for all, in return for the beneficial and pleasant exercise of their physical and mental faculties.

As these new family associations extend, they will unite conveniently for local and more general purposes; first in tens, then in hundreds, afterwards by thousands and tens of thousands, according to the objects and interests which will require their care, consideration, and direction.

There will be no first or last among them, no large kingdoms or empires to make war upon, and swallow up by violence or fraud their less powerful neighbours; no expensive and wasteful diplomatic arrangements; no watching, with destructive standing armies, the movements of other nations or people, for fear of some treacherous proceedings, or undue advantage to be taken if not upon his perpetual guard.

No! so different will this plain, simple, united, and rational state of society be, from the present complexed, confused, chaotic, disunited, irrational state, that there will be one universal confidence settled in the mind of each and of all throughout the whole population of the earth. There will be no motive to arouse any of the now created inferior feelings and passions; none of the rank insanity which these three errors are so admirably adapted to force into every mind from birth.

Peace, and an ever joyous activity will be always present in every family; wealth will everywhere superabound; money will be useless; priests, lawyers, and medical men being worse to society than useless, will not be trained for such worthless purposes; wars will of course entirely cease, and the enormous expense of these wasteful professions in time, labour, and destruction of the rational faculties, will be altogether saved. Neither will there be buying or selling, nor even any necessity to exchange by the estimate of value for value, after the system has advanced so far as to render the practices of the present chaotic system useless. And this period will not be distant after the three fundamental errors shall have been abandoned, and the three true fundamental principles shall have been made to supersede them.

To produce and enjoy wealth, and create a rational character for the population of the world, whose business and pleasure will be continually to improve its salubrity and beauty, will constitute the chief business of life. It will be all that society will have to do, except to increase continually in all kinds of useful knowledge, so as to diminish the necessity for any unhealthy or disagreeable occupation during the lives of all parties. And sufficient scientific knowledge is already discovered, if society were properly based, scientifically arranged, and well directed, even now, to render human existence, in the life of every individual, a superior pleasurable existence, with a fair commencement to make this earth, as population increases, a terrestrial paradise, in which peace and happiness might be made universally to prevail.

By these large families, thus united in tens, hundreds, thousands, etc, all aiding and assisting each other in all manner of ways, without motive for counteraction or opposition, the increase of knowledge, from all being well educated and well situated to try experiments in the best manner in every art and science, with no necessity for secrecy so as to have only isolated aid in making discoveries, the progress in new inventions and improvements would annually exceed all present conception.

When it is recalled to memory the difference between a population educated, trained, employed, and placed as the British population are at present, and the same number educated, trained, employed, and placed as they will be in a rational state of society, then some idea of the annual progress which the latter will make over the former may be imagined; but the most advanced minds, trained under the present system, will fail to approach a just estimate of the immense difference between these two most opposite states of existence. Therefore the fifteenth law will be, that –

'As these new communities, or large families, increase in number, unions of them shall be formed for local and general purposes, in tens, hundreds, thousands, etc, according to the more or less extended objects and interests which shall require their consideration and direction.'

In the formation of society, as it has hitherto existed, there has been no foresight or wisdom; no first principles understood and followed out consistently, to construct a system that could be explained and made beneficial for any portion of the human race, or for individuals, except for a momentary period of their lives by contrasting great misery and suffering around them.

Every part of society, when examined on scientific principles and dissected into its several opposing divisions, will be found, at this supposed advanced period of human knowledge, to be a chaos of the most absurd, opposing, and hostile notions, not only not based on facts, but in opposition to them, and in direct contradiction to every sound principle connected with human nature and with society.

The desire of all men, in common with all that has life, is to attain the greatest amount of happiness that their nature, or original constitution, can be made to enjoy.

The conditions necessary to the most permanent happiness of man have been stated in the third part of this book.

Instead of making foreseen and wise arrangements to secure these conditions, it would rather appear that plans had been devised, and measures purposely adopted, to render the attainment of these conditions not only difficult but utterly impossible, as long as those plans and measures shall be pursued.

The present state of society over the world is proof that man, society, and nature, have not been understood by man, at any period, and that, instead of adopting, from the beginning, sound principles, and pursuing them in practice, he has imagined false principles respecting humanity, society, and nature, and carried those false principles to their utmost bearable extent of error in practice – that, in thus acting, he has, in the most direct manner, opposed human nature, malformed society, and, in these respects, he has disregarded all the most plain and palpable general laws of nature.

Man requires for his happiness a security that he shall never want the necessaries and reasonable comforts of life. There are no arrangements to give this security to any under the present malformation of society.

Man requires for his happiness that all his faculties, powers, and propensities should be well cultivated, in accordance with his nature, and duly exercised at the proper periods of life. No provision has ever yet been made to secure this happiness for any portion of the human race.

It is only by the adoption of these large united families, with land around them sufficient, by their well-directed industry, of themselves to supply for ever the necessaries and reasonable comforts of life for the whole family, and to spare, that they may never have the fear of want, and that they may have also within themselves the means to form the superior character for each, and to afford due exercise, during life, for the physical, mental, moral and practical nature of each, according to the faculties and powers given to each at birth. And this land must be sufficient in quality and extent to afford the means to secure these results to the family, when full in number, for ever. And when thus filled, common sense arrangements will be required, by judicious well devised regulations for swarming, if the term be allowable, to prevent them ever being over filled, to the detriment of any of the family, or to any portion of the population of the world; to drain, cultivate, and beautify the earth, as it will be for the health and happiness of all that it should be drained, cultivated and beautified; the number of these swarms will be deficient for many thousand years, if not for ever. That there should be contests about land or wealth, when the first so abounds beyond any possible rational wants, and when the second may with so much benefit and pleasure be made to superabound, is only another proof, to the millions existing, of the wretched state of irrationality in which erroneous first principles have ever hitherto kept the tribe of human animals. Therefore the sixteenth law will be, that –

'Each of these communities shall possess around it, land sufficient for the support, for ever, of all its members, even when it shall contain its maximum in number.'

Having attained the period when, through a right application of scientific power, wealth may, with ease and pleasure, be made more than abundant for the human race, all necessity for contests respecting it may be made to cease over the world; as all, by judicious arrangements, may be secured in more than the full advantages that can be now given to any one, however favoured the individual may be under the existing system.

Whatever may have been said or written respecting virtue and justice, neither the one nor the other will be understood until arrangements shall be made to give to all equal advantages, according to age, as far as the capacities of each can use and enjoy them.

The dwellings of the human race will be so constructed, the employment of all will be so arranged, and their training and education from birth will be so conducted, that equal advantages will be ensured through life to each. And by foresight at the commencement of this change from the system of falsehood and evil, to that of truth and good, such results may be obtained, sufficient for all practical purposes; so as to give, evidently, to all, the utmost extent of advantages that highly cultivated and well-placed human beings can enjoy.

By such arrangements, which may be now easily effected, all motive to contest, all inferior-made human character will be withdrawn from society.

And it is well that contest should not cease until this justice shall be done to humanity.

It may be asked, Who has a right to individual rewards, distinctions or privileges?

Only the man who has discovered the means of creating his own faculties, organs, and propensities, who, by his will, can believe or disbelieve, and love, be indifferent or hate at his pleasure, and who can create or decide upon the time and circumstances in which he shall be born and live.

The man or woman who has achieved these matters may claim the highest individual rewards, privileges, and distinctions, and none other. Those who do not, who could not make their own organization of body and mind, who are compelled to believe or disbelieve according to the strongest evidence made on their minds, who must love that which is most agreeable to their individual nature, and dislike that which is most disagreeable to it, can have no rational pretension for individual rewards, privilege, or distinctions above their fellows. Nor will any one, when made rational, either desire or accept of any such unjust proceeding. But how, in a rational state of human existence, can any such difference be made, when all shall be secured from birth in all the advantages that human nature is capable of receiving and enjoying at each period of the life of every individual.

Therefore the seventeenth law will be that –

'The large family associations or communities, shall be so arranged as to give to all the members of each of them, as nearly as possible, the same advantages; and to afford the most easy communication with each other, by pleasant walks through groves, and other most improved modes of travelling that have been or may be invented.'

CHAPTER V

Government of the Population and Duties of the Council.

WHEN men and women shall be placed, from their birth, within rational and superior circumstances only, and thus trained from their birth to become rational beings; when they shall be made equal in education and condition according to age, age in employment according to age and capacity, there will be no difficulty in the government of such a population, when it shall be divided into the large families previously described, in which each, from birth, will be well cared for, and always under the kind care of all. And to those extensively experienced, it is known that no one can *govern* well unless he has previously served well, and has made himself master of those things respecting which he has to give instructions to govern.

The arrangements proposed for these large families have been devised that each one should pass, gradually, according to age, through the general business of each family first; and afterwards, of the more extended affairs of a number of these families united to supply each other with their respective surplus wealth, in order that the stores of each should be always filled as rapidly as they may be emptied. Or, in other words, that the supply should be made always to exceed the demand, that there may never be the most distant fear of want by any family or individual of any family.

This is the first evil to be overcome, and society now is in possession of the most ample means to remove for ever the cause of this evil, therefore it should not be allowed by the governments of civilized men and women any longer to exist.

The fear of want is, at this day, over the world, producing evil upon evil in endless succession, and is one main cause of misery to man.

It is not the interest of any of human kind that this fear of want should longer exist anywhere, or by one individual, and it is intended that it shall be made to terminate in the shortest period practicable.

That period will depend upon the wisdom and energy which shall be evinced in removing the *causes* which have hitherto made the population of the world irrational, and introducing those *causes* which can alone make man a rational being.

As it will be necessary, and therefore the interest of all, to serve, and to be trained to serve well, so it is necessary and therefore the interest of all to become governors, and to be trained to govern well.

The age for producing wealth and acquiring practical knowledge will be from infancy to twenty years of age; for instructing others in the higher departments of knowledge and practice of the business of these families, from twenty to twenty-five; and in preserving and distributing the wealth which they had previously acquired the knowledge to produce, from twenty-five to thirty. By this mode of forming the physical, mental, moral, and practical character of each man and woman, they will be well prepared to enter upon the government of the home department, and to become a member of the home governing committee, and to continue in this department ten years, or to the age of forty.

This committee to divide itself into subcommittees, and each subcommittee to take the more immediate direction of some one of the general departments into which the business of the family will be divided. The superintendence or government of these departments, under this arrangement, will be a constant source of interest, pleasure, health, and high enjoyment. There will be but one spirit of charity and kindness among all the members of the family, from the youngest to the oldest; all with most willingly aid; none will ever have any motive to oppose. Onward, onward, in knowledge, unity, charity, kindness and happiness, will be the perpetual motto of each family. And each separate association will become again the member only of an external extended family, to which there will be no limit east, west, north, or south.

Having thus acquired experience, during ten years, in directing the departments of a single family, they will be, at the age of forty, sufficiently experienced to commence the business as one of the great council to govern the external business of these large families, when united for more local purposes in tens, or hundreds; or for more general and extended interests, into thousands or tens of thousands without limitation.

For the great object of these associations will be to concentrate, as far as possible, the knowledge of all into each family; that all may be thus essentially benefited by each, and thus each family be made to contain an epitome of the past and present knowledge of the world, and, if practicable, that each individual should possess it, and be made to know his exact position with respect to the past, present, and future of human existence.

By this outline arrangement, when it shall be perfected, each man and woman may, with pleasure to themselves and their instructors, be made to acquire much more real useful knowledge than is at present known by the irrational-made population of the world.

Under this arrangement, the home and foreign government will never cease, but be always in the maturity of experience; – there will be no pupillage or old age, but youth, and vigour, and experience always united; – there will be none of the evils inseparable from contests for office and power; – there will be no hereditary imbecility in the government of nations; but all who govern will have passed through the practical operations of society, will have been a full time in serving, and been previously well instructed in the knowledge and spirit of governing justly, without force or fraud. Therefore, the eighteenth law will be, that –

'Each family shall be governed in its *home* department by a general council, composed of all its members between the ages of thirty and forty; and each department shall be under the immediate direction of a committee, formed of members of the general council, chosen by the latter in the order to be determined upon; and in its *external*, or *foreign* department, by all the members from forty to sixty years of age.'

There have been no individuals, in any part of the world, yet trained and educated on rational fundamental principles, and, therefore, could not be taught to acquire any rational notions of themselves, human nature, or society. A most lamentable, false direction has been given to the feelings, thoughts, and conduct of all from birth, and a most irrational spirit, in consequence, made to pervade the human race. It is useless longer to attempt to hide the fact, that man has never yet been enabled to attain the knowledge to make him a consistent or rational being in his feelings, thoughts, or conduct.

There is nothing rational, or without a great intermixture of error and inconsistency, in all the affairs of the human race, this day, in all nations, whether called barbarous or civilized. Although a moment's calm reflection, by one made rational, would exhibit, in the strongest colours, the fact, that it is the highest interest of each one of the human race, that the greatest amount of happiness that human nature can be made to enjoy, should be secured for every one, yet the conduct of all is such, that it might be readily imagined that all deemed it for their interest that the greatest obstructions to the happiness of all should be created that the faculties of man are capable of inventing.

Under this malformation of the character of man, it is not to be expected that many can be found with even tolerable faculties to govern any portion of their fellow men or their affairs with knowledge, or in a spirit of justice, or without force or fraud. But a government there must be in the transition state, the best that can be obtained until a generation shall be trained from birth to become rational men and women.

Until this can be effected, the individuals the most experienced and successful in governing should be selected, or elected, to govern the change from the present chaos of inconsistency to the rational state which the change from the fundamental principles of error to those of truth will effect.

It must not, however, be hidden that this is *the most difficult task* that man will ever have to perform; it is *the step of* difficulty and danger. It is far more hazardous than that in which physicians are now placed, who consent to superintend and direct a great lunatic asylum. The physician has his patients disarmed, and he himself may be armed; but in this case, the patients are armed, and have the power of life and death in a thousand ways over their unarmed supposed enemy, – and supposed enemy, because he is compelled to use the language of truth to them, or no cure could be accomplished. The language of truth, although applied in the strongest spirit of kindness, is to them a sharp-edged tool, which they have the greatest objection to be applied to themselves, even in the most gentle manner.

To be told, that which is now most evident, that all of the human race from the beginning have been made to become irrational, and that there are no exceptions to this rule, is an act more likely to arouse the ill-will and anger of those made to be irrational, than any word that can be spoken. And yet these words of truth must not only be spoken, but reiterated again and again until the leaders of the human race shall understand the causes which have made themselves and all others to be from the beginning irrational.

Those, then, selected or elected to govern in the transition from the irrational to the rational state should be made conscious of these facts, and be thus prepared, in the spirit of undeviating charity and of untiring kindness, to overlook all the infirmities produced in the governed, by an education from birth in irrational principles, and in the midst of irrational external circumstances.

It is by the application of this knowledge alone on the part of those who govern and direct the change, that man can be made to become a reasonable and consistent being, or to feel, think, and act rationally. And, therefore, the best and most experienced should be selected to govern and direct the change from the one state to the other.

But when a generation shall be born and educated from birth in the new state amidst the rational circumstances which will thence arise, there will be no difficulty about governors or government. All the causes which have hitherto created these difficulties will have been removed, and the most experienced hereditary governors, properly trained for their office, will be everlastingly provided without selection or election.

Therefore the nineteenth law will be, that –

'After all the members of the community shall have been rendered capable of taking their full share of the duties in the general council of government, there shall be no selection or election of any individuals to office.'

Contrary to the practice now so universal, office will never be sought for in a rational state of society. It will be viewed as a necessary part of the business of life, and to which, parties will regularly grow up through much practice and experience; and when so prepared, they will be called upon to perform the business of first, home, and afterwards, of foreign or external government, in the same manner that they had been previously called upon to perform the business of the preliminary stages, or divisions of life, from infancy to manhood. Thus will all pass through what may be called the lower, middle, and upper ranks of human life; all will thus contribute, in the most efficient and substantial manner, to promote the well-being, well-doing, and happiness of all, without any opposition of interest, or of feeling, much less of contest or competition for office, emolument or privilege, or desire for individual distinction of any kind.

At thirty, after the parties shall have passed through the regular business of early superior education, of producing, preserving, and distributing wealth, through the first six divisions of life, they will, in the due order of a scientific formed society, be called upon to undertake their fair share in governing the home department, all of which, by their previous education and practice, they will fully understand, and know how to direct in each of its departments. In these offices they will continue for ten years, aided always by those who have been longer experienced in this department, and thus will it be made easy to all, as they approach to the age for commencing the practice of governing.

At forty, their official business as governors of the home department will cease, and their official business as governors of the external or foreign departments will commence and continue for twenty years. During this period and to the end of their lives, having been gradually prepared from birth for this high station, in the general affairs of the world, they will be elevated to a condition greatly to be envied by any sovereign who has yet lived. The world will be open to them to add in the highest degree to their knowledge and happiness. They will be nature's genuine and unopposed aristocracy, improved physically, mentally, morally, and practically, to the utmost extent that the accumulated knowledge of the period in which they live will admit. To these, all the latest inventions and discoveries, ascertained to be improvements, in all the arts and sciences, and in every branch of knowledge, will be made known, not only without let or hindrance, but with a pleasure in giving it, equal to that by which it will be received.

What irrational beings have the human race for so many thousand years been, not to have seen the advantage of this unity of power, and to have acted upon it!

The progress in knowledge, and the amount of happiness thus lost during the past ages, are far beyond the powers of calculation or of irrational man's conception.

The change from the crude, irrational, and most injurious classification of society, as now existing, to the natural classification according to age, as it will be arranged in the rational state of society, will prove to be the difference between the extremes of error and misery, and of truth and happiness.

Therefore the twentieth law shall be, that 'All the members of the family at thirty years of age, who shall have been trained from infancy in the communities, shall be officially called upon to undertake their full share of the duties of management in the home department; and at forty, they shall be excused from officially performing them; at forty they will be officially called upon to undertake the high duties of the external or foreign department; and at sixty they will be excused from officially attending to them.'

The members of these large families, having passed through the six first divisions of life; having been made to acquire good dispositions, habits, language and manners, and the genuine spirit of the Rational System of society; having become experienced and well taught in the practice of all the parts of domestic life, according to age, strength, and capacity; having been well instructed in the science and practice of producing, preserving, and distributing wealth; in forming a superior physical, mental, moral and practical character for the rising generation, with a useful outline of the knowledge of the latest improvements, inventions, and discoveries in the arts and sciences; will be thus prepared to commence being rational governors of their immediate family affairs. The government of each family will be of deep interest to every other family; in the same manner that the character of each member of the family will be a matter of great concern to the family of which he is member. And thus, when the population of the world shall be divided into these rational families, each individual of the human race will discover that he has a substantial and abiding interest in the superior formation of the character of every other human being.

With this knowledge in theory and practice, and with the spirit of illimitable charity and kindness, which belongs alone to the Rational System of society, will the members of each family at the age of thirty, commence their important official duties of home government.

Important they will prove to be; yet not arduous, but highly gratifying and pleasurable.

They will commence their business by joining a council already well experienced in the duties of their office. With the practice of the details in every department, their previous educated and superior instruction has made them familiar. They will now have to assist to govern all the circumstances within the boundaries of the immediate family estate, comprising perhaps from two thousand to three thousand acres of land, sustaining a population of as many persons, including all ages, in their due proportion of young, middle-aged, and old.

The object of governing will be to have the estate made as beautiful and fruitful as its locality will admit; to have the most superior characters formed for each one of the rising generation that his original organization, physical, moral, and mental will admit, when placed under the most favourable circumstances that the knowledge obtained by the family can create; to have the most complete arrangements that the localities of each family will allow, for producing, preserving, and distributing wealth aided by the most perfect machinery that the latest discoveries and inventions in the arts and sciences will enable the parties to acquire, in order that all severe, unhealthy, or disagreeable labour on the part of the members may be rendered altogether unnecessary, and to secure to each a life of rational existence in health, and with daily increasing enjoyment.

To effect this result, the members must be taught the ALL-GLORIOUS SCIENCE of the influence of circumstances over human nature, for good or bad – for misery or happiness. This is the science, hitherto so little understood, that will in due time, according to the order of nature, ensure the future excellence and happiness of the human race. It is destined, ere long, to give what are now deemed superhuman powers to man, and enable him to adjust circumstances, with the skill of a superior chess-player in arranging his chess-men, to produce his foreseen and well-calculated result. Through a knowledge of this science he will learn, with the certainty of a law of nature, the immediate, and, to some extent, the more remote causes of good and evil, and by his training, education, and acquired experience in practical operations, he will know how to remove the causes of evil, and to replace them by those causes which will produce good. And thus, at length, through the slow experience acquired during ages, of fact after fact, and comparing the aggregate of these facts, to attain the knowledge of extended consistency in earthly matters, will the means be discovered to change the pandemonium in which the human race has alone hitherto existed, and produced by error, for a state of continually increasing happiness, or a paradise produced by a knowledge of the laws of nature respecting man and society.

Having for ten years assisted to create and maintain peace, order, and the true spirit of harmony among the members of the home colony, or united family of two thousand, more or less, and having attained the age of forty, the next advance is for such members to become one of the general council for conducting the external or foreign interests of the associated families, to the extent to which it may be the most convenient to unite them, to facilitate the well-being and happiness of all. Not that there will be any real limitation to the interest or union of these families; for on the principles on which all of them will be based and constructed, there can never be but one clearly perceived interest among all the members of each family, and among all the families, even until they shall extend to every part of the globe.

The more immediate business of the members of this department will be to receive visitors or delegates from other families, or association of families; to communicate frequently with other families; to visit and arrange with them the best means of forming or improving roads and conveying surplus produce to each other; to travel far and near to give and receive information of new inventions, discoveries, and improvements, and upon every subject that can add to the knowledge and happiness of the families separately and unitedly; and also to assist in the formation of new families, to be composed of the surplus population arising from the previously established families, and to send delegates to the more or less extended circles of families to which their family shall be attached.

By these means the most advantageous and friendly communication will be perpetually maintained between these families, however far they extend; for, with the facilities already acquired for travelling by land and sea, and those which, in such a state of society, may be soon anticipated to be added to them, the intercourse even round the globe will become, under rational arrangements, a pleasurable and beneficial excursion. In these families *home* will be everywhere, and the general business of each will be familiar to all. Confidence will be universal; for falsehood and deception will be unknown; and the universal spirit, pervading the character of every one trained in a knowledge and practice of the Rational System of society will be that of charity and kindness, directed by judgment, produced by a correct and extensive knowledge of man and society. All will know that, by the education given to each, the ruling desire of every one will be to promote, to the utmost of his power, the happiness of every member of these families.

If the world could be made conscious of the misery which has been created, and of the happiness which has been lost, by all having been trained to act from a contrary spirit, it would not lose a day in now preparing measures to effect this change in the population of every country, that the misery may be made speedily to cease, and happiness be enjoyed by the human race.

By this superior cultivation of all the human faculties and friendly continual intercourse between all these families, with the facilities which would everywhere exist for the immediate examination and trial of every new invention and improvement in every department of life, the progress may be rationally anticipated to be many thousand times more rapid and efficient than heretofore, while under the numberless counteractions which have hitherto existed under the individual, opposing, and ignorantly selfish system of society.

Soon, by these measures, all would acquire the habit of thinking and feeling that the world was their undivided estate, and that all were the legitimate children of the family to whom nature had given this estate for their support, pleasure, and enjoyment. Those who thus travelled from family to family, and in each of which would find a hearty welcome, a home and all they would desire, would feel that they were always travelling on their own estate; having a right of use and enjoyment in it that no one would ever dispute, or endeavour to restrict in any manner. Each would feel, and think, and might most correctly say, 'The earth is my family estate, I have performed my family duty to it, and have a right, with all the other members of my family, to use and enjoy it, injuring no one, to give me the greatest number of pleasurable sensations through my life, while all my brothers and sisters and parents have equal right of use and enjoyment.'

But one everlasting source of active enjoyment to these sages of the new world will be, to improve the construction of the buildings, machinery, and general arrangements of every new family residence and appropriated property, superadding to them all the most useful discoveries which had been made since the latest family establishment had been completed. And after a certain progress had been made in new inventions, discoveries, and improvements, the oldest of these establishment would be reconstructed, with all the latest improvements included. The enormous productive power and materials, always at the command of these united families, would be a temptation to prevent any old inferior establishment from remaining, without measures being adopted to create a new one, with all the improvements that extensive experience had elicited. Then a new interest would be created by the meeting of the more local or general delegates, to adjust and decide upon all matters that could improve the family estate within their jurisdiction, or add any newly acquired facilities, to make more perfect the character of the rising generation, either physically, mentally, morally, or practically.

How different would be the knowledge, spirit, and conduct of these delegates, when compared with the delegated members to the parliaments, congresses, or chambers of the existing chaotic and irrational state of society? The former, by their accurate and extensive knowledge; their cordial spirit of union, having but one interest; their direct truthfulness and straight-forward proceeding, would effect far more important business in one week, than the latter can accomplish in many sessions of six months duration. The delegate meetings of the new world will be family meetings of brothers and sisters, educated and practised to become highly intelligent. Long speeches will seldom be made; real knowledge will be alone expressed; crude ideas, or ill-digested schemes will never be brought forward; the most experienced will be listened to, their plans adopted, and all will be well informed upon all matters to be discussed and decided upon. Should doubts arise upon any points of difficulty, a committee of the oldest, assisted by the most experienced upon the particular subject under discussion, will decide according to their matured judgments, and all will willingly acquiesce, as children in the decision of their parents. It is, however, under such education, training, and practice, difficult to imagine any point of difficulty that could arise, especially as there will be no private interest to create a difference of feeling. Therefore the twenty-first law will be, that –

'The duties of the general council of the *home* department shall be to govern all the circumstances within the boundary of the family; to organize or direct the various departments of production, preservation, and distribution of wealth, and formation of character, through all the previous divisions of age; to remove all those circumstances which are the least favourable to happiness, and to replace them with the best that can be devised among themselves, or of which they can obtain a knowledge from other families. The duties of the *external*, or *foreign* department will be, to receive visitors or delegates from other families or strangers; to communicate with other families; to visit them, and arrange with them the best means of forming roads and conveying surplus produce to each other, that the stores and warehouses of each may be always over-supplied, that the *fear* of want may never be experienced; to travel to the most distant parts of the world, to give and receive information of inventions, discoveries, and improvements, and of every kind of knowledge that can be useful and add to happiness; and also to regulate and assist in forming new families, when the surplus population of any family or families may require their establishment; and to send delegates to the more or less extended family circles, to transact the business required within their district.'

The best governing principle is age and experience, while retaining physical and mental vigour, and when the parties possessing those qualifications have been previously well educated from birth, and well employed from childhood to manhood. When man shall be trained to be rational, arrangements will be made to remove the causes of all contests about governing, or for exclusive power of any kind, to the exclusion of others of the same age. There will be therefore no selection or election for governing, either in the home or external departments of the Rational System of society. The capacity and experience on the one hand to govern well, will be so greatly increased by the rational education and employment that will be given to each male and female according to age, and the diminished difficulty, on the other hand, to govern in a rational-made society, that all, at the ages stated, will be far more than competent to the easy task which they will have to perform.

And as these governors will have but one clearly perceived interest with the governed; as the direct object of both will be always to increase the knowledge and happiness of each, there will be no contest of any kind between those who, by their age and experience, become the natural governors of society, and those whom they naturally govern because they are younger and less experienced. The governors by age and experience will therefore have the full powers of government *in all things under their direction*, as long as they shall govern according to the laws of human nature, which laws shall be their guide upon all occasions.

But with parties trained from their birth in a knowledge of the laws of nature, educated under the immediate influence of these laws, and daily and hourly familiar with the inestimable benefits derived from their application in devising and directing all the business of life – and seeing the wisdom and benevolence of those laws in providing, by their effects on society, for all the wants of humanity, in the best possible way for each individual, and for their most permanent enjoyment through life – there never will be a shadow of temptation to induce these enlightened, experienced, natural governors, to govern contrary to the known and well ascertained laws of humanity.

The internal and external government of these large families and circles of families, will never be an affair of any difficulty to those who shall have been prepared, as described, to govern first the one and afterwards the second.

From the ages of thirty to sixty, the governing period, men and women, under the Rational System of society, will be in their prime of physical and mental vigour – in the best of both to do full justice to the important offices which, by their rights as men and women, they will be called upon to fill.

The guide to direct their proceedings will be ever present to them; – they will themselves be ever governed by that guide. The laws of nature will have been their first study – to apply them continually to practice, their education. They will have been familiar with the principles and application of them to practice from early childhood; – they will have discovered them to be alone of divine origin, and calculated to make all who study and apply them wise and happy. There will be, therefore, no motive on the part of these governors to deviate, in the slightest degree, from governing in every instance according to these divine laws.

Nor will there be cause to doubt about the application of these laws to practice; for these laws are few, and when no error has been previously forced into the mind, or habits opposed to them acquired, easily to be understood and acted upon. False principles, or principles opposed to nature, are indeed difficult, nay, impossible to understand, and equally difficult to continue to attempt to carry into consistent practice. The ways of nature, cultivated and well understood, may correctly be stated to be ways of pleasantness, and that all her paths are peace, and lead, without devious courses, to knowledge, health, and happiness. It is only by disregarding nature, and opposing her divine laws, that strife, war and violence, poverty, injustice, and oppression become known among men.

The governors will be trained and prepared from their birth to understand, when they shall attain the proper age, to govern in all things and on all occasions, in perfect unison with the laws of nature; and the governed, knowing this, will willingly, and with the greatest pleasure, obey them, and, as far as possible, anticipate their wishes in all that they may desire to have done.

Therefore, the twenty-second law will be, that

'The general councils, home and foreign, shall have full power of government, *in all things under their direction*, as long as they shall govern in accordance with the divine laws of nature, which will be their sole guide.'

Man does not form himself; he knows not nature's laws of mechanism and chemistry, by which his wondrous machinery is contrived, united, and continued for so many years in action, without the mind of the individual taking thought upon the matter, or the will having anything to do in setting these compound movements in motion, or in continuing them until they run their course.

The capacity of humanity to be made irrational and miserable from birth, or to be made rational and happy through life, is now discovered; – the *causes* which effect the one, and which may be made to produce the other, are now known, but known for the first time, apparently, since man existed upon this globe.

This knowledge opens a new and glorious field of action to the human race; – the adult man, through this knowledge, will be enabled to become, to a very great extent, before and after the birth of each individual, the creator of man; for he will understand how to create a new man, with a new mind and spirit, and with much increased knowledge and power over his progeny, and the external circumstances by which they shall be surrounded from birth to death. The knowledge of good and evil to man is thus given to man, with power to remove the causes producing the latter, and to supersede them by causes which shall alone produce good to the human race. This is that knowledge which gives the most valuable power to man; – this is the knowledge which the most advanced of past ages have sought for, and till now in vain; – this is that knowledge which will redeem the world from sin and misery, and enable man to make the earth the abode of health, union, knowledge, charity, goodness, and happiness.

Man makes not himself, physically or mentally; his powers of humanity are created before his birth for him, without his knowledge or consent in any way asked or given, and for them he cannot have merit or demerit; nor can he rationally, or in any manner justly, be made responsible to man for them, whatever they may be. But the creating power of the universe has made man, and all things having life, responsible to it by the pains inflicted and the pleasures experienced by every action of the instincts of each separate existence, as long as the existence possesses life. These are wise and most benevolent punishments and rewards, always beneficial to the individual and to society; while man's laws, emanating from his ignorance respecting the laws of his own nature, of humanity generally, and of the real *causes* of good and evil to his race, are unwise, unjust, cruel, and always productive of sin and misery. While man shall remain under the delusion that he forms his own powers, and is responsible to insane man for his notion how they should be exercised, that he can believe or disbelieve, and love, be indifferent, or hate at his will and pleasure, and that he has merit or demerit, and deserves rewards or punishments for any particular belief or disbelief, or for loving, being indifferent, or hating – so long must he remain an inconsistent, irrational, or insane animal.

He has been, through his whole history up to this period, the most inconsistent, irrational, and insane of all the animal creation, and at this hour, over the earth, his conduct is yet the most inconsistent, irrational, and insane. And therefore is man most unjust to man, and yet more unjust to himself, through the excess of ignorant, selfish feeling, limiting the mind and action of each to the atom, when it would be for the high permanent advantage of all, that they should be expanded to the aggregate of humanity. But this period of human infancy is about to pass away; man is in progress to know himself, and to understand the general laws of his own nature, and of humanity in the aggregate. Man will then be no longer the most cruel of all animals to man; he will no longer be so insane as to destroy his own high happiness and joyous existence, by destroying the happiness of others. He will, ere long, clearly perceive that this high happiness and joyous existence can alone flow to him through the high happiness and joyous existence of his race; that he may see and feel their irresistible influence wherever he may go, and there partake of it, in its full measure, and without the limitation of ignorant man's interference. The knowledge of the laws of humanity, and of the true nature of man, which the population of the world is beginning to acquire, will enable the more advanced in this inestimable knowledge, to adopt measures in practice to prevent the rising generation being trained to become the irrational, and insane animals which all previous generations have been, through error, forced to become. The path is now opened which, if steadily pursued, will lead one and all to a full rational state of society, in which principles and practices will always be consistent, and ever in accordance with the well ascertained laws of nature. Man will thus, from his birth, be carefully trained and educated, amidst rational-formed external circumstances, to become gradually, at maturity, a full formed rational being, when, of necessity, he must, at all times, think and act rationally, and by the consistency between his principles and practices, exhibit to all, the certainty that the old, irrational, and insane conduct has been abandoned, and with it the ignorance, poverty, division, sin and misery, which have hitherto held the human race in chains of the most degrading bondage, through the errors of imagination opposed to demonstrable facts. This new creation of the human character will speedily enable the population of the world to change the pandemonium state of human existence, the necessary consequence of the previous irrationality of man, into a real and substantial paradise, subject to the evils only of accidents, disease, and death, with the two former greatly diminished, and the latter divested of all its irrational terrors.

It is possible that accidents and disease may effect and derange the physical, intellectual, or moral part of the constitution of some individuals; but as this would be a heavy misfortunate to them – the cause of more or less mental or bodily pain – they will call for the sympathy of their more fortunate brothers and sisters, who will place them under the most favourable circumstances to effect their speedy cure and return to their society.

If any should be so far injured, mentally, as to endanger themselves or society, by being too much at large, they would be placed within the proper hospital for such patients, and there be attended with great care and kindness, and with the best skill to overcome the disease that the family could procure far or near. These poor individuals would never be blamed, or in any manner punished, for this would be irrational; but, on the contrary, they would be always treated mildly, and with genuine kindness, in order that the patient may not be made to suffer more than the pains inflicted by the disease, and that the cure may be completed in the shortest possible period. But, after two or three generations of rationality, there would be very few accidents, and very little physical or mental disease; for arrangements may be made to gradually diminish them to almost annihilation.

Therefore the twenty-third law will be, that –

'All individuals trained, educated, and placed in conformity to the laws of their nature, must, of necessity, at all times, think and act rationally, except they shall become physically, intellectually, or morally diseased; in which case the council shall remove them into the hospital for bodily, mental, or moral, invalids, where they shall remain until they shall be recovered by the mildest treatment that will effect their cure.'

It is intended, and confidently anticipated, that every one of these large families will have the best services of each and all of their members, in whatever way these services can be made the most efficient to promote the well-doing, well-being, and happiness of the family, or circles of families with which the family may be associated for general purposes.

If, therefore, any individual or individuals shall be discovered to possess superior faculty, and consequently knowledge, in any art or science, or on any subject whatever, useful to the family or families, to be called into more public action previous to the age for home or foreign government, the councils of either, as the case may be, shall have power to call such individual or individuals to their aid and assistance, and withdraw him or them, for the time necessary, from the duties of their respective divisions of age and employment. The services of all will belong to the family, circles of families, or to the human race, as circumstances may require; but none will be called upon, by the home or foreign council, to do more than will be beneficial for the health and happiness of the parties so called upon.

Therefore the twenty-fourth law will be, that –

'The councils, wherever it shall be necessary, shall call to its aid the practical abilities and advice of any of the members not in the councils.'

CHAPTER VI

On the Adjustment of Differences

Differences that will require the adjustment or interference of other parties, will never occur after the change from the irrational to the rational character shall be complete in all the members from birth. When the character of all shall be formed from birth on the knowledge of the laws of human nature; when the causes of opinion, and of attractive and repulsive feelings shall be clearly perceived by all; when the elements of society shall be understood and united in their due proportions in every family nucleus of society, and all producing a superfluity of wealth; then, when individuals and society shall be thus made to become rational in feeling, thought and action, which will be a necessary consequence of society being based on true first principles, it will be impossible that any differences, requiring the interference of third parties, could ever arise. All parties will be too well trained in a knowledge of the laws of human nature from their birth, to make it possible, except through the disease of mental derangement, that differences between rational-made men and women should arise to require the interference of third persons.

But it may be some time before all the injurious influences arising from the fundamental errors on which all human characters have been yet formed, can be removed from the entire of society; and until this change can be effected, and the influence of these old errors shall be altogether rooted out to the lowest foundation to which they penetrate, it will be a wise precaution to make substantive arrangements to adjust immediately, in the most effective manner, every difference that may arise in the transition state between any members of any family, or between family and family, or between circles and circles of families.

It will be true wisdom, while men are in training to become rational beings, that all differences requiring the interference of third parties should be adjusted with the least possible delay; in fact, if possible, as soon as the difference has arisen, that it may not be increased by the parties retaining unpleasant feelings – which feelings on every account, especially respecting health, should be avoided, and the *causes* producing them should be as speedily as possible altogether removed from society.

Many will for some time doubt the possibility of training man and forming society to be so rational as to overcome all unpleasant differences of feeling between individuals, and between associations of individuals; but this arises, and will remain until the influence of the knowledge of the laws of human nature shall be made obvious to the public at large, and *seeing* the effects produced by that knowledge, when the language of all shall be the plain, simple, and straight-forward language of truth, without any admixture of, or motive to resort to, falsehood or deception of any kind.

In fact, as soon as it shall be understood so distinctly as to ensure the application of the knowledge to practice, that man forms no part of himself – that he cannot decide by his will what he shall believe or disbelieve, what persons or things he shall like, dislike, be indifferent to, or love or hate – there remains no rational ground for anger or displeasure between individuals or bodies of men more or less in number. Those trained from their birth in this divine knowledge of charity and love, will not know how to be angry or displeased with their fellows, knowing so well that all their qualities, physical, mental, moral, and practical have been formed *for* them; and if well formed, so much the more fortunate for the parties, but without individual merit for them; if ill formed, so much the more will the parties require sympathy and aid to overcome the inferiority or defects of their formation, for which they cannot be justly charged with demerit, nature and society having so imperfectly created them.

After the transition state shall have been passed through, it will be utterly impossible, when all shall have been trained to understand the laws of human nature, and to have acquired the constant habit of applying them hourly to practice, that either the home or foreign council should ever think of contravening, or in any manner acting in opposition, or otherwise than in strict accordance with the ascertained laws of man's nature. The supposition that either council should so act, can exist only while the minds of men are passing from error to truth, from the irrational to the rational state of society.

However the possibility that from some inconceivable cause or other the councils should be induced, in the transition state, to act contrary to their own interest and to the interest of all – for in a rational state there can be but one interest for the human race – the evil is by the succeeding law provided for, through the extent of power which each family will possess within itself, to be derived from the wisdom of the sages above sixty, aided by the energy of the young, previously well instructed from the age of sixteen to thirty.

It will be readily perceived by those who reflect, that the members of the these councils will never be placed, as so many are often under the existing system, in opposition to their duty to themselves and others; for their interest and duty will be always the same, without a single arrangement being formed to oppose one to the other. This error, in a rational state of society, will never exist. The unity of interest, from the most single to the most extended operations, even to include those of the population of the world, will be, at all times, carefully preserved. It will ever be the interest of all to attain the highest degree of happiness within the reach of humanity, and it will be always the interest of all to assist each to advance as near to this point as shall be practicable by the aid of all. And when each shall be thus engaged in promoting the happiness of all, it is impossible yet to say the extent to which the happiness of each may be secured through life. Let the old errors of the world be once fairly abandoned by the governments of the world – and it is now their interest immediately to abandon them – and the difference between individuals and between states will rapidly terminate, and be superseded by unity and harmony in all their future proceedings; – let the population of the world be once made clearly to understand that no one can form himself, his convictions, or his feelings; – let the characters of all be formed consistently on this knowledge, and let all the institutions of society, as surely they ought, be based on this knowledge, and the peace and harmony of the world will be secured for ever.

There will then be no necessity for creating and largely paying a class of men trained by society to have a direct interest in creating repulsive feelings between man and man, and another class to create hostilities between nation and nation; – absurdity cannot proceed farther.

Let truth, according to undeviating past and present facts respecting the laws of human nature and of society, be proclaimed to the nations of the world by their respective governments; – let all the institutions of those countries be formed consistently with those laws, and soon will peace, with knowledge, order, and happiness become universal among mankind.

Therefore will the twenty-fifth and last law be, that

'All differences of every description, between individuals, if indeed it be possible for any to exist in families so trained, educated, employed, and placed, shall be immediately determined and amicably adjusted between the parties, by the decision of a majority of the three senior members of the council for the home department, except when the difference shall exist between the members of the council, when it shall be in like manner decided by the three members who have last passed the council. But if the general council should ever attempt to contravene the laws of human nature, which is scarcely possible, the elders of the family who have passed the councils shall call a general meeting of all the members of the family, from sixteen to thirty years of age, who have been trained from infancy within it. This meeting shall calmly and patiently investigate the conduct of the general councils, and if a majority shall determine that they have acted, or attempted to act, in opposition to these divine laws of nature, the general government shall for five years devolve upon the members of the family who have passed the councils, and are above sixty years of age, united with those who have not entered the councils, and are between twenty and thirty years of age. It is scarcely possible to conceive that this clause, after the transition generation shall have passed off by death, will ever be required; but if required, it will be only of temporary application.'

Now here are twenty-five substantive laws, all deduced from, and in unison with, the ascertained *laws of nature*, which are alone wise laws for the government of humanity. These laws will be found to be sufficient for the government of the human race, when it shall be made rational, by the character of each individual being formed, from birth, on the THREE GREAT FUNDAMENTAL LAWS

OF HUMAN NATURE, and when all the arrangements of society shall be made consistent with those laws.

Those twenty-five substantive laws are plain and simple, and will be readily understood by every one made rational from birth. They all emanate from, and accord directly or indirectly with, the three great fundamental laws of human nature; and when any doubt shall arise as to the true meaning, or right application of these twenty-five laws, the doubt will be removed by reference to these unchanging fundamental laws of nature. A part, and an essential part, of education of every member of these families, will be, to teach them a knowledge of these laws, the *causes* for them, and the importance of applying them uprightly, whenever their application may be called for.

How truly absurd is it to make innumerable laws opposed to nature's laws – inconsistent among themselves, too complicated for the most learned to comprehend, and then to call upon poor human beings who, from their birth, have been kept profoundly ignorant of these innumerable, inconsistent, opposing laws, and also of almost everything else that rational beings should know, to obey these laws, or be punished for their infraction by imprisonment, or fines, or often with death?

The accumulation of nonsense and absurdity in what are called *codes of law*, formerly or now in practice throughout the irrational-made nations of the world, proclaim aloud the wretched state of ignorance and brutality in which, alone, the population of all countries has yet been permitted to exist, and proves, at this day, the extent the barbarism which yet covers the earth, to keep it a pandemonium occupied by irrational-made animals.

When these six parts of 'the book' shall be studied, so as to be understood, and these twenty-five laws shall be made familiar to the public, it will be prepared to comprehend the seventh and last part, when the world will learn the difference between its population when trained in error from its birth to make it irrational, and trained in truth from its birth to make it rational in thought and conduct.

For convenience to the reader, the laws shall be now restated without the reasons previously given for each.

UNIVERSAL CODES OF LAWS, OR GENERAL CONSTITUTION FOR THE GOVERNMENT OF THE HUMAN RACE UNDER THE RATIONAL SYSTEM OF SOCIETY. THIS code is based upon, and emanates from, the now ascertained fundamental laws of human nature; namely,

1. That individual man forms no part of his physical, mental, or moral organization, or character.

2. That he must feel pleasure or pain, love or hatred, as his natural organization and educated character compel him to feel. And –

3. That he must believe in obedience to the strongest impressions made upon his mind.

Man cannot, therefore, be responsible to man, in a rational state of society, for his feelings, thoughts, or actions; but he will ever be guided aright by the pleasure or pain which, by nature, he is compelled to experience through his feelings and thoughts, and from his actions.

The following laws are in accordance with those of nature.

UNIVERSAL LAWS.

1. All shall have liberty to express their opinions upon all subjects, as nature compels them to be received by the strongest impressions made upon the mind.

2. No one shall have any other power, than by fair argument, to control the opinions or belief of another.

3. No praise or blame, no merit or demerit, no reward or punishment shall be awarded for any opinions or belief.

4. But as the human race has been made to become variously superstitious over the world, all shall have equal right to express their opinions respecting the incomprehensible power which moves the atom and controls the universe, and to worship that power under any name or form, or in any manner agreeable to their consciences; not interfering with the equal rights of others.

5. All shall be equally provided, through life, with the best of everything for human nature, by public arrangements; which arrangements shall give the best known direction to the industry and talents of every one.

6. All shall be educated, from infancy to maturity, in the best manner known at the time.

7. All shall pass through the same general routine of education, domestic teaching, and employment.

8. All children, from their birth, shall be under the especial care of the community of families in which they are born; but their parents shall have free access to them at all proper times, so as not to interfere in the formation of a superior character for them.

9. All children in the same community, shall be trained and educated together, as children of the same family, without partiality; and shall be early taught the fundamental principles of their nature, and how to apply them, on all occasions, consistently to practice.

10. All shall be encouraged from birth to express their feelings and convictions only; or, in other words, to speak the truth solely on all occasions.

11. All, of both sexes, to have equal education, rights, privileges and personal liberty; the union or marriage of the sexes to arise from the general sympathies and natural feelings of affection, uninfluenced by artificial distinctions.

12. Under the Rational System of society, – after the children shall have been trained to acquire new habits and new feelings, derived from the laws of human nature, – there shall be no useless private property.

13. As soon as the members of these families shall have been educated from

infancy in a knowledge of the laws of their nature, and to apply them rationally to practice, and surrounded by circumstances in unison with those laws, there shall be no other individual punishment or reward than the wise and benevolent punishments and rewards of nature.

14. Society to be formed of a union of single families into communities, or associations of men, women, and children in the usual proportions, with not less than about five hundred, nor more than from two thousand to three thousand.

15. As these family unions increase in number, unions of them shall be formed for local and general purposes, in tens, hundreds, thousands, etc, according to the less or more extended objects and interests which shall require their consideration and direction.

16. Each of these associated families shall possess in perpetuity around it land sufficient for the support, for ever, of all its members, even when it shall contain the maximum in number.

17. These communities shall be so arranged as to give to all the members of each of them, as nearly as possible, the same advantages, and to afford the most easy communication with each other.

18. Each community shall be governed in its *home* department by a general council, composed of all its members between the ages of thirty and forty; and each department shall be under the immediate direction of a committee formed of members of the general council, chosen by the latter, in the order to be determined upon; and in its external or foreign affairs, by all its members from forty to sixty years of age.

19. After all the members of the community shall have been rendered capable of taking their full share of the duties in the general council of government, there shall be no selection or election of any individuals to the governing councils, either in the home or foreign department.

20. All the members, at thirty years of age, who shall have been trained from infancy in the communities, shall be officially called upon to undertake their full share of the duties of management in the *home* department; and at forty they will be officially called upon to undertake the duties of the external or foreign department; and at sixty they will be excused from officially attending to them.

21. The duties of the general council of the home department shall be, to govern all the circumstances within the boundaries of its community – to organize the various departments of production, distribution, and formation of character – to remove all those circumstances the least favourable to happiness, and to replace them with the best that can be devised among themselves, or of which they can obtain a knowledge from other communities. The duties of the general council of the external or foreign department will be, to receive visitors or delegates from other associations or communities – to communicate with other similar associations – to visit and arrange with them the best means

of forming roads and conveying surplus produce to each other – to travel, to give and receive information of inventions, improvements, and discoveries, and of every other kind useful to promote the happiness of society; and also to regulate and assist in the establishment of new associations, composed of the surplus population of the community from among themselves, and to send delegates to the circle of communities to which their community shall be attached.

22. The general councils, home and foreign, shall have full power of government in all things under their direction, as long as they shall act in unison with the laws of human nature, which laws shall be their sole guidance on all occasions.

23. All individuals trained, educated, and placed in conformity with the laws of their nature, must, of necessity, at all times think and act rationally, except they shall become physically, mentally, or morally diseased; in which case the council shall remove them into the hospital for bodily or mental or moral invalids, where they shall remain until they shall be recovered by the mildest treatment that can effect their cure.

24. The council, whenever it shall be necessary, shall call to its aid the practical abilities and advice of any of the members not in the council.

25. If the general council should ever attempt to contravene the laws of human nature, which is scarcely possible, the elders of the family who have passed the councils shall call a general meeting of all the members of the community between sixteen and thirty years of age who have been trained within it. This meeting shall calmly and patiently investigate the conduct of the general council, and if a majority of the young and old shall determine that they have acted, or attempted to act in opposition to these laws, the general government shall devolve upon the members of the community who have passed the councils, and are above sixty years of age, united with those who have not entered the council, and are between twenty and thirty years of age. It is scarcely possible to conceive, that men and women trained to be rational beings from their birth, should render it necessary to resort to the application of this clause; but if required, it can only be for a short period of temporary application.

All other differences of every description, if, indeed, it be possible for any to exist in these families, shall be immediately determined, and amicably adjusted between the parties, by the decision of a majority of the three senior members of the foreign council; except when the difference shall exist between members of the councils; when it shall be, in like manner, determined by the three members who have last passed the councils.

When the human race shall be trained from birth in strict consistency with the three great fundamental laws of human nature; shall be placed within external circumstances in accordance with those laws, and shall be classified and employed according to age, there will be no necessity for any other laws than the twenty-five now enumerated and explained. During the transition state from irrationality to rationality, regulations in conformity with these laws will be required; but when all shall be educated from birth to be rational beings, they will, under every change of circumstance, and on all occasions, without additional laws, act rationally.

END OF THE SIXTH PART

THE BOOK

OF THE

NEW MORAL WORLD:

CONCLUSIONS DEDUCED FROM THE FOREGOING PRINCIPLES, CONSIDERED IN REFERENCE TO THE PRESENT EXCITED AND UNSATISFACTORY STATE OF THE CIVILIZED WORLD, SO CALLED.

BY ROBERT OWEN.

TRUTH WITHOUT MYSTERY, MIXTURE OF ERROR, OR FEAR OF MAN, CAN ALONE EMANCIPATE THE HUMAN RACE FROM SIN AND MISERY.

PART SEVENTH.

London:
PUBLISHED FOR THE SOCIETY, BY
J. WATSON, 5, PAUL'S ALLEY, PATERNOSTER ROW;
AND ALL BOOKSELLERS.

1844.

THE BOOK

OF THE

NEW MORAL WORLD

SEVENTH PART

CHAPTER I

'The period for introducing the Rational System, for remodelling the character of man, and for governing the population of the earth in unity, peace, progressive improvement and happiness, is near at hand; and no human power can successfully resist the change.'

What are the signs of the times which indicate the arrival of the period for the introduction of the Rational Society over the earth?

These are now numerous. The most prominent, and the most influential to make the change immediately necessary, is the present state of the British empire; – the most advanced in scientific knowledge, wealth, and power of any empire yet known; and yet exhibiting not more than the mere germs of the knowledge, wealth, and power which it contains the means to increase to an illimitable extent; even to an extent sufficient rationally directed, to ensure permanent prosperity to the world. And while thus abounding in the elements of riches, and in the means of an enormous increase, its millions, of the most industrious population of the world, are suffering more from actual poverty and from the fear of it, than any other nation or people.

It is then the anomaly of the extremes of knowledge and ignorance, of wealth and poverty, of extravagant magnificence and the lowest state of degradation and destitution, when the destitution, degradation, poverty, and ignorance may be, most beneficially for all, removed for ever, that constitute one certain sign of the times that this most inferior condition of society cannot be allowed long to remain.

The mechanical inventions, the chemical discoveries, with the innumerable improvements in other arts and sciences to render human labour less necessary to the production of wealth, and to reduce continually its commercial value; with the impossibility of supporting the increase of population with the decrease in the merchantable value of labour, is another sign of the times that a great organic change cannot be much longer delayed. The injustice, oppression, and cruelty, which arise from this progress, are already too apparent to the public mind to permit it to acquiesce in the continuance of the misery thus hourly created, and of necessity increasing. The agitation, in consequence of this increased misery, which has been exhibited in England, Ireland, Scotland, and Wales, is another sign of the times, that a great change in human existence is near at hand.

The producing powers derived from science by the inventions, discoveries, and improvements, of a population advancing slowly through a century from fifteen millions to twenty-eight millions, have increased during that period from an amount equal to the labour of about twelve millions of trained adult men, to an amount that, without such new aid from scientific knowledge, would now require the labour or industry of more than eight hundred millions of well trained adults, to execute the same work in the same time; an extent of new productive power that, without this aid, would require four times the manual labour at present to be obtained over the world.

What folly that this enormous power should be so misdirected, under an irrational system, as to produce poverty and crime, instead of riches and virtue! But this productive power, enormous as it appears when contrasted with its amount a century past, is but the mere germ of a power to the increase of which man can set no limits; for its increase appears to be inexhaustible, and its power of growth to increase with its growth.

But this miraculous new power has been discovered and brought into action by a population less than thirty millions; while, now that the discovery has been made, the knowledge of creating similar power and its increase may be given to every population of equal numbers; or in proportion to any greater or less population; thereby securing an inexhaustible and ever-growing power to render wealth as easily attainable as water, and as much in superabundance, for all the rational wants of the human race, as air. This is another of the extraordinary signs of the times, indicating the immediate necessity for a reorganization of society.

But this new, enormous, and illimitable power to create wealth, and remove poverty or the fear of it for ever from the human race, has been and is now applied to limit wealth for the millions, to create poverty for them, and the fear of it in almost all.

That a power calculated, under a wise direction, to produce wealth far more than sufficient to saturate the population of the world, should be so far misunderstood and misapplied as to be made the cause of greater poverty and the fear of it in the millions inhabiting the most advanced nations in the world, is a sign of the times that a great change in human affairs is demanded at this period, no sane mind can doubt.

When it can be demonstrated that the means abundantly exist to fertilize and beautify the earth, so as to make it a highly pleasurable scene, and to saturate the world with the most useful, valuable, and desirable wealth; and that these very means are applied to inflict every kind of misery on the millions in the most powerful nations of modern times, then may it be predicated that the existing system of society is worn out, and that a great change in the affairs of men is urgently demanded.

The failure of all attempts in the most wealthy and powerful empire yet known to have existed, in providing common sense arrangements for its poor, so as to prevent poverty or the fear of it in future, is another sign of the times that the present system is altogether inadequate for the period now attained, through the knowledge of facts acquired by experience.

Again, the extraordinary disclosures of the destitution and degradation of humanity, daily brought forth and published by the press, exhibiting the most certain evidence that, in the most advanced nation in the world, such occurrences, in all the horrors of slow starvation under the most appalling circumstances, are frequent even in the metropolis of the British empire, as well as in all the provinces, as proved by the new charitable associations for the *houseless* poor,[a] etc, are proof, if further proof could be required, that the present system of society is quite unequal to its government under the extraordinary changes which have occurred in the last century. The poverty, destitution, and degradation of the mass increasing, while the national wealth and power are increasing, constitute a sure sign, as the happiness of each individual is the rational object of society, that the period has arrived when a reorganization of society has become an act of necessity, which, ere long, will be irresistible.

When society has attained the knowledge of the means through which, by scientific arrangements, the creation of superior wealth, in superfluity for the wants and desires of all, may be made a pleasure and pastime, a most delightful recreation for the young and middle-aged; and when, at the same time, under the existing system, the creation of wealth is made a slavery to the many and a subject of contest to all; when it is made the cause of every kind of fraud, violence, injustice and oppression, dividing men into opposing classes, and thus making the conduct of all most irrational; it may be certainly perceived, by those whose minds have been expanded by the acquirement of much varied knowledge, that a great organic change is of necessity near at hand for the benefit of the human race.

When the world is made a great scene of contest about the possession of wealth, territory, and power, while, by simple and beautiful arrangements, beneficial for all, more wealth, territory, and power may be secured for all than

[a] E.g., the Metropolitan Association for Improving the Dwellings of the Working Classes, formed in 1841. In the 1840s the Society for Improving the Condition of the Labouring Classes was also active in this area.

any will desire to possess, is again an evident proof or sign of the times that a revolution or great change in the affairs of men is of necessity approaching.

And when the great object of all is the acquisition and accumulation in perpetuity of wealth, while the practice of the world is to misapply, to waste and destroy it upon the most magnificent scale of error in all the present proceedings of man over the world, and when that error has been discovered, this is again another sign of the times that the period has arrived when a new state of human existence has become greatly to be desired for the well-being and happiness of all, and that a rational system for conducting the affairs of men should be introduced, to terminate the present irrational proceedings of the human race.

The ignorance in which the human race has been so long detained, becoming at this period obvious to certain minds, who have been made conscious of the innumerable evils thence arising, and of the necessity for its removal, is another evident sign of the times, that the period for a fundamental change throughout all the ramifications of society is near at hand. The present system, having been based from the beginning on ignorance, and hitherto sustained solely by ignorance, should this ignorance be superseded by real knowledge, the whole of the existing system and organization of society would appear so monstrous, contradictory, and absurd, that none, after a short period, could be otherwise than greatly ashamed to remain an advocate for the continuance of such an heterogeneous mass of sin and misery, of gross irrationality, and obstruction to human happiness.

It is evident the time has arrived when this ignorance can be continued no longer. The axe has been applied to this tree of evil, and it must soon give way, root, trunk, branches, and fruit. It has been fairly undermined, its roots laid bare, and no power can much longer sustain it. The lowest class in society is becoming better informed upon some of the most important subjects than the highest class were but a short time since, and than many of them are at present. The rapid increase of knowledge among the inferior class, compared with their knowledge at any former period, is another sign of the times that a change in the arrangements and classification of society is necessary, which change cannot be effected without an entire reorganization.

In this progress from ignorance to real knowledge, the millions have discovered the fallacy of the foundation on which all the various superstitions of the world from the beginning have been constructed. Many of them now know that these superstitions have one and all emanated from inexperienced, and often greatly diseased imaginations of individuals, influencing first a few, and afterwards numerous associations, comprising nations extending over large portions of the globe.

These superstitions are calculated so far to create a disease of the imagination of those who imbibe them, that they speedily overcome and destroy their powers of judging with truth and accuracy on all subjects having reference to the particular superstition, under the name of religion, with which the individual has been afflicted.

And the effects produced by these various, and often strongly opposing superstitions, are much the same generally in the disciples of all, wherever they may be found in any part of the world. If a stranger should ask any one of them respecting these superstitions, the uniform answer from all would be – 'Our superstition,' which they call religion, 'is true, it is divine, or from God himself, and *therefore* we know it to be true; but all the other superstitions, which the disciples of them call religion, are so contradictory and absurd, that if the disciples of them had not been trained to believe in them from their childhood, and thus made to be insane and quite incompetent to judge of our religion, or to perceive its truth and divine origin, they could never commit the errors and mistakes of so momentous a nature as they do.' Thus demonstrating that all these superstitions destroy the rational faculties of all who are trained to believe in their contradictory absurdities.

But the belief in, and reverence for, these systems for deranging the faculties, and creating the most vile and violent of human passions, are rapidly decreasing throughout the world; and that decrease is mightily hastened by the establishment and progress of the British and Foreign Bible Society.[a] It was seen at once by those whose minds had escaped the derangement produced by these superstitions, that the most sure mode of first disturbing and then destroying these superstitions would be, by devising the means to compare the contradictions and absurdities of one with another; and the wealth and activity of the British and Foreign Bible Society have enabled its missionaries over the world to accomplish this task in the most clever and extensive manner, in comparatively a very short period.

To those who by singular good fortune escaped the derangement of their rational faculties, through disbelief in any of these wild superstitions, it was evident that no chance existed to save the human race from this humiliation of deranged intellects, and all its dreadful consequences, as long as the children of every generation should be compelled, before they possessed powers of mind to judge between insane notions and common sense, to receive as divine and eternal truths, the most absurd vagaries of some disordered imaginations, having no reference whatever to *facts* or divine truths, which are always consistent and unchanging.

The rapidly growing disbelief in these superstitions, and the almost miraculous decrease in the public reverence for them, are certain signs of the times that their entire downfall approaches, and that society must be new based on principles of common sense in accordance with facts, to supersede the absurdities on which all these superstitions have been based and constructed.

[a] Missionary society, founded 1804.

The discovery of the false base on which all human laws have been made; of their direct opposition to nature's laws; and of their gross injustice and oppression of the weak when opposed by the strong; of the evils which their fallacies are hourly producing in all directions and among all classes; with the folly, now becoming evident to the public, of training and extravagantly paying a class of men to have its interest made to be, to divide and estrange the feelings of man from man, and to keep society in a state of continual hostility and turmoil, when it is the true interest of one and all that men should be cordially and permanently united, and that litigation should be unknown among them; – the evils thus produced by the professors and advocates of these insane laws, framed in direct opposition to nature's just, wise, and beneficent laws, are becoming too glaring to be long continued, as appears by the daily growing desire to adjust all differences by a just and friendly arbitration; which is another sign of the times that a great organic change in society is coming upon the world, to terminate the miseries which these old errors have increased until they are no longer bearable.

The increase of crime, arising from poverty, superstition, and human laws opposed to nature's laws, has increased to an extent which begins to alarm society in various ways, so as to force the attention of many to enquire into the causes of the rapid and extensive increase to this cause of misery, and into the justice of human punishments upon the individuals who commit the crimes.

In consequence, those, the most freed from superstition and from the errors on which society has been hitherto based, are beginning to discover, that these crimes are the necessary effects of the ignorance, poverty, superstition, and laws, with which the world, through error, has been so long afflicted; that therefore, these crimes are the crimes of society, and not of the individual, who is most unjustly punished for the ignorance and error of society. The irrationality of these proceedings is becoming daily more and more glaring, and will ere long be discovered by the public generally, to be so contrary to common sense and honesty, that they must be abandoned. And this change in public opinion, as to ignorant men being longer permitted to punish ignorant men, according to the extent of ignorance between them, is another sign of the times, that the present system, formed of such a mass of errors, requires to be superseded without loss of time, by a new organization of society; an organization, from which the causes of these errors shall be removed, and by which their return will be rendered impracticable.

But the most evident sign of the times, to indicate a revolution in the affairs of mankind, and the necessity for an entire reorganization of society, is the new general public opinion in favour of educating the millions; to give them a new character, instead of the old one of ignorance and coarse vulgarity. All now admit that the *people* must be educated; but the dispute between the most powerful parties in the state now is, Who shall educate them, and upon what principles shall their education be based? Short-sighted irrational mortals! Can public opinion be now staid upon this all-important subject? The real question is, shall the millions, the great mass of the human race, be continued in worse than Egyptian darkness[a] with regard to their nature, or position in society, and be crammed with some of the horrible imaginary wild fancies of some one of the existing irrational superstitions which have hitherto destroyed the reasoning faculties of the human race, divided man from man, people from people, or be made rational in their feelings, thoughts, and actions? Yes! Error shall be now abandoned and truth adopted: the light of knowledge has commenced, superstition will be abandoned, and with it will disappear the endless miseries which it has produced, and which are still suffered by the population of the world.

It is now known that the character of each individual is formed *for* him, and chiefly by society. It is true, nature prepares the material before birth; but it is now known that even in this respect nature may be materially aided by lately acquired knowledge. It is also known that society, and not the individual, has the full power to make, or manufacture, the human material from birth into a very inferior or superior man or woman at maturity. Inferior, by entire neglect, or by filling the mind from infancy with any of the superstitions of the world; or superior, by laying a solid foundation of truth, and building up the mind with the most useful knowledge of facts, all in accordance with that foundation.

Foolish, irrational man! to suppose that the knowledge now acquired of human nature, with the means of training and educating all from birth to the inferior or superior, can long exist without destroying the ignorance which has hitherto left the human race in darkness respecting its own nature, and thus made man a violent, passionate, revengeful, inferior being, without signs of any qualities approaching to rationality!

No! man must now be educated. But how? No longer to be a mental and physical slave to imaginary fears; the days of ghosts and hobgoblins are passing with the superstitions which gave them birth, and man must have his character henceforward based on demonstrable truth, and must be made an intelligent and superior rational being, fitted to create the circumstances to ensure happiness to his offspring, and to live a long life of healthy joyous existence.

Who or what shall now form the character of the subjects of the British Empire? The Hindoo, Christian, or Mahomedan sectarianism? Or shall the future subjects of this extended and all-influencing empire be so placed and trained from birth by society as to become full-formed men and women, having all their natural faculties, propensities, and powers well cultivated and duly exercised through their lives? Or, in other words, shall they be made opposing, fighting, ignorant, irrational beings, or to become well informed, consistent,

[a] See for example Exodus 8:6.

rational men and women, with all their physical, mental, moral, and practical powers, well trained from birth, and exercised through life up to the point of temperance?

No! fortunately for poor long-abused and vilified human nature, man is indeed about to burst the shell of ignorance, in which all his rational faculties have been hitherto confined and imprisoned without a ray of light being permitted to enter. But an aperture has at length been made, light has penetrated into the interior of its dark recesses, it is hourly increasing, and, ere long, man will come forth into a new existence, a new creature, with a new heart, a new mind, a new spirit, and with new knowledge that will prepare him to give happiness to, and receive it from all around him. But to effect this great and glorious change for the human race, man must not have his character formed by the sectarianism of any superstition; his imagination must no longer be made his ruling faculty, to the destruction of all his superior rational faculties. His mind must be based, not on imaginary notions opposed to facts; but on facts never known to change, on eternal truths, always capable of immediate demonstration, and which no powers of sophistry can ever impugn, or with any chance of success contend against.

Yes, the signs of the times make it now evident, that man must be educated; and that, after much useless superstitious contention, by various parties striving to have him made a weak or bigoted sectarian of some irrational creed or other, all will at length unite in the conclusion that he shall be rationally educated from birth, and be no longer made a mere localized, contending animal, opposed to nature, reason, and common sense; but a being with the full-formed powers of humanity, exercising his physical, mental, moral, and practical faculties rationally, to secure his own well-being and happiness, through the superior well-being and happiness of all around him.

This great change in the character of man is evidently in rapid progress of preparation; but this change can never be effected under the existing mal-organization of society; no, it is impossible that any great and permanent good can arise to man so long as society shall be organized on the false principles on which alone it has ever yet been based. On these principles man can never be made rational; there must be a new organization and classification of society before man can be made to become rational; and the signs of the times indicate that the great circumstances of society are in progress of formation to render this change not only practicable, but greatly to be desired by all of the human race, of every rank and condition, in all countries.

Another great and overruling sign of the times, rendering it necessary that another organization of society should be made, is, the universal dissatisfaction of the governed, with all the past and present governments over the world. Each form of governing has now been tried again and again, under every conceivable modification, and all have been found incompetent to produce a superior character and happiness for the governed. It is a superior character and happiness which are required from governments; yet they have not and cannot produce them; they are, one and all, unequal to the task required from them. And why is it thus? evidently because the present organization of society will not admit of either being attained as long as men and nations shall be so irrational as to desire to be governed on false principles.

Where, in what part of the world, has despotism, limited monarchy, oligarchy, aristocracy, republicanism, or democracy, ever produced a superior character or happiness for the people governed by either of these forms?

The whole system of society, under any of these forms, is a compound of ignorance, injustice, and gross absurdities; it is therefore, whenever trial has been made of any one of them, that the governed have soon found its mode of acting incompetent to produce wisdom and happiness among the people.

The population of the world is now tired of these unsuccessful attempts to govern them wisely, and no longer expect permanent prosperity from any of these old forms or modes of governing. The superior character for all is not created, the superabundant wealth for all is not produced and distributed, and these results are the only criterion of a good government. There is a clamour for and against all these modes of governing, because those governed by any one of them are dissatisfied, and wish for the trial of some other, expecting any change to be an improvement; but for any of these modes of governing no experienced person, with a sound judgment, will now contend. Universal dissatisfaction with governments therefore naturally exists, and will continue until there shall be an entirely new organization of society, one based on the principles of truth respecting human nature and society, and in which the classification shall be alone the classification of age; seeing that by simple, beautiful, scientific arrangements, giving health and pleasure to all by their operations in action, more wealth may be produced, of superior qualities, than the population of the world will require. And that from the individual organization at birth of each human being, a useful, good, and to society, valuable man or woman, according to its sex, may be formed by society; and thus, that no necessity will longer exist, after the present generation, for an inequality of education or condition among men; the sciences being made the superior slaves and servants of the human race. The government of society over the earth will be in accordance with this new state of human existence, and will perform its proper part and proportion in the new organization, which the times, or the changes which it has produced, now to irresistibly require.

All the governments hitherto have been governments of force and fraud; and the governments to direct the creation of wealth and the formation of character being required to be governments of charity, reason, justice, and kindness, without individual rewards or punishments, the necessity for an immediate new organization of society becomes daily more and more urgent, for the benefit of the present and all future generations.

The population of the world having been so classified and divided as continually to require force and fraud to keep it, hitherto, in a bearable state of existence, and so opposed and excited, universal war became an almost unavoidable result. But now the gross folly and madness of wars are become so glaring to the millions, who were before blind to their iniquity and endless miseries, keeping the human race in a continued state of the grossest immoralities, in addition to its wholesale butcheries and robberies, that another organization of society to terminate war, its immoralities, its miseries, and its insanities, is become necessary and irresistible. The real wants of society, are, as previously stated, a superior character for all, wealth for all, and unity, charity, and kindness, to pervade the minds of all people and nations; while war is the most powerful engine now to prevent the formation of a superior and rational character, to destroy wealth, and to limit its production, and to render it impracticable for charity, kindness, and unity to exist among beings irrationally trained to war, or to support war by their contributions. This great change of public opinion in opposition to war, especially in the more civilized parts of the world, is another sign of the times that a new organization of society is required in the course of nature, and that, in consequence, it cannot be far off.

The deranged state of the monetary system in all countries the most advanced in wealth and the means of its illimitable increase, is another sign of the times that a new organization of the system of society is required.

The God of the world is wealth, individual wealth; the great stimulus to action among men is to obtain it; all the superior or happiness-producing qualities of our nature are held in abeyance, that the wealth-obtaining qualities may have unrestrained action. And yet all this is rank insanity or downright madness.

The monetary system of society is in a great degree the cause of this species of insanity and madness; it blinds the reasoning faculties of the race, making them suppose that money is wealth, and that each man can never accumulate too much of it. While, on the contrary, this monetary error, prevents, more than any single cause, the creation of wealth, and its just distribution beneficially to every one. It prevents the perception by all, that were it not for money accumulated and kept by individuals, under the individual system of society, wealth would soon become as superabundant for all rational purposes as water is at present, where it continually superabounds.

While wealth was scarce, and the means of its annual reproduction difficult, artificial money was useful; but now that over-production, or an over amount of wealth can be so easily arranged for the world, money, except during the transition from a false to a true organization of society, can be of no use to beings made rational, placed in a rational state of society, and governed on rational principles.

The world is in universal action to gain gold and silver, regardless of the misery created and experienced in the pursuit or when they are obtained; while the only rational object that man can require is happiness for himself and others. All this action to obtain artificial wealth, or a mere shadow mistaken for happiness, is uselessly wasted. It is altogether a thorough mis-application for the faculties of the human race. Simple arrangements, pleasurable for all to superintend, may now be made every where to create wealth of superior qualities, illimitable in amount, and far beyond the possible wants of the population of the world, and to be increased annually ten, or if useful, twenty times more rapidly than population under any circumstances can be made to increase.

This disorder and confusion in the monetary system of society is, then, another indication that the present organization of society is wholly unfit to meet the increasing advance in the knowledge of the sciences, to enable man to create wealth without any laborious, unhealthy, or disagreeable manual exertion; or to distribute the wealth so created, well and wisely, without the intervention of gold or silver or artificial money.

The disrepute into which all governments depending upon talking legislative assemblies, have gradually fallen, and the almost contempt in which the millions now hold them, is another most powerful sign of the times, that the present organization of society is rapidly dying its natural death. To govern the world well, requires acting, not talking; to form a superior character, to create wealth, to unite all in charity, kindness, and in one interest, and to remove the inferior and to replace them with superior external circumstances, are all that is required to govern the human race well and wisely. To do this requires but little more talking, and the action may be made very simple and straight forward.

More may be done to govern the world well and wisely in one year, when the proceedings shall be based on true principles, and all the measures adopted shall be uniformly consistent with them, than has been effected by all the legislative assemblies in the world for the last five hundred years.

The trash of inconsistencies which is daily poured forth in the speeches of the members of three great leading public legislative assemblies in the world, is well calculated to create the disrepute into which they have universally fallen. Their speaking is like the writings and speaking of theologians, which, at the end of thousands of years leave the subject more confused and in the dark than it was when ignorance commenced its task; for religion and politics are now where they were at the beginning, except, that both subjects are perhaps less understood in consequence of being far more complicated. The modern speeches in the three great legislative assemblies of the civilized world are ever redundant with words without utility for any beneficial practice. The members of each of them are trained so wretchedly ill from birth, that they can only speak the result of this malformation of the human character from birth. Instead of enlightening mankind by sound principles calculated to produce valuable practice, a knowledge which would be thus so speedily spread throughout society; they send forth into all lands into which the publication of their proceedings is admitted, most useless personal and local prejudices, well conceived to perplex and confound the faculties of all who read them. The whole business of life, which may be made so plain and simple, that all could understand in principle, and beneficially act upon in practice, is made so complex that none comprehend the principles or can apply them with general advantage to practice. This error is daily becoming more and more obvious to the millions, and the reading of these worse than useless speeches are being gradually abandoned by those who desire to improve the permanent condition of all classes. This is another sign of the times that a change is required in the general organization of society, and that truth is about to supersede falsehood and error. But one of the most sure signs indicating the necessity for this change is the direful effects upon the millions of this class legislation.

With the most abundant means to make the populations of all countries now, highly intelligent, cordially united, abounding in wealth, surrounded by superior circumstances only, charitable kind, truly good, and permanently happy, these class legislative assemblies pass laws and adopt other methods to keep the millions in ignorance, disunite all classes and individuals, keep the mass in the most inferior and the very worst circumstances, create the most uncharitable, unkind, and unjust spirit in all; and thus ensure permanent misery, instead of devising plain, practical measures to remove the causes of these evils, and to ensure a superior state of human existence over the earth. The mass are too strongly justified by their severe sufferings to call for the termination of class legislation, but they are yet too ignorant to know what should be substituted for it. If popular assemblies were elected from and by all classes in England and France, as in the United States of North America, and the present organization of society to remain in these countries, they could produce no more wisdom and benefit than the members of Congress in North America have hitherto produced.

The immoralities, poverty and miseries produced, and daily augmenting, by the extent to which individual and national competition is now carried throughout the civilized world, and the much greater evils and misery which it is yet calculated to inflict upon the human race is another of the innumerable signs of the times which prove the necessity for an entire change in the organization of society.

All that individual and national competition could effect to prepare a foundation for the future prosperity and happiness of society has been attained. To accomplish this prosperity and happiness, and to make man intelligent, rational and happy, individual and national cordial unity and co-operation are now required. This change is proceeding step by step, but in a most imperfect isolated manner, as evinced by railway, steam navigation, gas, water, banking, and other extended companies now in action and extending throughout Europe and America. The extreme folly of opposition and disunion, and the illimitable advantages of the most extended unions will soon become so glaringly obvious that the latter must be universally adopted, and the former altogether abandoned.

In fact, the signs of the times indicating the necessity for a change in the organization of society multiply so rapidly, as the subject comes under consideration, that this part of it must be concluded with one more striking proof in confirmation of the principle of change from necessity promulgated in this chapter. And this proof shall be drawn from the deteriorating effects produced upon the general character of mankind by the immoral consequences proceeding from the practice of all individuals directly or indirectly being trained from childhood to endeavour to buy cheap and sell dear.

This is a principle destructive of all sound or pure morality; it is a principle opposed to the cultivation of all the superior qualities of humanity; it places all individuals in covert enmity to their fellows; it makes man an ignorant and selfish being, and creates disorder throughout the mind and conduct of all; it is opposed to sincerity, to charity, and to kindness; it engenders a spirit always inclined to take an advantage of others, and while its practice shall obtain, it will be useless to expect that men will endeavour to promote, in the extent in their power, the well-being and happiness of every man, woman, and child, without regard to their class, sect, party, country, or colour.

As all now, from the highest to the lowest, endeavour to buy the services of others at the least cost of value, and to dispose of their own at the highest advantages they can obtain for them, deception must be, and is as universal as the practice. Truth and deception cannot govern society; one or the other must prevail: deception produces misery; truth will produce happiness: the formation of minds trained to endeavour to buy cheap and sell dear must be therefore abandoned before man can be educated, to become rational in his feelings, thoughts, and actions, or the Rational System of society can be adopted in practice.

CHAPTER II

'That the governments of the world will soon be compelled, in their own defence, to adopt this superior system, to prevent their being involved in anarchy, civil war, and ruin.'

It is not the interest of one human being that the present most irrational state of society should be continued for one day longer. It has been proved to be based on error – of error that perpetually generates falsehood and deception; that it maintains ignorance, deranges the human faculties, creates poverty, division, anger, jealousy, and all the other evil passions; instigates to war and rapine, injustice, oppression and cruelty, every kind of vice and crime; has ever been upheld by force and fraud, and will now require a greater and a continually increasing amount of both to permit its feverish longer existence. It is directly opposed to the future progress, well-being and happiness of the human race, involving them, through the derangement of their mental faculties, in the folly and madness of one superstition or another, until all are actively and most efficiently engaged in destroying the rationality and consequence happiness of all. And thus is the earth, while superabounding in all that is necessary to secure health, wealth, a superior character, and high enjoyment for all, made a pandemonium to torment the human race, and prevent man changing it into a terrestrial paradise for the permanent enjoyment of his race.

The acquisition of facts, aiding the rapid progress of scientific knowledge, has given man new powers never conceived as within the sphere of possibility by the past generations, and thus has prepared materials to give the population of the world new powers which must give a new direction to all its future proceedings, and render all the present cumbrous system for carrying forward the business of life far worse than useless.

With the new means and illimitable scientific powers at the control of man to fertilize and beautify the earth; to create wealth beyond any assignable limit; to ensure a rational and valuable character for each and all; to prevent disunion and all crime or motive to contest or competition among men; to govern without force of fraud, but solely by reason, charity, and kindness, what need will there be for armies or warlike navies? for superstition under any name? for punishments by men or any of the absurd paraphernalia of what are called courts of justice, when they are in reality courts of the most gross injustice, cruelty, and oppression? or for any of the professions to keep the population of the world in ignorance, divided and dependent upon most injurious mysticisms? or that the many should be most ignorantly governed by a few united, made, by external circumstances, more powerful than the many disunited? There is now no longer any necessity for this monstrous waste of physical and mental power in conducting human affairs. It is a waste of means so misapplied as to be destructive of the health and happiness of the millions, and of the common sense of all.

But this ignorance of what is now good for man, – this demon of evil, cannot much longer continue this horrible power over the human race. The public mind is aroused; it now asks whence the power or right of ignorant man over ignorant man? It is discovered to be assumption all, and that, to this day, *might has been alone right*, and that hitherto might has been with the united few over the disunited many. But the many are on the way to unite, and then the *might* will be with them. How necessary, then, for the existing governments of the, so called, civilized world to educate, employ and make rational, the many, before they discover their might, and the gross injustice and cruelty of the manner in which the might of the few has hitherto exerted its powers over the natural rights of the many?

With the new knowledge elicited by the discovery of new facts; with the enormous new powers thus attained; with the illimitable increase to them that may now be made, is it possible to suppose that the population of the world can continue to be governed as heretofore? Can injustice, oppression, and cruelty prevail, when it has become the perceived interest of the many that they should cease to exist, and to be remembered no more in the transactions of man with man?

War, and rapine, and bloodshed, and destruction of wealth, and of the means of creating it, of ignorant man in his blindness, punishing ignorant man; and all this maintained indirect opposition to right reason or common sense, while the mass are rapidly adding fact to fact and deducing obvious conclusions from them, exhibit a state of society in progress from all that is erroneous and pernicious, to all that will be true and beneficial for the race of man.

Truth has gone forth and is now extending its invaluable knowledge in all directions around our globe, and truth will make the nations of the earth free from the demon of error and his legions of evils with which he has hitherto tormented the human race, and kept man ignorant, and made him irrational in his feelings, sentiments, and conduct, and held him a slave in the mental chains of superstition.

This progress from all that is erroneous and evil to man, to all that is true and good for man, cannot continue without it becoming soon obvious that the existing organization of society is a false one, and most injurious to the few and many; that a necessity has arisen for a change to be made and a new organization given to the world by the present *few* who govern, or, if not by them, then by the *many*, who have been so long misgoverned by the few, under the old organization of the world.

Blame or recrimination between parties for the past miserable government and conduct of mankind is useless; it is now clearly seen that they were the *necessary* effects of circumstances, over which the governors and the governed had no control. These past circumstances were necessary to produce the present, as the present are necessary to produce the future. The past has been, from causes yet inexplicable to man, a state of great suffering and misery to the millions; the present is evidently a period preliminary to a great change in the condition of the human race, and as all the materials are most amply provided for a state of permanent general prosperity and happiness, it is reasonable to infer, that the change will be one from ignorance, division, and poverty, to one of increased knowledge, unity, and wealth, producing a superior and rational existence for mankind.

To those who understand human nature it is now evident that there can be no peace, no unity, no permanent prosperity and happiness, so long as there shall be inequality of education or condition. The inequality will be, of necessity, a perpetual source of disquiet, discontent, and of exciting agitation, as long as it shall be unwisely continued. But until the late discoveries, inventions and improvements in the sciences and arts, and especially the inventions in mechanism and the discoveries in chemistry, this equality of education and condition was impracticable. Manual power, without the aid of great scientific power, could not produce the wealth and the leisure requisite for an equality of a superior education and condition of the human race. Until this new scientific power was secured to be applied on the most extensive scale for the universal service and benefit of man, slaves and servants were necessary to give leisure to some to discover, invent, and improve. This has now been done to as great an extent as is necessary to change the present inequality of education and condition into an equality of both, and each much superior, for the formation of character and a creation of better external circumstances, than any class in any country has ever yet attained.

The new scientific powers already brought into practice, if they were wisely applied, are far more than are required to terminate all slavery and servitude among the human race, and to attain and secure a superior education and condition for all. Why, then, should not the change from universal physical or mental slavery and servitude be now commenced systematically, in peace and order, by the existing governments of the more civilized and powerful nations of the earth? It is beyond all ordinary calculation for the interest of these governments to commence and direct this change. It is necessary now that they should thus act, for their safety, prosperity, and happiness, and for the peace of the countries over which they govern. It is most unreasonable to expect that when it is made evident to the millions, that there are ample means to secure, without evil to any, a very superior state of existence for all, that they will be content and quietly allow the *few* to prevent the attainment of this happiness for all.

Enormous as these scientific powers are, which have been already discovered, invented, and improved, to render future inequality of education and condition unnecessary and highly injurious, the power of increase to them is illimitable. Our ancestors, in Great Britain and Ireland, only a century ago, had to commence their progress in obtaining these new powers with an aid not exceeding the labour of fifteen millions of adults. Less than double that population have to proceed with the extension of these powers, by a new aid obtained within the century, from science, equal to the labour or more than eight hundred millions of adults; with this power daily increasing, upon a magnificent scale, in a continually increasing ratio, and to which increase man can put no assignable limits.

Why then, backed by such power now in existence and illimitable store to draw upon to anticipate all future wants, should the governments of the world hesitate to place full reliance upon their power, with these means already secured and in active progress, to relieve mankind from the fear of want, from ignorance, from disunion, with all the crimes and miseries necessarily engendered by and emanating from poverty, ignorance, and disunion.

Now that these extraordinary powers for the production of wealth, knowledge, goodness and happiness, among the human race have been discovered, and are in progress of being made known to the people of all countries, it will be utterly impossible for the governments of these countries to continue to govern them on the principles of military force and superstitious fraud, and to keep the people in the mental slavery and physical servitude in which they are, producing real benefit to none, but misery or danger to all.

There is no reason, but the dire effects of an irrational formation of character, and the creation of irrational institutions and human-made external inferior circumstances, why this false, and most wretched system of inequality of education and condition should be longer maintained through force and fraud by the existing governments. It can be continued only by increased force and fraud; for as knowledge progresses among the millions, and it is daily advancing, there must be a continual increase of these misery-producing irrational powers, to keep in check, if it be possible for a short period longer, the growing intelligence of the nations of the world.

It is possible by a temporary unholy alliance between the leading governments of Europe, and by an annual increase of force in the armies and navies, and of fraud in their superstitions, to maintain, for a short period, the reign of the present irrational system, opposed as it is to the well-being and happiness of the race of man in all climes and of all colours; but the increase of pain and misery thus extended would, in nature's own time, create the circumstances to aid the suffering millions to enable them to say, in the language of the public opinion of the world, 'So far shall this system of misery and rank insanity proceed and no farther.'

Should the governments of the more civilized and powerful nations of the earth continue blind to the irresistible progress of nature's great changes, and most unwisely endeavour to maintain, by increasing force and fraud, the present chaotic and perplexed condition of human existence, then is the day near when the nations of the earth shall arise in their might and say 'that man shall be no longer governed by force and fraud, be trained from his birth to become a mental and physical slave to the few; but shall be made a rational being, equal in education and condition according to age, and be governed only by laws of knowledge, charity, and kindness, in accordance with, and without deviation from, nature's wise, beneficent, and just laws, which adhered to, will for ever increase the knowledge and happiness of every succeeding generation.'

But surely the leading governments of the more advanced nations of the earth, are not so blinded by the errors of the past, as not to perceive this change which is now in rapid progress. The revolutions of the United States,

South America, and France, and the general disturbance of so many old established governments, customs, and institutions, are strong indications of the forthcoming great and universal organic change to relieve the world from the degradation of ignorance, superstition, poverty, and disunion, with their necessary consequent crimes and miseries; and to establish, upon a solid and everlasting foundation, the permanent system of nature, based upon unchanging facts, which never err, or are inconsistent with themselves and all other facts, and which facts lead alone to real knowledge and substantial happiness, both to increase, as one generation shall succeed another.

The governments which do not yet perceive the unerring indications of this change in the discontent of the masses of the people in so many countries, arising from the ignorance, poverty, and division, which, by their rulers, they are made, most unwisely now for all parties, to submit to, and unnecessarily suffer; must be in worse than Egyptian darkness,[a] and made blind in their own destruction.

But it is hoped, that the most enlightened among these powers will discover their present real position, and use their best efforts to remove the error from those the least advanced in a knowledge of the signs of the times, and that they will unite to act with foresight and wisdom to effect those changes peaceably, willingly, with order, and beneficially for themselves and the world, and thus prevent the necessity of the revolution from error to truth, or from misery to happiness, being made by the people, instead of by wisely foreseen and devised measures of the governments.

It is by such rational measures, on the part of the leading governments of Europe and America, that anarchy, war, and ruin for an indefinite period will be avoided, and the endless evils thence ensuing be prevented. But it cannot be, that such facts as the actual misery of the world, with the abundant means to remove and in future prevent its recurrence, should be so glaring to the public, and not be strongly felt by the governing party, and all who have influence in society. Should this blindness really exist, then it is evident, that all existing governments are doomed to contend with difficulties, which must ultimately overcome and overwhelm them in anarchy, war, and ruin.

Let the governments of the world enter fairly on the investigation of the principles and the consequent practices of the existing system of society, and examine the foundation on which it rests, and then ask themselves the single and simple and yet now most necessary question, 'Is this system, in its principles or practices, now or in future, calculated for the interest, well-being, and happiness of the human race, either for the governors or governed?'

The reply must be No! on the contrary, it is admirably calculated to keep the population of the world in ignorance, the masses in poverty or the perpetual

[a] See for example Exodus 8:6.

fear of it; to establish falsehood and hypocrisy, to instigate to all manner of crime; to pervert the natural propensities and superior qualities of humanity into violent and degrading passions, and to make men and women into irrational contending and fighting animals, when, under another system, based on well ascertained laws of nature, they may be trained from birth to become superior rational beings, living in peace and harmony with all their fellows, with the inclination and power by their well-directed industry to make the earth a terrestrial paradise.

It is, therefore, not the interest of any one government in the world to maintain the present order or organization of society. In fact, it is not the interest of one individual upon the earth to continue the present chaotic, random, confused and mystified state of existence called human society. It might more truly be termed, a state of human contest about irrational objects; when far superior may be abundantly obtained without contest and in perfect peace and harmony.

How desirable it is that the faculties of the governors of the world should be now opened to the light of common sense, and cultivated to enable them to understand the great and permanent interests of humanity; that they could be induced now to perceive the path, the only path to happiness for themselves, their offspring, and the population of the world, and to pursue it ardently and perseveringly, without ceasing, until this pandemonium, which now extends into and over every quarter and lesser district of the earth, should be, as it now easily might be made to be, a delightful abode for rational beings, whose knowledge and happiness would everlastingly increase through every succeeding generation.

Could the governments of the world be now made to understand the revolution in rapid progress in public opinion against the present unjust, oppressive, and cruel system of governing society, and forming the character of men and women in all countries, they would not continue to govern as they do in any of those nations deemed the most powerful and advanced in modern civilization. No! they would hasten to acquire a correct and comprehensive knowledge of human nature and of society, and to govern in undeviating accordance with the science of each; sciences drawn from facts which have remained unchanged since man's knowledge of the history of his race commenced.

Could they be made to perceive that individual man cannot make his own organization; that he cannot make himself to believe to disbelieve, to feel or not to feel love or hatred, pleasure or pain; that society is a beautiful and simple science, when once understood, of four elements, now easily be combined, every where, in their due proportions to produce knowledge, health, wealth, unity and happiness, in great perfection; they would no longer attempt to coerce the population of the world to believe falsehoods and to act contests and destructions to continue the present chaos of insanity and misery which, through their errors of governing, they now inflict upon the whole race of man. How easily, with the transmitted powers now possessed by these governments, were they united for good instead of evil, could the entire change from all that is erroneous in principle and injurious in practice, be made, to all that is eternally true, uniformly consistent, and most beneficial in practice? And what a mass of suffering would this change prevent, and how much happiness would it ensure to the present generation, and how much more to all future generations?

Surely when these truths shall be placed before them, with a desire for their safety and future happiness; when they hear on all sides around them the cries of misery and the consequent louder and louder cries for change to relieve them from those miseries; they will not hesitate to adopt the right course, and save the effusion of human blood, of anarchy, and ruin to themselves and families. For ruin to themselves and families must ensue; nature is against the continuance of the present irrational system; and they who oppose nature, who never gives up the contest, must sooner or later be defeated. Let the existing governments then not persevere in gross errors until force shall compel them to desist.

CHAPTER III

'That this change will root up and utterly destroy the old vicious and miserable system of ignorance, poverty, individual competition and contest, and of national wars of opposition throughout the world; and will introduce, in place thereof, the Rational System of society, in which strife and wars will cease for ever, and all will be trained, from infancy, solely to promote each other's happiness.'

Is it indeed true that a change can be made in human affairs, competent to 'root up and utterly destroy the old vicious and miserable system of ignorance, poverty, individual competition, and contests, and of national wars and opposition throughout the world?'

Yes, it is most true, and may be easily accomplished by the governments and people of the world, if they will turn their attention to the investigation of plain, simple, and unchanging facts, and from these facts form a science of society in the same manner that, by carefully observing other facts, the population of the civilized world has been enabled to form so many other valuable sciences, so as to acquire fixed and unchanging knowledge upon astronomy, geology, chemistry, mechanism, etc, etc, which may now be applied to produce the most beneficial results throughout society. The facts have been discovered which may be now formed into a fixed science, to give to every one, from birth, such knowledge as shall prevent any one growing up in ignorance, or with a mind otherwise than filled with useful and valuable facts or eternal truths, so connected and arranged, as to form a consistent association of ideas that will constitute a rational well-informed being; rational and well-informed to the extent that the natural qualities or faculties of the organization of the individual will admit, when placed under the most favourable circumstances from birth.

As soon as men can be made a little rational in the general outline of their minds, they will discover, that it will be for the highest and permanent interest of each one, that *all* should now be thus placed and educated; that the science of forming a rational and superior character for *all*, should, in the shortest time, be made universal. Ignorance, of the most lamentable character, respecting man and society, at this hour, pervades all nations. This gross ignorance has been, and is, the bane of the world, the curse of humanity, the evil spirit which continually seeks whom it may render wretched and miserable, and which instigates to destroy the first approaches to happiness among the nations of the earth. There is not a human being who is not now grievously injured by the continuance of this foul enemy to man; it blights the effects of the most promising discoveries for man's happiness, and turns them to the production of misery. It is an unmixed evil to all, the fatal effects of which are, at this day, experienced to a great extent by every one over the earth.

The sufferings which it continually creates, and the happiness which it prevents, are far beyond all human calculation or conception; it permeates into all districts, among all families, and is the real cause of torment to every individual. It is the sole foundation of all falsehood and hypocrisy, and while falsehood and hypocrisy shall be thus, through ignorance taught to man, there will be neither virtue nor happiness known among the human race.

And yet this hydra of evil, father of lies, and tormentor of man, may now be most easily destroyed root and branch, and the earth be for ever freed from the endless miseries which it has hitherto perpetuated.

All that is required is, that the governing powers of society should adopt efficient arrangements that every infant born under their influence should be well trained and educated from birth, physically, mentally, morally, and practically, and taught to acquire a knowledge of the most valuable *facts* now known throughout society, without any of the mystifying superstitions, creeds, or dogmas of the present ignorant world, and to give this training, education, and knowledge to each and all, under every government. This conduct would be, by far, the most economical, and the wisest mode of governing man and the world. Look now, what, under a combination of very irrational circumstances, is effected in the most liberal and best conducted infant schools, as a proof of the ductility of infant human nature to receive impressions good, bad, or indifferent, wise or foolish, true or false, and then say, if truth, and the most valuable useful knowledge for practice, could not, by yet a much superior arrangement of external circumstances, be impressed upon and made the habit of all?

To instil the layers of knowledge according to the natural growth of intellect, layer upon layer, in due order, to build up a sound, consistent, and rational mind, together with superior habits, manners, and conduct, and to infuse a universal spirit of charity and kindness, necessarily emanating from that superior knowledge, would now be an easy and most delightful task, if man's ignorance of himself and of humanity were once effectually removed, and proper measures were adopted to instruct all in the sciences of human nature and of society. Let, then, the concentrated powers of those who have a disinterested love of their race, and who, as far as is practicable, desire to render happy all that has life, be directed to remove ignorance from the world, and to give real knowledge to every individual in it. It is knowledge alone that can make the population of the world healthy, intelligent, good, wealthy and happy; and knowledge can ensure these results, after a certain period, to *all*. Who then can be now benefited by the longer maintenance of ignorance over the mind of our fellow being? Not one in reality. Yet those trained and placed to become most ignorantly selfish, will, for sometime, contend for the continuance of ignorance in what they call the lower classes. These blind and most ignorant selfish advocates for the continuance of ignorance in some classes, that they may keep them their slaves and prey upon their industry and rights, are called the higher class, and members of professions, who now are supported by the ignorance of their fellows, to be their tormentors, and the destroyers of their happiness.

This upper class, and these members of the military and civil professions, are, however, far from obtaining any thing approaching to a superior state of permanent happiness, through their ignorant injustice over their more ignorant and most grievously oppressed fellow mortals.

It is from a knowledge that ignorance inflicts misery on *all*, whatever may be their station, profession, or calling, and that the removal of it from the population of the world would add, most essentially, to the happiness of men and women of all ages and degrees, in all countries, that its entire abrogation from society is now desired and so strongly recommended.

The destruction of this monster-ignorance, will prove the precursor of all that will be permanently beneficial to future generations to the end of time. The hitherto all-powerful enemy to the introduction of the most useful knowledge, and the great ally of ignorance, has been the mentally deranging influence of the various superstitions which have deluged the earth with their conflicting insane creeds, dogmas, and doctrines, all so well calculated to make and keep man an irrational and contending animal.

But this hitherto all-powerful influence for evil has at length received its death-blow, by an accumulation of the knowledge of unchanging facts, which demonstrate that these superstitions are, one and all, the mere emanations of disordered imaginations, introduced when man was under the dominion of inexperienced imagination, and before he knew how to observe unerring and unchanging facts, and to draw accurate, and therefore just, conclusions from them.

But now these facts are so multiplied, and all consistent one with another throughout our terrestrial globe, that when viewed and considered as a whole, forming undoubted laws of nature or *divine* laws, those who can thus contemplate them, have their eyes opened; they perceive the folly of their ancestors, in always sacrificing the substance of knowledge and happiness to mere words, or the empty shadow of both; and they strongly feel the necessity of putting an end to this wretchedly insane state of human existence, by terminating the reign of these superstitions, and of all ignorance, as far as facts will enable them to effect both.

Ignorance being the primary and remote cause of error and of almost all human evils, every thing that man can accomplish to remove it from humanity should be now done. It comes into the world at the birth of every infant; and substantive arrangements should be formed in every country to supply each infant from birth with real knowledge, as he advances in age and acquires mental and physical vigour. Let this original sin of humanity be thus attacked and carefully watched from the hour of birth of each, and the progressive improvement and happiness of society will be secured through all future generations.

But as the mind of each infant at birth is ignorant of itself, and of all things around him out of himself, the greatest care becomes necessary not to allow error of any kind to enter. But error has already entered most largely into the minds and habits of the existing adults over the earth, and none can be found without great error; and the difficulty of excluding all error, as the old instruct the young, will be, at least for one generation, almost insurmountable, yet to make man an intelligent, good and happy being, this task must be entered upon, and persevered in until all errors shall be abandoned by the inhabitants of every part of the world. And this result may be now obtained in a shorter period than the men of the present generation imagine to be practicable.

The immediate cause of human error has been discovered; the means of removing the cause are perceived; it is the interest of all that the cause should be removed with the least delay. All that will be required is to adopt measures to make this knowledge, now known only to a few, universal; and the means of extending valuable knowledge over the world have latterly been wondrously increased, and are daily increasing. The labours of the Bible Society, intended for a very different purpose, by forcing comparisons with other scriptures, will hasten and aid materially in shaking to their foundations all the present superstitions of the world, with their opposing mysteries, creeds, dogmas, and doctrines. No measure could more surely break up this darkness, so long forced on the human mind, than the adoption of means to induce parties to compare these superstitions one with another; and the publication of the Old and New Testament of the Christians, through the wealth and superstition of the pious throughout Great Britain and other christian countries, will aid to effect this object in a manner which may be considered as a modern miracle. This result was foreseen by some at the commencement of this Society. The cause which has so long implanted ignorance at the foundation of the human mind, has been the origin of all the superstitions which have deranged the human faculties and tormented the human race through every period of its known history.

This cause, then, being removed, the endless errors producing misery will also speedily disappear, as well as the misery itself; for it is error alone with very trifling exceptions, which has produced, and which now produces, the misery suffered by man.

All are, then, deeply interested that the cause of error should be withdrawn from the inhabitants of the earth, as early as means can be devised for this purpose.

It has been stated, that ignorance arises from each infant being born without any knowledge of itself or any external object, and that the foundation of the endless errors which have hitherto afflicted the human race, has been the imaginary notions, contrary to every known fact, that each one has the power to form himself to be good or bad, to believe or disbelieve, to like or dislike, or love or hate, at his pleasure, and the errors thence ensuing – of forming superstitions, laws, governments, and institutions, and all human affairs upon these erroneous and unreal suppositions.

The intellects of man, and, in consequence, all human affairs, have been in a state of continual derangement; so much so, that all being compelled by their nature to desire to be happy, every expedient that insane cunning could devise to torment mankind has been adopted and tried in practice; and now, the human race appears, with greatly increased attainments to ensure human happiness, to experience more misery, during universal peace, than has been suffered by the nations of the earth during periods of almost universal war.

These painful results are the means which nature creates to force men to reflect, and to trace effects to their ultimate causes, that the sufferings may be removed and pleasure enjoyed. Let the greatest exertions, then, be used by all, to remove error from the human mind, which, when effected, will soon make itself evident in the improved spirit and conduct of all.

The suffering from ignorance is universal; it is the cause of poverty, which is, perhaps, with the fear of it, the next most general evil which afflicts man in all parts of the globe. While poverty shall be experienced or dreaded, man cannot enjoy anything approaching to permanent happiness; yet, the true object of all society is, to discover and adopt the means that will ensure this happiness.

Poverty being an universal evil, and the dread of it being almost equal to actual poverty in the mental suffering which it produces, the remedy should be universal. And now it easily might be made so.

The general contest of the world is to obtain riches and to avoid poverty, and to ensure so much individual wealth as to exclude the fear of poverty. This object occupies the greater portion of the thoughts, time, and capital of the population of the world.

But, as has been stated, the new means obtained from the progress of science within the last century, have given to man the power of creating wealth beyond his wants to an illimitable extent; poverty, or the fear of it might, therefore, now be made not to exist among any portion of the human race, in any part of the world.

No one circumstance can prove the general ignorance, or rather irrationality, of the human race, more than the fact that there is so much fear of want, so much suffering from actual destitution, so much contest about wealth, and so many crimes committed to obtain it, and so much expense incurred and punishments inflicted to prevent what are called crimes against property. Imprisonment and transportation, on this account, are, in Great Britain, in many respects the most advanced of nations, common occurrences.

And yet, without slavery or servitude, property might easily be made as superfluous beyond human wants as water, and every anxiety respecting it might be removed for ever from the human race.

The present English poor laws, with their union workhouses, spare and inferior diet, separation of the sexes, and treatment of females respecting illegitimate children,[a] prove how little British senators yet know of human nature, nature's laws, the science of society, or how to conduct public affairs, or to govern with the first degrees of knowledge requisite for the purpose. Even now, all the essential interests of the human race, to produce national permanent prosperity and happiness for all, are by them utterly neglected; while they waste their time, and the capital of the country, in vain babblings about the means to perpetuate ignorance, injustice, and gross oppression.

How much real permanent good might they now effect for the human race in a short period, while session after session of their sittings is most ignorantly misapplied, in various ways, to attempt the perpetual subjugation of the mental faculties of the mass of the people, and to keep them ever as slaves to their passions, injustice, and oppressions?

What different beings would the members of the British Parliament become, were they occupied in the direct enquiry how the enormous powers, now at the

[a] Under the Poor Law Amendment Act of 1834, husbands and wives receiving relief in workhouses were to be separated. (This was widely ignored by local authorities.) Women bearing children out of wedlock were liable to be removed from relief (at least to their native parish) if they were deemed to be a likely long-term burden on the parish.

control of society, to produce wealth for all, and a superior character for all, could be the most speedily and advantageously applied!

Here is a nation, under a system of individual contest and competition, inflicting all manner of evil upon each other in support of these contests and competition to obtain private and public wealth, which, by an ignorant and vulgar scramble for it, is limited to the amount, among the whole population of Great Britain and Ireland, of not more than the value, at present prices, of about five hundred millions of new wealth created annually, upon which the inhabitants of these islands now live; and some in addition, accumulate surplus wealth, by industry or economy, or by great public swindling, or by committing great crimes too powerful for the laws to reach; laws made to entangle the poor and ignorant.

And yet all this contest, injustice, and oppression, take place in the scramble for this small national amount of wealth; when, by a wise, quiet, peaceable, and just direction of the mechanical, chemical, mental, and manual powers at the control of the government, four, five, or six, and many more times that wealth could be annually produced, with health, comfort, and pleasure to all parties.

The creation of wealth, under rational or common sense arrangements, may now be made a perpetual source of health, pleasant occupation, and high enjoyment to all of all ages throughout life; and thus may individual contests, competition, and national wars, throughout the world, be made to cease for ever.

But this change can be effected only by the introduction of the Rational System of society in the whole extent of its principles and practices.

It is in vain to expect that the principles and practices of the present irrational system for forming the human character, and governing the affairs of the world, can ever be combined with the principles and practices of the Rational System of society, so as to make them unite and work harmoniously together.

When the fundamental principles of the two systems are known and fully comprehended, and compared together as to the consequences necessarily proceeding from each, it will be at once perceived that the two systems are in direct opposition to each other, that they never can be made to amalgamate, and that society must, after such comparison, decide to have the one system entire or the other. And as one has produced all manner of error and evil, so as to create a pandemonium of falsehood and hypocrisy, of force, fraud, and all kinds of injustice and oppressions; and the other, when fully and fairly introduced, must of necessity dispel all these evils, and terminate strife, wars, and contests, private and national, and perpetuate happiness for all of the race of man, there can be no doubt which of the two systems will be adopted and permanently preferred, as soon as the great public of the world can have their minds opened and enlarged, so as to enable them to understand the Rational System in its principles, and their consequences in practice.

When this system shall be adopted and generally introduced into practice, as it now soon must be, all will be trained from infancy solely to promote each other's happiness.

Instead of the human faculties being so generally occupied in measures to accumulate individual wealth, the great business of the world will be to devise means to increase the *happiness of all;* and no beings will appear more opposed in mind, spirit, countenance, and conduct, than those trained to desire and to practise the means to accumulate individual riches, and those who have been formed to desire, and to be actively engaged in daily measures to promote the happiness of all.

The former will have the inferior faculties of human nature cultivated at the expense of the superior, and this will be strongly evinced in their mind, spirit, countenance, and conduct; while the latter will have all the faculties of their nature duly cultivated and exercised to produce happiness, and this will be equally indicated in the mind, spirit, countenance, and conduct of the individual.

CHAPTER IV

'That this system can be best commenced by convincing governments of the truth of the principles on which it is founded. There must also be a sufficient number of individuals imbued with the spirit of genuine charity, affection, and philanthropy, and instructed in the best mode of applying it to practice. They must likewise possess patience and perseverance, to overcome all the obstacles which prejudice will oppose to their progress; and, above all, they must be united, have full confidence in each other, and be directed by one heart and one mind.'

To change the system of the world from all that is most erroneous in principle and injurious in practice, requires a proceeding little understood by those who have been educated to have their characters formed upon those erroneous principles, and in the daily habit of those injurious practices.

These principles and practices have deranged the rational faculties of *all*, and introduced disorder and counteraction to happiness, in all the affairs of life.

All, therefore, have been trained and placed, from their birth, under circumstances opposed to their own happiness, and to the well-being, prosperity, and happiness of all their fellow-men. *All* having been thus placed, it may well be asked, How, then, can a change from all that is wrong in principle and pernicious in practice, be expected, when all, from their birth, have been made to become, through error, most irrational in mind and conduct?

It is evident that this total change in the mind, spirit, and conduct of men, and of all private and public affairs among individuals and societies, whether more or less numerous, cannot be effected by any ordinary minds or proceedings.

The ascertaining that the world has been based on error, that, in consequence, all have been made, through past generations, to become irrational in mind and conduct, is itself a new discovery of more magnitude than all previous discoveries made by the human race.

It is a law of nature, that that which is new and different to established institutions and previous habits, shall be, at first, opposed, and opposed with virulence and violence in proportion to its newness, and to the prejudices or ignorance of the parties to whom the discovery is stated, until they can be taught to comprehend it.

The discovery of the causes of human error and misery, is a discovery the most opposed, of all discoveries, to the oldest and deepest established prejudices in the human mind, and may, therefore, be naturally expected to be the most virulently and violently opposed by all of the human race, but especially by those trained to become the most superstitious, and who, by being placed in the most unfavourable circumstances, have been made the most ignorant, and are, therefore, the least acquainted with general facts, or how to deduce accurate conclusions from them.

The combination of faculties and circumstances necessary to make the discovery that the population of the world has been in error respecting man and society from the beginning, and to discover the means to remove that error, was also made to be conscious of the extent of the obstacles, a rising from the prejudices of ignorance, that might be anticipated to be opposed to a change that would require the minds of men to be born again to comprehend it, and the entire organization of society to be reconstructed from its base through all its ramifications. And these obstacles were then duly appreciated and more than anticipated. These obstacles, and this opposition, have never yet equalled those which were expected and prepared for, before one sentence, upon this most exciting of all subjects, was given forth to the world, to meet and sustain its attacks.

The denouncer of the principles and practices of the world, of its mental ignorance and superstitions; of its consequent ignorant and immoral practices; of its erroneous organization and classification; and of its gross irrational mental and physical proceedings throughout all the ramifications of society; could not, of course, be otherwise, in the estimation of an irrational-made population, than mad, and a very bad man; so bad, according to the published estimated calculation of one reverend person, as to be 'Fifty thousand millions of times worse than the devil.'

The natural faculties and combination of external circumstances acting upon those faculties from birth, which elicited the discovery of the errors of the old, and truths to form a new, mind of man, and to prepare a new world for that new mind, also made it evident, that the truths were unchanging laws of nature, and therefore unassailable, with success, when fairly and fully examined; and that their introduction into general practice throughout the population of the world, would be of incalculable permanent benefit to every child of man through all coming generations.

That, therefore, the principles being eternally true, and the practices, thence ensuing, being permanently beneficial to all of human kind, if measures were adopted to bring forward these principles and practices before the contending and opposing superstitions and malpractices of mankind, to place them in a simple form before the public mind; to advocate them with firmness and boldness, yet in the spirit of charity, kindness, and forbearance, naturally emanating from these eternal truths of nature, and to continue these proceedings with patience and perseverance which should know no limits, there would be a *chance*, a *hope*, a *prospect*, nay a *certainty*, that, in the end, truth would overcome error; and that the malpractices of the old ignorant immoral world would, gradually, give place to new arrangements, purposely devised to secure the well-being and happiness, through a comparatively long life, of every individual, through all future generations.

It is not by opposing governments with violence, or with wordy abuse, that this change, from the false to the true in human existence, can be effected. The change advocated is one beneficial for the human race, or it is not. If it be beneficial, then it will be their interest that it should be made; men are formed to attend to and adopt that which is for their interest when they know it. This change will be most advantageous for all of human kind. This knowledge they cannot acquire of themselves, and therefore they cannot act upon it. Those who have discovered it, have to instruct those who know it not; and all have been prejudiced from their birth against it. That prejudice has to be overcome. But the best mode to overcome prejudice is not by violence or abuse.

Knowledge, charity, kindness, and affection are the powers given by nature to overcome prejudices; and these powers, wisely applied, will overcome prejudices the most deeply rooted, and of the longest duration, when truth alone shall be advocated.

These are the true weapons with which to assail the prejudices of the present ruling influences throughout the world. Let these qualities be evident in the advocates of truth; let no error be mixed with these truths, and by patience and perseverance all the errors of the old world must fall before them.

When governments can be made to understand the fact, that other principles of governing society than those hitherto known and practised, will be far more beneficial to the governors and their children and connexions, there will be no great difficulty in inducing them to assist to effect the change, when the mode of effecting it shall be made plain and easy and not injurious to them. And knowledge, charity, kindness, and affection, united, will be enabled to accomplish this result.

None will willingly act contrary to their supposed happiness; or interest, which is in fact the same. Nor should they be forced to do so. It is a law of nature for each living being to desire to be happy; and these beings will always contend, according to their knowledge, strength, or power, to accomplish this object. Governments have the power at their control, to secure, as they suppose, to the parties governing, as much happiness as they can attain in this world. While this impression remains upon the minds of governors, they will tenaciously use their power to maintain their authority; and while the impression on their mind is allowed to continue, it is wise in them so to act.

Governments are now assailed in the most ignorant manner, by those who are opposed to them. It is not by a unity of knowledge, charity, kindness, and affection, applied to convince the parties that by other principles than those practised, their happiness and the happiness of the public would be permanently greatly increased, and by giving the reasons to demonstrate this result; but, on the contrary, some faction with very limited knowledge, and less charity, kindness, and affection, adopt the most hostile civil, if not military, measures to overpower the existing parties who govern; and if they succeed, continue the same principles of governing by force and fraud; adopting some slight change only in the mode of applying the principles. And thus is society kept, over the world, in a constant state of ignorance, turmoil and suffering from one generation to another, without apparent benefit from all the useful discoveries which experience produces; governors and governed remaining in the most irrational state; and all in a most miserable and pitiable condition. The parties who desire to change the present irrational system of society, for the Rational System, will not so act; but will adopt the only rational course to effect an object of so great magnitude, and of such vital importance to the human race.

The change from the one system to the other is essentially to benefit all of every clime and colour, and to introduce knowledge, peace, and happiness, to all the inhabitants of the earth; to the governing powers as well as to the governed.

The first rational step towards effecting this change, which is to reorganize society, and recreate the human-made part of the character of man, is to convince the governing powers of nations, as well as the governed, of the unchanging truth of the principles, and of their inestimable value when wisely applied to practice. Without this base, on which to raise the superstructure, there can be no solid foundation for success; but once convince the governors and governed of the truth of the principles, and the incalculable benefits to be derived from their universal adoption in practice, and a great difficulty will be overcome. When this task shall have been accomplished, another most formidable difficulty is to be met and conquered.

The mode by which the change is to be effected, from the false principles to the true, from the injurious practices emanating from the false principles, to the superior practices which will proceed from the true principles, must be made plain, easy, and beneficial for the governed and the governors. And this task, formidable as it may at first appear, must be accomplished, if the change is to be effected in peace, with order, wisdom, and foresight, and advantageously for the human race. Each step of this change in practice, without prematurely disturbing the existing state of society, must be made evident to the governors and governed.

The parties who desire to produce this change from all that is erroneous and injurious in principle and practice to all of human kind, for all that is true and most beneficial in principle and practice, must, without petty personal considerations, patiently persevere in this righteous course, until this great and glorious result shall be secured for ever for the race of man.

This is the course which wisdom dictates, by which the Rational System of society can be alone rationally introduced to the population of the world, and motives can be created in the present governors and governed, to induce them to listen to, and to endeavour to learn, these words of truth and this practice of happiness, and willingly to consent that the change shall be made, to ensure the well-doing and the well-being of all future generations.

Let then factions and all violent hostilities to governments cease, and let all endeavour to acquire knowledge, charity, kindness, and affection, and with these qualities patiently persevere in the instruction of the governments, until they shall discover the necessity for, the advantage of, and the wisdom in, making the change from the present to the full Rational System, in the shortest time practicable.

But other measures may be adopted materially to facilitate this change, by parties who now severely suffer from the existing irrational system; or who, if not now suffering thus severely, have the prospect sooner or later of doing so: but indeed, under this system, all from the highest to the lowest suffer more or less of varied evils.

There are, however, those who now suffer grievously from the effects of ignorance, poverty, and division; many from actually experiencing these evils in their own persons, and many from witnessing them in others without having the power to afford them any permanently effectual relief.

To put an end to this most ignorant and vulgar state of suffering, measures may be immediately adopted, by those who have capital, with hearts and minds to employ it most usefully, profitably to effect the greatest good to their suffering fellow men.

These vulgar sufferings arise immediately from the want of an education in accordance with the laws of human nature, of employment wisely directed, and of the creation of those external circumstances which would admit of such education and employment.

It is most useless to waste more time in finding fault with any part of the present sectional state of things, when the system itself is erroneous in principle, and through all its ramifications in practice. There is no difficulty in finding fault with particulars, when all is contrary to what it should be, for the well-being and happiness of the race. The only useful practice is to *adopt measures* that will effectually aid to exhibit to the eyes of men and women what is right, and how they may, by their own mental and physical exertion, relieve themselves, almost immediately, from the more common and vulgar sufferings arising from ignorance, poverty, and division.

The rulers of the world have been taught that the most easy mode to govern, under the false system in which all are placed from birth, is by the division of the governed into classes, sects, and parties, and by keeping up the opposition in interest and feeling between them, to retain all in their power by a nice balancing of parties.

Thus are the upper, middle, and lower classes separated and opposed to each other, by education, feeling, and apparent interest, forming by their compound the present irrational and insane system of society. Irrational and insane, because all, unperceived by themselves, are opposed by it to their own happiness, while society enormously superabounds with all the materials necessary to ensure a state of happiness for ALL, very superior to that which *any* can attain under the pandemonia system which alone has hitherto prevailed over the earth.

Now there are useful, necessary, and advantageous qualities of character in each of the three general divisions of society as it exists; and there are also great defects in each. That which is required, is to unite in the character of each individual, the superior qualities of each class, and to avoid forming any of the inferior qualities of any class, in the character of any individual.

Those who the most immediately suffer severely from ignorance, poverty, and division, are the most industrious among the lower and middle classes. These are, therefore, the most immediately interested to have a change of the system effected. Cordially united, they could speedily introduce the change, and by its universal superiority over the present, in all that is essential to the unity, excellence, and happiness of the human race, they could exhibit these advantages to the eye, and thence, through the understanding of all who witnessed these results in practice, the public would adopt the change more eagerly than they adopted that from the old gravelled roads, to the new railway system of travelling; the difference in the benefits between the change from the one system of society to the other being far greater – greater beyond all comparison – than that between the worst of the old roads and the most improved of the railways.

But the middle and lower classes have been, by their false education and unfavourable position, made very generally too blind to discover their own defects, and too ignorant to perceive how to apply their respective advantages to effect the change in themselves for ignorance, poverty, and division, to knowledge, charity, kindness, and affection, – or, in fact, from the misery which they now suffer, to the happiness which they might enjoy permanently during their lives.

The middle and lower class united could easily effect the change, as soon as they acquired a knowledge how to commence and proceed with it; for between them they possess all the essential useful qualities to form a rational state of society. The middle class to direct, the lower class to follow their directions in a unity of design, from its commencement through all its ramifications.

To unite these two classes, cordially, in this new measure, is the task to be performed, to immediately exhibit to the world the practical means by which ignorance, poverty and disunion, are to be exchanged for knowledge, charity, kindness, and affection.

It is ignorance alone which keeps them separate; the greater ignorance, of course, is in the lowest class, although there are some of the most superior of the working class better informed than are some of the inferior sections in the lower divisions of the middle class, and especially among the inferior retail traders.

Whatever is, must be taken as it is, and made the most of. To commence this change the most advantageously, there should be a choice selection made from the middle and working classes, in due proportion for the business to be performed and the work to be executed. They should be instructed in a knowledge of the principles of the system to be carried into execution, and they should be well taught now, upon all occasions, and under all circumstances, to apply those principles consistently to their every-day practice.

A sufficient number of such selected individuals, so taught and trained, united upon these principles, and determined to apply them faithfully to practice, could be now made easily to be emancipated from ignorance, poverty, and division, and soon be made, not only to acquire knowledge, charity, kindness, and affection for themselves, but, by their enjoyment of superior happiness, to force all the nations of the earth to imitate their example. To effect this union, the members thus uniting of the middle class must acquire patience and charity of the lower class, and adopt the best practical arrangements gradually to change them into the new character required. And the lowest class must submit to be taught how to overcome their ignorance, vulgarity, and most disgusting assumptions, as soon as they are taught to acquire a very little more knowledge than it is customary for their class to possess, and thus commence their future progress towards the attainment of the extent of improvement in habits, manners, spirit, and conduct, which can alone make them desirable associates and companions for those now their superiors in these respects.

Ordinary minds and habits are very unsuitable for the commencement of measures so important to the future well-being and happiness of the human race; but were the commencement fairly made, and the example of one full association, based on the principles of nature, in practice before the public, the advantages would be so far beyond the present state of human existence, that all would rapidly follow it, and the entire change of the system of society would be effected peaceably, and without disorder among all people and nations.

But, as many little petty obstacles and obstructions may be expected to arise from the defects of the old system, more or less annoying the progress of the new, the parties commencing this new state should be prepared to expect, to encounter, and to overcome them, by illimitable patience and perseverance.

The system which they unite to introduce, should be fully understood by them, and they should make up their minds, honestly and faithfully, to apply the principles to practice; and, with patience and perseverance, there could be no doubt of complete success, provided they were united, had full confidence in each other, and were directed, in all their proceedings, by one heart and mind.

All these qualifications are essentially necessary to speedy and straightforward success.

Without patience and perseverance to overcome prejudice and all obstacles opposed to their progress – without full confidence in each other – without unity of feeling, of design, and operations – and without the parties being directed by one mind, having the interest of the system paramount to all other considerations, and the well-being and substantial comfort of all at heart, the progress will be of necessity slow and uncertain; but with these, rugged and unpromising as the path may appear, it will soon become smooth and most delightful to pursue; until success will crown the efforts of these pioneers in the greatest attempt, for the good of the human race, ever yet made by man.

This unity of purpose, in mind, spirit, heart, and practice, is essential to the success of a first experiment, if it is to proceed as rapidly as the present sufferings of society require; and all have an interest that these sufferings should not terminate at the earliest period practicable. Great care should be therefore taken in the selection of the parties who are to be the pioneers in this great work. There should not be one counteracting mind in the whole party, nor one unimbued with a knowledge of the principles, or without a fixed determination to apply the principles, on all occasions, to practice. It is true, that with principles and practices so directly opposed to the prejudices forced from birth into the mind and habits of the human race, there will be, at first, a difficulty in obtaining such selection, and more especially by reason of the gross falsehoods published by the designing opponents of the system, to procure those from the superior middle and upper classes, who so much dislike to lose caste, and to descend to be associated with the general ignorance, inferior habits, and narrow-mindedness of the lower class.

But these difficulties, to whatever extent they may arise, must be fairly met, and by patience, perseverance, and charitable and kind conduct, overcome.

The object to be gained is the eternal happiness of the race of man, from the period when the Rational System shall be spread and established over the earth; and it requires only to be made known, in its entirety of principle and practice, to supersede the present irrational system, by which the world has been so long governed, kept in an inferior state, and made miserable.

It is ignorance, and the petty selfishness produced by ignorance, that can alone give any lengthened existence to the system of error by which the character of all individuals is now formed, and the nations of the earth are governed. Let every measure be, therefore, now adopted to dispel ignorance and falsehood, and introduce knowledge and truth.

CONCLUDING REMARK

'Under the past and present irrational system of society – devised in opposition to experienced nature – nineteen out of twenty, or perhaps, more truly, ninety-nine out of one hundred of the external circumstances formed by man around society, are of an inferior and vicious character: but under the Rational System of society now proposed, which is formed in accordance with experienced nature, all the circumstances under human control will be of a superior and virtuous character.'

In one sense, every thing, past, present, and future, may be said to be emanations from nature, because all things exist only through and by nature. Ignorance and knowledge, vice and virtue, falsehood and truth, violence, contests, robbery, bloodshed, and murder, along with forbearance, charity, kindness and affection, folly and wisdom, good and evil, misery and happiness, have proceeded and must proceed, alone, from the powers of nature as they grow, or advance just in proportion as nature gives experience to man.

Ignorance, vice, falsehood, violence, contests, robbery, bloodshed, murder, folly, evil, and misery, proceed direct from nature inexperienced in man; while knowledge, virtue, truth, forbearance, charity, kindness, affection, wisdom, goodness, and happiness, proceed direct from nature by slow but extended experience in man.

The want of knowledge or experience in man produced the past and present irrational system of human society, with all its accessary miseries; the increase of knowledge, or experience acquired through the past ages of human existence, has produced the dawn, and will produce the meridian of the Rational System, with its never-ending but always increasing happiness. Experience, then, is nature's great teacher of mankind. And there is no demerit for what experience has withheld, nor merit for what it now gives to individuals or nations. All things that exist in their present state, are the necessary or unavoidable consequences of nature's, to man unknown, operations.

We say, nature; but it is only a word used to express the cause of all consequences or effects; a cause utterly incomprehensible to man, and respecting which, experience declares, by all past events in human history, that it is folly and madness for men to dispute, or in any manner to excite unpleasant feelings between them.

Suffice it now to say, that the past has been grossly irrational, and that experience has supplied facts and knowledge to enable man to apply the wisdom thus acquired to create a reasonable prospect that a speedy rational future is before us.

The irrationality, arising from past inexperience, has created the inferior and injurious past and existing circumstances of man's formation. These evils to humanity, experience now commands to be made to cease as speedily as they can be superseded by a new class of circumstances, superior and beneficial for the race.

It is the deficiency of experience only, of these who rule society, which prevents this change being made immediately over the earth. It is the interest of all, and for the happiness of all, that external circumstances, superior for use and beauty, should alone be now created to surround all from their birth to death, and as man is the creature of circumstances, he will become in the same proportion as these are improved, superior and beautiful. In every point of view, it is most desirable, that the human race should abandon the practice of permitting any inferior circumstances to exist, which, by the union of human efforts, can be removed and replaced by superior. And the new powers latterly acquired through the progress of scientific discoveries and inventions, have so multiplied the means of the human race to supersede the one by the other, that, with ease, all might soon be placed within far superior, and more beneficial and beautiful circumstances, than any have ever yet been, and to an extent, for the advantage and enjoyment of each, which none have ever yet experienced; which none have ever yet imagined to be within the possible powers of humanity to attain.

This is the great work which the world has now to perform, and for which purpose, wars must be made to cease, 'swords must be turned into ploughshares and spears into pruning hooks'[a] and man must be made to become rational from his birth, to be full of strength and activity, and filled with knowledge and true wisdom. And why should this change not now be effected? All the means requisite to accomplish it are in the greatest abundance, ready, as raw materials, within and upon the earth, waiting for the intelligent industry of man to

[a] See for example Isaiah 2:4.

manufacture and apply them, each to their best purpose. Railways and steam-boats will now rapidly convey them from where they are superabundant to supply those places in which they are deficient.

The present excited mind and wandering imaginations of the searchers after truth, must now be brought to anchor, and concentrated in practical measures, aided by the new tools of modern society, to effect this magnificent change for the world.

Why, now that these great physical, mental, and moral discoveries have been made, should individual man, with his individualized scanty powers, limited means, and petty local notions and ideas, all tending to low, grovelling, and individual results, longer be left to be thus miserably isolated, opposed to his fellows, and with his fellows opposed to him?

It is a state of madness; of rank insanity; in which all desire to be happy, but in which all are so placed as to be energetically active in measures to produce daily and hourly misery to all around.

This must not continue to be; humanity, male and female, possess by nature all the internal materials or pre-requisites for the attainment of superior happiness, without retrogression. These qualities require to be known in their varied variety, and to be so placed from the birth of each individual, that each one of these varied qualities shall have a right direction given to it through life. The means to effect this long-looked-for result are fast ripening for action and for universal application. Let none, therefore, longer continue to put obstacles in the way of this progress for universal good; but, on the contrary, let one and all exert every faculty given to them to remove whatever obstruction yet exists to the attainment of this advent for the human race. It is, simply, *to remove all the removeable inferior circumstances, and to supersede them with superior only, to the extent that human means will now or in future admit.*

What sect, or class, or party, in any country, can now, with a little plain instruction given in the spirit of charity, with kindness and forbearance, object to this change from all things inferior around themselves and their children, through all future generations, for those which shall be so greatly superior, as to ensure the permanent continually increasing prosperity and happiness of all?

Let those who acquire a knowledge of the principles of the Rational System of society be taught, also, how, in the spirit of forbearance, kindness, and charity, to apply those principles, consistently and efficiently, to practice; and the great and glorious change for the world – the emancipation of the human race from sin and misery – will be effected in a much shorter period than those trained and remaining in the errors of the old world can at present imagine, or believe to be possible.

This change will ensure to every child of man, from birth, by comparison with the present malformed character of the human race, a very superior physical, mental, moral, and practical cultivation of their natural faculties to attain these results.

And before it can be known what humanity is, all the faculties of human nature must be duly trained from birth, and, in the due order of nature, exercised, regularly, to the point of temperance for each faculty.

'Under the existing religious, political, commercial, and domestic arrangements of Great Britain, two hundred and fifty individuals cannot be supported in comfort on a square mile of land: while under the proposed system, with much less labour and capital than are now employed, five hundred may be immediately supported in abundance; and in a few years after the new arrangements shall have been matured, one thousand, fifteen hundred, and, probably, without any additional new discoveries to those already made, two thousand individuals may be also supported on every square mile of an average quality of soil.'

The religious, political, commercial, and domestic arrangements of all countries, are opposed to human progress and happiness, and are grossly irrational; but the arrangement of these divisions in the British Empire is the most irrational to be found over the earth; and, in consequence, with the most abundant means to ensure the greatest amount of happiness to all, these means are now so insanely applied, as to produce the greatest amount of misery to a great majority of its population. The religious arrangements of the British Empire, including Protestants, Catholics, Jews, Mahomedans, Hindoos, and Pagans, constitute an heterogeneous mass of as much opposition to facts, contradiction to each other, inconsistency, folly, and madness, as appears possible to be generated in the human brain and introduced into practice, without actually destroying the human race by the excess of violent contentions, robberies, massacres, and universal disorder.

These varied insanities of the early growth of the human brain, keeping it in a high state of fermentation, appear now to be subsiding and cooling down to a new condition approaching to rationality. The symptoms of this change, so long looked for by the most advanced minds in every generation, are many, and daily increasing in all parts of the world. These exciting changes in men's minds are the forerunners of that glorious and happy change which has been anticipated by what has been expected to arise in a state which has been attempted to be explained by the term millennium; but it will be a change of progressive improvement, and of increasing happiness, generation after generation, as long as man shall exist upon the earth. There will be no stay, much less retrogression, to the onward steady advance of this glorious and joyous existence. More joyous, by reason of constant progress, to which no limit can be assigned, except the attainment of the knowledge of the causes of all things and their consequences, and the means to regulate and control all things within the universe, if the term within can be rationally applied to that which can have no boundaries.

The various phases of insanity, called religion, in the British Empire, are requiring, daily, a greater waste of mental and physical power and capital than, if wisely applied, would ensure the permanent prosperity and happiness of every subject of that empire. This anything and everything which any insane-made individual chooses to call religion, not only destroys the rational faculties of all who are so unfortunate as to be placed under circumstances to acquire any one of its divisions, but it *prevents* the creation of new wealth to a greater amount, by far, than all the sums now expended in charities over the world. It professes to do every kind of good, while it does nothing but injury to the population, and is now, alone, *the* obstacle to the attainment of the highest excellence and happiness by a people who, from their present position over the globe, might speedily disperse knowledge, charity, and happiness in all directions, until every quarter of the earth should be filled with these virtues.

The causes which maintain these endless mental aberrations, must be removed, ere man can have any chance of becoming a rational being, or of doing otherwise than wasting the enormous powers for good now at his control. The easiest, the best, and most rational mode of doing away with this monster evil to man, is to make plain the absurdity upon which all these mental aberrations are founded, and to place before the public the gross absurdity of any man, or combination of men, pretending to know anything whatever of that Power which everywhere acts, to compose, decompose, and recompose, everlastingly, the materials of the universe; forming and destroying, without ceasing, all the varied, organized, animate and inanimate things, which exist throughout the universe; or to devise means to glorify a power so far beyond their comprehension, or to do any manner of good to that existence, by whatever name called, which pervades the universe; an existence, the qualities of which, or mode of action or rest, have not entered into the heart of man to conceive.

In fact, the religious mania of man ever has been, now is, and while it remains, will be, the curse of humanity. It will destroy all human rational faculties, continue to make the human race more vicious than the brute creation, and keep the earth, while possessing all the means to ensure human happiness, a pandemonium, to torment man and his offspring. And these evils will continue until the germs of what has been hitherto called religion, through all generations, in all parts of the world, shall be utterly abandoned, without a vestige remaining. And it must be evident now to all who reflect, that there can be nothing deserving the name of rational economy as long as what is now called religion shall be supported.

If the religious mania of the world be so injurious in preventing the creation of wealth, so wasteful of mind, and time, and so extravagant in worse than useless expenditure, how much better and wiser are the so-called political institutions of the world?

These, also, are said to be established to promote the happiness of the human race, and yet, next to the mania produced by the superstitions of the world, they have been, and are the second curse of man. They not only sanction, but foster and encourage this superstitious mania; and aid it to keep the mass of mind in the darkness of ignorance, or filled with errors, often much worse than mere ignorance. The enormous direct expenditure of the armies and warlike navies of the world, the waste of life and wealth of which they destroy, but the far greater amount of wealth of which they *prevent the creation*, are evils of such magnitude as the puny-formed minds of men, as they have yet been made, cannot comprehend. These are evils which greatly exceed the trained incapacity of the race to encompass. This subject, so large and ramified, yet unperceived, enters into every department of life.

The wealth thus *expended, wasted, destroyed,* and *prevented* being created, is a larger amount, than, if directly and wisely applied for the benefit of man, would be much more than abundant to supply all the wants of the human race, and to remove poverty, or the fear of it, for ever, from them.

But the useless and now easily preventable wars of the world are not the only senseless modes of wasting enormous wealth, and preventing an incalculable greater amount being created; for in addition to the same enormous waste and loss incurred by governmental support of the superstitions of the world, there is another source of incalculable waste and loss of the creation of wealth, in devising and supporting political laws, called civil and criminal.

As stated in former parts of this book, all the codes of laws, given hitherto by man from the beginning of human history, have been based in misconceptions respecting the unchanging laws of humanity, and in ignorance of what society may be made to become, when the laws of man shall not be opposed to the laws of human nature, but shall each one be in perfect unison with those laws.

Then will the world, for the first time, learn what man may be made to become, and what society will be, when man's laws shall emanate solely from nature's laws.

The insane laws of man are not only erroneously based, unjust, oppressive, and cruel, but are, especially in Great Britain, enormously extravagant in the waste of the best feelings of humanity, of time, talent, and money. They are one of the existing monster evils of society, which sorely afflicts it through all its ramifications. They are, with the superstitions of the world, one of the great dividing and repulsive powers among men; a repulsive power emanating, as all do, from ignorance of man's nature, and of the enormous means at the hourly disposal of society, to render all superior in excellence, and wealth, and wisdom, and power, through the adoption of nature's laws.

Generally speaking, the best natural talent among the individuals of the educated families, is selected, to have his own mind first destroyed by the study of human laws, which, being based on notions directly opposed to nature's laws, can never be comprehended by any mind. He is then trained in the sophistry of these artificial laws of man, to advocate any side of any question, and to endeavour to puzzle and confound the minds of his opponents, and the judges and juries before whom he pleads. It is, through all its phases, a system of universal repulsion and disorder, and hence a most injurious and extravagant waste of talent, time, good feeling, and real wealth.

The time and talent thus grossly misapplied and far worse than wasted, might be made, if wisely directed, to instruct the world in the most useful and valuable knowledge, and to unite all in one kind and charitable spirit, instead of dividing so many, to their pecuniary and mental ruin; while the capital, thus expended for ever, might be applied to effect the most substantial permanent good to all not of the profession of the law, and save the poor lawyers themselves from the feelings which they are compelled to have, arising from the consciousness that their profession is opposed to the well-being and happiness of society. So well are many of them aware of this false position, that they would be delighted to see a new organization of society that would render their profession unnecessary, and give a rational direction to their faculties, physical, mental, and mortal.

But the extravagance and enormous waste of time and of physical and mental power under the direction of politics, end not here. The insanity arising from not well educating and employing the people who are un or ill-educated, or un or ill-employed, while all profess to desire to have a good character formed, and an increase of wealth created for all, is proof to demonstration of the pitiable condition in which ignorance retains the human faculties, misdirecting all the natural valuable powers of the human race.

Again, the numbers now left uneducated or who have been ill-educated, who are unemployed or ill-employed, were they well-educated and well-employed, could, under wise direction, produce sufficient of the most useful and intrinsically valuable wealth for all. Within the range of these two evils, may be included, in addition to the ignorance and want of any employment among the paupers and working classes, all who have been ill-educated, uselessly or injuriously employed, or who spend their time in idleness, among the middle and upper classes. The waste and useless expenditures thence arising exceed man's present means of calculation. It is greatly more than, if wisely applied, would be required to render the population of the empire, if not of the world, permanently prosperous and happy.

Ignorance and ill education, idleness, or injurious employment, are now, as they ever have been, the bane of society, misapplying all its energies and valuable powers to make a pandemonium of the earth, when the same natural powers, wisely directed, would create speedily an earthly paradise.

Another of the extravagant political evils afflicting the human race, is the necessity which has arisen, from the errors of the principles from which political power has emanated, that populations thus educated, employed, and classified, should be governed only on principles of the most gross injustice, oppression, and cruelty, by a powerfully organized system of force and fraud, the most extravagant mode of governing that can exist. It most injuriously wastes the wealth which is annually created to a most extravagant extent, while, by the necessity of the system to act upon the misery-producing principle of 'dividing to conquer,' an immense amount of wealth – an amount far beyond the comprehension of minds formed as they have been in the present generation – is *prevented* being annually produced, – an amount, again, far more than sufficient to amply supply all the wants of society when it shall be made rational.

The difference of expenditure between arranging and governing society upon principles to divide and oppose feeling and interest, and upon the principle of uniting feeling and interest, is a greater amount than between universal poverty and wealth, independent of its being the difference between universal crime and virtue, and misery and happiness.

In fact, the present political system of the world is extravagant beyond estimation, through all its ramifications, in the waste of means to give wealth, prosperity, and happiness to the human race.

The *commercial* arrangements of society, as far as their influence extends, are equally extravagant in the waste of wealth, as well as otherwise so injurious to the character of all who are engaged in producing, preserving, distributing, and consuming wealth. The whole of the arrangements of individualized society, for these purposes, creates a waste of talent, skill, time, and capital more than sufficient again, if these departments were united on sound principles and properly conducted, to supply society, when made rational, with all that would be required to ensure permanent prosperity and happiness to all its members.

The details of these errors have been given so often in previous parts of this book, that they need not be again here enumerated. And it will be sufficient to state, that the waste arising from the present mode of producing, keeping, distributing, and consuming wealth greatly exceeds all the wealth which is now annually created by all the ill-directed labour and toil of the human race, amidst all its contentions for individual riches. There is yet *an entire absence of wisdom* in all these departments.

In the general domestic arrangements of society, the waste of wealth, and of the means for its creation, are in accordance with the waste and loss in every other division of the present crude and random organization of society for conducting the business of life. And the *most* injurious and wasteful are those in the highest and lowest classes, but the arrangements in the middle class, although by far the most economical, are abundantly extravagant.

Under a wise economy, upon the united principle and interest of society, it is probably that greater domestic comforts of benefits will be obtained for an expenditure of five hundred pounds annually, than are now procured for five thousand, and that for the former sum all the advantages of society of the highest order will be permanently ensured, in such a manner that each adult will have all the enjoyment of individual privacy whenever desired, with the best society, without trouble or inconvenience, whenever society shall be preferred to privacy.

Under these arrangements, also, every foot of soil will be the best applied to produce abundantly, and to contribute, by the superior building, and park-like, and pleasure-grounds which will be formed in every variety, to the greatest enjoyment of the higher faculties of humanity.

By this new organization, reclassification, and arrangement of society, every square mile of land will be made to support four, five, six, seven, and gradually eight or more times the number of superior individuals, in far superior circumstances than those which now anywhere exist, or than can be maintained under this wretchedly organized and classified state of human endurance. By this change, misery will be everywhere removed, and happiness made universal, the ultimate object of all human desires.

Such is the difference between the irrational system of society and the Rational System, based on *Truth*, each part a part of one consistent whole; each part separately, and the whole collectively, purposely formed to promote the well-being and happiness of every man, woman, and child, of every clime and colour, and by degrees to amalgamate the human race into one cordially-united, intelligent family, with one language, one interest, and one object, namely, the permanent happiness of all: and science to be made the slave and servant of the human race.

With this new view of society in prospect of easy attainment, shall the present system, based on falsehood, be no longer supported? – a system organized, classified, and arranged in accordance with the fundamental errors on which society is based – errors producing all manner of inequality, vices, crimes, and misery, making man an inferior and irrational being, and the earth a pandemonium. Will the human race longer insanely maintain such an heterogeneous mass of folly and absurdity, and doom their offspring, through succeeding generations, to be inferior, irrational men and women, filled with every injurious notion, and governed by most ignorant and misery-producing institutions, while excellence, superior external circumstances, and happiness lie directly before them, and of easy attainment?

RECAPITULATION

Nature vindicated; or, The Second coming of Truth

The First Truth, given through the spirit of the most advanced mind in former periods of the history of humanity, declared, 'That to make the population of the world wise, good, and happy, there must be universal charity, and universal kindness – men must be trained to love one another as they love themselves, and then there will be peace on earth and good will towards men,'[a] and not before.

This is the announcement of the First Great Truth to mankind.

But the causes which continually prevented the creation of universal charity, of universal kindness, – which kept men ignorant, wicked, and miserable, – which made men hate or dislike each other, and maintained war and ill-will among the human race, were hidden until now in impenetrable darkness; and, much more, the *causes* which can alone create universal charity and universal love, make man wise, good, and happy, and ensure, for ever, peace and good will among mankind.

The second coming of truth is to announce this all-important knowledge to the human race.

This knowledge is contained in this book, which, with 'The Development,'[b] explains the outline and details of the Rational System of society in principle and practice.

GENERAL RECAPITULATION

MAN makes not himself, nor any of his organs, faculties, qualities, or physical, mental, or moral powers.

He is created with qualities which compel him to believe or disbelieve according to the strongest convictions made on his mind: to love, be indifferent, or to dislike, persons and things, according to the impressions which these make on his individual constitution.

From ignorance of these great and everlasting truths, man has been, through all past ages, taught that he makes his own qualities, can believe or disbelieve, love, be indifferent, or hate, at the caprice of a free will within him, and thus have uncharitableness, hatred, and unkindness, been universally created, and wars and ill-will been perpetually engendered, fostered, and encouraged.

The removal of these errors, unknown as such at the first coming of truth, and the introduction of the knowledge that will arise from the second coming of truth, will destroy the *causes* of all evil among men, and create the *causes* which will ensure love, peace, and joy throughout the world.

To effect these results, society must be reorganized on the fundamental principles of nature, as declared in 'the Book' of the second coming of Truth.

---

[a] See Luke 2:14.

[b] See *infra*, vol. 2, pp. 339–415.

This organization to be on the principle of universal unity, interest, and attraction; and, of course, to supersede, but peaceably, quietly, and orderly, the present organization of individualism, opposing interests, and repulsive feelings of disunion.

That man is formed, prior to and from birth, by the circumstances which surround him, animate and inanimate.

That if these are inferior, the character of each individual will be inferior, physically, mentally, morally, and practically.

That if the circumstances are of a compound nature, some inferior and others superior, so will be the character.

That if the circumstances shall be superior, such will be the character of the individuals having the benefit of them.

Yet no two characters will ever be the same; because nature makes a difference between all individuals at birth; and because no two can be placed, day by day and hour by hour, much less minute by minute, under exactly the same circumstances. Both these causes everlastingly operate on all individuals, and will for ever, fortunately, prevent any two being the same, physically, mentally, morally, or practically. As individuals do not make themselves, nor the circumstances which form their character from, or prior to birth, no one will ever be praised or blamed, rewarded or punished, in a rational system of society; but the adults of one generation will be, through this new knowledge, so trained, physically, mentally, morally, and practically, that they will form the succeeding generation to be superior, through the superior circumstances which this knowledge will give them the power and inclination to create.

These superior circumstances will be created through the knowledge developed in this book, first of the 'Conditions requisite to Human Happiness' – secondly, 'Of the Principles and Practices of the Rational Religion' – thirdly, of 'The Elements of the Science of Society or of the Social State of Man' – fourthly, of a 'General Constitution of Government, and Universal Code of Laws' – fifthly, of 'Liberty of Mind' – sixthly, of 'Providing for and Educating the Population' – seventhly, of 'General Arrangements for the Population,' – eighthly, 'On the Adjustment of Differences' – and ninthly, 'Conclusions deduced from the foregoing.'

To effect these changes, there must be not only a new organization of society on the principle of *attractive union*,[a] instead of *repulsive individualism*, but there must be, also, an entirely new 'classification of society,' according to age, and not according to the birth or wealth of individuals. The classification of age is the essence of justice to the human race, and will produce universal charity, kindness, peace, and happiness; while the classification of birth and wealth,

[a] Here, and elsewhere in this period, Owen adopted the notion of 'attractive' association popularised by the French socialist Charles Fourier and his followers.

will, so long as it shall be most unwisely permitted, produce uncharitableness, unkindness, wars and misery.

The classification of age will permit and require the creation of superior circumstances around all from birth to death.

The classification of upper, middle, and lower classes, will, as long as continued, require permanent inferior circumstances more or less around all classes.

The question, then, which the human race has now to decide is, whether they will persevere in maintaining a system based on ignorance of human nature, and therefore false and irrational, requiring the continual maintenance and re-creation of inferior circumstances for the lower class, and never having better than very mixed circumstances for the middle and upper classes; and many of these circumstances creating continually injustice, oppression, and cruelty of the upper upon the middle and lower, and of the middle upon the lower class?

There can be no doubt that, as soon as the public mind can be imbued with one clear rational view of society, it will decide upon having the principles of nature for its foundation, its organization in accordance with those principles, and arranged in accordance with the unity attractive, instead of the individual repulsive, arrangements of society; its classification, the classification of age, in order that all the external circumstances may be superior around all of the human race.

What then does the Rational System of society now require for the creation of these superior circumstances, from those who govern the most powerful and influential nations of the world. Simply,

1st. That they should unite, for their own safety and happiness, and for the safety and happiness of all those over whom they now govern, in order that peace and good will may become permanent and universal over the earth.

2nd. That this union shall be first directed to form substantive arrangements to rationally train and educate physically, mentally, morally, and practically, every child that shall be born.

3rd. That it should form arrangements, connected with the preceding arrangements, to permanently employ and duly exercise, physically and mentally, according to age, each of these children, as they advance in years, during their lives.

4th. That these results, which will be for the eternal happiness of all, through all ages, can be effected, and can only be effected, by an entire change of society in principle and practice, throughout all the ramifications of its divisions, – a change in its fundamental principles, in its organization, in its classification, in its education, in its employment, and in its government.

5th. That this entire change, in principle and practice, can be effected, but can only be effected, by superseding all the inferior circumstances of human creation by the most superior that human knowledge and means can, when united, be made, through the pure and genuine spirit of the Rational System, to create, for the permanent happiness of our race.

Thus, then, the SECOND COMING OF TRUTH declares to the world, that all which is now required to ensure the permanent progressive improvement, and consequent happiness of every succeeding generation, is,

To rationally *educate* and *employ* the human race, from *birth* through *life* to *death;* and to effect this change immediately, by scientifically superseding *all existing human inferior circumstances*, by the *most superior* that mankind, united, can now create. Or in other words, an organization TO RATIONALLY EDUCATE AND EMPLOY ALL, THROUGH A NEW ORGANIZATION OF SOCIETY, WHICH WILL GIVE A NEW EXISTENCE TO MAN, BY SURROUNDING HIM WITH SUPERIOR CIRCUMSTANCES ONLY.

Then let the capital, skill, and industry of the population of the world be now employed, with energy and wisdom, to adopt efficient measures to change the *inferior* for *superior* circumstances, and to form a scientific arrangement of society, to ensure the *greatest amount of happiness to all through every succeeding generation.*

Education, employment, superior circumstances, all calculated to produce charity, equality according to age, and happiness, from birth to death, for all. Such will be a rational system of society; and it is THE ONLY REMEDY which can remove the CAUSES OF EVIL, and ensure *the attainment of all that is* GOOD *for man*.

THE END